Enrique Alvarez Córdova

To Richard,
With love –
Mom + Dad
9-9-20

Enrique Alvarez Córdova

Life of a Salvadoran Revolutionary and Gentleman

JOHN LAMPERTI

Foreword by Charles Clements

McFarland & Company, Inc., Publishers
Jefferson, North Carolina, and London

Library of Congress Online Catalog data

Lamperti, John.
Enrique Alvarez Córdova : life of a Salvadoran revolutionary and gentleman / John Lamperti ; foreword by Charles Clements.
p. cm.
Includes bibliographical references and index.

ISBN 0-7864-2473-7 (softcover : 50# alkaline paper) 

1. Alvarez Córdova, Enrique, 1930–1980. 2. Revolutionaries—El Salvador—Biography. 3. Politicians—El Salvador—Biography. 4. El Salvador—History—20th century. I. Title.
F1488.A48L36 2006 2006008888

British Library cataloguing data are available

On the cover: Enrique Alvarez Córdova at a 1980 Washington, D.C., press conference *(Sandoval/Maryknoll Missioners)*

Manufactured in the United States of America

McFarland & Company, Inc., Publishers
Box 611, Jefferson, North Carolina 28640
www.mcfarlandpub.com

Contents

Foreword

by Charles Clements

Many Americans know about Archbishop Oscar Romero, the modern martyr of El Salvador. Few know about Enrique Alvarez, who belonged to one of the *catorce*, the fourteen families that ruled El Salvador through their extreme wealth. He, too, was a modern martyr, but not because of his religious faith. It was rather because of his rationality, his sense of fairness, his generosity of spirit, all of which caused him to be called a communist.

Enrique Alvarez didn't need a philosopher like John Locke to explain that the right to accumulate private property should be limited by a universal right to subsistence. He could know it by observing the lives of the peasants who helped accumulate his family's wealth. It is the reason that toward the end of their lives Enrique Alvarez and Archbishop Oscar Romero became close friends. They had come to understand that the structural violence that the poor in El Salvador often call "our daily bread" was becoming a vortex of inevitable revolution.

In the fall of 1980 Alvarez was president of the Revolutionary Democratic Front (the acronym is FDR in Spanish), a group of civilian leaders who openly opposed the military installed junta that was abetting the terror in El Salvador. He had three times been the minister of agriculture. He had been a popular national basketball star. He was one of the largest coffee growers, and hence also one of the wealthiest men, in El Salvador.

Sometime back, Alvarez had begun to convert his profitable coffee plantation, *El Jobo*, to a cooperative. According to his friends he used to say, "We who have the most must share a little. That would be the life insurance for this country to avoid bloodshed."

But El Salvador's life insurance of which he spoke had been spiraling out of control for some time. On Thanksgiving Day, November 27, 1980, Enrique Alvarez was one of six civilian leaders abducted at gunpoint as they prepared to hold a press conference at a Jesuit high school in downtown San Salvador. Later reports that day indicated their mutilated bodies had been found and that a "death squad" boasted its responsibility for the kidnappings.

One thousand was the monthly average that year — that is, of civilians that were kidnapped, murdered, mutilated or "disappeared" by security forces— the same security forces who, when they changed their uniforms for civilian clothes, changed their name to "death squads."

For many North Americans, as people in Latin America refer to us, one thousand is just another statistic, not even a significant one by most standards. At that time the population of El Salvador was about five million, one-fiftieth that of the United States. So in proportion to the United States, El Salvador was experiencing the equivalent of fifty thousand deaths a month — nearly the total of America casualties in a decade of warfare in Southeast Asia. That was the monthly carnage in El Salvador in 1980 — and the civil war had not yet begun. This is the context for the story of this remarkable and gentle man.

Privilege generally weaves a cocoon around itself. When the protection and isolation it affords fail, an individual can be considered a traitor to his class. Such was the case of Enrique Alvarez. What enabled him to first hear the voices of the poor who toiled on the extensive coffee plantations of his family? Why did he begin to identify with the plight of peasants rather than the concerns of those with whom he played polo? And when his life was repeatedly threatened, what led him to ignore his own safety and continue to fight for land reform?

These are a few of the questions that John Lamperti explores in his compelling biography of Enrique Alvarez, a work that delves deeply into the events that led to El Salvador's most recent civil war.

Not long after Alvarez died, I worked as a family physician serving a dozen villages in rural El Salvador. The area became a free fire zone and was bombed, rocketed, or strafed daily by American supplied aircraft. The guns on some of those aircraft could put a bullet in every square foot of a football field in sixty seconds. As the aircraft swooped down spewing destruction, the Salvadoran peasants would respond with rifle fire. Later when I led Congressional delegations to El Salvador, instead of trying to understand what conditions could fuel such determination in the face of overwhelming firepower, too often the question would be, "Where did they get the rifles?"

In his last speech the day before he died, the one entitled "I've been to the mountain top," Martin Luther King, Jr., said, "...in the human rights revolution, if something isn't done, and done in a hurry, to bring the ... peoples of the world out of their long years of poverty, their long years of hurt and neglect, the world is doomed."

I believe the places in the world where people grow tired of being plunged across the abyss of humiliation, where they experience the bleakness of chronic despair, where they grow bitter from watching their children die as they can do little to protect them from dirty water, common diseases, and insufficient food, become breeding grounds for resentment and hatred, for spawning violence.

In his preface, Lamperti says, "I hope this book will help preserve the memory of a good man who should be counted among his nation's true heroes." I think it does more than that. It vividly illustrates John Kennedy's belief that those who make peaceful revolution impossible make violent revolution inevitable. The message herein is not historical; it is current.

Charlie Clements, M.D., M.P.H.
President and CEO of the Unitarian
Universalist Service Committee
Author of *Witness to War*
Cambridge, Massachusetts

Preface

It used to be said of El Salvador that fourteen families, "Las Catorce," controlled the economy of the country and owned most of its resources. The number fourteen was arbitrary and the saying seems to have originated with a cocktail party conversation followed by an article in *Time* magazine.[1] Still, there is no question that for many years a relative handful of extended families largely ran El Salvador and enjoyed most of the fruits of its coffee-based wealth, using the nation's armed forces as their private police.

One of those oligarchy families bore the surname Alvarez. On my first trip to Central America twenty years ago, I heard of a rich man from "the fourteen" who had rejected the privileges of his class and joined the cause of the impoverished and oppressed common people of El Salvador. I learned that in April 1980 Enrique Alvarez Córdova became president of the Democratic Revolutionary Front (FDR), a broad coalition of nearly all the center/left civilian opposition to the regime. This made him the top political leader of the country's radical movement and potentially its first post-revolution president. But Enrique Alvarez did not become president of El Salvador, nor did he head the FDR for very long. In the fall of that same year Alvarez and five companions were kidnapped and murdered by elements of the armed forces and their ultra right-wing backers.

I learned too about Archbishop Oscar Romero, the conservative cleric whose honesty and loyalty to his people led him to struggle against the growing oppression by the military-dominated government and brought about his martyrdom. This surprised me less, for it seemed to be the logical consequence of his Christian faith and the theology of liberation. *Of course* Christians must oppose repression and work for justice — the big surprise was that this could be a controversial position. But many (not all) of the Salvadoran oligarchy put greater faith in the theology of wealth, and were ready to defend their interests and privileges by any means necessary.

Why was one member of the Alvarez family so different? What made Enrique Alvarez Córdova the exception — a "traitor to his class"?

This book is the result of my attempt to answer that question. Writing it was delayed many years after my "discovery" of Central America, for I knew that during El Salvador's civil war people could not talk freely about political questions. Also I had to learn Spanish, and that took a long time. At first I looked for some simple formula, some exclusion or resentment that might explain why this man didn't follow the pattern. As I learned more about him, I had less and less expectation of finding any such explanation. Enrique Alvarez was a highly successful member of his social class, and to the advantages of family position and wealth, he added great personal qualities. He was an outstanding athlete. In addition to intelligence he had charm and charisma, and was popular with both men and women from different levels of society. He was not a resentful loner or outsider.

I soon realized that Enrique's life could not make sense without some understanding of Salvadoran history and of the social and political setting in which he lived. That history is fascinating; a lot can happen in a very small place. Moreover, the career of Enrique Alvarez is a vital part of the story of his country. According to journalist Raymond Bonner, "His life and death mirror the history of El Salvador, the forces that have polarized and radicalized, the causes that have forced democrats to unite with the armed revolution."[2] In addition, El Salvador provides the stage and illustrates the key elements of much recent United States involvement in Central America, involvement that has often been based on inadequate understanding of the region and its people. Describing some of El Salvador's evolution thus became another major purpose for this book.

Enrique Alvarez was not a born radical. His ambition and lasting passion was to transform El Salvador's system of agriculture and improve the often-miserable conditions of the nation's rural workers. But unlike the legendary Salvadoran revolutionary Faribundo Martí, who was devoted from his early youth to radical change and to socialism, Enrique Alvarez spent most of his adult life working for practical reforms within the existing system. He was superbly qualified to do that, by means of his social position and his own abilities. Although he always insisted he was not a politician, he plunged into his nation's politics and served as minister of agriculture in three different governments. He also demonstrated a working model for agrarian reform by turning his profitable ranch "El Jobo" into a successful worker's cooperative. In the end, he found that fundamental change was beyond the reach of these efforts; the landowning class and its military allies could not be persuaded to accept even gradual reforms that weakened their control over the nation's wealth. The whole system had to be rebuilt, and the name for that is "revolution." Like his friend and advisor Monsignor Romero, Enrique always hoped that real reform could be achieved peacefully. But he was prepared to support the path of armed struggle when at last it seemed clear that there was no other way.

El Salvador is, of course, a Catholic country, and in the 1970s new currents within the Church affected it profoundly. Liberation theology contributed far more than Marxist theory to the growing demands of the poor for justice and dignity. I wondered about the role in all this of a wealthy man such as Enrique Alvarez. In his class, wealth — especially the ownership of land — was almost sacred. Enrique must have thought about Jesus' admonition (Matthew 19:23–24) that "it will be hard for a rich man to enter the kingdom of heaven. Again I tell you, it is easier for a camel to go through the eye of a needle than for a rich man to enter the kingdom of God." Whatever that teaching meant to him, Enrique Alvarez did not reject his inherited wealth. Instead, he *used* it. His life exemplifies the related but simpler Biblical instruction: "From everyone to whom much has been given, much will be required..." (Luke 12:48).[3] Something similar is inscribed on his monument at El Jobo.

One Salvadoran theologian has linked Enrique Alvarez with widely known Church martyrs through a concept of spiritual "poverty" akin, perhaps, to simplicity and the Biblical "purity of heart." Lutheran Bishop Medardo Gomez believes that the "eye of the needle" verse does not refer specifically to the possessor of material wealth, but to "the proud, the haughty, the tyrannical, the exploiter, the hypocrite, the traitor." These are the "rich," regardless of their bank balances. Poverty, on the other hand, could describe the person who "is humble, faithful, who identifies with others, is loving, is inclined to give and to share." "In our Salvadoran historical process," Bishop Gomez has written,

> We have a history of "poor" people. For example, one of them was Enrique Alvarez Córdova, because although he was a millionaire he was a converted and understanding person, ready to be of service to others, prepared to give and to share. Another such was Monsignor Romero; other "poor" were the Jesuit priests who were compelled to offer their words on behalf of those without a voice....[4]

Today Enrique Alvarez Córdova is not well known even in his own country. A majority of Salvadorans were born after Enrique's death in 1980, and to them the years of his lifetime are ancient history. At the cooperative El Jobo, however, his memory is revered. People there understand the words of Monsignor Ricardo Urioste of the San Salvador Archdiocese: "Enrique Alvarez was the first rich man who died in El Salvador for the poor ... for his country, for his people."[5] I hope this book will help preserve the memory of a good man who should be counted among his nation's true heroes.

A Note About Gender-Specific Language

Women played a major role in the movement for change in El Salvador, and in particular were prominent, often as leaders, in the revolutionary forces during the civil war of 1980–1992.[6] There were, however, very few women in visible or leadership positions in the government or big business sectors or with the government armed forces. The reader should know, therefore, that expressions such as "armed forces spokesmen" do indeed refer to *men* and are not meant to be understood as inclusive.

Acknowledgments and Sources

The personal story of Enrique Alvarez could not be found where I began looking for it, in documents and libraries. Some speeches and official statements are there, for example the platform of the Democratic Revolutionary Front, but even the basic facts of Enrique's life were not easy to learn. Freedom of Information Act (FOIA) requests to the U.S. government did not help much either. The State Department did (in the course of time!) supply some useful items, especially cables to and from the U.S. Embassy in San Salvador, but the CIA replied with a flat refusal to even consider my request. After an appeal they admitted holding one item related to the murder of the FDR leaders—but said it must remain secret, supposedly for reasons of "national security."

For the most part, then, the life story of Enrique Alvarez had to be sought in the testimony of people who knew him, or knew about him. I am grateful to all who contributed their time, their memories and their thoughts to this project, and a list of their names can be found toward the end of this book. All those listed were helpful, and some were essential. I also received contributions of photographs and graphics, only a few of which could be included in this book. More photos can be seen at my web site, found at www.math.dartmouth.edu/~lamperti.

Several people must have special mention. Enrique's close friend and one-time basketball teammate Antonio Cabrales invited me to his home and spoke with me at length several times. It was the first of those conversations that showed me that my dream of telling Enrique's story would be possible. Likewise, Enrique's long-time friend and coworker Lino Osegueda was an essential informant and a gracious host to me on several occasions. Mauricio Alvarez, Enrique's cousin and (with his brother Dr. Emilio Alvarez) the historian of the Alvarez family, was also helpful and hospitable, and the first chapter of this book would have been impossible without the family history *Los Alvarez* which I obtained from him. Damián and Carolina Alegría, both former revolutionaries now politically active with the FMLN, did much more than provide me with a comfortable and secure base from which to work with their San Salvador guesthouse "OASIS." They were also my primary bridge to the Salvadoran left, and I am especially indebted for two important interviews that Damián arranged for my benefit (or for the benefit of the project). And of course I am very grateful to Dr. Charles Clements for his generous foreword.

Finally, muchas grácias to my *compañera* Arlene Ash for reading drafts and for her patience with my obsession during many years of on-and-off work on this book. Thanks too to many other friends for criticism and suggestions, and to other members of my family for their long-range tolerance and help. I hope you will all think one day that your contributions and efforts were worthwhile.

John Lamperti
Norwich, Vermont
March 2006

Prologue: A Bad Day in San Salvador

San Salvador, November 29, 1980. From *El Diario de Hoy*, page 1:

Enrique Alvarez Córdova Found Shot 12 Times

Yesterday morning along the highway to Corinto ... the body of Enrique Alvarez Córdova, President of the Democratic Revolutionary Front (FDR), was discovered. He had sustained twelve bullet wounds: ten in the back, one in the head and one in the arm, plus three other wounds in the back.

Alvarez Córdova, former Minister of Agriculture, was kidnapped Thursday at 11:30 AM by a group of unknown men who arrived in two vehicles, a pickup and a large truck, while Alvarez, together with other leaders of this leftist organization, were located at the Legal Aid Office of the Archdiocese in the San José High School. ...

The corpse was found by a group of quarry workers. They notified the authorities who arrived promptly where the ex-minister lay dead, at a site overlooking a beautiful landscape including part of Lake Ilopango.

Alvarez Córdova was dressed in a white shirt with red stripes, beige trousers, brown belt and socks, and shoes of the same color. The cadaver was lying in an east-west direction on the left side of the highway leading to Corinto beach, between quarries one and two. Its right arm was destroyed by a gunshot....

Enrique Alvarez Córdova, fifty, was a member of a prominent San Salvador family. He served as Minister of Agriculture in the administration of Col. Arturo Armando Molina, at which time an attempt was made to implement an agrarian reform in our country. Alvarez Córdova resigned this position and seemed to distance himself from public life.

When the first Revolutionary Governing Junta took office after the coup d'état of October 15 last year, he was again named Minister of Agriculture. Early this year he resigned and later became known as the principal leader of the FDR, a coalition of left-leaning organizations.

Frank McNeil, a former U.S. State Department official, gave this assessment of what the Alvarez murder — one more among thousands that year — meant to El Salvador:

> Military units, presumably contracted by members of the oligarchy, in November 1980 assassinated leaders of the newly formed Frente Democrático Revolucionario (FDR), including its much-respected president, Enrique Alvarez. More than any other single event, this mass murder condemned El Salvador to protracted conflict by wiping out most prominent politicians of the political left at one stroke....
>
> I have little doubt that the assassination of the FDR leaders aimed at forestalling the United States from working with the political left. In Latin America, moderates are the meat in the sandwich. The right wants moderates out of action in order to tell local elites and the United States that the only choices on the political menu are Communism and right-wing repression. The Leninists mirror this desire.[1]

The government junta condemned the murders, denied that it had any responsibility for the crime, and promised to pursue the killers:

> **Communiqué**
>
> The Revolutionary Governing Junta condemns the assassinations of the Señors Enrique Alvarez Córdova, Juan Chacón, Enrique Escobar, Humberto Mendoza and Doroteo Hernandez, members of the FDR.
>
> Assassination is not the way to combat political delinquency, and the Junta has always advocated legal procedures for this struggle....
>
> This atrocious crime is a sample of the lengths to which extremist groups will go in grabbing for power and trying to impede the revolutionary process now underway which seeks to construct a democratic, egalitarian and participatory society in which there will be room for all ideas within a legal framework.
>
> But this process is opposed both by the extreme right and the extreme left, since both are attempting to achieve political power at any cost, the former in order to regain their lost privileges and the latter in order to install a totalitarian government.
>
> From this ambition for power arise two terrorist forces, from the right and from the left.... The Government has suffered attacks from both extremes....
>
> On another front, we [the Junta] face a noisy world disinformation campaign which tends to maintain a climate favorable to more violence, while, internally, irresponsible rumors are propagated which aid the cause of terrorist violence.
>
> To the foregoing is added the irresponsibility of certain international press agencies which distort the news, as when in the case of the kidnapping of the FDR members they reported the presence of men in uniform —

while witnesses have testified to the investigating authorities that no such thing occurred.

Because of all this, and reaffirming its condemnation of the assassination of the FDR members, the Revolutionary Governing Junta has reiterated its orders to pursue the terrorist bands from both extremes and bring them to book for their crimes, in order to pacify the nation according to the laws of the Republic.

November 27, 1980, San Salvador.[2]

That statement was quickly followed by another from the Armed Forces:

Communiqué

The Armed Forces profoundly regret the fatal outcome of the kidnapping yesterday of Señores Enrique Alvarez Córdova, Juan Chacón, Enrique Escobar Barrera, Manuel Franco and Humberto Mendoza, who were seized yesterday at noon by a number of heavily armed men....

At this time the Armed Forces condemn these assassinations, which can do nothing to resolve the problems that afflict Salvadoran society.

Erroneously, certain elements of the national and international press have reported information about the supposed participation of members of the military and security forces. This was officially denied, since it has been established that no element of the Armed Forces had anything to do with this shameful and repugnant crime.

The Armed Forces, respectful as they have always been of the principles of freedom of thought and action, have repeatedly shown by their conduct respect for human rights, and at no time could any military or security body have participated in any way whatsoever [in the crime against the FDR members]....

In the case of the kidnapping perpetrated yesterday against the persons mentioned, the administration of the National Police acted immediately, ordering a minute investigation of the events at the very location where those gentlemen were kidnapped and who, lamentably, later were found assassinated.

In conclusion, the Armed Forces always have maintained a strictly professional course, distant from the swings of politics, and remain firm in complying with their duty as the true guarantor of national sovereignty, peace and the progress of the nation.

November 28, 1980, San Salvador

If the military did not carry out the kidnappings and murders, who did? As usual a "death squad," composed of unknown persons and claiming to operate solely on its own authority, stepped up to claim responsibility. The "Maximiliano Hernández Martínez Brigade" issued its own statement on the day of the crime:

Communiqué

We wish to announce to the citizens that today we, a squadron of the General Maximiliano Hernández Martínez Anti-Communist Brigade, claim responsibility for the execution of the communists of the Democratic Revolutionary Front (FDR) Enrique Alvarez Córdova, Juan Chacón, Enrique Escobar, Humberto Mendoza and Doroteo Hernandez, whom we charge with the responsibility for the murders of thousands of innocent people who did not wish to be communist. We also warn those priests affiliated with the Marxist terrorist bands that they will meet the same fate if they continue their preaching which poisons the minds of Salvadoran youth.

Our brigade will continue to execute traitors to our fatherland.

United always for liberty, family and God: General Maximiliano Hernández Martínez Anti-Communist Brigade.

In all their essentials these three statements were lies. One branch of the government's armed forces, the so-called Treasury Police *(Policía de Hacienda),* had sent some 200 uniformed troops to surround the school where the FDR leaders were meeting, while policemen in plain clothes entered and took them away at gunpoint. The government, including its civilian members, knew this. Finally, there was never any real attempt at investigation.

A week after the killings, United States Ambassador Robert White met with junta member José Napoleón Duarte. Duarte had been a friend of Enrique Alvarez since the 1950s and later described him as "a noble man with a big heart."[3] White wrote about that meeting in *The New York Times:*

> I wasn't surprised to hear that the security forces of El Salvador's military rulers had kidnapped and assassinated six leaders of the opposition Democratic Revolutionary Front; the identity of the murderers had been openly discussed on the streets and in the markets for days. But to hear it confirmed by José Napoleón Duarte himself, as we sat together in the ornate halls of the Presidential Palace — that was a surprise. Duarte was then the top civilian member of the country's reform-minded junta; he was to become the junta's president within two weeks. In response to my remark — half question, half accusation — he nodded, and sadly admitted that certain elements of the armed forces were guilty of these brutal murders.[4]

Outside of El Salvador, at least some of the press got it right. From Mexico City the liberal newspaper *Uno Más Uno* issued this report:

Cooperation or approval of armed forces in assassinations, archbishop declares

[San Salvador, Nov. 29] The Salvadoran Catholic Church condemned the assassination of the leaders of the Democratic Revolutionary Front (FDR),

> carried out with the "cooperation or approval" of the government armed forces. Meanwhile in a clandestine press conference, the FDR announced the membership of its new provisional executive committee.
>
> The U.S. ambassador here, Robert White, described the murders as "one step further" toward civil war, a step which "reduces the possibility of dialog" between the junta and the opposition, while the *New York Times* commented that "El Salvador's Government now faces another severe challenge to its credibility" and suggests that the Organization of American States should participate in an investigation of the crime.[5]

In less than two months the long-simmering civil war broke into the open with the guerrilla offensive of January 1981. It ended eleven years later when a peace agreement brokered by the United Nations was finally signed by the FDR/FMLN rebels and government representatives. That agreement established an international "Commission on the Truth" to clarify the war's worst human-rights abuses. The Commission's report was unequivocal about the FDR murders:

> **Report of the Commission on the Truth for El Salvador**
>
> The Commission on the Truth concludes that [the FDR kidnap/ murder] was an operation carried out by one or more public security forces and that the Treasury Police were responsible for the external security operation that aided and abetted the perpetrators. By commission and, in failing to properly investigate the incident, by omission, the State failed to comply with its obligations under international human rights law to protect and guarantee the enjoyment by individuals of their most elementary rights.
>
> March 15, 1993, New York[6]

The year 1980 in El Salvador saw an unending parade of horrors. Political killings included the murder in March of one of the nation's finest and best-known men, Archbishop Oscar Arnulfo Romero, as well as thousands of campesinos, workers, teachers, and organizers of many kinds. People of all ages and conditions of life were massacred by military and paramilitary forces. Even so, the assassination of Enrique Alvarez by agents of the right was remarkable, for he was a son of one of the most prominent and wealthy families in El Salvador, one of "the fourteen." Before assuming the presidency of the opposition FDR, Alvarez had served as a cabinet minister in three different governments. Like that of Monsignor Romero his spiritual journey had been a long one, from the pampered child of a rich family to the top political leader of his country's revolutionary movement.

But the story begins a century earlier, when the first of the Alvarez family arrived in El Salvador.

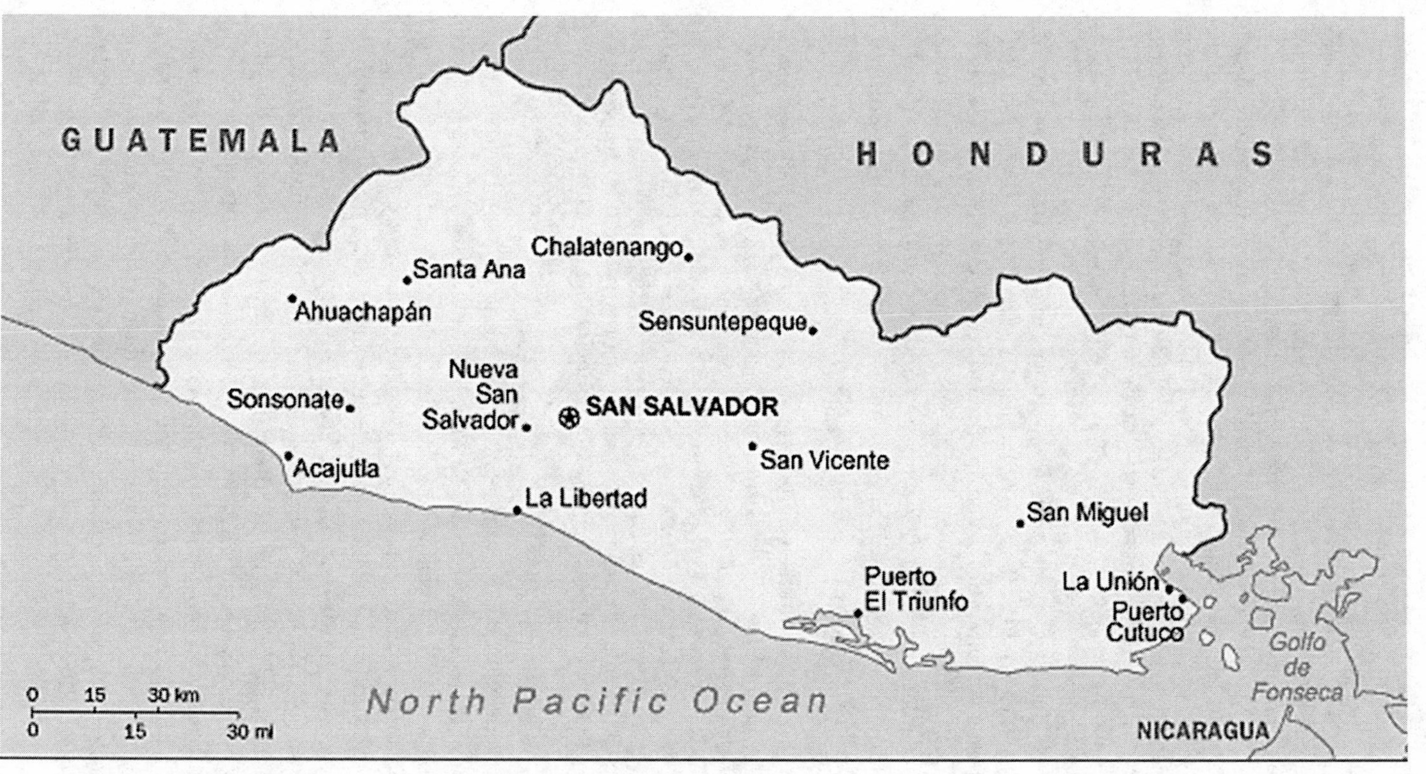

Map of El Salvador

The Murder of the Polo Champion

They killed the polo champion.
The man of a thousand suits,
the same one who had mansions
and yachts
and rich and pretty women almost the world over.
They shot him dead
and threw him, hands tied,
into a ditch.
They killed him because he abandoned his suits,
his horses and polo,
his yachts and mansions,
and above all because he began to walk
like a poor man among the poor.

—Alfonso Quijada Urías,
from *They Come and Knock on the Door*,
Curbstone Press, 1995 (Spanish and English).
Used by permission.

❖ ❖ ❖ ❖ ❖

"... Todos los oligarcas aquí están cortados por la misma tijera. Lo único que les preocupa es hacer más dinero, no importa a costa de qué. ¿Quién en El Salvador es distinto? Quique Alvarez y pare usted de contar. Qué odio le tienen al pobre Quique. Un traidor a su clase. No les queda más remedio que tomarlo en cuenta. Es uno do los suyos y no un resentido cualquiera."

[All the oligarchs here are cut from the same cloth. The only thing they worry about is making more money, no matter what it costs. Who in El Salvador is any different? There's Quique Alvarez, and then you can stop counting. How they hate poor Quique! A traitor to his class. They can't help taking him into account. He is one of their own and not some resentful outsider.]

—Claribel Alegría,
from *Despierta Mi Bien Despierta*
UCA Editores, 1986, page 32.

1

A Salvadoran Family

On June 17, 1995, the Alvarez family held a gala reunion. The Jade Salon of Hotel El Salvador[1] provided an elegant setting for more than 400 adult members of the clan, including seven who traveled from Colombia to attend. On one wall the Alvarez coat of arms was created out of flowers for the occasion. Each guest received a scroll with a family tree, where twenty-two portraits hanging like fruit from the branches illustrated the migration of a generation of Alvarezes from their native Medellín to the greener pastures of El Salvador. Above the branches was this explanation:

> **And all for a girl !!!**
>
> It was a maiden named Isabel Pérez Lalinde who captured the heart of Uncle Emilio and caused him to abandon his country and family and set out for unknown lands. This is the beginning of the history of the Alvarezes in El Salvador. Here are those old-timers named Alvarez Lalinde.

The day of the reunion a leading newspaper retold the romantic story of a young Colombian student who fell in love with his cousin and followed her and her family to their new home in a foreign land. Emilio Alvarez Lalinde[2], then 25 years old, received his medical degree in Bogotá in 1872 and quickly set out for San Salvador. With three years of hard work he established himself professionally in his new country, and finally married his beloved cousin Isabel. In some 30 years of practice, study, and teaching, Dr. Alvarez so transformed medicine in El Salvador that he is remembered as the "father of Salvadoran surgery" and the founder of the medical faculty at the national university. His death in 1906 was officially declared a national misfortune, and Emilio's statue in bronze still stands heroically on a tall pedestal near San Salvador's Hospital Rosales where he practiced surgery more than a century ago.

The official accounts picture Emilio's career, and his great impact on Salvadoran medicine, as the inevitable result of merit and hard work:

Above: **Alvarez family tree (courtesy Mauricio Alvarez).**

For three years [after arriving in El Salvador] he worked furiously, and at the end of that time entered into matrimony with the object of his love. In the year 1875 the San Salvador Hospital lacked any scientific organization. The surgical patients were mixed with the medical ones, and ... one surgeon was able to attend them all. But two factors contributed to establishing separate surgical and medical clinics, the [earthquake] destruction from 1873 and the increasing pace of medical studies.

Dr. Alvarez, with his generous nature and solid scientific education, did not hesitate in accepting the two posts which were offered him, that of Professor of Medicine and of Surgeon at the hospital.

Left: **Statue of Dr. Emilio Alvarez Lalinde**

> With the first he could fulfill his desire to teach and help prepare disciples, while the second would provide an extensive field for his investigations.
>
> Not much time passed before his intensive labor showed results. The students were inspired by his teaching, and new breezes were felt in the Hospital and the [medical] School.[3]

A private family history gives a different impression, for Emilio's early years were not easy and his success appears inevitable only with hindsight.[4] As a medical student in Bogotá he took turns sharing textbooks with friends since he lacked the funds to buy his own, and he worked a night job to be able to help his mother in Medellín. She needed what he could send. Having borne 11 children (including two who died in infancy), Doña Matilda Lalinde "worked all day and even at night" to sustain her family. Her husband and Emilio's father, Juan Francisco Alvarez Lopez, was for many years a professional actor. Don Francisco

> was a personage worthy of folklore. He loved the theater and nightlife. *A History of the Theater of Medellín* says that "Señor Alvarez possessed an arrogant figure, a resonant voice, reasonable style and he was not without talent, but for lack of study or attention his roles did not turn out well." He was much admired by women, and it was said that some of them loved him for himself, but others were attracted by the characters he represented. Without any doubt he was the origin of the popular family phrase [when someone misbehaved] "that's the 'Juanpacho' coming out!"[5]

Clearly Doña Matilde's problems did not end with the family finances!

When Emilio Alvarez moved to El Salvador, along with his new medical degree he brought his brother Jaime, younger by three years. Not long after their arrival the capital was devastated by an earthquake, a recurring theme in the nation's history. The brothers came through this one unhurt and found a new home in nearby Santa Tecla where Emilio continued his medical practice. Financially, at least, these early years were difficult; it was not easy for an unknown foreigner to establish himself. Worse, Jaime contracted a severe form of tuberculosis and died in 1876.

Emilio's medical career changed suddenly in 1875, when he was on the spot at a dramatic and very public accident. Units of the army were giving an exhibition at the "Field of Mars" (now Plaza Libertad) in San Salvador when one soldier stabbed another in the head with his bayonet, very close to one eye. No one dared to move the wounded man and bystanders clamored for medical help. Dr. Alvarez humbly offered his assistance. Although he was completely unknown to the authorities, they had no alternative and accepted his offer. At the city hospital, then quite primitive, Emilio operated with such success that the soldier recovered completely. Word of this incident greatly boosted his reputation, and the job offers plus numbers of paying patients soon followed.

Dr. Alvarez's status and fortune now soared, to the extent that in 1883 he could undertake a long-desired trip to Paris to work and study with French physicians. The trip had another purpose, to seek the best care for his wife Isabel who was suffering from heart disease. The visit was a scientific success but a personal tragedy for the family, for Isabel died in France leaving her husband with four children. Another trip to France in 1887 saw Emilio visit Italy too, and there he found a second Isabel (or Isabelle) and remarried. After a few years back in San Salvador the growing family returned to Paris in 1891, bought a house, and remained for ten years. Finally, with Emilio himself in failing health they returned to El Salvador for good in 1901. Dr. Alvarez died five years later of a cerebral hemorrhage. He was buried in San Salvador's General Cemetery with an "impressive and magnificent" funeral procession including an "uncountable number" of elaborate wreaths. He was 59.

Without doubt Dr. Emilio Alvarez did much good with his contributions to Salvadoran medicine. He also did very well for himself. At some time in the 1880s he was able to purchase two promising properties ("fincas") on the north-facing slopes of the San Salvador volcano; these would soon become highly productive coffee farms.[6] He then invited his younger brothers Esteban, Francisco and Roberto to travel from Colombia and aid him in managing these properties. (Another brother, Rafael, would make the same trip in 1889.) The brothers together founded the "Agricultural Company of El Salvador" (*Compañía Agrícola de El Salvador*), and the newcomers took over running the coffee farms. Francisco and Roberto soon moved from the capital to the western city of Santa Ana where they founded "Alvarez Brothers Hardware." Francisco became manager of the "Western Bank" *(Banco Occidental)*, created a little earlier by Emilio. Roberto—whose grandchildren would one day include Enrique Alvarez Córdova—was only 18 but he competently took charge of the hardware business. By this time the family's prospects in their new country were promising, if not assured.

The last brother to arrive, Rafael Alvarez Lalinde, would make an impact on El Salvador's coffee economy comparable to Emilio's contributions to medicine. His early life in Colombia hardly seems to foreshadow what he later became. Born in 1860 in Medellín, Rafael married Julia Angel in 1880; she was then 19. By his own account, the day after the wedding his entire capital was the 10 pesos in his pocket. His sister and brother-in-law lived in Manizales, a growing town of some 12,000 people, and with their help Rafael opened a shop on the plaza. It soon became popular with many townsfolk—especially women, it seems—who found his prices reasonable and his company congenial. Life was peaceful until 1884, when friends and the Liberal Party called upon Rafael to join an armed uprising against the Conservative government. Off he went to fight, leaving his wife and at least two very young children on their own at home.[7] Rafael was then 24 years old.

Stories of Rafael, the uprising and its aftermath became classics in the Alvarez family. In house-to-house fighting during the battle for Salamina his regimental commander was shot through the heart, and by acclamation of the troops Rafael received a battlefield promotion to acting colonel. Soon afterward the Liberal army was defeated, and he had to flee for his life. He found shelter with a shopkeeper in a tiny village, who hid him under a box behind the counter of her store. From there Rafael heard the conversation of the soldiers looking for him, and he struggled not to sneeze while they were still in the shop. His rescuer, coincidentally named Rafaela, built him a hiding place among some plantain bushes in the patio of her home where Rafael endured several days of tense inactivity. More than a week passed before he could appear at home, alive and well, to relieve his wife's anxiety.

Somehow the family hung on in Manizales, lying low politically and adding a child each year. There were five (one died in infancy) by the time Emilio's letter arrived urging them to join him in El Salvador. As Rafael's son Carlos later wrote, "My uncle [Emilio], clear-sighted as he was and knowing the political conditions in Colombia at that time, wanted to prevent my father from compromising himself further. Wishing for his good as he had done with the other brothers, he called [Rafael] to his side to begin a new life." It was hard for Julia to leave her home and family, but with her "characteristic self-denial and angelic faith in God" she agreed to undertake the journey.

The trip itself was not simple. First, several days of travel by hired mules carried the family and its baggage as far as Onda, a river port on the Magdalena. A small river steamer—for which they waited in Onda eight days—took them to Barranquilla on the Caribbean. From there they sailed, somehow,[8] to the Salvadoran port of La Libertad, arriving on June 5, 1889 after a journey from Manizales lasting over a month. The final stretch, some 50 miles to San Salvador, was covered using ox-drawn carriages—which fortunately had leather roofs, since those days brought a heavy rain, the first in six months.

Emilio was then living in a large house in the capital, which he shared with Esteban and his family. The newcomers crowded in too for a while, until Rafael moved his wife and children some ten miles north to the coffee finca "Colombia" near the village of Quezaltepeque. Here, with no knowledge whatever of coffee growing, he began his agricultural career managing "Colombia" and "Santa Isabel," Emilio's properties on the slopes of the volcano.

By all accounts Rafael was intelligent and very hard working, and he soon saw how to improve production. His son Carlos remembers spending long days at age 10 helping his father install a huge tank high up the mountain at Santa Isabel, which would store winter rainwater for the dry months to follow. Nearby on the Rio Claro the brothers set up El Salvador's first water-powered machinery for depulping coffee beans. The Alvarezes pioneered a new stage in Salvadoran coffee production by preparing processed coffee for export instead of selling it in a cruder state. The value of the coffee and the profitability of the enterprise leapt upward.

Rafael was always eager to expand the coffee holdings. His zeal brought him into conflict with his older brother, who paid the bills but complained that Rafael was going too far, too fast. Nevertheless they purchased properties lying between the two fincas they already owned, and eventually a chain of five more farms joined Colombia and Santa Isabel. Emilio's reservations seem to have been overcome, and in a few years production reached the level of 10,000 quintals of "green" (processed) coffee (*café oro* in Spanish), ready for export. This equaled roughly 50,000 quintals of berries (*uva fresca*), an unheard-of quantity for that time. The Alvarez coffee industry, always to be the backbone of the family's fortunes, had been launched in earnest.

In Santa Ana, Francisco took a step that also enhanced the family's position; in 1891 he married a young woman named Rosa Valle. She was said to be a beauty, but in addition had inherited from her wealthy father four substantial fincas producing coffee, sugar cane and cattle. One of these properties, "El Molino," would become one day the site of the largest coffee processing plant in Central America. Rosa died in childbirth along with her baby only a year after the marriage, leaving Francisco alone as the new owner of the four farms. His misfortunes continued. Suffering from what was apparently a severe stomach ulcer — never successfully treated despite a visit to Emilio in Paris— Francisco lived only until 1898. The new properties near the Santa Ana volcano, however, remained in the Alvarez family and gave another push to its expanding empire.

A Difference of Opinion

The family history written by Carlos Alvarez Angel *(Memorias)* makes no mention of political affairs in El Salvador prior to 1890. Of course family and not politics was Carlos's theme and he doubtless saw no need to mention matters that were entirely "normal"; after all, every Salvadoran government during the 1870s and 1880s amply supported the interests of coffee growers like the Alvarez clan. But in 1890 there was a sudden change, and politics enters the story for the first time. Carlos writes of the early 1890s that

> Bitter times had come for El Salvador. The brothers Carlos and Antonio Ezeta had come into power, Carlos as President and Antonio as Vice-President. Carlos had been the right hand man of the preceding president General Menéndez, but he betrayed him and brought about his assassination in order to take power himself. A man of bad intentions, he imposed arbitrary taxes on individuals and jailed those who didn't want to obey his orders. One victim of these taxes was my uncle Esteban who was still in El Salvador while they were in power; they took 10,000 pesos away from him.[9]

"They earned the hatred of all the people," Carlos continues, but fortunately help was on the way. As he describes the events, a group of 44 brave men, some of them just returned from exile in neighboring Guatemala, assembled on the night of April 29, 1894 and attacked the Santa Ana army barracks by surprise. Having succeeded in taking it over, they aroused the fighting spirit of "the whole city" and proclaimed the end of the Ezetas' illegitimate rule. Antonio Ezeta, who had made himself the "boss" of western El Salvador, was roused from bed where he was sleeping with an actress of the Santa Ana theater, and (so the story goes) he had to flee in his underwear back to the capital to avoid capture by the rebels.

In San Salvador, Carlos Ezeta mobilized units of the national army and set out to bring the rebellious city to heel, threatening to leave no stone upon another when he captured it. But the people of Santa Ana—women included—resisted courageously and well, and after 42 days the government forces had to abandon the siege in defeat. The Ezeta brothers saw the handwriting on the wall and fled into exile, where they died years later in misery and ostracism. These actions of "the Forty Four" earned Santa Ana the title of "Heroic City" by which it is still known.

The Alvarez brothers are not listed among the 44 but there is no doubt where their sympathies lay. Rafael had come with his family to Santa Ana a short time before the rebellion broke out, and told of making a shelter inside his house, using sacks of coffee beans as sandbags for protection against bullets and shell fragments. One day during the siege he climbed into a church tower and with binoculars spotted the enemy beginning to withdraw, news which he passed on to the rebel leaders. One of the younger brothers had a more dramatic experience. Roberto took part in attempts to bribe certain officers of the (pro–Ezeta) army but was betrayed, captured, and for some reason placed on a ship headed for Europe! A little while later Roberto encountered in Paris none other than Carlos Ezeta, now an exile himself. Ezeta tried to greet him as a fellow countryman, but Roberto would have none of it; he spat in Ezeta's face and broke a walking stick over his head. "You should know this fact," writes Carlos Alvarez in his family memoir, "because it shows the indomitable character of the Alvarezes, who knew how to render unto Caesar that which was Caesar's and to God that which was of God." No doubt the spirit of these tales is true, even if certain details may be questioned.

This version of events is roughly consistent with more detailed accounts of the period given in standard histories.[10] But while the basic facts are not in dispute, there are very different ideas about what it all meant. The legendary left-wing activist Miguel Mármol was born in 1905, the first child of a poor, single, teenage mother. Since he came into the world a decade after the Ezetas were overthrown he had to learn about them second hand. Much of his history came orally from a blind former farm laborer whom Mármol called "Archive." Archive remembered the Ezeta period this way:

> Contrary to what's been said in El Salvador during these last years, the Ezeta government was one of the most progressive in our history as a Republic.... General Carlos Ezeta, acting as President of the Republic, ordered the landowners to modernize their estates, he forced them to build adequate housing and to introduce various improvements in the living conditions, and he passed a law forcing them to use all their land to grow coffee.... The 'work-loads' in the fields were reduced and the same wage was fixed for each one.... The bosses also had to provide three nutritious meals a day.... Money spilled over everywhere in the countryside.... Peasants also began buying hats, machetes, candles and many handcrafted items. There was a sudden flowering of craftsmen in the cities. From the 75 centavos a day they had been earning, they were now earning four or even five colons a day.... Our class and all the poor people were happy under the Ezetas.

Something like that could not be tolerated for long by the landowners and the rest of the elite:

> The Church, the feudal bosses and the conservative Guatemalan government began to conspire together.... Finally there was an insurrection in Santa Ana, backed by the Guatemalan government, which was successful. It was the famous "rebellion of the 44," a reactionary mob that defended feudal interests and that bourgeois historians couldn't record by its true name, because those 44 were 44 rich good-for-nothings and 44 traitors and 44 sons of bitches.... One of those 44 rich boys, Rafael Antonio Gutiérrez,

> became the provisional President, and the city of Santa Ana was named "The Heroic City." An absolutely oligarchic title, though, and today when the poor people of Santa Ana brag about it they're only putting a noose about their own necks.... The economic situation became miserable for the people, including Santa Ana, because in spite of everything the Ezeta government was more for the people, while that of the 44 was fundamentally an enemy of the people.[11]

Which of these accounts is "true"? Even if that question has a meaning, it won't be answered here. Perhaps both are. On Mármol's side of the argument, it is notable that among the rebel 44 were men bearing the names of El Salvador's richest land-owning families, and in contrast the surname "Ezeta" is today hardly to be seen. In any case these divergent views of the Ezeta period are a dramatic reminder that "history" depends, among other things, on the class and social position of the observer — and that position is usually nearer the top than the bottom.

Attending to Business

Talk of politics now disappears from the Alvarez family history for many years. It was about this time that Esteban returned to Colombia with his wife and children. As a mining engineer he established offices and labs in Medellín that in 1951 still bore the Alvarez name, managed by one of his grandsons. With Esteban's departure and Francisco's ill health, Emilio arranged for Rafael to move to Santa Ana and take over running the farms there, including the fincas which Francisco had inherited from his wife. Roberto in turn soon transferred to the capital to run the *Compañía Agrícola de El Salvador*, which dealt with the properties near the San Salvador volcano. A new company, *Alvarez Hermanos* (Alvarez Brothers), was created for the Santa Ana interests. Both firms dealt principally with coffee and did business in England, France and Germany.

Coffee was always the basis for the family's success. Occasional forays into other fields (aside from banking) did not turn out well —*Alvarez Hermanos* lost a substantial sum one year when the price of sugar didn't behave as expected. Some time later Rafael ventured into silk production, but the project came to a disastrous end when most of the silkworms were destroyed by a plague. Coffee remained. Despite those setbacks the brothers did well enough to enable Emilio to buy a chateau in the French countryside in addition to his residence and office in Paris, and to send Rafael's son Carlos to study in England. Not bad for children of the actor from Medellín.

This did not mean that life always flowed smoothly; in fact the family encountered serious problems along their way. There were numerous illnesses, and several children died in infancy despite the best medical care then available. Santa Ana suffered an epidemic of yellow fever, and Rafael was one of those afflicted. He pulled through thanks to the devoted care of two family friends, physicians from Colombia, and he sailed in their company to France for an extended convalescence. Meanwhile in Paris, Emilio's son Jaime, a promising student at age 21, was suddenly stricken with severe epilepsy. The disease was quite untreatable at that time and Jaime died five years later. Voluntarily or otherwise, so many of the brothers found themselves in Europe during the 1890s that Emilio had to invite still more relatives from Colombia to help manage family affairs in El Salvador.

Nor did the coffee business always move straight ahead. The brothers hoped to start a factory to produce the sacks for their exports, but the project failed when the government would not grant them the tax breaks they sought in order to import the machinery. In 1898 there was a sharp fall in the price of coffee on British and French markets and their firms took heavy losses. Carlos comments: "This was a year of severe crisis for El Salvador, a monoculture nation then as it is today. I don't recall if it was a world crisis like that of 1929-30, but the coffee-producing countries passed through a very difficult time."[12]

Due to these setbacks Emilio couldn't afford to keep Carlos at school in England for another year, and told him he must return home to help his father. But despite their problems, thanks to excellent credit in Europe and to some new financial dealings—for example Emilio and Roberto formed The Santa Ana Central Coffee Company ltd. in London to hold some of their Salvadoran assets—the Alvarez brothers pulled through intact.

The family worked hard for what they gained. Carlos recalls that his Aunt Inés ran a commissary in each of the family fincas on the San Salvador volcano and traveled hours each day by muleback to take care of these small businesses. On his return from France, 17 years old, he himself began a daily routine of visiting all the fincas in his father's charge, and says that 24 years passed before he had a real vacation! Still life was not *all* work. As a student in England Carlos had begun playing tennis and soccer, and with cousins and friends in 1900 he helped found the first *fútbol* club in El Salvador. He played in the evening after a full day's work, and kept it up during the five years of his engagement to Teresa Lemus and for six years after his marriage. Love of sports was a common thread in the family, and years later would be a big factor in the life of Carlos's second cousin Enrique Alvarez Córdova.

In 1898, Francisco died in Paris; only 33 years old, a second operation had failed to cure his chronic ulcer. Roberto brought the body home to El

Salvador so his brother could be buried beside his wife in Santa Ana. This left only Emilio still in Europe, and he too returned in 1901, having sold the two houses in France at a considerable loss. The three brothers now dedicated themselves to the coffee industry. Low coffee prices lasting several years had reduced the value of land, and Rafael repeatedly took advantage of opportunities to acquire more properties in the Santa Ana area. Emilio and Roberto were skeptical, but Rafael insisted that times and prices would improve and that coffee was "the only profitable business in the country." In the long run, his faith was richly rewarded.

Rafael's contributions to coffee cultivation went beyond faith and hard work; he made important innovations. One spring day he and his family were taking a stroll on a farm neighboring their finca Malacara. Rafael noticed some unusually fine coffee bushes growing near a patio where beans were drying. This patio was surrounded by a plant growing wild—it was considered almost a weed—called Izote. Could there be a connection? From the neighbor Rafael learned that this plant grew easily from cuttings, and he offered to buy some. "Take all you like," he was told, and Papa, Mama and all the children carried away bundles of Izote to plant on eroded areas of their own farm. This proved a brilliant idea. For a time other growers ridiculed Rafael's new trick, and his wife accused him of "acute izotitis." But he was nothing if not persistent. The plant was excellent for holding soil and fighting erosion, and its use has become widespread. Izote is now recognized as El Salvador's national flower.[13]

In these final years of the old century, the youngest Alvarez brother, Roberto, was still a bachelor. He managed the *Compañía Agrícola* and frequently visited the coffee fincas that were the company's main assets, but he lived in San Salvador. Perhaps it was love of music, perhaps also boredom or loneliness, that often took him to the *Parque Bolívar* to hear public concerts performed by a 65-piece orchestra called *La Banda de los Altos Poderes.*[14] The director of this group was a German immigrant named Heinrich Drews; his wife Elena Ashoff was German as well. It happened that this couple had an attractive daughter, who also attended these concerts.... Roberto and María Drews were married in 1900, and spent their honeymoon on one of the family's coffee fincas near Lake Coatepeque, not far from Santa Ana. This marriage produced five children born between 1900 and 1908, although the youngest died when he was only four. Their third child and second son, Enrique Alvarez Drews, was destined for a long and eventful life, succumbing to a heart attack in 1992, aged 88. It was this son who in 1930 became the father of another Enrique, the central figure of this history.

The year 1906 was a hard one for the Alvarez clan. Emilio's sudden death was a severe blow, since he had always been regarded as the head of the family. His funeral was celebrated with many honors, and Colombian poet Julio Flores read verses composed for the occasion. President Escalón proclaimed the passing of Dr. Alvarez to be a "national misfortune." After the oratory and the flowers, however, the widow was left in a difficult position. She was not experienced in business matters, and there were three daughters from Emilio's first marriage, now young women, plus three small children of her own to consider. And despite Emilio's many successes, he did not leave them in an easy financial situation.

Both the *Compañía Agrícola* and the Santa Ana Central Coffee Company Ltd. were heavily in debt. The surviving brothers considered liquidating all these businesses and continuing each on his own, but Rafael, always the optimist, convinced Roberto they could hang on. They did divide their responsibilities, with Rafael and his sons managing the Santa Ana interests. Roberto then took over the *Compañía Agrícola* with all the properties on the San Salvador volcano. The Central Coffee Company had large debts in England, France and Germany and soon had to be liquidated after all. Nevertheless Rafael obtained new credit (at high interest) from the *Banco Oriental*, and proceeded to buy more coffee lands and improve the existing milling facilities, especially at "El Molino." It must have been an anxious time — but the eventual payoff was lavish.[15] In the end these enterprises firmly established the Alvarezes as leaders among El Salvador's elite, one of the "fourteen families."

Roberto was not idle in the meantime. He obtained loans from the *Banco Salvadoreño* and invested in a great quantity of chemical fertilizer, which at that time was not used for coffee growing. The San Salvador fincas soon were yielding nearly twice the previous quantity of coffee from the same land. Roberto also purchased more up-to-date machinery for the processing plant on the Río Claro. Here he made one big mistake; in seeking to economize, he neglected to insure the Río Claro installations. There was a fire and the entire plant, together with part of that year's harvest, was reduced to ashes. Even so Roberto was not stopped. He obtained more loans and rebuilt.

Despite the fire Roberto's affairs prospered, and in 1913 he took his family to Paris and enrolled his children in school there. Things at home went well under the management of two reliable administrators, and Rafael and his son Carlos made an occasional inspection trip to keep an eye on the fincas. But no amount of care could prevent what came next. On June 7, 1917, the San Salvador volcano erupted from its northern slope, producing a powerful earthquake. The two administrators watched in terror as the house at Finca Colombia crashed to the ground, then ran on foot toward the capital to escape the choking gases. They arrived at 1:00 AM to find the city in ruins and the populace panic-stricken, camping in parks and plazas.

The first shock was felt strongly twenty-five miles away in Santa Ana and threatening noises were heard in the distance. As soon as he could confirm what had happened, Rafael set out from Santa Ana with wagonloads of water and food. He found that the Alvarez relatives in the capital were safe, but the devastation was enormous. Within a few days a lava flow cut the rail line from San Salvador to Santa Ana. All vegetation on the volcano appeared dead, the animals had either burned to death or vanished, and most of the population had fled. The house at Colombia had now burned completely, together with nearly 100 acres of their best coffee. The farms seemed a desolation, the coffee and shade trees mere skeletons.

The day after the eruption a cable arrived in Paris: "San Salvador volcano erupted; fincas apparently destroyed." This was a blow indeed; Roberto believed himself ruined. It was not easy to travel from Paris to London (in 1917!) but he managed it somehow, then with still more delay obtained passage for El Salvador. In the meantime, Rafael had once more been the optimist, and once more had been right. Other landowners in the area were cutting back their coffee bushes so they could sprout again from the roots, but Rafael gave orders that this should not be done on Roberto's fincas. The hope was that the plants could recover on their own, and he decided to wait and see. In 15 days Rafael and Carlos visited the volcano again, and to their joy could see that the tips of the burned branches were swelling with sap. Rafael was immensely relieved, and fired off another cable to Roberto who was still in London, telling him that although that year's harvest was gone the fincas were not ruined. The rainy season was beginning and when Roberto finally arrived the coffee trees were fully leafed and promising a good yield—for the year after the next one. Losing two years of production was a serious blow, but the neighbors who cut their trees all the way back lost three years and even then their yields were reduced. Roberto looked around, decided to "diversify" and bought another finca a little further away.

The years of World War I brought the family problems and opportunities. They lost their German coffee markets but began to sell much more in the United States. The Alvarez firms paid off most of their European debts; some of them were owed in German marks and these were eliminated when the mark fell to one ten-thousandth of a dollar. In 1918 Rafael and his sons had a rare chance to sell their harvest at the unprecedented price of $28.50 per quintal. Rafael insisted on holding out for $30, and for once his judgment failed him. They missed the moment and prices fell sharply. Their debt with the *Banco Occidental* rose, instead of being eliminated as it could have been with a timely sale.

Despite occasional reverses the Alvarez family continued to flourish. In 1922 the Santa Ana firm *Rafael Alvarez L.* was reorganized as *Rafael Alvarez L. e Hijos* (Rafael Alvarez LaLinde & sons) to acknowledge the passing years and changing family responsibilities. Also that year Carlos and Teresa were able to take their first real vacation in 24 years, a three-month trip to and around the United States. (Carlos's mother cared for eight of the couple's ten children while the parents were traveling.) They left a daughter at school in San Francisco; Rafael earlier had sent another of his sons, Carlos's younger brother, to study in Switzerland. Of course it was only coffee that made all this possible.

By the early 1920s don Rafael no longer visited the fincas regularly himself. He was not as strong as he had been, and left the day-to-day management to his sons Carlos, Jorge, and Rafael Jr. The first two looked after the fincas and the mill — the actual production of the coffee — while Rafael Jr. managed the office and the sales side of the business. His own health was declining, however, and doctors in San Salvador diagnosed pernicious anemia. Finally father and son traveled to San Francisco in search of the best medical help. Rafael Sr. bought a house there that would remain his principal home for the rest of his life. The son's health did not improve, and he called for his wife to join him in San Francisco. Rafael Sr. also sent for Doña Julia who had remained behind, worried, in Santa Ana.

Rafael Jr. died soon after his mother's arrival. The shock was severe and grief aggravated her own condition; she had felt poorly since leaving El Salvador. Finally she underwent an operation in the Dante Hospital from which she did not recover. Julia died some four months after her son, at the age of 65. Rafael brought both bodies back to El Salvador, where Carlos recorded that their funerals were celebrated "with a great attendance of both rich and poor, for Mamá was much loved in Santa Ana."[16]

Following the deaths of his wife and son, Rafael's life took an unexpected turn. After the funerals he returned to his house in San Francisco, and ten months later sent word to the family in El Salvador that he had remarried! Pauline Kearns was a U.S. citizen, divorced, and not yet 30 years old in contrast to Rafael's 67. In his family history Carlos admits, no doubt with considerable understatement, that the surprise was "disagreeable." Some time later, however, Roberto visited the couple in the Unites States and reported that he thought Pauline a fine person. Their marriage produced one child, and when little Carmen Patricia won the hearts of her Salvadoran relatives the reconciliation was complete.

Rafael never returned to live in El Salvador. He and Pauline spent two years in Guatemala, and did make an extended visit to Santa Ana on the way back to the United States. Upon returning to San Francisco Rafael fell seriously ill and was largely bedridden for the last ten years of his life; Pauline cared for him loyally. In 1939 the government of Colombia decorated the one-time rebel with its Cross of Boyacá in recognition of his many contributions to the coffee industry. Rafael died of a cerebral hemorrhage on January 6, 1949.

"The years 1927 and 1928 were years of abundance in El Salvador, a one-crop country. With the high prices of coffee it was easy to obtain credit," wrote Carlos. The facts bear him out, for the value of El Salvador's coffee exports tripled between 1915 and 1928, reaching nearly $23,000,000 by the end of that period. Those were also years of abundance for most members of the Alvarez family. Carlos and his wife took an extensive (and expensive) trip to Europe, touring in a new Packard limousine that they ordered shipped from New York to Paris, and leaving several Alvarez children enrolled at boarding schools in France and England. It was also a time of new investments in coffee growing and processing, financed with more loans from the *Banco Occidental*. Carlos' brother Jorge visited Europe too, combining business with pleasure as he carried the plans for coffee processing equipment to discuss with manufacturing firms in England. The grand new mill "El Molino" was to be ready for the 1929-1930 season.

Roberto Alvarez Lalinde died from cancer during the Christmas holiday of 1927, after a short illness. His death left the family divided into two main branches, centered in Santa Ana and in the capital, San Salvador. Roberto's holdings on the San Salvador volcano and in nearby Alegría consisted of at least 9 properties, including Emilio's first fincas Santa Isabel (named for his wife) and Colombia. Nearly 2500 acres were planted in coffee on those farms, and their production had increased to around 18,000 to 20,000 quintals per year. These assets were divided among Roberto's widow María Drews and his four surviving children, leaving all of them well off. Enrique Alvarez Drews, the second son, inherited the fincas Miranda and Antioquia on the volcano plus part of another property. He was 23 when his father died, and his career was just beginning.

A Larger Picture: The Coffee Republic

A bird's eye look at the political landscape of El Salvador is in order. Independence from Spain, gained in 1821, brought neither peace nor prosperity to most of the new nation's people. There were many reasons for fighting. In the beginning, the struggle for and against Central American unification repeatedly involved El Salvador in armed conflict. Liberal versus Conservative rivalries were often disputed by military force, both within

El Salvador and in battles involving neighboring countries, especially Guatemala.[17] A third source of conflict was the oppression of farm workers. Class and labor issues about working conditions and low pay were complicated by racial and cultural resentments between Indians and Spanish-speaking Mestizos, often called "Ladinos." In 1832 a major Indian rebellion headed by Anastasio Aquino won control of the central part of the country and threatened to capture San Salvador before it was defeated by government troops. Interventions from outside the region also played a role, and in the mid 1850s Salvadoran soldiers joined the fight against the U.S. "filibuster" William Walker in Nicaragua.[18]

In the 1700s and early 1800s, El Salvador's leading export crop had been the dye indigo, cultivated by Indian and Mestizo laborers often forced to work under miserable conditions. Large planters made fortunes, but as the nineteenth century advanced it became clear that indigo's days were numbered. The world demand fell sharply during the U.S. Civil War because of the blockade of Southern cotton, and it dropped nearly to zero a few years later when good synthetic dyes were developed. However, a new export crop was waiting in the wings, ready to take indigo's place at the center of El Salvador's cash economy. This was the "golden grain"—coffee.

A Brazilian immigrant named Antonio Coelho is credited with first demonstrating coffee's commercial potential for El Salvador, and as early as 1846 a government decree gave preferential tax breaks to coffee growers. From the 1850s forward all Salvadoran governments promoted the new crop. President Gerardo Barrios, who had just led El Salvador's troops against William Walker's forces, stepped up government backing for coffee with land grants and road construction. A few years later with the presidency of Santiago González — which began in 1871, just before the arrival of Dr. Emilio Alvarez in his adopted country — a 56-year stretch of nearly uninterrupted "Liberal" government was underway. Among other things, Liberal rule meant that demands of the market were given primacy in a trade-oriented economy. During these years, the government actively supported the planting of coffee to replace indigo as El Salvador's chief export. Land was made available cheaply, sometimes free, to farmers who had the resources to plant coffee and tend the plants during the three to five years until the first harvest. The national government also built the infrastructure — roads, railways, and port facilities— necessary for the industry. These policies were enormously helpful to newcomers such as the Alvarez brothers who, starting with very limited capital, sought to establish themselves as growers.

The Liberal measures did not benefit everyone. Indigo cultivation had coexisted with traditional subsistence agriculture, but the rapid rise of coffee made far greater demands for land and labor. Before and especially during the presidency of Rafael Zaldívar (1876–85), lands that had long been farmed collectively were privatized or confiscated in order to make way for coffee production. An early consequence was another Indian rebellion in 1872 in the area around the western town of Izalco. This uprising was put down with considerable repression, adding to Indian/Ladino resentments in the region.

For large growers, the privatization of collective lands had a double advantage. It ended the village subsistence farming which the growers (and their government) considered an archaic and inefficient system of land use. This in turn forced formerly self-sufficient campesinos to seek paid work on the coffee fincas, and so helped provide the large seasonal labor force which coffee production required. In March 1882 the national legislature enacted a definitive law:

> CONSIDERING:
>
> 1) That agriculture is the Nation's chief source of life and prosperity and that it is the duty of the Legislature to remove any obstacle to its development;
>
> 2) That a principal obstacle is the communal land system in that it annuls the benefits of ownership of the larger and most important lands in the Republic now used for less intensive forms of cultivation, or causes the abandonment of land due to its precarious and uncertain tenure by its holders, thus preventing them from the right of developing the said land;
>
> 3) That resolutions passed to abolish the common land system by indirect means have not achieved the purpose intended by the Legislature....
>
> [The House of Representatives] HEREBY DECLARES THAT:
>
> Article 1. The *ejido* system [village ownership of land] in El Salvador is hereby abolished....[19]

This decree was a disaster for much of the rural population, especially in areas where the land was most suitable for coffee. The way of life of many villages was overturned, and dispossessed small farmers had to seek a living as landless laborers. The blow fell hardest on the communities that were mostly Indian in population. The foundation was now laid for El Salvador's continuing land conflicts and rural misery, problems that would long be at the root of the national condition. And the door was open wide for great wealth to be acquired as coffee assumed the dominant position among the nation's exports.

The Coffee Elite

The saying that El Salvador is owned and governed by fourteen families was always dubious, and events since 1980 have changed the traditional picture even more.[20] But in 1961 an article in the conservative magazine *Bohemia Libre* described *Las Catorce* this way:

> The political and economic life of El Salvador has always been controlled by influential and powerful families—feudal lords, masters of all the wealth of the country, who remove and install presidents with the help of ambitious military men who serve as their hired private police. *Time* magazine summarized the Salvadoran powerful as 14 families. Since then, in spite of the number of rulers being more or less, they have been known both within and outside the small republic as "The 14." Here is a succinct history of those families who have ruled El Salvador for more than half a century as their private hacienda, while the native people survive in the worst misery found on the soil of the Americas.[21]

Not a flattering picture! The article lists 14 surnames; in order they are Dueñas, Regalado, Hill, Meza Ayau, De Sola, Sol Millet, Guirola, Alvarez, Meléndez, Menéndez Castro, Deininger, Quiñónez, García Prieto, and Vilanova. (*Bohemia Libre* mentions several other names that could deserve inclusion in the list.) Of the 14, all except Meléndez are said to base their fortunes at least partly on coffee.

There are sketches of the families themselves. The thumbnail description of the Alvarez clan concentrates on the Santa Ana branch:

> ALVAREZ: The Colombian don Rafael settled in Santa Ana to undertake the business of coffee. Currently his descendants harvest more than 50,000 quintals of coffee each year, and own the coffee mill ["El Molino"] that Salvadorans proudly call "the largest in the world." The brothers Ernesto, Ricardo, Rafael and Carlos Alvarez Lemus [grandsons of don Rafael] have carried out social reforms and are popular among their workers for their generous character....

Families of the coffee elite controlled the government of El Salvador during most of the years from 1860 to 1930, and several family names listed among "the 14" are those of former presidents: Dueñas, Menéndez, Regalado, Meléndez, Quiñónez. Not Alvarez. Members of the extended Alvarez family did not take visible roles in national government prior to 1948, when Enrique Alvarez Drews served briefly as Minister of Industry and Agriculture.

The Alvarez brothers (and one sister) came to El Salvador at a propitious time to make their fortunes, a time when their indisputable intelligence and drive were matched by highly favorable social conditions. Their success, of course, was also based on the labor of many nameless Salvadoran workers. It appears that the Alvarez family treated their workers justly, even well—by the standards of that time and place. Mauricio Alvarez explains that his great-grandfather, don Rafael, insisted when he bought a major finca in 1908 that he planned to build "not only a big coffee farm but a community." And in fact Rafael eventually had constructed some 400 workers' houses, a hospital, two schools and a church on the family's farms.[22] Mauricio adds that these concerns and benefits made the Alvarez family popular with working-class people in Santa Ana but were resented by other landowners, who even called them "socialistic."

Like the more recent use of the word "communism," that is a very peculiar conception of socialism! Recently the writer Claribel Alegría, a former Santa Ana neighbor whose father used to play billiards with Rafael's son Carlos, described Carlos Alvarez far more accurately as "a very good man, but very *paternalistic* with his employees."[23] The word seems apt for his father as well. Rafael and Carlos surely expected their workers to follow orders without much discussion, but they were also concerned for their needs, including the education of the children.

To put this sort of paternalism in context here is a contrasting story. This incident was recorded years later by one of El Salvador's progressive priests, a leader in implementing the "theology of liberation." He writes that the "immense majority of the haciendas" had no school, since the owners saw no need for the campesinos to enjoy such luxuries.

> Regarding schools, I recall a story told me by my friend Father Abad, a Colombian descended from cattle raising people in Medellín. Abad attended to the "spiritual" needs of many rich families in San Salvador. On Sundays he used to visit their haciendas, and on occasion he celebrated mass for the local campesinos. On one such occasion he asked them if their children had a school, and the congregation answered that they did not, because the *patrón* had no interest in the children learning to read and write. He then asked if they would like to have a school, and of course the campesinos said "yes." Later while having lunch with his friends in the manor house, he commented ingenuously on what had happened during the service, his dialogue with the congregation. The owner, Fr. Abad's good friend, his face red with anger, stood up and shouted, "But where did you get the idea of talking about a school to these ignoramuses? Don't you see that if they learn to read they're going to get big ideas and make problems for me? For a long time now I've seen to it that they aren't interested in anything, and now you come along with this! Father, we are good friends, but all the same I want you to leave here right now. I don't want to have communist priests as friends of my family." Abad had to say farewell to the Señora and the children and leave that place for good.[24]

Father Abad's experience sounds extreme, but it was closer to the norm than Rafael Alvarez's vision of founding a "community."

With or without luxuries such as elementary schools, however, agricultural production in El Salvador was based on the abundance of low-wage manual labor, and the system was designed to make sure that sufficient labor was always available and always cheap. The growers' *Asociación Cafetalera* acted almost as a second government, putting their own needs at the top of national priorities. One cog in that system, the National Guard, was created in 1912 in order to serve as a rural police force that could replace the private guards of the owners and combat ordinary crime. It began well, but President Manuel Araujo who introduced it was assassinated midway through his four-year term and the Guard soon acquired what has been its primary function ever since — suppressing labor organization and enforcing whatever working conditions the landowners saw fit to impose. The National Guard was empowered to arrest any person whom the *patron* claimed was suspicious or causing unrest. Later on, small units of Guardsmen actually lived on some of the large fincas and were paid by the owners to serve as enforcers of "labor peace."[25]

El Salvador — especially rural El Salvador — was a rigidly divided society. The wealthy elite were separated from the working poor by a small middle class of tradesmen and technicians, but the gap from top to bottom was unbridgeable. A fictional description of a 1931 trip through the countryside near Santa Ana, including a conversation between an American visitor and a Salvadoran with progressive politics, helps to visualize the scene:

> We had a graveled road most of the way, so the trip was pleasantly dust-free. The highway bore a surprising amount of traffic: oxcarts laden with sacks of coffee berries, barefoot women stepping along gracefully with water jugs or bundles balanced on their heads, tiny donkeys almost invisible under mountainous loads of kindling wood or fresh-cut grass, and now and then a herd of lean cattle which choked the road and reduced our progress to a crawl. The panorama had an air of vitality and bustle, and I said so to Eduardo. He clucked his tongue dubiously.
>
> "You see it with foreign eyes as a quaint, picturesque scene, Frank," he told me. "Try looking at it my way for a minute. Those cattle we just passed don't belong to the men who were herding them. Neither the coffee in those oxcarts nor even the carts and oxen themselves belong to the cart drivers. We are passing through don Jaime Dominguez's estate just now, and almost everything you've seen along this road belongs to him. And everything in sight except the gravel, the telephone poles, and this car, remains just as it was 200 years ago. Our people live in the 18th century, not the 20th." ...
>
> I ventured that unemployment couldn't be as terrifying in a tropical country like this, where most people lived on the soil and raised their own food. "I'd much rather be out of a job here than in the Chicago slums, where you have to buy groceries and coal and heavy clothing to survive," I told him.

My comment was a mistake. Eduardo bounced up and down on his seat and became nearly incoherent.

"Put yourself in their place, Frank," he sputtered. "Your country may have an unpleasant climate, but is it any more pleasant to die of disease or to waste away of vitamin deficiency than to die of cold? Could you stand to be treated like a burro all your life and watch your children grow up to be denied schooling and treated the same way? These people are human beings like you. Think of that!"[26]

The elite at the top of this society, especially the major coffee growers, formed a class apart. Historian Thomas Anderson wrote of them that

> The descendants of the powerful coffee families tended to marry foreigners; they were educated abroad, and in time became almost a new race, differing from the rest of the Salvadoran nation not only in social mores and prejudices, but even in color and other physical characteristics. ... During the thirties the newspapers were full of stories of their long, slow steamship rides to Europe. Today they would be part of the jet set.[27]

Anderson cautions against thinking of this class as totally frivolous, pointing out that it supplied the physicians, engineers and other professionals that the nation surely needed. Still, he says,

> during the early decades of the century, the existence of this group tended to be parasitic. The young women were purely decorative and given chiefly to gossip. The young men, the *señoritos* as they were derisively called, spent most of their time playing pool or dominoes, or with their lower-class mistresses, while waiting for their fathers to die so that they could inherit the family estates.

Even those who wanted to work hard — and that included most members of the Alvarez family — were limited by tradition to a few professions, especially law and banking, in addition to their role in managing family enterprises.

More recently sociologist Jeffery Paige has studied the thinking of this Salvadoran elite. He reports that

> The poor were discussed as almost a separate nation or species to be assisted, to be led, to be employed, to be helped toward a higher standard of living in an industrial future, but were never regarded as legitimate claimants on societal resources or power. Labor organizations might be accepted in the mills, but only as long as they had no political ambitions. Democracy was accepted but not the notion that democratic power might be used to change the relative balance of social and economic power.[28]

Paige interviewed members of the coffee elite around 1990, but these attitudes that they freely expressed go back many years. They represent the climate of opinion of the class and family in which Enrique Alvarez Córdova was born and raised. And yet, remarkably, Enrique would learn to set aside the barriers of class and see his world through different eyes. How that happened is the theme and inspiration for the chapters that follow.

2

Social Explosion; Peaceful Childhood

> Cuando la historia no se puede escribir con la pluma, entonces debe escribirse con el fusil.
>
> [When history cannot be written with the pen, it must be written with the rifle.]
>
> — *Augustín Farabundo Martí, Salvadoran revolutionary, executed 1932*

Enrique Hernán Alvarez Córdova was born in San Salvador on March 3, 1930. His paternal grandfather, Roberto Alvarez Lalinde, had died in 1927 but the baby's father, Enrique Alvarez Drews, was 26 years old, able and energetic. Years later, a younger man who knew well both Enriques, father and son, described Enrique Sr. this way:

> His father was an extremely intelligent man, and he had a mathematical mind. He went to college in France, but the depression hit, coffee went under and he had to come back, so he never finished.... [He] was an extremely hard working person, and then he was so gifted intellectually, and such a good businessman, that he went into other things; they went into banking and insurance companies, this and that. So Enrique was born into an already pretty wealthy situation.[1]

Enrique's mother Carmen Córdova Lardizabal was one of four sisters, and there was also a brother who died in infancy. Their physician father, Salvador Córdova, had moved from neighboring Honduras with his wife Luisa Lardizabal and established a medical practice in San Salvador. The Córdovas were prosperous but not really wealthy; they did not own coffee properties and lived from Salvador's professional earnings. Enrique Alvarez Drews and Carmen Córdova had met in San Salvador and married in 1926, shortly before the final illness of his father Roberto. The new baby boy, Enrique Jr., was the couple's second child. Their daughter Carmen Elena had been born two years earlier, and another son, Ernesto, would follow in 1940. The family was still well off in spite of the depression, and young Enrique's prospects in life seemed golden.

The Gathering Storm

Despite the favorable auspices of Enrique's birth, a deadly storm was gathering over the family's world. By 1930 very hard times had come to El Salvador; the recent era of prosperity for the coffee economy had ended with the financial crisis. Historian Thomas Anderson writes that

> Even before the great crash, coffee prices had started downward. With the start of 1930 this downward trend grew markedly worse and most producers preferred to let the harvest of 1930 rot in the fields.... As many of the fincas, or coffee plantations, were heavily mortgaged, the owners often lost their land. Some 28 percent of the coffee holdings in the country changed hands during the early years of the depression, the small growers generally suffering more than the large.[2]

Of course unsold harvests and unpaid mortgages for the growers meant unemployment and desperation for their workers. According to Miguel Mármol,

> Conditions all over the country were terrible from the economic point of view, because the worldwide crisis of capitalism that broke in 1929 lashed out at our country in a particularly disturbing way. In the countryside the situation was extremely miserable, there was real starvation and true despair among the peasant masses. These masses began to intensify their political work, channeling their unrest into our [Communist] ranks.[3]

Major A. R. Harris, a U.S. military attaché in Central America, offered this astute commentary when he visited in December 1931:

> About the first thing one observes when he goes to San Salvador is the number of expensive automobiles on the streets.... There appears to be nothing between these high priced cars and the ox cart with its bare-footed attendant. There is practically no middle class between the very rich and the very poor.
>
> From the people with whom I talked I learned that roughly ninety percent of the wealth of the country is held by about one-half percent of the population. Thirty or forty families own nearly everything in the country.

> They live in almost regal splendor with many attendants, send their children to Europe or the United States to be educated, and spend money lavishly (on themselves). The rest of the population has practically nothing....
> I imagine the situation in El Salvador today is very much like France was before its revolution.... The situation is ripe for communism and the communists seem to have found that out....
> A socialistic or communistic revolution in El Salvador may be delayed for several years, ten or even twenty, but when it comes it will be a bloody one.[4]

But the revolution did not wait for years; it erupted in less than two months! The uprising, poorly coordinated and with its plans betrayed by informers, was quickly put down by the government army. The ferocious, far more deadly reprisals that followed became known simply as *la matanza* (the slaughter) and left a heavy imprint on Salvadoran society that persists today. And the name of one revolutionary leader lives in El Salvador's major political party of the left: the Faribundo Martí Front for National Liberation (FMLN).

The fundamental causes of the uprising were, of course, structural. Anderson notes that

> When one combines all the reasons for peasant discontent — the breakdown of the *ejidos* [collective lands], the miserable treatment of *colonos* [live-in farm workers] and hired hands, the social problems and dislocation caused by the coffee economy, the cultural hostility between Indian and Ladino, and the class hostility between campesino and landholder — and then, when one adds the economic disaster of the depression, it is not hard to see the basis of the revolt of 1932. That some movement would arise that would seek to harness this discontent and provoke a rebellion was almost inevitable....[5]

But there had to be proximate causes as well; a brief look at these begins with the political situation. In March 1927, don Pío Romero Bosque took office as President of El Salvador. He seems to have been a man with liberal views and humanitarian instincts who hoped to preside over a moderate degree of peaceful democratization and social progress. Perhaps absent the 1929 crash he could have done just that. But the desperate economic conditions and the increasing militancy of workers' organizations and the left made quiet evolution impossible, and increasingly don Pío resorted to repression —forbidding "subversive" propaganda, prohibiting or violently suppressing demonstrations and jailing hundreds of protesters. A number of organizers were murdered by police. During the final months of 1930 and the first months of 1931, some 1200 persons were imprisoned for labor agitation or leftist activity. One of them was a young man named Augustín Farabundo Martí.

As his presidential term drew to a close, Romero Bosque decided on one final, radical act: to determine his successor, he would permit a free election with no government-backed "official" candidate. The immediate result was confusion. Such a thing had never happened before, so there were no political parties ready with candidates and platforms. Soon enough, however, several wealthy men threw their hats into the ring. Their ideas ranged from moderate to far right, and none were to the liking of the increasingly conscious labor movement.

On July 4, 1930, a new candidate declared himself. Don Arturo Araujo had studied engineering in London, an unusual choice for a wealthy young Salvadoran. After obtaining his degree he moved to Liverpool, worked as an engineer in local industry, and boarded at the house of a shop steward active in the Labor Party. Araujo also married an English woman from a middle class family, Dora Martin, who would be his companion for some fifty years. He returned to El Salvador in 1900 and established a reputation as a benevolent landlord and progressive civic activist — he is reported to have paid twice the usual miserable wages to his farm workers, and (like Rafael Alvarez Lalinde) to have built schools, houses, a medical clinic and chapels for the workers on his finca.

By 1930 Araujo was widely known as an able and decent man. For the campaign don Arturo and his supporters created a Salvadoran Labor Party modeled on the British one, which he admired. The party's ideology, far from Marxism, followed closely the thinking of the popular Salvadoran writer and journalist Alberto Masferrer who championed a sort of capitalist welfare state which would provide all citizens with the "vital minimum" necessary for a decent life.[6] But in spite of his wealth, class origin and moderation, Araujo was at most marginally acceptable to the ruling elite who were suspicious of his known sympathy for El Salvador's workers and campesinos.

The campaign was confusing, with six candidates trying to clarify, and sometimes to obscure, their programs. (The least popular of the six, General Maximiliano Hernández Martínez, dropped out late in the race and announced his support for the Labor Party.) Nevertheless, Araujo persuaded thousands of workers and campesinos that his candidacy offered them some hope for a better life. Masferrer's active campaigning for Labor must have helped with students and intellectuals. President Romero Bosque kept his promise of non-intervention and Araujo won a strong plurality, receiving about 101,000 (46.5 percent) of the 217,000 votes cast, far ahead of the second-place finisher's 63,000.[7] Since the constitution required an actual majority the formal decision went to the national legislature, where in February Araujo was declared the winner by an unanimous vote. Don Arturo took office as president on March 1, 1931.

Things went badly from the beginning. Miguel Mármol commented that Araujo "had risen to power with the support of the people, but then quickly fell out of favor." The problems came from several directions. Desperate workers and campesinos demanded immediate reforms and relief, which no government could have provided. Appointments presented difficult problems. Since he received little cooperation from the better-educated sector of the population, Araujo had to give important government positions to political supporters who were sometimes poorly qualified or openly self-serving. This cost him the support of Alberto Masferrer, who refused a cabinet appointment and criticized the administration from the floor of the National Assembly. And despite the moderate reformism of Araujo's program and his explicit rejection of Marxism, much of the landowning oligarchy did not hesitate to attack him as "communistic."

Araujo chose General Hernández Martínez as his vice president, and also appointed him to the cabinet as minister of war. The president insisted he had made no deal to gain the general's support, but he apparently considered him to be one military man he could trust. During April and May, Martínez[8] used the armed forces to repress peasant attempts to protest, organize, and strike. Dozens of civilians were killed in these actions, with scores more wounded and arrested. Demonstrations against government policies continued, and in July the administration declared a state of siege and suspended civil liberties. This meant little to campesinos who had enjoyed few liberties in any case, and new conflicts soon erupted, often to be "settled" by the guns of the police and National Guard.

Popular unrest was only one part of the government's difficulties. Nothing it could have done would have altered the fact that by 1931 coffee prices had fallen to less than half of their 1926 values. Despite that low price coffee still represented 94 percent of the value of El Salvador's exports in that year, so the terrible state of the economy can be readily imagined.[9] Government revenues declined in proportion, and payment of salaries, both civilian *and military,* fell months in arrears. The government negotiated a $1 million loan from the United States, a move that proved widely unpopular. Araujo did attempt to implement certain rural reforms, but his resources were totally inadequate and the efforts were too little and too late. By the autumn of 1931 the government of this decent and well-intentioned man found itself with enemies on all sides and few supporters except the armed forces.

Their support soon proved illusory. On December 2 a military revolt erupted, seeking to overthrow Araujo's government after a tenure of only nine months in office. Some loyal military units resisted for a while and great confusion resulted, but within two days the coup plotters prevailed and don Arturo had to seek refuge in Guatemala.[10] A junta was formed to govern temporarily, and acting with the "advice" of a U.S. envoy it quickly decided to seek the closest available approximation to a legal succession of power. By the evening of December 4, the transfer of authority to the former vice president had been arranged. Except for a brief pro-forma break, General Maximiliano Hernández Martínez would remain El Salvador's president for the next 14 years.[11]

Farabundo Martí and the Left

Among the most influential leaders of the left, and certainly the most colorful, was Augustín Farabundo Martí. The sixth of 14 children, Martí was born in 1893 to a land-owning family. His father's properties amounted to almost five square miles, and Martí grew up among children of the *colonos* who lived and worked on those lands. According to his biographer Jorge Arias Gómez,

> From an early age, his childish understanding could never explain satisfactorily the differences he saw at every step — between his own shoes and the bare feet of the workers' children who were his playmates, between the clean, good-quality clothes of his parents and the dirty rags of those who worked every day from dawn to sunset.
>
> There are credible stories about Martí, telling how as a child he would give away almost everything he had to young and old.[12]

It is striking that these very things were said years later about the childhood of Enrique Alvarez Córdova. Perhaps it was inevitable that children of wealthy families should first encounter and question social inequality in their own homes. Most quickly learned to accept or ignore it, but a few, like Martí and Quique Alvarez, struggled with these contradictions all their lives.

In any case Martí was an excellent student, received his *bachillerato* (high-school diploma) with high honors in 1913, and entered the national university to study law and social science. His academic career there did not run smoothly. He was disillusioned by the rigid, old-fashioned curriculum and customs he encountered at the university and often argued with his professors about the program. One such discussion "passed the limits of propriety and led to personal insults. These produced a challenge to a duel, an event which was avoided through the intervention of friends of both parties." Not surprisingly, Martí never received his degree. Arias Gómez explains that "On embracing the struggles of the Salvadoran people, Martí would permanently cut off his university studies."[13] Still, he remained at the university for some time to comply with family obligations and to study the Marxist and anarchist texts available there in the company of a small group of like-minded young people,

In 1920 Martí was arrested at a largely student demonstration and sent into exile for the first time, to Guatemala. Most of the young demonstrators rounded up by the police were released after President Meléndez met with the group to warn them to behave. During this encounter Martí was unable to remain silent at what he saw as injustice, and he demonstrated the firmness of character, or the stubbornness, for which he would later become famous. This earned him and one companion the severe penalty of exile.[14]

In Guatemala Martí took menial jobs to experience the lower side of society, and joined in left-wing discussions and organizing in the capital. In 1925 many of the exiles, including Martí, were expelled from Guatemala. Back in San Salvador he was exiled again, this time to Nicaragua, but soon returned secretly and plunged into the work of the newly formed Regional Federation of Salvadoran Workers (FRTS). The FRTS had a moderate program calling for land reform, popular education, and the eight-hour day, and in 1927 it was represented at a congress of the A.F. of L. in the United States. President Romero Bosque (1927–1931) was initially well disposed toward the FRTS and met with its leaders, reportedly telling them that labor organizing in the cities was acceptable but to leave the campesinos and rural workers alone. His government introduced reforms including legal recognition of labor unions and the eight-hour workday, but none of these applied to farm workers. Even a liberal president had to recognize that abundant and dirt-cheap rural labor was an essential part of the coffee economy.

Labor and political organizing was never a comfortable profession in El Salvador, not even in the early days of don Pio's government. Martí was arrested once more in 1927, but a hunger strike plus agitation by university students contributed to his release. In 1928 he again left El Salvador, this time voluntarily. Martí then surfaced in New York, where he was briefly imprisoned following a police raid on the offices of the Anti-Imperialist League. Soon after that he made his way to the mountains of Nicaragua in order to join the forces of César Agusto Sandino resisting the occupation by U.S. marines and their local allies. Arias Gómez reports that Martí "took part in armed actions and soon became the confidential secretary of the great Nicaraguan patriot.... For his distinguished participation in the movement,

Martí was awarded the rank of Colonel in the 'Army for the Defense of the National Sovereignty of Nicaragua.'" Widely published photographs show him at Sandino's side together with other international volunteers and members of Sandino's staff. A famous story asserts that one day U.S. aircraft began to bomb Sandino's positions while Martí was writing a report. Martí then put aside his typewriter saying, "If history cannot be written with the pen, it must be written with the rifle." With that he took up his weapon, positioned himself behind a tree and began to fire at the attacking planes.[15]

In October 1929 Martí parted from Sandino during a trip to Mexico, returning the next year to El Salvador. The full cause of this break is not clear, but basic political differences played a role. Sandino was above all a patriot and nationalist, who struggled to expel the foreign (U.S.) troops occupying Nicaragua and reestablish his country's independence. He explicitly denied seeking to impose a social revolution, and refused when Martí urged him to add a communist plank to the movement's anti-imperialist platform. Despite this disagreement and his public criticism of Sandino's "incorrect" policy, Martí maintained great respect for the Nicaraguan, and on the eve of his own death praised Sandino for his patriotism and his firm resistance to Yankee imperialism.

The Communist Party of El Salvador (PCS) was officially founded in March 1930, without the participation of Farabundo Martí who had not yet returned to his country. When Martí did arrive he assumed the leadership of another organization, the "International Red Aid" (Socorro Rojo Internacional or SRI), a sort of politicized Red Cross of the left. The two groups worked together closely, and it was through the SRI rather than the PCS that the Salvadoran left maintained some contact with the international Communist movement and even received a little aid, amounting to about $50 per month.[16]

The desperate economic condition of the Salvadoran people favored the work of labor organizing, and on May 1, 1930 the FRTS together with the PCS put together an impressive demonstration of some 80,000 workers and campesinos on the streets of San Salvador. (The population of the entire "department" of San Salvador, containing the capital city, was then only 190,000 people; that of the whole country about 1.43 million.) By this time the left had rejected President Romero Bosque's warning to stay out of the countryside, and organizers had gained influence among the peasants in the western part of El Salvador. Many rural schoolteachers helped to spread the call for a new social order; their participation partially made up for the largely urban and ladino nature of the PCS, 80 percent of whose 400 or so members lived in San Salvador.[17] The rights of farm workers now took their place among the demands of the labor movement. Demonstrations continued during the summer and fall, and increasingly don Pío resorted to repression, including large-scale arrests. This gave the SRI its cue, and campaigns to "free the political prisoners" brought pressure on the government at home and abroad.

Miguel Mármol returned to San Salvador on the last day of 1930, fresh from a difficult but inspiring trip to the Soviet Union. He spoke about the USSR to enthusiastic groups of workers, and plunged into union and political organizing as well. Years later, Mármol told Roque Dalton about this work:

> The people were so interested in what I had to say that the Central Committee of the Party decided we ought to inform the masses at public gatherings. Therefore I wrote a very broad and detailed report (which was later lost, in 1932) and I read it at several massive gatherings, some legal and others clandestine ... and at several secret meetings for peasants, political meetings that we called "ravine meetings." At this kind of gathering we would meet with 300 or 400 peasants in a ravine or gorge, under darkness, and we'd talk all night long.... The atmosphere in these meetings was truly moving due to the obvious fervor and revolutionary hope that welled up in the people....
>
> Of course the authorities were going around hungry after us and we had to use more than a thousand tricks to guarantee our safety and the continuity of the work. What times those were! To hold meetings at night we placed oil lamps all around in bordering camps, and to guard the meetings even the local children helped out, signaling us with little firecrackers or bells when the National Guard patrols or the Army, etc., were approaching....[18]

Farabundo Martí was not at hand when Mármol returned. He had been arrested on November 27 and in December was placed, under guard, aboard a steamer plying the Pacific coasts. He was allowed off when the vessel reached California, only to be held in jail for two weeks and then placed on board once again by U.S. authorities. Finally in February, when the Salvadoran elections had been held and Arturo Araujo elected president, Martí was able to leave the ship in Nicaragua. By the 20th of that same month he had made his way back to San Salvador and was ready for action. Organizing mass demonstrations, agitating for the release of prisoners, hunger striking for twenty-six days when jailed himself, and even negotiating in person with President Araujo, Martí and his companions of the left were a force to be reckoned with throughout that tumultuous year.

During the summer and fall of 1931 the workers and the communist movement intensified their pressure on the government. In western villages, the ancient grievances and traditional institutions of the Indian population partially meshed with the organizing and propaganda from the urban left to produce an explosive mixture. In addition to class and economic issues, ethnicity played a major role. An important figure in each town was the *cacique* or chief, a leader of the Indian community although not formally recognized by the government. One of the most influential was the cacique of Izalco, José Feliciano Ama, who was therefore a prized ally for the communist cause. Other caciques were also attracted by visions of what a revolution might bring to them and their people, even though the communist organizers stressed class conflict and largely ignored specifically Indian issues. Local Ladino leaders joined up too. For them, the seemingly hopeless economic situation must have been a strong motive as a further sharp fall of world coffee prices in August 1931 increased rural desperation.

In early December the government fell. The PCS was not involved in the coup which was carried out from within the armed forces, although of course the persistent attacks on the Araujo administration contributed to the latter's weakness and disorganization. Even so the left's reaction was surprisingly moderate, even cautiously positive. The student editor of *Estrella Roja* ("Red Star") actually congratulated General Martínez on the coup, and stated that the "blunders" of Araujo's government had imposed on the military the "moral obligation" of overthrowing him.[19] This remarkable opinion was combined with unjustified optimism about the possibility of radical reforms from the new government. Farabundo Martí was not so naive, but he also expressed complacency about the coup, believing that "the conditions for the success of an insurrection would be even better under a criminal government."[20]

Within the Communist Party, serious planning for an armed revolt began late and indecisively. Of course the party was united in the desire to gain power, but it was held back by internal divisions over strategy and had even purged some members accused of "reformism." PCS organizing among campesinos was also hampered by its rigid opposition to all forms of private property, even though party leaders knew that many rural workers owned small parcels of land and longed for more. As late as December 1931 several strategies were still under consideration. A large part of the Central Committee wanted to participate in elections, possibly to be followed by a general strike; this group argued that the basis for a successful insurrection did not exist. But the anger and desperation of the rural poor could not be held back for long, and an explosion was coming whatever the decision and plans of the PCS.

Voting for mayors and city councils had been scheduled for mid–December, to be followed in a few days by an election for the national legislature. After the coup these were postponed until early in January 1932. The organizations of the left had intended all along to take part, and decided (not without internal struggles!) to enter their candidates in January in spite of serious obstacles in the way of effective campaigning. At least, the leadership thought, if the elections were widely seen as corrupt it would increase the support for the more drastic course of armed rebellion.

That is more or less what happened. In San Salvador the official count put the Communist candidates in third place. In some other towns the PCS claimed victory, but the results were not reported for several days and then conservative candidates were declared the winners. In several towns where the left obviously had strong support the elections were simply suspended with no result at all, or else annulled. Much the same thing happened the next week in the legislative elections, for which in any case the voting was extremely light. At the same time, repression increased sharply. The student paper *Estrella Roja* was banned by the police, and the military killed dozens of campesinos while putting down rural disputes.

The left made a final attempt to avoid war; after much debate, the PCS Central Committee sent a delegation of five members to try and negotiate with the government. They offered to calm the workers (which in reality they could have done to a limited extent at most) and to use only legal methods of protest, in exchange for a halt to the repression and some emergency benefits for the poor and unemployed. President Hernández Martínez declined to meet with the delegation, sending word that he was suffering from toothache. The group talked instead with his secretary and with the Minister of War, but no agreement could be reached. This was the last effort to prevent an armed conflict. It left the PCS with the choice of joining and attempting to guide the coming rebellion or trying, without much hope of success, to abandon the campesino rebels and get out of the way. By January 10 the Central Committee had decided to try and lead, and its attention now focused on how to carry out the insurrection.[21]

Insurrection and Matanza

The revolt, twice postponed, broke out on the night of January 22/23, 1932. It seemed that Nature joined the upheaval, for the Izalco volcano was in full eruption with flames visible for many miles and lava running down its slopes. If everything had gone perfectly the rebels might have had a chance, but in reality their cause was lost by the time the fighting began. Three main things went wrong. First, Farabundo Martí and several comrades in the revolutionary leadership were betrayed and arrested on January

19. Second, a government crackdown in Guatemala broke up plans for diversionary attacks from across that border. And finally, plans for mutiny within the government armed forces were discovered in advance, and the rebellious soldiers disarmed and arrested. This last was probably the fatal blow sealing the fate of the uprising.

The Salvadoran government counted on its army of some 3000 men, plus police and National Guard units amounting to another 3000. They had vehicles and machine guns as well as rifles, and the untrained and poorly armed rebels could not hope to face these forces. However, the revolutionaries had been at work among the troops persuading some to join the uprising, presumably explaining to the soldiers, with reason, that their interests lay far more with the workers and peasants, the classes from which they came, than with the government and the landowners. Miguel Mármol lists an impressive number of units that were expected to join the uprising, and concludes that "In short, we had more than enough strength in the Army, together with the active support of the insurrectionist masses in the countryside and cities, to smash the bourgeois state apparatus."[22] But plans for capturing several key barracks were reported to officers loyal to the government and they anticipated the action of the dissident troops—executing some, putting others under arrest and keeping a firm grip on the important weapons. In the major western town of Ahuachapán, for example, the captain commanding the machine gun detachment, whose loyalty was suspect, was arrested just before the attack and many soldiers were disarmed and expelled from the barracks. The armed forces, reduced in number but under firm government control, were soon ready to move against the rebels.

In the meantime the revolutionary groups, in the majority Indians, captured a number of towns in Western El Salvador. Izalco, Juáyua, Tacuba and several smaller towns were under rebel control for a few days. A sizable force attacked Sonsonate, the provincial capital, but the army garrison drove back the attackers with heavy losses. Nearer to San Salvador, Colón and Santa Tecla were also attacked but not captured, as was Ilopango, immediately to the East of the capital. By January 25, government forces had taken the offensive everywhere, and the towns under rebel control were quickly recaptured. Within another day the armed uprising was essentially over, although a few incidents continued to arouse fears and provoke counterattacks during the following month.

What was the toll of the "red wave," as one novelist called it? There were some battle casualties among the government troops and police, and there were several cases of cruel murders of civilians in towns captured by the insurgents. There were rapes as well, but apparently only a few. Thomas Anderson made careful estimates, and concludes that "certainly the total number of those who fell to the machetes and guns of the rebels could not have been more than thirty five." That number does not include soldiers and police killed in the fighting, and these were harder to count. In all, Anderson concludes that the number killed by the "communists" may have been about one hundred.[23]

As frightening and bloody as the uprising had been, the aftermath was incomparably worse. Once the rebellion had been thoroughly put down, the real reign of terror began. Government forces killed prisoners without trial, and often without interrogation. They killed campesinos en masse and with no warning. The reprisals had two main parts. In the cities, especially San Salvador, hundreds of real and suspected leftists were rounded up and summarily murdered, often after torture and without any sort of trial. The victims did include some of the actual Communists who had participated in organizing the rebellion. One of these was Miguel Mármol himself, who miraculously survived his attempted execution by firing squad and later provided an eyewitness description of this part of the repression. Many of those killed, however, were simply organized workers who had no part in the uprising, or merely unfortunates who got in the way of police sweeps through poor neighborhoods.

The other side of the "punishment" inflicted on the rebels was the great *matanza,* an indiscriminate slaughter of campesinos, largely Indians, in the western areas of the country where the uprising had been strongest. Since the rebellion had been completely suppressed when most of the killing occurred this was not counter-insurgency warfare; it was pure terrorism. Villages became "free fire zones" (to borrow a term from a later era) where after machine-gunning the houses, any survivors were lined up and shot. Innumerable rapes were committed by the soldiers. Military commanders issued orders for all "innocent" people to report in order to receive a safe-conduct document; those who believed this story and came forward were then murdered. Unquestionably thousands of people who had no part in the rebellion were slaughtered along with many others who did participate.[24]

The number of the victims is hard to determine with any precision. Anderson gives a conservative estimate: "...about ten thousand rebels may have lost their lives afterwards in the *matanza* or in the course of the fighting, with easily 90 percent falling in the *matanza.* This means that the government exacted reprisals at the rate of about one hundred to one."[25] Other estimates put the death toll much higher. In El Salvador, it is widely believed that as many as 30,000 people were murdered after the revolt was over. This would represent over two percent of the nation's population at that time.

A few deaths among the thousands merit special mention. The Indian leader José Feliciano Ama was captured by soldiers and imprisoned in the Izalco town hall, then taken out and lynched by the bourgeoisie of the town. Farabundo Martí was granted the luxury of a trial. He and two young comrades captured with him, Mario Zapata and Alfonzo Luna, appeared before a military tribunal on the evening of January 30. Of course the outcome was predetermined, and despite Martí's plea that he alone was responsible and not his companions, all three were shot early in the morning of February 1, 1932. Their bodies still lie in the General Cemetery of San Salvador.

The events of 1931 and 1932 changed Salvadoran society for generations to come. "Indians" as a visible group nearly disappeared, since the open manifestation of Indian culture had proved fatal to thousands during the *matanza*.[26] The dictatorship of General Hernández Martínez was cemented in place and he remained in power until 1944; military government would be the norm in El Salvador for the next 50 years. (The story of this extraordinary man, whose character combined intelligence, extreme ruthlessness, and exotic religious and pseudoscientific ideas (he was a Theosophist), is worthy of a book yet to be written.) The subjection of the campesinos to the will of the landowners was confirmed in blood, and the organizations of the working class were crushed for years to come.

The revolt and the *matanza* left deep spiritual scars as well in the Salvadoran people. Miguel Mármol spoke for many when he described their reaction:

> I think the drama of '32 is for El Salvador what the Nazi barbarism was for Europe, the North American barbarism in Vietnam, a phenomenon that changed completely, in the negative sense, the face of a nation.... After that damned year all of us are different men and I think that from then on El Salvador is a different country. El Salvador is today, before all else, a creation of that barbarism.[27]

Finally, a persistent myth was created and grew in the absence of reliable information. That vacuum was no accident. As the Salvadoran writer Claribel Alegría said in a 1991 interview, "...in 1932 a cultural lobotomy was performed on the entire nation by the dictator Martínez when he ordered the burning of all magazine and newspaper files dealing with the peasant massacre, and it was done. Our book *Ashes of Izalco* was the first historical novel written about the events of 1932."[28]

Thomas Anderson once again, writing around 1970, put it this way:

> Like most ghosts, the specter of 1932 prospers best in twilight and shadow. For this reason, the ruling military powers have deliberately tried to keep the true nature of the events of that year from the people. They have fos-

tered a legend of bloodthirsty mobs butchering thousands of middle-class citizens, and of a heroic army that barely managed to turn back the barbarian wave. Little has been written on the revolt, except propaganda.[29]

This legend of the Red Menace inspired lasting fears among the wealthier classes. It contributed to the nearly total intransigence of most of the elite toward all proposals for social change, and to the labeling of any reform benefiting the poor as "communism." Anderson notes that "The savage way in which the military and the wealthy have treated the peasants since that time is owing to a fear of repetition. This fear effectively stifles any thought of agrarian reform."[30] Such attitudes helped make inevitable another violent upheaval, an even greater one, which would break out half a century later.

A Peaceful Childhood

These terrible events had no direct effect on a baby growing up in a wealthy household of San Salvador. The Alvarez family's home was on Avenida España in the heart of the city, where grandfather Roberto Alvarez Lalinde had settled. Quique, as Enrique was known all his life, was a healthy boy who escaped the perils that took the lives of many children even of the upper class. One friend remembers the early years this way:

> We were neighbors. Maybe I was 5 and his sister was more or less my age. He was 3 or 4. We went to grammar school together. We lived in the same neighborhood so we walked together all the time. We lived near the San Francisco church, near the children's park on Juan Pablo II Boulevard. My house was by the Majestic Theater; in front was his grandmother's house, a big house. Around the corner were the grandparents from the mother's side. The Córdova family came from Honduras; a very good family, well known, they came to live here. The father's family came from Colombia.[31]

Inevitably Enrique encountered social inequality in his own home and neighborhood, and he found it hard to reconcile with the moral teachings of his parents and Church. Even as a small child Enrique worried about human needs and inequality: "Why don't those kids have shoes? Why do I have nice clothes and the boy across the street doesn't have them? What's the difference?" He used to ask his parents about that. After Enrique's death 50 years later, the Argentine/Mexican commentator Adolfo Gilly wrote this about him:

> The road to this point has been long. Raised in a land-owning family of a liberal strain, his first encounter with injustice was in his own house, where he was one of the masters. That vision of inequality, painful and guilt pro-

> voking for those few of his class who don't have anesthetized souls, conflicted also with the liberal ideas he heard from his father. This liberal tradition in our countries has often been the initial seed of revolutionary radicalism in those who undertake to adjust their lives to their beliefs and carry out this liberalism to the end....[32]

The problem stayed with him all his life. One early attempt to cope with it was told later by a friend:

> I used to admire [Enrique's generosity], the guy had a very big heart. One day after his death I was commenting on these things to his mother, and she said, "Tony, let me tell you a story. We went with his father to New York when Enrique was about 9 years old, and I bought him his communion suit, white pants and white coat and everything, because he was preparing himself at the Church for his first communion. Well, the day came when he was going to receive his first communion. I told him we had to get everything ready and he had to get up at least at 6:30, had to be out there at 7:30. We used to do first communion with a group of other children. So here it was 7:30 and we couldn't find Enrique's little suit. I called him over, and said 'Enrique, what did you do with your first communion suit?' He said, 'Mom, I gave it away.' I said, 'Son, what did you do? Why did you do that?' He said, 'We always have to give away the best things we have.'"
>
> Can you imagine? Nine years old! When she told me that, I said Holy Smokes! No wonder — when I met him, twenty-some years old, I thought, "Now I understand. He was *born* that way!" He was just born that way. It was his destiny to end up the way he ended up. He just had a heart this big. And that was much of his frustration to see all the poverty and the people....[33]

Enrique's first school was *Santa Teresa del Niño Jesús,* managed by two Spanish ladies. It was coed for the earliest years, and he attended *Santa Teresa* together with his sister Carmen until the fourth grade. (According to a family friend, "That's where 'everybody' went; they had good professors."[34]) After that he studied at the Jesuit-run *Externado de San José,* located in the center of the city. ("Externado" means day school; students commute to attend classes and don't reside at the school.) 1942 was his final year of elementary courses, and his school records show many good grades, with a "9" average. ("10" is the highest grade.) In 1944 an issue of *Externado,* something like a yearbook, lists Quique in the "first course" and shows that he received first prize in Religion and ranked first in his class in History and second in Arithmetic. He had no prizes for "conduct" or "punctuality," although these were liberally awarded.

In the summer of 1944 Enrique left the *Externado* and, like most young men of his social position, set off to study in the United States. His first

The Hackley School, Tarrytown, N.Y.

destination was The Hackley School in Tarrytown, New York. The school sits on a hill above the town, which lies on the east bank of the Hudson River less than an hour's drive north of the City. In those years the students were all boys, 50 of them in Enrique's class, and most of them lived at the school. There were one or two other Latin Americans, which must have helped since Enrique spoke very little English when he arrived. He learned! He also had to adjust to a new name, since his Anglo classmates for the most part called him "Henry" or even "Hank." It seems clear that he soon won their respect and affection. One classmate writes: "I remember him as a handsome, strong man who was liked by all." He adds, "That was unusual for Hispanic students at that time; most were looked down on." Another remembers him "well and with great fondness. The memories include his warm smile, an enchanting accent, his good will toward everyone, his modesty."[35] Others also recall Enrique's popularity at Hackley, and his blurb in the 1948 school yearbook sums it up this way:

> "Hank," from El Salvador, joined our class in his freshman year, and has now become one of the most popular boys in the Senior Class. ... His athletic prowess is well known, and on the social side he is found at the head of almost all the school dances. The opposite sex finds him very attractive because he is "quiet and handsome." Little do they know!

> Henry's pleasant personality and his ability to get along well with other people will make him a success in whatever business he enters.

The same edition of *The Hilltop* also reports that Enrique's peers considered him the "Best Looking," the "Best Dresser," the "Best Dancer," and the "Biggest Lady Killer" in the Hackley class of 1948.[36] In those years the word "charisma" was little used, but there's no doubt that Enrique had it to spare.

The comment about "athletic prowess" was not idle, for Enrique Alvarez really was a remarkable natural athlete. He won letters playing on the school's soccer team in his first and second years; of course *fútbol* is the major sport in El Salvador and Quique must have played it as a child. But soccer was not taken very seriously in the United States at that time, so in his junior and senior years Enrique switched to American-style "football" and played halfback on Hackley's team. He also enjoyed basketball and won letters in three of his four years. Quoting again from the yearbook, in 1948 "Hackley had perhaps the best basketball team in the history of the school. The team broke six records.... Besides breaking the record for wins in one season, the team set a new record for consecutive victories with a string of twelve in a row.... Henry Alvarez set a new individual scoring record for one season with his 193 points, breaking the previous record of 177...."

But tennis was Enrique's best game; he was on Hackley's team all four years and was its captain for three of them. In his junior year the team won ten matches and lost one. The 1948 team was just as good. Again from *The Hilltop:* "In Captain Alvarez, [the coach] probably has one of Hackley's best all-time players, and there is little doubt that he will again be playing number one singles, a position which he has held for the last two years. The opening meet will no doubt find him playing on the number one doubles team also...." A junior-year tennis teammate (who "defected" to baseball in 1948) commented that "Whether or not [the 1948 tennis team] was undefeated, I do not recall, but with Enrique in his senior year and just getting stronger, smarter and better, I am pretty sure he himself went unbeaten."[37]

Classmate Jerry Nolan told a remarkable story. He remembers once asking Enrique how he became such a good tennis player. The answer was that his father had arranged for U.S. singles champion Ted Schroeder to spend some time in El Salvador and give him lessons! Alas, it didn't happen that way. Asked for his version, Mr. Schroeder wrote that "I hate to dash your hopes, but there isn't a word of truth" to the tale, adding that he had never been farther south (into Latin America) than Mexico City.[38] It's not clear whether Nolan's recollection was faulty (he himself suspects it was another leading player rather than Schroeder) or if it was just Enrique's joke, based on the fact that something of the sort *could* have taken place.

Hackley Seniors, 1948. Enrique Alvarez is standing, Freeman Day seated at the right (courtesy of Freeman Day, Jr.).

In fact, Enrique's father was himself an excellent tennis player during the 1940s ("Central America champion" according to family history[39]), and there may be no need to look beyond the family to find Quique's principal teacher.

Clearly "Henry" Alvarez was a thoroughly likable young man, one who would have been popular even apart from his athletic skills. The word "gentleman" was often used to describe him. Classmate Perry Edgar remembers that Enrique "was very much a ladies' man, which became apparent when you saw him at a dance. He loved to dance." Mrs. Edgar, who is the twin sister of another classmate as well as Perry's wife, described Quique as "Such a gentleman, and a wonderful dancer! ... He was certainly well liked, absolutely charming.... We wouldn't have known he was a rich kid, he didn't act as you might have expected, or show off. He was just an awfully nice fellow." Her husband summed it up: "We all thought he was a splendid guy."[40] There were no dissenting opinions.

After Hackley, Enrique's U.S. education continued at Rutgers University in New Brunswick, N. J. In 1948 Rutgers was swollen with returning World War II veterans studying under the G.I. Bill of Rights. Its men's colleges enrolled about 4200 students that year; the university's total was over 8600. That is not large by today's standards, but it must have been a major change for 18-year-old Quique Alvarez after his high school years as a "big man" on a very small campus.

Enrique joined Kappa Sigma fraternity and lived in its house on the edge of the campus. His roommate there was Leon (Lee) Pierce, a young man Enrique's own age. (Many of the fraternity brothers were veterans, several important years older.) Lee remembers "Hank" as a "first-rate person," a wonderful guy, handsome, pleasant and well dressed but not flashy. He had a fine singing voice, which he would sometimes demonstrate at informal fraternity beer parties; he was an outspoken fan of Frank Sinatra. But despite his talent and amiability, Enrique did not fully fit into student life at ΚΣ. He frequently left the campus on weekends, not offering much explanation except that he was meeting friends in New York. Even at this stage of his life, Enrique was an essentially private person.[41]

His major was business administration. Enrique was not a good student at Rutgers, and with the exception of courses in Spanish literature he earned mostly poor grades during his freshman and sophomore years.[42] The environment at the fraternity house didn't encourage serious study, and living there was probably a mistake. Lee Pierce thinks he didn't study very hard, almost certainly true since Enrique could have done well academically if he'd applied himself more seriously.

Enrique chose not to participate in organized university sports, but his housemates did discover that he was athletically talented. Lee Pierce was impressed by Enrique's technique when they played informal soccer on the fraternity lawn. Another friend, Carl Fleming, was a Rutgers athlete who played on the university's football and baseball teams and thought of himself as a "fair" tennis player too. Carl recalls that he once asked "Hank" for a game, and got a big surprise. "He was really a terrific tennis player," he writes. "Every ball was hitting those back corners. In desperation I began sending high lobs back in order to break his rhythm. No good! He had a devastating overhead smash that was unreturnable." After the match in which Carl won "maybe one or two games," he asked Enrique why he didn't go out for varsity tennis. He answered that he didn't have enough time. Enrique with characteristic modesty never mentioned that one-sided match to the other guys at the house.[43]

It's impossible to know how Enrique's university career would have developed, for he stayed at Rutgers only those two years. His father was

Enrique's fraternity at Rutgers University.

suffering from the aftereffects of a riding accident that limited his activity, and he needed the help of his older son to manage the family's affairs. Enrique Sr. was also worried about his son's poor grades and the possibility that he might be drawn into the U.S. military and the Korean War. Enrique returned home in the summer of 1950, and soon plunged into the very different life of a wealthy young "gentleman farmer," sportsman, and socialite in El Salvador. He played those roles to the hilt during the next 15 years.

El Salvador in 1950

El Salvador was not the nation it had been in 1932. After the *matanza*, General Hernández Martínez ruled his nation as a military dictatorship with little room for political dissent. Not only the Communist party (the PCS) but *all* opposition parties were banned, along with labor unions and labor organizing. Martínez governed largely in the interest of the agricultural elite, and usually enjoyed its acceptance and cooperation. A debt moratorium passed in 1933 was a vital help for many landowners who would otherwise have lost their farms to the banks. United States recognition was essential and had been withdrawn after the 1931 coup as was required by treaty provisions. No problem. In 1934 Martínez briefly yielded the presidency to an associate, then staged an election in March 1935 with himself the only candidate. This "victory" was good enough to regain U.S. recognition for his government.

The generally sensible economic policies of President Martínez during the 1930s contrasted with his eccentricities in other areas, which included a serious flirtation with Fascism. El Salvador got in ahead of both Germany and Italy in recognizing Franco's regime in Spain, and it was also the first nation to recognize the Japanese puppet state of Manchukuo in occupied Manchuria. A German colonel was appointed to head the military academy, and Salvadoran officers trained in fascist Europe. In 1940 it was even declared illegal to criticize the Axis. Under strong U.S. pressure, however, these policies were abandoned and El Salvador joined the Allied side, declaring war on Germany and Japan shortly after Pearl Harbor. (Martínez was eccentric but not crazy!) The general's government was then rewarded with a flood of lend-lease armaments, which of course saw no service against the Axis. (Some of them were used in the 1969 war with neighboring Honduras.)

The years of World War II brought other changes. An economic boom was accompanied by a cautious renewal of labor organizing. Allied war propaganda about the "four freedoms" and the fight for "democracy" could not be kept out of El Salvador, and these ideals, which Martínez had to endorse in word if not in deed, contrasted with the realities of his long-lasting regime. Gradually Martínez alienated many of his supporters among the younger military, who resented their lack of chances for advancement, and among the wealthy, who distrusted increasing government involvement in the economy as well as some populist directions it seemed to be exploring. But although relaxed restrictions on labor and talk of social reforms worried the rich, they failed to win support for the regime from workers and campesinos. The memory of the *matanza* and the repression of the 1930s could not be so easily erased.

General Martínez had continued in the presidency with the aid of a dubious political maneuver in 1939, but his subsequent term was due to end in January 1945. In late 1943 and early 1944 he prepared to grant himself another extension, and arranged for a Constituent Assembly to make the necessary changes in the constitution. This was duly accomplished. On February 25, 1944 the Assembly declared Martínez reelected to serve as president until the end of 1949 — it had not only changed the law of succession, but had also granted itself the power to make the actual "electoral" decision without troubling the public with any need for voting! Just such a move had worked in 1939. Its repetition in 1944, however, was not successful, and outrage over the fake election added to the growing general discontent. In contrast to the rebellion of 1931, this time members of the middle and upper classes, students, professionals and officers of the armed forces, for their own differing reasons, were among the opposition to the General's regime. An U.S. official reported that the Alvarez family "was undoubtedly active in preparing and swinging" the city of Santa Ana to join the cause.[44]

On April 2 a military revolt broke out. President Martínez and other top officials had left the capital in order to celebrate Holy Week, and the uprising had considerable initial success. But the rebel leaders failed to follow up their advantages. They made many errors, including a radio broadcast that prematurely claimed victory. This broadcast gave the dictator's forces vital information; from it Martínez learned that the police in the capital remained loyal to him. He was then able to elude troops sent to capture him and reach police headquarters in San Salvador to take command of the resistance there. The Air Force, which had joined the uprising, tried to bomb the police barracks but succeeded only in destroying part of the city center. *Time* magazine reporter William Krehm wrote that Martínez's "unworldly sangfroid gave new heart to his men." The general personally visited *El Zapote,* a key fortress near the presidential palace, which had not declared for either side. "If you are not with me," he stated calmly to the officers there, "then go right ahead and shoot me." They pledged their loyalty to the government.[45] Miguel Mármol, who did not take an active part in this uprising, stated that President Martínez "simply changed cars and zoomed on into the capital. He went right through the ambush without anyone seeing him. And on sheer balls, he took over all the vacillators who wanted to give up to the 'revolution,' he organized the resistance.... There's no doubt that he had a good time through the whole rebellion, he played ping-pong with it."[46] By April 4 the fighting was over, the rebellion was crushed, and its organizers were under arrest or in flight.[47]

Military coups, successful or unsuccessful, are far from rare in the history of El Salvador. This one was utterly defeated, and most of its leaders were being executed, with or without trial, by the dictator's forces. Yet in only a little over one month, Hernández Martínez was gone. What happened *was* something rare — rare in world, not just Salvadoran, history. A mass movement of civil disobedience, almost entirely non-violent, succeeded where armed rebellion had failed and made it impossible for Martínez to continue in power. The basic strategy was a general strike, known as *la huelga de los brazos caídos.* In contrast to the rebellion of 1932 the movement had support from all social classes, with students and professionals taking the lead; also unlike 1932 its greatest strength was in the capital. As the strike continued to grow, transportation stopped, most businesses, banks and shops were closed, and even civic employees and personnel of some government offices joined in. The population largely stayed home during the strike; marches and demonstrations were discouraged in order to avoid bloody confrontations with the armed forces.

By the first week in May, the president was finding it impossible to govern. He saw only the options of ordering a massacre (which in any case might not have saved his government) or resigning. As he explained later in an interview:

> In the first days of April, I defeated the insurrection with arms, but finally they provoked a strike. Then I no longer wanted to fight. At whom was I going to fire? At children and youths who did not completely realize what they were doing? Women also were enlisted in the movement, and thus there was no longer a target at which to fire.[48]

On May 9, 1945, General Hernández Martínez resigned the presidency of El Salvador. Two days later he left for exile in Guatemala, never to return.

The More Things Change...

The rebellion that ousted General Martínez was not a revolution. Most of the personnel of the Martínez regime, including members of the legislature, judges, and the senior officers of the armed forces, continued in the jobs they had held. Hernández Martínez's vice-president and crony, the former general Andrés Ignacio Menéndez, assumed the presidency. There was no instantaneous return to democracy.

There *was*, however, an opening that permitted a revival of labor and political organizing and free speech. Acting president Menéndez was an elderly man without dictatorial ambitions, and several parties and candidates prepared to dispute the elections scheduled for early 1945. A moderate reformist party led by a popular physician, Dr. Arturo Romero, seemed headed for success with clear majority support.

In October the tentative democratic opening slammed shut. A successful military coup overthrew the interim government and installed Colonel Osmín Aguirre y Salinas as president. The new leader, a former police chief, averted the alleged threat of "anarchy" by sending Romero and other opponents into exile and making sure that the upcoming elections would have only one candidate. When the voting took place in January 1945, that candidate — General Salvador Castaneda Castro, another early Martínez collaborator — became the nation's "legal" president. Although General Martínez was gone, the continuation of military rule was assured.

Castaneda Castro almost managed to serve out his term. When that term approached its scheduled end, in December 1948 he tried the same tactic with which Martínez had succeeded in 1938 and failed in 1944 — using a constituent assembly to extend his time in office. It didn't work. Dissension within the military would not permit a continuation of that government, and a coup the next day was quickly successful. This became known as the "majors' coup"; it was also sometimes called, with much exaggeration, the "revolution of 1948." Again there was talk of the "military youth" who planned to implement reforms. The administration would be headed temporarily by a Revolutionary Government Council (CGR), which promised a renewed democratic opening, trials for corrupt members of previous governments (both Osmín Aguirre y Salinas and Castaneda Castro were accused and arrested), as well as other reforms including honest elections. As its Minister of Industry and Agriculture the CGR appointed Enrique Alvarez Drews, who apparently became the first member of the Alvarez family to hold a high-level post in any national government.

One of the members of the CGR, Oscar Osorio, was elected president when the date arrived in March 1950. This time the election was contested by a serious opposition party, and Osorio's PRUD (Partido Revolucionario de Unificación Democrática) won with a comfortable but not overwhelming margin. A constituent assembly was again chosen to write a new constitution. This assembly was actually elected by popular vote, and the opposition gained substantial representation. Osorio's administration would prove to be moderately successful, enacting some worthwhile reforms and limiting the repression of its opponents to selected cases. It had the advantage of a substantial rise in coffee prices that produced a modest economic boom and a temporary lessening of social conflicts.

This was the situation to which Enrique Alvarez Córdova returned after his years of U.S. education. It was a time when a well-connected, energetic and bright young man could prosper. Enrique found many ways to enjoy himself, but as the years passed he also took good advantage of his chances.

3

Young Man on the Go: Socialite, Sportsman, and Farmer

Enrique Alvarez was twenty years old when his father called him back to El Salvador in 1950. He was expected to become involved in family business, especially farming, and he did. He wanted to get back into the sports he loved, and he did that too. Then there was the social life, obviously a temptation for a wealthy, popular and dynamic young man. Enrique did not neglect this either.

But first came a grand trip to Europe, an almost obligatory experience for young men of his class. A letter sent from Paris to a friend in El Salvador late in 1951 gives the flavor of the trip. "It seems impossible that the time passes so fast, and in only 15 days we'll be leaving for New York," Enrique wrote. He thought Paris beautiful, and wanted to see everything; his list included "museums, gardens, shops, and above all places to enjoy oneself." Rome, which he said seemed even prettier than Paris, only smaller, also impressed him and he reported that the Coliseum and the other ruins were more striking than he could put into words. Finally, he was delighted by the Swiss countryside, and called it the most lovely he had ever seen. "There are moments when you can see a snow covered mountain, a green pasture and a crystalline river between the two," he wrote. "One wants to lie down and gaze at the panorama for hours."[1]

Enrique was an active and popular young man during the early 1950s in El Salvador. A woman a year younger, who knew him since their teen years and who later became a professor at San Salvador's Universidad Centroamericana (the UCA), remembers those years:

> Around this time we became friends, companions; we'd go out dancing together, we'd go for excursions, played cards during vacations, things like

> that.... He was the heir to one of the biggest fortunes in El Salvador. He was very good-looking, athletic, danced wonderfully. He was *simpático,* a good person; he was— any woman would have been happy to have a relationship with him.

But there was much more to him than that, she says. Enrique was a "very sensitive" man who was moved and concerned by the conditions of the poor majority of people in El Salvador. She felt that concern too, and says she did things then that would "cause her problems" later on:

> Not that I regret them at all! But the fact was that he understood how things were, that he saw that in this country there is a minority highly privileged, which has all the advantages. Here the people have nothing, no choice in their lives, because the others have it all.... And me, I'm one of the group who have the advantages, not because my father was extremely rich but because of the structure of the country. My dad was a doctor, so I had opportunities.... I had the chance to travel and study abroad and to learn about things, which the people here can't do.[2]

Another longtime friend, Coralia Godoy, has similar memories of Enrique:

> I came back [from school in the United States] in 1949; we met, we went to parties together, we were very good friends. Quique was very good looking; he was a gentleman, a very wonderful man, very honest. He worked with his father, at the bank, at the office. He had a hobby, he liked bicycle [racing]. He was very keen on sports, and he helped the poor people to do bike riding, etc. He used to promote football [soccer]; he was always trying to help people that way, to promote people who didn't have money. He gave them suits, and everything. Things like that. He was very different from most of his high-class friends.
>
> One example: He used to give parties at his house; he was very sociable, he had his own personality. He danced beautifully. When he had a party at his house he usually invited many girls; some of them had boy friends, others didn't. He danced with every girl he invited to his house, every one. And all his friends could visit him.[3]

She added, "Any girl whom he would court would be *loco* to marry him!" Of course she meant "eager," not insane!

Enrique's close friend Antonio Cabrales, a few years younger and a basketball teammate during the 1950s, remembers Enrique at parties:

> He'd walk in, you know, and there would be about 30 people there and he'd just take over. He just oozed charisma! Oh, and he sang beautifully. He had a beautiful voice for popular songs. The only thing the guy had left to do

> was play the piano or the guitar, but he didn't go that far, he was involved in so many other things.... There was practically nothing he couldn't do; he was a remarkable guy. And here his friends just loved him, all of his peers, and the girls were all trying to be near him and be his girl friend.[4]

Family historian Mauricio Alvarez agrees.[5] Mauricio also went to The Hackley School, a few years later than Enrique, and met him sometimes in the United States as well as in El Salvador. He feels he knew him well. "He was incredible. He was a wonderful dancer, sang, was a great sportsman. He did everything well! Socially we saw each other a lot because he dated my sister too. All the girls here were in love with him." But Enrique was hard to capture. "He would date her, they would fall in love with him, and then he wouldn't call them for six months. Then he'd call again," Mauricio said. He was referring to his sister "Chiqui"—and quite a few others as well.

"The Most Beautiful Girl in El Salvador"

In 1953 or 1954 Enrique met a girl that he didn't treat so casually. María Isabel Arrieta Gálvez, always called Maribel, was a remarkable young woman, and, as several people commented, undoubtedly "the most beautiful girl in El Salvador." There is objective backing for that claim. In 1953 she was chosen "Miss Latin America" from among 43 contestants and rode on a float in Pasadena's Rose Parade. Then in 1955 Maribel represented her country as "Miss El Salvador" at the "Miss Universe" competition in Long Beach, California. She came in second to the entrant from Sweden.[6] Maribel was a national celebrity when she returned to El Salvador after the competition, and a considerable crowd, including Enrique Alvarez and his brother Ernesto, was on hand to meet her at the airport.

In fact Maribel's friends had expected her to win the top spot in the contest. One of her classmates from Los Angeles still has a firm opinion on the subject:

> She was NOT the second most beautiful girl in the world. She was the MOST beautiful (inside and out). We were all certain that she would become Miss Universe. Why didn't she? She did a very stupid thing. The day before the big judging, she went out on the beach and got a sunburn!!!!! Her skin was pink, pink, pink in that swimsuit! In fact, one of the judges did tell her that she lost points for that, and that's what cost her the contest.[7]

A history of the pageant found on the internet confirms that 1955 produced an unusual "scandal" because "a group" questioned the final judgment, insisting that Maribel Arrieta, described as "the most exact double of Marilyn Monroe," ought to have won. In any case, Maribel had a couple of consolations in addition to her second place finish. First, she was voted "Miss Congeniality" by the other contestants, their own choice for the nicest person among them. She also obtained a short-term contract and acting lessons at Hollywood's Universal Studios, and in November of that year co-starred in the Mexican comedy film *Nos veremos en el cielo* ("We'll meet in heaven"), which was screened in 1956. Unfortunately the film was less memorable than Maribel's Miss Universe appearance, and it seems to have been the only one she made.[8]

Maribel was also a serious artist, and she studied at Los Angeles's College of Art during the early 1950s. In 1953 she received a prize for one of her lithographs and was accepted as a member of the Watercolor Society of Los Angeles. Decades later her paintings appeared in international shows in France, Spain, Belgium, the United States, and Italy. In 1983 one of her pictures won first prize at the International Exposition of Monaco.

One more testimony to Maribel asserts that she unintentionally played the role of Dante's Beatrice for a young Nicaraguan poet in exile:

> There in San Salvador, Rigoberto fell in love, with the most passionate Platonic love I have ever seen, with a beautiful young Salvadoran named Maribel Arrieta, the only Central American to win second place in the global contest "Miss Universe."
>
> One day he showed me an exquisitely lettered album full of manuscript poems dedicated to Maribel. I believe that she never came to know Rigoberto personally, since all this happened by way of us.[9]

The Nicaraguan poet was Rigoberto López Pérez, who in 1956 assassinated the dictator Anastasio Somoza García and lost his own life in the act. For many (but of course not quite all) Nicaraguans he is a beloved national hero. The fate of the album of poems written to Maribel is, unfortunately, unknown.

For several years Maribel Arrieta and Enrique Alvarez were frequently together, and friends expected them to marry. Maribel was more than just good-looking; "she was a beautiful person inside and out," says Tony Cabrales.

> She was fair, blonde, looked something like Marilyn Monroe, that type, but much more beautiful. Marilyn was more sexy, this girl was very humble, very nice — a beautiful girl. She used to come to the games, and that was his girl friend. I used to go with him to give her serenades, guitar playing and love songs, and he'd sing and everything.... I remember all those years.
>
> He really liked this girl. For some reason something happened and he

didn't continue with her. Otherwise I think his life might have changed, gotten married.... He never married.[10]

Another friend and colleague, Lino Osegueda, had this to say about Enrique and Maribel: "They were really in love and planned to marry. But her finish in Miss Universe opened for her a year of modeling and touring in Europe, and this led to their breakup. A bit later, Enrique was very upset to read that she was going to marry a nobleman."[11]

And so she did. In December 1956 Maribel was appointed chancellor of the Salvadoran consulate in Antwerp, Belgium, where she served until 1963. There she met Baron Jaques Thuret. When the two were married in April of 1961 Maribel herself became a member of the Belgian nobility as the Baronesa de Thuret. The marriage, which took place in Genoa, between a Latin American beauty queen and a European nobleman was a glamorous event and received international attention.

Maribel's marriage with Jaques Thuret produced three children, but their relationship was not a happy one; "Jaques was not a nice man," according to one of her friends. Fortunately Maribel had other interests. She kept up diplomatic work in various positions, and in 1977 became a cultural attaché for the Salvadoran mission to the European Community. Living in Europe also allowed her to continue to study and work as an artist—with considerable success, achieving her first international show in 1974 in France. Maribel expressed her religious and compassionate feelings by caring for seriously ill people making the pilgrimage to Lourdes in search of help. She even studied nursing (in Brussels) in order to do this work, and made many trips at her own expense. The Order of Malta in El Salvador honored her devotion with the "silver medal of merit Melitense" in 1981, and with the title "Dama Magistral de Gracia" in 1985. Maribel died in 1989 at the age of 55 years.

Opinions differ on why Enrique and Maribel separated. Her movie role and other career choices may have been part of the story, but if so were they the cause or the effect of the breakup? Antonio Cabrales suggested that Enrique's parents may have opposed a marriage between the two, since Maribel's family, although they were far from poor, had a lesser social position than the Alvarez's. "At that time society here was very, very closed," he added. "Of course she was a very beautiful girl ... but they expected *everything.* It was like Diana and Charles...." Ernesto Alvarez discounts this idea, commenting that their parents liked Maribel very much.[12] The full truth is probably impossible to establish. But after Enrique's death 19 years later, Lino Osegueda received an envelope from Maribel with a photo from the 1950s showing the two of them dancing. She couldn't keep it anymore, she explained, since seeing it made her too sad. Lino also speculates that the frustrated love affair with Maribel could be the reason Enrique never married, but he isn't sure, and neither is anyone else.

Athlete and Sportsman

Sports were a strong current in Enrique's life during the fifties. He kept up the tennis he played so well at Hackley, and was considered the number two player in El Salvador. The strongest player was Federico Aguilar Meardi, also the son of a wealthy family, and they tested each other often. In those days relatively few Salvadorans played tennis; to play at all meant belonging to a club and the whole country had only a handful of courts. There were national tournaments, but formal international competitions were a thing of the future.

Basketball was more important, and El Salvador had many amateur teams. In a small country sports could bring together surprising sets of people, and a club called "Arco Iris" (Rainbow) was the arena where Enrique Alvarez and José Napoleón Duarte became friends. Duarte's political trajectory was to be dramatic. As an organizer and leading activist of the Christian Democratic Party during the 1960s he became for a time the country's foremost opposition politician. He was three times elected mayor of San Salvador, and almost all observers believe he was cheated of the nation's presidency in 1972 after a hard-fought campaign (see chapter 4). Eventually Duarte did achieve his dream of being El Salvador's president, but only under very different circumstances when his Christian Democratic Party, much changed from its idealistic beginnings, provided a civilian facade for the military/political project backed by the United States during the civil war of the 1980s.

But all that came much later. "That decade of my life, the 1950s," Duarte recalled in his autobiography,

> was filled with my family, my career and private community service. I had come back from Notre Dame ready to build the highest buildings, the wonders of concrete and steel, banks and hospitals. I saw myself purely as an engineer and wanted to build bridges and roads in my country ... my mind was on engineering, not on politics. My activities were all apolitical, like Scouting. I coached the basketball team that would become the Latin-American champions....[13]

That team was the Arco Iris. Enrique Alvarez helped organize the team and became one of its star players. He and Duarte were close friends at the time, although politics and history were to drive them apart.

In fact the Arco Iris was not merely a basketball team but a multi-faceted sports club. According to Napoleón's older brother Rolando Duarte, it was founded in 1947 by both brothers.[14] Rolando then left to study in England, but Napoleón kept up the club and Enrique Alvarez joined soon after he returned to El Salvador in 1950. At its peak the Arco Iris had about 80 young men and boys (no girls) as dues-paying members, and they played tennis and volleyball as well as organizing basketball teams at several levels. The club had its own facilities, constructed on some land belonging to the Alvarez family that Enrique arranged for them to use without charge. There they built basketball and volleyball courts, with lights and a grandstand and a sign proclaiming the complex as the "Arco Iris Sports Center." Often after practice at the Center Enrique would take everyone out for food and drinks, picking up the check for them all as a matter of course.

The players who formed the senior basketball team had been students at different U.S. and Salvadoran universities and schools, and when they first got together each brought his own uniform from his old team. The variety of colors suggested a rainbow and the name stuck, although once organized the team wore yellow uniforms and were sometimes called "Los Dorados" (the golds) in the sports pages. Enrique and the Duarte brothers were all on the team in the early 1950s. (Rolando played volleyball too until sidelined from both sports by a knee injury.) The Arco Iris did win the Salvadoran basketball championship and for several years they were clearly the nation's strongest team. Arco Iris players formed the nucleus of the national team later in the 1950s.

It was the Arco Iris that brought Enrique together with Antonio Cabrales, who became one of his closest life-long friends. Cabrales was a Salvadoran national, but he grew up in the United States. In the 1950s he lived in New Orleans where his father was El Salvador's consul, and Tony became a teen-aged basketball sensation (the "dribbling magician") playing for the "Saints" of St. Martin's High School. One day he received an unexpected telegram from Napoleón Duarte. As he told the story,

> ... both of them [Enrique and Duarte] were sponsoring this team, and I remember that one day I got a telegram in New Orleans from Duarte, saying "We need you here for a championship game. Take the plane...." I went to my father and asked if I could go. He said OK since it would only be for a couple of days, so I came down here. I was still in high school. They all came to meet me at the airport, Duarte and Enrique and all, and it was a big game because it was one of these turning points. There was this team that had been the champions here for about 20 years, and then this new generation of boys was being pushed by Duarte—you can imagine Duarte, all of his energy was going into sports at that time. Later all that energy went

> into the Christian Democrats, but he was ... always revved up to 2000 revolutions per minute. And Enrique was very energetic too. So they were all excited about the chance of beating this Buitres ["Vultures"] team.
>
> We ended up beating this team 2 out of 3 games, and I'll never forget: Duarte said to me "You're going to start and you'll be the captain." I said fine. Then I didn't see any clipboard or anything like that, and it was getting close to game time. Finally we got in a huddle, and Duarte said, "OK, you're going this way and they are going that way. Go in there and fight!" [This seemed to Tony a bit sketchy as game strategy!]
>
> When he became president we used to say, "That's probably what he's telling them up there at the White House: We're going this way..." Even in those times we used to call him "El Loco Duarte" ... he'd get in fights with the referees; he was always so energetic and so hyper, you know. He was quite a guy.[15]

Another reminiscence about those years was recently published in a novel entitled *La Conexión Gringa (The Gringo Connection).* The central figure is a wealthy self-made Salvadoran who remembers the team, and especially Enrique, fondly:

> Yes, I miss those times, especially the years of the Arco Iris.... They were maybe the best of all....
>
> We were national champions for several years. It was a great bunch of guys. Social differences didn't exist; we were all friends ... but maybe the best of all as a person, and the one who helped me a lot, the way he helped anyone who asked, was Quique Alvarez.
>
> To Quique money wasn't important....[16]

The hero in the novel explains that Alvarez found him a job so he could support himself while studying, then put him in touch with possible employers after graduation. He even met his wife at one of Quique's parties. Later Enrique helped him get started in business. Without this help his success would have been impossible, he explains, since "in this country a poor man, no matter how much he works and how capable he is, lives and dies on the same mean street unless he has access to higher levels." The story quoted is fiction, but the comments about the Arco Iris, and about Enrique Alvarez, have the ring of truth.

Something parallel happened with Antonio Cabrales in real life. When he first came to El Salvador to play basketball he didn't speak much Spanish. He stayed at the Alvarez home and Enrique introduced him to Salvadoran society. Later, after Cabrales graduated from Delaware Valley College in Pennsylvania and returned to live in El Salvador, Enrique helped him buy a cattle farm. Tony remembers it this way:

> I went to him and said, "Should I buy this farm?" And he looked at it and said, "Yes, go ahead and buy it." I said, "Well, can you help me?" And he replied, "Sure, what do you need?" I said, "I don't want any money, but I need your collateral, your signature, or they won't want to lend me any money." He said, "OK, you tell me where to sign and I'll sign."
>
> Well, I have my farm because he gave me his signature. It was the only favor I ever really asked of him. And I worked my tail off because I didn't want to cause a problem here. If they foreclosed on me, he would have to pay the debt. I never had to do that. And he saw me, for at least 15 years, buying my farm and getting ahead. So I know he used to feel very proud, because he would tell people "Look what Tony's done," and so on, because he felt in a way that he had been my mentor. So I was happy to show him that I was able to do what I had done.
>
> What I did was not easy; not too many people here have done it. Go out and buy a farm, and buy cattle, and do everything that I did, on zero money. I didn't put up one penny. I went and borrowed 100 percent. I didn't even have money to pay the lawyer to make the deed. And we just don't do that here, nobody does it. You have to have at least 30, 40, 50 percent up front, or else your interest payments become terrible when you have zero and you owe 100 percent. I did it! But the reason I did it was that I went out and I lived on the farm, with my children. For about 10 years ... and I broke my back to make it work. One of the reasons I broke my back was because I couldn't let [Enrique] down.[17]

Cabrales became a successful rancher and businessman, served as Minister of Agriculture in the late 1980s, and has been the vice-president and is currently (2005) president of FUSADES (Salvadoran Foundation for Economic and Social Development), an influential private-sector thinktank closely tied to U.S.A.I.D. He is a man who "made it" in Salvadoran society starting without inherited wealth—but not without a helping hand from "higher levels."

Back in September 1955, both Enrique Alvarez, a "veteran" at age 25, and newcomer Tony Cabrales (19) were preparing to play for the national team in the Fifth Central American Championship of basketball. First came a two-game preliminary round versus Honduras. Playing at home the Salvadorans won them both; Enrique had 10 and 11 points in the two low-scoring contests. But when the team moved on to the finals in Guatemala, perennial favorite Panama defeated El Salvador twice; in the first game the score was 88 to 61. A San Salvador sports columnist wrote that "Nothing availed, we repeat, the vitality and experience of our "cracks" Pineda, Alvarez and Guzmán Cucalón, nor the mischief, craftiness and shooting of newcomers Cabrales, Salomón, Matheu, Rivera and others. The Panamanians, strong cagers by tradition, dominated our lads the way they know how to do in these competitions, by comfortable scores."[18] Still, the Salvadoran team acquitted itself honorably by splitting its two games with Guatemala and taking both from last-place Costa Rica. Underneath a picture of the starting five (which included both Enrique and Tony) *La Prensa Gráfica* commented that "in spite of pessimistic expectations, our team exceeded itself and did an excellent job...."[19]

Just once, in 1959, the Salvadoran basketball team managed to beat Panama and win the Central America championship. After that they traveled south to play Venezuela and beat them too; that qualified El Salvador for that year's Pan American Games, held in Chicago during September. Neither Alvarez nor Cabrales can be found in the box scores from those Games. Enrique went to Chicago as a non-playing coach (*entrenador*), while Tony didn't go at all. It was his senior year in college, he explained, and participating with the team, including the months of preparation, would have cost him a year's delay in graduating that he couldn't afford. "And to tell the truth," he adds, "I wasn't too eager to go because I knew we'd get our pants beaten off up there, when we had to play the U.S. team!" And so they did — El Salvador was crushed 101 to 42 by a U.S. lineup loaded with future N.B.A. stars including Hall of Famer Oscar Robertson. The U.S. team won all its games and the championship while the Salvadorans finished last, losing to each of the six other teams in the tournament although the rest of their games were far closer than the loss to the United States. Alvarez and Cabrales at their best would have helped, but couldn't have reversed that decisive outcome.

After 1959 Enrique's days as an international basketball player were finished. Tony Cabrales continued to play with the national team until his marriage in 1961, and Enrique helped coach some of those teams together with Napoleón Duarte. Cabrales remembers an occasion, probably in 1961, when the team was getting ready for a practice. Duarte turned to Alvarez and asked mysteriously, "Quique, shall we tell them what we're doing?" Enrique said no; they should talk about that another time. Tony had no idea what was going on, but later found out that Duarte was deeply involved in organizing the Christian Democratic Party of El Salvador (the PDC) and had talked it over with his friend. Their basketball companion Napoleón was on his way to becoming the leading popular politician of the nation. In 1964 in his first campaign Duarte was elected mayor of San Salvador, usually considered the second most important elected post in the nation.

Enrique also played polo. The sport was something of a family tradition, for "the Alvarez brothers" of an earlier generation were among the founders of Salvadoran polo in 1926.[20] After a decline, enthusiasm for polo was revived in 1950 and Enrique, age 20, was among this generation of players. A few years later a new group, including Enrique's younger cousin

Jaime Alvarez, replaced some of the 1950 cohort—but not Enrique, who stayed active for many more years. Starting in 1955 a Central American polo tournament was held yearly, and Enrique's name was listed for El Salvador that year and the next. He missed the next two competitions (Jaime did play in both), but returned in 1960 and played each of the next five years, and again in 1966. Along the way Enrique suffered a serious injury in which he broke ribs and a collarbone and needed surgery to repair the damage to his body—his spirit wasn't touched. Tony Cabrales described Enrique's style:

> El Salvador had a good polo team and used to win competitions. [Enrique] was a tremendous polo player and I admired him there too because he could really ride, he was a daredevil rider.... You'd see him dominating this 1500 pound horse. He was very well built, very strong. He was very gifted. You'd go to the swimming pool and he'd get up on the high diving board and would be doing all kinds of things—somersaults. You'd get him on the dance floor and people would think he'd studied at Arthur Murray's.[21]

As that comment suggests, basketball, polo, and tennis were not the whole extent of Enrique's athleticism; he tried many things and was good at all of them. Water skiing, for example, not then a team or competitive sport, still gave him a chance to show off. Watching him, a friend commented, you might have thought you were at Cypress Gardens!

In all of this activity Enrique's athletic ability was matched by another quality—his generosity. He used his wealth to sponsor teams and players, sometimes at a very personal level. Antonio Cabrales mentioned one example, one among many. In the 1950's Enrique's father and other family members founded a shoe company. It was in competition with "ADOC," started around the same time by another group of investors. ADOC succeeded and is today a major seller and exporter of shoes, while the Alvarez's company "La Calzadora" failed after a few years. But during those years, Enrique carried 30 pairs of shoes in the back of his car. Tony says that "Every time we'd go someplace and poor people would be around, he'd give them shoes."

> I remember at that time our houses didn't have walls outside—now it's like a walled city, you know—so people used to come into the yard of Quique's house over there, especially kids. I used to stay at his house when I'd come to play, and I remember he'd take shoes—someone would say, "Quique, do you have any shoes to give me?" And he'd go to his closet and get shoes out; he'd get shirts out. I remember that all of his clothes were good quality clothes, bought in New York ... and he'd give them away! I used to say, this guy, his biggest problem—it wasn't really a problem, it was a noble attribute—was he had a very big heart.[22]

A Painful Scandal

In 1957 an unpleasant incident interrupted the flow of Enrique's life. Exactly how it began is obscure, but rumors circulated about one or more bizarre parties involving Arco Iris basketball players and other young men, some of them, like Enrique Alvarez, from prominent families. These affairs involved a lot of drinking (this was not unusual!) and, it was claimed, also gay sex among the men. By some accounts, a resentful member of the team that Arco Iris had just defeated made public the story of one such party, including the accusations of homosexuality. Whoever was responsible, a list of names was published in a gossip and scandal column called *El Machete* that appeared on the back page of *El Independiente,* a small "alternative" paper. That column did not actually accuse those it named of homosexuality or anything else, but to anyone who had heard the rumors the meaning was clear. The story was then picked up in a highly guarded form by the mainstream press as well.[23]

For a time, this minor incident became the gossip of the nation. There wasn't much to it, but sons of famous families were involved and in the Latin America of the 1950s homosexuality was scandalous in a way that is hard to understand today. The affair was noted three times in the Jesuits' journal *Estudios Centroamericanos (ECA)*, which in those days was far from the progressive voice it later became.[24] The first comment was this:

> Without giving credit to the lies and exaggerations of a certain yellow press, the fact is that our "good" youth, certain young people from distinguished families, have become the theme of daily comment in all circles, particularly because of the shameful acts with which they occupy their long periods of idleness.... It was truly deplorable conduct on the part of those who by their position, their comfortable economic circumstances, and the education which they have received, should be obligated more than others to give an example of order and morality, the necessary condition for them to command respect from members of the public who have not had their advantages....

The second mention by *ECA* reported that the national legislature had taken certain measures because of the scandal. The law it passed, which *ECA* hoped would lead to "concrete steps" and not be allowed to become a "dead letter," was aimed at the *publishers* of material which "in any way offends against modesty and good manners" or against "public morality," and it provided penalties up to three years in prison plus substantial fines. The third note was headed "Repudiation of the immoral press" and stated:

> An occasional paper called *El Machete* recently created a public scandal, offending the norms of social morality by publishing certain obscenities

> and by brazenly defaming a number of persons worthy of consideration, accusing them of immoral acts. This scandal shows the measure of the laxity and greed of certain bad journalists, who will do anything to make money even if it causes great harm to society....

In two months, *ECA* had moved from denouncing the "shameful acts" of idle, privileged youths to condemning the publisher of the scandal! Printing that list of names in *El Machete* does seem malicious, and it certainly caused pain to those involved, including Enrique Alvarez. Nevertheless, the National Assembly's response set up a new and dangerous obstacle for anyone trying to practice critical journalism—a civic virtue for which El Salvador was not greatly noted in any case.

Dr. Ruiz Izaguirre, the novelist whose hero fondly remembered the Arco Iris, has his character describe the events this way:

> Sometime in 1957 there was a scandal when there was uncovered a group of ... homosexuals ... who got together to enjoy themselves. They did it in private, trying to be discrete, but accidentally the thing got too big and became known all around. There was even an article in a fourth-rate newspaper, which listed the names of the supposed members of that group. Today [1994] this doesn't seem so terrible, but at that time various families fell into disgrace because their sons were mentioned as part of the group. Quique was mentioned among them. There were those who didn't see him any more, but we stuck with him. The friendship among the team members was too strong for us to leave him by himself. We went on playing, and winning....
>
> The team broke up years later, for other reasons. What hurts me now, and always will, is that Quique—who was Minister of Agriculture in the years of the government junta, who organized a model agricultural cooperative on family lands, who was generous to so many people ... years later they kidnapped him, they tortured him atrociously, savagely, and finally they killed him.
>
> There are things that just have no name! But even these things are forgotten in this country. I've often thought that even by dying for it one can't accomplish anything.[25]

Enrique was hurt by the scandal, but he was also enraged and looked for a way to strike back. Friends recall that he wanted to fight a duel with the publisher of *El Independiente,* a young man named Jorge Pinto Jr. There was no duel, but a fight between the two did take place. Antonio Cabrales is the only witness still living; he remembers it this way:

> And then one time this other team that we beat, they were really mad ... and so when we beat them they started coming up with defamatory type of

> things, saying that all of the Arco Iris guys, we were all queers. It came out in the papers, and this one paper put in a list of all of us. I wasn't on the list because they didn't know me too well. I was one of the best players, but since I wasn't living down here for some reason I escaped. But the rest of them were all on this damned list....
>
> One day, all of a sudden — all I remember is that we were driving down the street in San Salvador, Quique was driving, Duarte was next to him in the front seat and I'm in the back seat. All of a sudden Quique says to Duarte, "Take over, Napoleón." Napoleón jumps over and takes the car, you know, Quique gets out and sees this guy coming down the sidewalk, and Boom! He just hit him two right hands right to the jaw. The guy goes over, [Enrique] jumps back in, and we take off like a group of gangsters. I didn't know what the hell was going on at all!
>
> It was the owner of this newspaper ... one of the third-rate papers, like a supplement, 2 or 3 pages, that had come out with this list of all the players, most of the team. And Enrique didn't like that at all, and wanted to show him, look, if I'm queer, let's see if you're man enough to do something about it. We came back to Enrique's house about an hour later, and a police car had been going around looking for us.
>
> You know I'll never forget that. Can you imaging me sitting in the back there, and there were Duarte and Enrique Alvarez, two figures who later in history were going to be what they were.... If I'd known at that time who they were going to end up being! It was amazing![26]

This scandal marked Enrique for life. It was never completely forgotten and the idea that he was gay followed him always. It remained a *suspicion,* never confirmed, and it started with the Arco Iris accusations. The fact that Enrique never married was a contributing factor, even though he had many attractive women friends in addition to Maribel. Moreover, it was widely commented from his Hackley years onward that he was a "gentleman," especially in his relations with women. As his many sports successes demonstrate, Enrique was anything but effeminate, but he failed to display some of the traditional *machismo* common among men of his social cohort. These factors seem to be the grounds for the persistent rumors of his homosexuality.

Enrique was a private person who exchanged few intimate confidences. He was highly discrete about his personal life, to the extent that even close friends and some family members were never sure of his sexual orientation.[27] But the suspicion that he was gay, once planted, could never be undone, and this in itself had an impact on his life. After 1957 Enrique cut back some of his social activities, and the scandal distanced him from certain members of his economic class and social circle. Perhaps to some extent it forced him to grow up and take life more seriously. The scandal itself, and possible questions about his sexuality that it raised, may also have been factors in his separation from Maribel, although that is pure speculation. Certainly this episode added to the growing difficulties in Enrique's relationship with his father, differences which would turn explosive and bitter with their political disagreements in the years to come.

Jorge Pinto Jr.

Enrique's anger toward young Jorge Pinto was natural and justifiable. Nevertheless, Pinto's scandal mongering becomes more understandable, even if not excusable, when events in his own life are taken into account. He was also a character worth knowing.

Jorge Pinto Jr., like Enrique Alvarez, was born to wealth, into a family linked to the coffee oligarchy. His maternal grandfather was Mauricio Meardi, a leading coffee exporter and perhaps at one time the richest man in El Salvador. On the other side, Pinto's father, and his father before him, were important journalists and publishers. As Pinto tells it in his autobiography, both were dedicated to defending the interests of the poor and to fighting against corruption within El Salvador and against imperialism from without. When his parents married in 1929, the mother was a young widow with considerable education and experience of the world. (Her first husband had been a Spanish diplomat who died of appendicitis two years after their marriage.) Through her astuteness, Pinto writes, "the contradictions in the union of a person from a highly conservative family with a young journalist belonging to an old line of ultra liberals" were kept in the background. He adds that "A hundred elegant guests drank toasts to the happiness of the couple [Pinto-Meardi] in a land submerged in misery."[28]

Their son was born in 1937. His father was editor of the San Salvador newspaper *Diario Latino,* and he was arrested in December 1943 for the paper's opposition to the Hernández Martínez dictatorship. While still in prison in 1944, when the boy was seven, Jorge Pinto Sr. was shot by guards and badly wounded. He never recovered his health, although he lived thirteen years longer until February 20, 1957. By that time the son, just completing his teen years, had launched his own career as a journalist and militant opponent of the military-dominated government of Oscar Osorio.

In 1954 Jorge Jr. began publishing a paper called *Epoca* in which he denounced "the electoral fraud of the government, the thievery by its high officials and the demagoguery with which it used the word 'revolution' for a regime that was no more than the continuation of the evil dictatorship of Martínez." It is hard to imagine that *Epoca* represented any real threat to Osorio's government, even though Pinto claims that "its success was complete" since it "filled an information vacuum and broke the silence imposed by fear." In any case, *Epoca* was effective enough to land its young publisher in jail. He was roughly arrested by plain-clothes police in September 1954; at the same time his printing equipment was confiscated from his mother's house. In the Central police station young Jorgito was beaten, stripped, thrown handcuffed into a cold and filthy cell, and tortured with the *capucha*,[29] treatment that might have broken many an older man. After some days Pinto was transferred from the police cells to the penitentiary. There the physical abuse stopped, but conditions of food, sanitation, etc., were miserable and such luxuries as showers and a weekly movie had to be purchased from corrupt officials by those prisoners who could pay. Significantly, perhaps, Pinto was disgusted by the open homosexual cruising of some of the men, who sought partners each night in the dormitory where they all had to sleep.

Jorgito was charged with defaming President Osorio, and his chances for release rested on the president's whim. Those chances appeared to be poor. In early December Pinto undertook a desperate measure, a hunger strike in which he declared he would refuse all food and drink until his death or his release. Amazingly, he won. On December 18 the Supreme Court ordered his freedom and he was carried out of captivity on a stretcher, weak but triumphant. A crowd of supporters was there to greet him, some 50,000 as he claims although such a high number seems unlikely. But no doubt he is right that it was strong popular pressure around his case that made the government back down and decide to free him.

Naturally Pinto felt like "a triumphant David confronting a defeated and humiliated Goliath." His dedication to crusading journalism was stronger than ever, and on April 2, 1955 he launched a new paper. *El Independiente* would publish until 1981, when it was finally closed down by bombs that destroyed its facilities and by military terrorism against its staff. During its final years *El Independiente* was one of very few news sources in El Salvador that dared to criticize the military-dominated government and its projects.[30]

Two remarkable young men, both soon to be well known as writers and revolutionaries, served as reporters and columnists with Pinto's new paper. One was the Guatemalan Otto René Castillo, who achieved international fame as a poet in 1957. After years in exile Castillo joined the guerrilla movement in his country, where he was captured, tortured, and murdered by the army in 1967. The Salvadoran of the pair was none other than Roque Dalton, who, Pinto says, had been a friend since childhood and a fellow student at the Externado de San José. It was Dalton who, by pure luck, saw Pinto again being abducted by some 20 plain-clothes policemen on August 21, 1956 together with his editor and a chauffeur. "Probably it was the alarm raised by Roque," writes Jorgito, "that saved us from being definitively disappeared." That alarm worked well indeed, and Pinto was released to a crowd of supporters after only one violent day in captivity.

In the early months of 1957, *El Independiente* was investigating a particularly odious police official. The paper's reporting contributed to a most unusual outcome: Adán Torres Valencia was dismissed from his post, tried, convicted, and sentenced to the penitentiary for the torture and murder of prisoners in his custody. This was the same officer who had tortured Jorge Pinto Jr. himself during his first arrest in 1954. But Pinto was distracted from these events by something even more compelling: the final illness and death of his father on February 20. He writes that Pinto Sr.'s last words were to urge his widow and son to continue the fight for justice in their homeland.

At twenty years of age and with these experiences dominating his life, it is understandable that "Jorgito" would have been disgusted by the reported carousing of rich youths, including the allegations of gay sex, and that he wanted to shame those idlers and make them pay some price. After all, there was urgent and serious work to be done in El Salvador, and the *señoritos,* as Pinto saw them, chose instead to be part of the problem. Enrique's angry reaction to *El Machete*'[31] and to Pinto's scandal mongering was equally natural. Probably neither of the two young men could have believed then that they would meet again 23 years later as close political allies, and even, perhaps, as friends. But times and people do change—and one day Pinto would write of Enrique Alvarez that "very few Salvadorans, of whatever social class, would disagree about the noble principles and the honesty of this man."[32]

Becoming a Farmer

Enrique had to find his place in the family business affairs, and his place was not in the bank or the insurance office. He did not inherit his father's ability to see at a glance the meaning in numbers and data—qualities which helped Enrique Alvarez Drews run the Banco Capitalizador, in which the family had major interests as owners and managers, plus an insurance company, La Centroamericana S.A. So instead Quique followed the path of Emilio's younger brothers when they arrived in El Salvador in the previous century, and started learning to manage the Alvarez farming enterprises. As with his grandfather and great uncles, this meant learning about coffee and helping to oversee the fincas on the San Salvador volcano.

But Enrique loved dealing with animals, and he was eager to move into cattle and dairy farming. Of course the lands on the volcano had to remain in coffee, since conditions there were nearly ideal for that highly profitable crop. But there were Alvarez cattle interests as well, with a ranch near San Salvador and another in the eastern part of the country. Early in the 1950s Enrique senior, with his son's eager agreement, added promising farmlands a few miles south of Sonsonate in the Southwest. Tony Cabrales was visiting at the time, and he remembers accompanying father and son while they inspected the farm called "El Jobo."[33] All three of them rode around the property on horseback, and Tony says that Enrique was dying to buy that farm. In fact, he and his father first rented the property for a year, and then did buy it in 1953. At that time about 80 percent of the land was applied to growing sugar cane and the rest to grain. As manager, Enrique began a transition to "dual-purpose cattle," animals that are raised both for milk production and for meat, and by 1960 the acreage in sugar was down to 40 percent. In order to improve the farm technically, Enrique "sought advice and information from friends and growers with more experience," said his long-time associate Lino Osegueda, "and if he didn't know something he was smart enough to ask, even though he was a millionaire.... He had everything, but his money never went to his brains to block his mentality, his decisions, his way of being."[34]

By 1960 or so Enrique's sports career was winding down and he no longer played basketball with the national team. But he was still competitive, and he put a lot of that drive into farming. Tony Cabrales explains that

> ... we both took all our sports energy, both myself and him, and put it into agriculture. He went to the States, I went with him, and he bought his first pure-bred cattle, Brahmin cattle, and then he started his Brahmin herd, a real pure-bred herd, and he got the milking herd, also, for milk production, and beef production. And then he started doing showing, in Central America, and he became on of the best breeders in Central America. I got involved in showing related to dairy products, the Holstein group. That's why I went to Brattleboro [Vermont], because that's where the head of the Holstein association was....
>
> So we gave all our interest and energy from sports and focused on cattle. And then we got involved in showing, and that was making up for the void of competition. We used to go around together to Honduras, to Guatemala, to shows and everything.[35]

Some of the results can be seen at El Jobo. Pictures of prize bulls hang on the walls in the farm's office building, and a meeting room there also serves to display trophies that El Jobo's cattle have won — over two hundred of them! In addition there are some twenty sports trophies won by El Jobo teams, especially for *fútbol* (soccer). Enrique himself played sometimes, even when his friends told him he was "too old."

More evidence of technical progress at El Jobo appeared in *Agricultura de las Americas,* a Spanish-language farming journal published in Kansas City.[36] A photo of Enrique Alvarez inspecting one of the farm's pastures fills the cover of the January 1970 issue. The featured article entitled "Intensive Pasturing: More milk at less cost" explains how Enrique and Antonio Cabrales undertook a major experiment. They used 124 hectares of land usually considered "too good" for grazing, divided it into 40 small plots, and allowed their milking herd of registered Holsteins to graze a single plot for one day. Then the cattle were moved on to the next small field, and the plot they had just grazed was "rested" for 15 to 20 days. This scheme produced better nutrition for the cows resulting in nearly 30 percent more milk per day, plus equally important cash savings through lower outlays for diet supplements and fertilizer. "One couldn't ask for more," Enrique stated. "I hope the production will continue to go up as we progress with our program to improve the herd through artificial insemination." And it did—production at El Jobo continued to improve steadily throughout the 1970s. The farm is still productive and economically sound today.

Another Venture and Another Sport

The venture was a sporting goods store called "Estadio Centro Deportivo"; the sport was bicycle racing. The store was located in the center of San Salvador, and had its beginning in the middle of the 1960s. It lasted into the 1980s when the building that housed it was destroyed by an earthquake—but that was several years after Enrique's death.

The store began as a partnership between Enrique Alvarez and several young men, at least two of whom had worked for the Alvarez family in low-level positions. One of these was Víctor Villeda, now the prosperous owner of "Industrias Víctor," a sporting goods business in the capital. Villeda recalls[37] that he was managing various small operations for the Alvarezes, things like commissaries in the fincas that the family owned. Enrique liked his work and told him that he deserved to earn more but that he couldn't pay it himself. Instead, Enrique proposed a business partnership where he would put up the capital for a sporting goods store, and Víctor and several other partners could pay for their shares over time if the business succeeded. It did. They started with soccer equipment, Víctor says, and soon branched out into other sports.

Around that time the sport of bicycle racing was taking root in El Salvador. Villeda was a rider himself and Estadio Centro Deportivo soon moved into this field, not only as a supplier of equipment but also as a sponsor. Enrique Alvarez did not compete in bike racing himself; it was one of the few sports he passed up. Instead of riding he became a major patron of Salvadoran cycling. Since 1964 the famous "Tour de France" has had competition, the "Vuelta a El Salvador." The Vuelta is a six-day race through the Salvadoran countryside covering almost 800 kilometers and passing through all 14 "departments"; it was held 22 times during the years 1964–1994, and then renewed in 2004. It soon attracted individual riders and teams from all of Central America and from Mexico; later South Americans came to race also. The 2004 Vuelta included around 100 riders from 16 nations including Europe and the U.S., and was won by a Salvadoran.[38] Enrique Alvarez, together with Estadio Centro Deportivo, was among the earliest organizers and backers of this event.

Estadio sponsored a racing team as well as individuals, and its riders were always near the top. Víctor Villeda competed in the first Vueltas, as did another young man connected with the store, Francisco Antonio Funes, who won the fourth Vuelta in 1973. Of course they both rode for Estadio's team.

Soon a promising younger cyclist joined the group. Orlando Mungía placed second behind a rider from Guatemala in the first "Vuelta de la Juventud" (Youth Tour) held in 1971. He and the Salvadoran team, which finished eighth, were sponsored by Estadio. As the first Salvadoran finisher Orlando won a first-class racing bike; the prize was donated and presented by Enrique Alvarez.

Orlando Mungía continued to star in Salvadoran cycling for several years. Riding for the "Pílsener" (a popular beer) team instead of Estadio he had notable triumphs in national and international races. In 1975 Mungía moved to New York City where he has lived since. He remembers Enrique Alvarez well: "He was a wonderful man, a people's man," he says. Enrique drove a light blue Volkswagen Beetle, not the usual rich man's car that was likely to be a Mercedes. And he owned two Dalmatians. "Enrique was a very private guy who didn't want press coverage or fame for his activities," Mungía recalls. "But he was a big and generous backer of sports in El Salvador."

Bicycle racing was not a rich man's sport. Mungía himself started riding while a teenager working as a messenger, using a very cheap bike that he bought with a loan from his boss. He remembers that once when another rider, a rather poor man, won an important race, Enrique asked him what he would like as a prize. A refrigerator perhaps, or a TV? "No, Don Enrique," the rider replied, "I don't need those things. I'm trying to build a house and I really need bricks for the walls." A couple of days later a truckload of building materials arrived at his site—a gift from Enrique Alvarez.[39]

A Near-Death Experience[40]

It wasn't Enrique's death but Víctor Villeda's that came closest, although both of them could have been lost. Víctor with some others of El Salvador's best cyclists were getting ready for the Vuelta. One hot day the team was visiting El Jobo, and a swim seemed like a good idea. They all went to the ocean shore at another of Enrique's properties.[41] The sea was running high, but they were strong swimmers, especially Víctor who used to do laps in a pool for up to two hours at a time.

"I threw myself in as always," Víctor explained, "and then a wave came along. I went with it, and when I tried to stop I was already 100 meters away and it was still taking me." It was especially hard, he says, because the water was so full of sand that it seemed almost like a mixture of sand and cement. Víctor was in good condition and could ride a bicycle 200 kilometers, but struggling with the surf and riptide was wearing him out.

There were around 20 people in the group, still on the beach. A couple of local fishermen happened to come by, took a look and warned that it was "an ugly place where people drowned." These men had some ropes with them and Víctor's companions tried to get a line to him, but couldn't do it. That sea must have been truly bad, and no one wanted to go in to help.

But Enrique went in. He set out toward Víctor, who was struggling and seemed to be losing heart. While still trying to reach him Enrique was yelling, "Think about your wife, think about your children, think about Lorenita and Roxanita!" He nearly drowned himself, Víctor recalls. Finally, somehow the current altered and brought them closer to shore. This time their friends managed to reach them with lifelines and the two collapsed on the beach. They had been fighting the sea for at least half an hour. Enrique was exhausted, Víctor much more so; he passed out and was unconscious for about thirty minutes.

"This was the only time in my life," Víctor says, "that I saw the tunnel that comes when you are dying." He had read about that, and seen it in films. "There was a black, conical tunnel, and I saw my mother and some relatives who are dead. Then I came to a celestial place where people and beings seemed to be flying. My mother was there and my aunt, and they called to me, 'Son...' and I reached out my hand to them but I was flying and so were they and I couldn't touch them. Then I felt that I was falling, as if into a well. Before I could take my mother's hand, I woke up."

Later Víctor discovered that he had detached the retina in one eye, and after a month he could see nothing from it but blackness. When Enrique heard about it he immediately sent Víctor for a medical exam. That same day the eye was operated on by the best surgeon they could get. There was no laser surgery then, and Víctor had to spend over a month totally immobile, a terrible ordeal for a young athlete. Enrique paid all the medical bills.

Back to the Farm

From the beginning Enrique was unhappy about the treatment of the workers on the Alvarez farms. He would ask his father, "How is it possible that we pay these people so little?" Enrique Sr. replied that they were complying with the laws of the nation and paying the minimum wage. (Many owners did not even do that since enforcement was lax.) Enrique would say, "Yes, but..." and his father would continue something like this: "Son, please understand; you can't do that. If you start paying what it would be possible to pay, you can't do it with only one or two men, you have to do it with everybody and then you just can't afford it. You have to be realistic. That [worker], if he had education he wouldn't be shoveling, he'd be driving a tractor and then his productivity would be higher. With higher productivity he would earn more." Enrique would constantly "have problems" with this argument, says Tony Cabrales.[42]

Enrique himself later recalled some of those feelings:

> I used to do a lot of sports, and there I had a chance to meet people that belonged to another class. And this was very helpful, to understand how different the conditions that they lived in were from the conditions of my life. I started working, after I got back from school, in agriculture. Coffee, mainly. And there it was very clear to me that the people that were making us so rich lived in such poor conditions. So we started doing many things to improve, to change those conditions, such as better houses, nurseries, schools, and so on.[43]

Lino Osegueda explains it this way:

> When he started supervising the farms, Enrique didn't like what was going on in labor treatment. He didn't like to see the workers at coffee-picking time sleeping under the branches of the coffee bushes. He didn't like to see the coffee pickers just eating beans and a couple of tortillas. He worried about the workers' conditions and talked to his father; they started improving the food and providing some shelter for pickers— it was cold; they were 5500 feet above sea level. He was one of the very first coffee growers in this

> country to provide that kind of facility to his workers. He even made some barns. He was more creative too; he collected rainwater to have enough so the workers could have a bath once a week.[44]

These sound like small things, but they made a difference. A former FMLN (revolutionary armed forces) officer recalled that during the civil war of the 1980s he once talked with a campesino who used to work on one of the coffee fincas Enrique managed (and later owned). This man explained that respect and better treatment were also good for business:

> ... he was telling me about working on a coffee finca belonging to Enrique Alvarez Córdova sometime 15 or 20 years earlier. ... He told me that he'd been working on this finca, and that the people preferred to work there because they were treated better there. For example, the food. Generally the workers got beans, tortillas and some salt. But in this finca there were beans, eggs fried or boiled, some cheese, platanos, and of course salt and 3 or 4 tortillas. Everyone saw the difference in the food they got.
>
> Another thing was the housing. Usually it's one huge building where everyone gets a bit of ground to sleep on. But in Quique's farm the conditions were better. Things were clean, and there was ventilation.
>
> He also said that the other finqueros [owners] were annoyed with Quique Alvarez, since of course most of the workers preferred to be on his farm. And it even paid off for him. The workers took more care with the coffee, picked the beans better, did a better job and produced more. So the other owners were angry with him, because he was a "bad example." It put pressure on the others to do some of the same things. But the tradition was to give the workers just the minimum in food, housing, benefits and so on.
>
> So it's interesting that Enrique gave a little more, but his people felt good about it and did a better job and so his production was higher than on the other fincas.[45]

To care about workers' welfare was unusual but not unique. Lino Osegueda comments that there were others: "Francisco de Sola, Víctor de Sola, Roberto Poma were other rich men who cared about the people. They were human-sensitive, not just money-making machines." The same could be said of several earlier members of the Alvarez clan. But Enrique's concern had an important extra dimension: he wanted to *empower* the workers, not just benefit them. "He thought about their potential to become efficient at farm management," Lino Osegueda says. There is ample evidence for this, and Enrique later summed it up himself. After commenting on the efforts to improve working conditions, he continued this way:

> But I found something which I think is the most important thing; that the more I did, the more the people depended on me. And I don't think that's

> right. I don't think anybody should depend in that way on another person. So I started then reading and studying other systems, and I made a decision then that the people should be let to decide their own future — that *they* should take the decisions of what to do.[46]

He took the lesson to heart, and years later it led to the long and successful effort to develop El Jobo into a worker-managed and owned cooperative. It was this attitude, not simply humane treatment, which was unique or nearly so among the big landowners and which constituted Enrique's real "treason against his class."

At the same time, Enrique Alvarez was ready to accept progress in small, practical steps, to work within the system to achieve limited gains—without losing sight of larger goals. His coming years as a government official testify to this willingness. He would argue that change should be regarded as a form of insurance, that moving rural El Salvador toward social justice would provide security and stability for future generations. With his wealth, family connections, and personal qualities, he was superbly qualified to persuade and lead his fellow landowners toward gradual but real reform. Nevertheless it proved impossible to make much progress, for most members of the oligarchy steadily refused to make concessions or accept meaningful change. In 1980, with political options closed, Enrique Alvarez would become president of the Frente Democrático Revolucionario, demanding fundamental social change for his country — by armed struggle if necessary. That was the last resort. Enrique would come to support the cause of revolution only when he believed that all possibilities for peaceful evolution had been exhausted.

But the 1960's were a time of hope. New political spaces were opening, and progress through the existing system seemed to be, if not certain, at least possible. Inevitably, Enrique Alvarez would be an important part of that process.

El Salvador into the 1960s

A brief description of El Salvador's next decade can help set the stage. The administration of President José María Lemus (1956–1960), like many others, began well and ended badly. Although Lemus assumed office after a fraudulent election, his administration undertook several moderate reforms and useful public projects. Falling coffee prices hurt the economy, however, while the Cuban revolution of 1959 raised popular hopes and demands that could not be met. The oligarchy called for a firm hand to maintain control, and Lemus responded with a bloody attack on the national university and a state of siege, among other repressive measures. On October 26, 1960 he was overthrown in a bloodless coup. His presidency left "a legacy of arrest, torture, murder, and exile of dissidents."[47]

To govern the nation, the coup organizers installed a six-man junta consisting of three junior military officers and three civilians. The junta's program consisted basically of a return to democracy. It lifted the state of siege, freed political prisoners, proposed new programs of public education, and promised to hold free and honest elections in the near future. It also declared, reasonably, that major social and economic reforms would have to wait since they should be undertaken by an elected government.

This simple program was too radical for the Salvadoran military, and just three months later the junta was removed by another coup in the name of anti-communism. Unlike the October coup this one was protested by large popular demonstrations; they were bloodily suppressed by military force leaving 96 dead.[48] The new junta, calling itself a civilian/military "directorate," soon abandoned any pretence that its elections would be open and honest. It dismantled the old official party, which by now had a bad reputation, and created a new one called the National Conciliation Party (PCN). One of the directorate's members, Lt. Colonel Julio Adalberto Rivera, then resigned in order to become the PCN's candidate for president. He won the "election" of May 1962 against the only other candidate, a donkey nominated by university students. Rivera went on to complete his term in office, and was succeeded in 1967 by the second PCN president, Colonel (later General) Fidel Sánchez Hernández.

It appears that the U.S. government also found the program of the 1960 junta too democratic for its liking. One member of that junta was Dr. Fabio Castillo Figueroa, a professor of physiology at the national university (UES) and later to be the university's president. Dr. Castillo testified at a U.S. Congressional hearing in 1977 about the role of the United States in El Salvador. Referring to 1960, he quoted two conversations in which the U.S. chargé d'affairs objected both to the proposed free elections and to the junta's plan for a literacy campaign. Castillo said that he rejected the chargé's "advice," and after that "members of the U.S. Military Mission openly intensified their invitation to conspiracy and rebellion."[49] Other accounts suggest that the first junta's willingness to establish diplomatic relations with Cuba may have been a crucial issue as well. The new "Directorate," in any case, was quick to placate the United States by strongly denouncing Fidel Castro, the Cuban revolution, and "communism" in general.

In spite of its undemocratic beginning, however, Col. Rivera's term as president was relatively peaceful and prosperous. Coffee prices were up, and U.S. aid was arriving under the Kennedy administration's "Alliance for Progress"—especially now that the threat of a Salvadoran government soft on Cuba had been avoided. The new Central American Common Market provided outlets for a growing light manufacturing sector. Modest liberal reforms granted organizing rights to urban workers; there were benefits for campesinos too (but not including the right to unionize), and useful government projects included schools, water systems and public housing. These policies were generally popular, and the United States approved of them as well. In agreement with Alliance for Progress rhetoric Rivera also offered some space to political opponents, and El Salvador's party politics became, if nothing else, much more interesting. The basic structures of land ownership and control were not touched, but even so some members of the oligarchy were outraged by these "Bolshevik" measures.

José Napoleón Duarte, the old basketball teammate of Enrique Alvarez, was one of a committee of eight men who, starting late in 1960, organized the Christian Democratic Party of El Salvador (PDC). Duarte has written that when the possibility of really free elections was raised by the 1960 junta, there were no organized parties prepared to take part except the right-wing military party on one hand and the Communists on the other. The PDC, he says, was meant to be a democratic party of the center, created to fill that gap. In fact the early 1960s saw a rapid growth of Christian Democracy throughout Latin America, with the 1964 election of Eduardo Frei to be president of Chile as the leading example.[50]

In El Salvador, once the PDC was given a chance to organize and participate in elections its advance was rapid. Napoleón Duarte served as the party's general secretary and was its first major candidate for office. Beginning in 1964 he won three consecutive two-year terms as mayor of San Salvador, where he did a good job with city affairs and gained a considerable popular following. The Christian Democrats also won substantial minority representation in the national assembly. The PDC fared less well in the 1967 presidential election, however, and after a dirty campaign it finished a distant second behind the PCN, not far ahead of the newly left-leaning Renovating Action Party (PAR) whose candidate was Fabio Castillo.[51] (The PDC and the PAR together received 36 percent of the votes nationwide, but a 54 percent majority in San Salvador.)

Reform with Repression

During the middle 1960s El Salvador seemed to be moving toward democracy and progress, but there was a much darker side to the picture as well. After John Kennedy's death in 1963 the constructive work of the

Alliance for Progress declined. Covert U.S. "security" aid, however, continued for twenty years—and after that time much of it simply moved into the open. All this reflected the contradictory priorities of U.S. policy, where combating popular movements, which the United States always saw as potentially leading to communism, often conflicted with support for democracy, welfare, and human rights. Outstanding examples in El Salvador were the creation of two organizations named ANSESAL and ORDEN (the names are acronyms, but the latter is also Spanish for "order"). The U.S. government was heavily involved in their founding and operation, and much of the "death squad" terror of the 1970s was a direct legacy of this kind of "foreign aid."

ORDEN was a paramilitary organization operating mostly in rural areas; founded in 1965, at its peak it claimed over 100,000 members. Some of these were ex-soldiers, but many others were simply campesinos who gained practical advantages from membership, especially protection from military and police persecution. Its roles included anti-communist propaganda and low-level "intelligence"—the identification of dissidents and organizers to be killed, either by its own members or by military units. In contrast ANSESAL, originally named the National Intelligence Service (SNI), was primarily for intelligence and based in the military forces; its supporters thought of it as a Salvadoran version of the CIA. ANSESAL maintained extensive files on thousands of Salvadorans, including information received from U.S. sources. It had counterparts in other Central American countries as well, all of them closely linked to U.S. intelligence agencies. Their personnel received weapons and also training from the United States, often at the U.S. Army's "School of the Americas" then located in the Panama Canal Zone. (The SOA training was reported to include interrogation techniques and the use of explosives.) Both ORDEN and ANSESAL were responsible for the organization and sometimes the direct control of the so-called death squads, which murdered thousands of Salvadoran civilians in the name of "national security."

The founder of ORDEN and the "godfather" of El Salvador's security/terror organizations was a National Guard officer named José Alberto "Chele" Medrano. General Medrano was proud of the work he did to "fight the plans and actions of international communism." He was well paid by the CIA for many years, and in 1968 U.S. President Lyndon Johnson awarded him a silver Presidential medal "in recognition of exceptionally meritorious service." The U.S. ambassador from 1964 to 1968 considered him a close personal friend "and a good friend of the United States." By any objective measure, however, Medrano was a leading terrorist—if that term may be applied to someone working for the U.S. side.[52] Major Roberto D'Aubuisson, who in the 1980s would be better known as the founder of the right-wing political party ARENA, had been Medrano's protégé and was deputy director of ANSESAL at the time of the 1979 coup. Although he was officially dismissed from the armed forces after the coup, D'Aubuisson soon became El Salvador's best-known death squad leader as well as the most charismatic political figure on the far right.[53]

Father José Inocencio ("Chencho") Alas (more about him later) became a friend of President Julio Rivera through a program of Workshops in Christianity which Alas helped conduct and one of which Rivera attended. After leaving the presidency Rivera served as El Salvador's ambassador to the United States, and Alas visited him in Washington in 1967. The two walked around the city and finally sat down to talk alone by the Lincoln Monument. "Julio began to recall the years of his presidency," Alas has written,

> and finally he said to me, "There is something I regret about my time as president, something which I will regret for the rest of my life." He sighed, and continued: "It's to have permitted the founding of ORDEN. That was my worst error, my greatest sin. Much harm will come to our country because of ORDEN." He knew its leaders and its financiers. He knew that with ORDEN he had officially created "the death squads."[54]

When Fidel Sánchez Hernández began his term as president in 1967, El Salvador stood at a crossroads. There had been encouraging economic and social progress during the decade thus far, the political system was opening up, and a measure of electoral democracy, greater social justice, and increased prosperity all appeared to be within reach. But the power of the super rich, the oligarchy, was intact — and was buttressed by new institutions for repression put into place with U.S. help. Reform or repression — or reform *with* repression — was the question facing the new administration and the nation.

4

National Reform: Minister of Agriculture

The reforms and relative prosperity of the 1960s had little effect on the tough lives of Salvadoran peasants. Quaker physician Charles Clements, who worked with civilians in rebel-held territory during the civil war a few years later, recalls trying to explain his belief in non-violence to members of a campesino family. One man challenged him from his own pre-war experience:

> "You gringos are always worried about violence done with machine guns and machetes. But there is another kind of violence that you must be aware of too.
>
> "I used to work on the hacienda," he went on.... "My job was to take care of the *dueño's* dogs. I gave them meat and bowls of milk, food that I couldn't give my own family. When the dogs were sick, I took them to the veterinarian in Suchitoto or San Salvador. When my children were sick, the *dueño* gave me his sympathy, but no medicine as they died.
>
> "To watch your children die of sickness and hunger while you can do nothing is a violence to the spirit. We have suffered that silently for too many years. Why aren't you gringos concerned about that kind of violence?"[1]

Apparently conditions hadn't changed a lot since the desperate times before the 1932 rebellion, when Claribel Alegria's fictional "Eduardo" told another gringo visitor much the same thing.[2]

The Problem

El Salvador's "First National Congress on Agrarian Reform" was held at the Universidad de El Salvador (UES) during January 5 to 10, 1970. The Congress was organized by members of the National Assembly, and it included representatives from the government, private enterprise, labor organizations, the Catholic Church, the political parties, and the two universities, the UES and the brand new Jesuit-run Central American University (UCA). The UES published the papers presented at the Congress in a special issue of its bimonthly journal *La Universidad*.[3]

The Congress had the blessing of President Sánchez Hernández, whose speech of welcome called for open and frank discussions: "The theme of Agrarian Reform can and must be discussed and analyzed without fear. It is no longer a taboo subject as it was before.... Agrarian Reform is an immediate necessity and we are going to carry it out firmly and gradually."[4]

The hopeful appearance of all social sectors coming together to solve the nation's worst problems didn't last long, for the representatives of private enterprise walked out the very first day. At issue was whether the Congress would vote on resolutions and issue recommendations. The owners' groups wanted to have discussions only, and objected to the idea that campesino and worker representatives could vote on conclusions that the Congress would put forward. *La Universidad* commented that "The problem passed beyond the halls of the Legislative Assembly and reached the television and the press. The public learned of the controversy to its surprise; merely to talk of agrarian reform had in other times meant political persecution, exile and prison for many citizens."

The simple fact that there could be public discussion of agrarian reform may have been the reason for the editors' optimistic conclusion: "Despite the absence of the leading figures of the managerial sector and of other delegates, the Congress successfully accomplished its tasks."[5]

The first paper was presented by the University of El Salvador itself, and described the existing agrarian situation. Some 61 percent of the population, almost two million people, were living in the rural areas. About 55 percent of people deemed "economically active" were working in agriculture. And 54 percent of the value of all El Salvador's exports in 1968 came from just two crops, coffee and cotton.

The ownership of agricultural land was highly concentrated. There were 2058 large farm units of 250 acres or more, which represented about 1 percent of the total number of farms. However, these relatively few large units accounted for nearly half (46 percent) of the nation's arable land. On the other hand, small farms working less than 7.5 acres, amounting to 78 percent of the total number of farms, were cultivating only 11 percent of the land (1961 census). Of course, the paper also notes, this concentration of ownership resulted in a highly unequal distribution of income. The wealthiest landowners accumulated capital and formed a special class that included the bankers, merchants, industrialists and politicians of the country. On the other hand, the lack of effective laws regulating farm work and the weakness or absence of farm labor organizations meant that the large landowners could dictate the conditions of work, including very low wages. A majority of the nation's workers therefore could buy almost nothing beyond their basic survival needs and thus contributed hardly at all to El Salvador's internal market. This was holding back the process of industrialization.

But the most important issue was the marginalization and misery of so many people. The poor received less, not more, than their share of such social benefits as education, health, and housing. This was reflected in the miserable living conditions of the rural poor, the campesinos: housing in small, crowded huts, poor food, minuscule incomes, worn-out clothing. It also showed itself through ingrained customs including unscientific or counterproductive farming methods, and in traditional attitudes of submissiveness and conformity. Campesinos had little hope that conditions could change for the better, and the fear in which they lived made them easily manipulable. There was almost no political consciousness.[6]

A second paper, offered by Church representatives, added specifics about the conditions of campesino life. Illiteracy in rural areas was around 65 percent, and over a third of school-age children were not receiving any education. Anemia was widespread due to poor diet. Infant mortality was nearly 60 per 1000. And an estimated 1,400,000 rural people, nearly half the nation's population, lived in "houses that did not deserve the name. These people were exposed to all the harshness of the weather, and as a result suffered from a variety of illnesses."[7] Several other contributed papers confirmed this general picture of rural injustice and misery.

The Congress then turned to solutions, and 22 papers dealt with various models and aspects of possible agrarian reform. Many of these were the work of labor organizations and of center/left political parties, including the Christian Democrats. The Ministry of Economy contributed a discussion of how the reforms might be financed. This was the only paper from the national administration. (One other government contribution came from the Social Security Institute.)

Surprisingly, perhaps, the Cabinet department[8] most directly concerned, the MAG (for "Ministerio de Agricultura y Ganadería," or Department of Agriculture and Livestock), did not take an active part in the Congress. The Minister of Agriculture was Enrique Alvarez, and Lino Osegueda was his undersecretary. Osegueda says that they simply weren't ready. Enrique had headed the department for only eight months, and that brief period was disrupted by the war with Honduras. Two months earlier, in October, he had announced that his department was going to work toward far-reaching reforms. A major planning process was underway, but January was much too soon to discuss any conclusions. The MAG was not responsible for the Congress and Enrique refused to be pushed into an action he thought premature.

The Agrarian Reform Congress put rural and agricultural issues prominently on the public agenda and demonstrated the pressing need for fundamental change. Leaders of the private sector strongly disapproved of the whole thing and, as noted, had withdrawn almost immediately. Some elements of the Right went further. One of the Church's delegates to the Congress, a young priest named José Inocencio ("Chencho") Alas, had been outspoken in advocating the organization of campesinos. On the afternoon of January 8 Alas was violently kidnapped from a parking lot next to the National Palace by police in plain clothes. Witnesses quickly called the archdiocese. Bishop Arturo Rivera Damas and Monsignor Ricardo Urioste visited the Minister of Defense, who denied knowing anything about the affair. The two churchmen then sat in the minister's office for several hours, refusing to leave until they were convinced that Alas was alive and would be released promptly. He was found the next day in mountains south of the capital, beaten, drugged, and naked — but alive. Such violence in response to a political challenge was a precursor of much more and worse to come, and was a huge obstacle to achieving genuine reform. This kidnapping was also, ominously, the first physical attack on the Church in modern El Salvador.[9]

Enrique Alvarez and Public Service

In the 1960s the population of El Salvador was around three million people, about a tenth of whom lived in the capital. Many Salvadorans were illiterate, most were ill educated, and most were poor. Only a small minority of the people were well educated and economically prosperous, and almost all the members of this set knew each other. It was inevitable that a rich, well-connected young man such as Enrique Alvarez who was also smart and personable would be tapped for national leadership. His chances were not long in coming.

During this decade Enrique took more and more responsibility for Alvarez family enterprises, especially the farms. (He was also a trustee of the Banco Capitalizador, but this took only a small part of his time.) One of his goals was improving production and efficiency, and he worked hard to learn modern farming methods. He learned fast, and it helped that he was never too proud to ask for advice when he didn't know the answers. The results were apparent in the increased productivity of the farms he managed. Along the way Enrique naturally joined the growers' associations for both cattle and coffee. In both of them he was noticed as a successful young man with good ideas in the field, and he served a term as president of each organization. He was popular with the other landowners—partly because he was not talking about agrarian reform at that time. And toward the end of the decade Alvarez was asked to take part in national government.

Enrique Alvarez and Lino Osegueda had met in the 1950s, but they became friends only after 1965 when Osegueda returned to El Salvador to direct the National School of Agriculture. (In the meantime he had obtained two degrees from the University of Florida and had taught for four years at the Escuela Agrícola Panamericana in Honduras.) The Salvadoran National School had been neglected, Lino explains:

> There weren't resources; there were a lot of problems involved. So I decided to nominate a special support committee, and I invited Enrique along with [several others]. They all accepted and used to come to meetings about once a month.
>
> Enrique used to listen to me about the problems we had—limited resources, lack of motivation of the staff and of the students.... As for resources, Enrique decided to form a special board of trustees to get some financial support....
>
> The first support I got—he asked, "What do you want to do at this moment?" I answered that I wanted to experiment with feedlot preparation. Two or three days later he came to the school and said, "Lino, I've got the cattle for you. Do you have money for the feed?" I said no. He left, and the next time he came to the national school he came with a truck loaded with cattle. He had convinced each member of the committee to donate two steers for this experiment, plus the money to buy the food. The results were so successful that he asked me to prepare a special seminar here in San Salvador sponsored by El Banco Hipotecario. It was the first cattle management seminar in the country. That's how we got closer and closer.[10]

In 1968 President Fidel Sánchez Hernández offered Enrique Alvarez the cabinet post of undersecretary of agriculture ("subsecretario"). He accepted the next day. Enrique assured Osegueda that he would continue to support the national school and would try to back that up with more resources. He also persuaded the minister, Antonio Berríos Mendoza, to organize an internal seminar to be attended by all department heads and assistant heads within the ministry. (Lino Osegueda was included since the National School was part of the MAG.) Osegueda says that "After those meetings we realized that there was duplication of effort, and there were a lot of items not being covered by the ministry that were the responsibility of the MAG." He adds that it became increasingly clear that Enrique and the minister had serious differences about what needed to be done.

Osegueda described Enrique's start as a government official:

> He had a commitment to prepare himself better. He thought he shouldn't consider whether his own enterprises were making money, but how the farmers of the country could make money without abusing the workers; how he could convince them to treat their workers better. He started working in the government, but his ideas were in conflict with some other officers in the government, and in 6 or 7 months he resigned. He said it was a very closed environment, like a coconut shell, hard to break. He didn't have the power to break it then and decided to go back to his own farm. He said he didn't have the power to make changes then.[11]

When Enrique Alvarez resigned, Lino adds, "a lot of people felt very discouraged because he was doing excellent work." Then in 1969 Enrique returned to the agriculture department, this time in the top job. Osegueda explains that at that point,

> We were having problems with agricultural output in El Salvador. Then [President] Sánchez Hernández asked Enrique to be the minister. Enrique put conditions; he said OK if he was given authority to work as he thought was needed. He said we needed to make changes in agriculture policy in this country, that strategies and extension service work should be different. Sánchez Hernández told him he was conscious of the needs, and said he was asking Enrique [to be minister] because he wanted change. He wanted solutions on his desk, not problems. So Enrique became the minister in March or April 1969.[12]

But almost before the new minister had settled into his office, everyone's attention was distracted from internal problems and focused in a different direction.

The "Soccer War"

Shortly after Enrique Alvarez became Minister of Agriculture, El Salvador was at war with Honduras. The actual fighting didn't last long and the conflict is also known as "the hundred hours war." Of course it was not really about *fútbol.* Three bitterly contested soccer matches had indeed helped inflame public feelings, but the war was about politics, land, and economics, not who would qualify for the 1970 World Cup.[13]

El Salvador was (and is) a small, densely populated, nation. Its export-oriented agricultural system left tens of thousands of rural families without land of their own and with minimal employment at best. Neighboring Honduras, in contrast, seemed underpopulated. By 1969 perhaps as many as 300,000 Salvadorans were living in Honduras, most of them without legal residence documents or land titles. Earlier in the century Honduras had welcomed such migrants, many of whom moved to the Caribbean coast seeking work in the banana industry. Thousands of others settled on unused land and undertook subsistence farming. By the late 1960s, however, these Salvadorans could be portrayed as rivals of local campesinos for land and jobs, and they offered a convenient scapegoat for Honduran governments facing serious domestic discontent and for large landowners resisting reform. Mistreatment of the immigrants and confiscation of their farms became widespread, often with the encouragement of the Honduran government. A number of atrocities were committed against Salvadorans, but most of the people who were affected, perhaps around 20,000, were simply forced or frightened into leaving their farms and crossing the border with the few possessions they could carry.

The plight of the Salvadorans in Honduras was also a useful distraction for the government of Sánchez Hernández. The persecution of these compatriots was played up in the press, and national indignation ran high. There were other economic factors behind the growing animosity; for example, Hondurans believed that the Central American Common Market favored El Salvador, which was well ahead of Honduras in industrialization. To make matters worse, the border between the two countries was not well defined and a number of incidents along the frontier further inflamed feelings of threatened national honor. The harassment of both nations' soccer teams when they visited each other's home turf for the first two qualifying matches provided only a small additional provocation to an already tense situation.[14] Patriotic feelings and hostility toward Honduras were intense in El Salvador, and historians have even suggested that there could have been a coup had President Sánchez not acted aggressively.

On June 26, the very day of the deciding third soccer game, the government of El Salvador broke off diplomatic relations with Honduras. The first shots were fired on July 3, and low level cross-border skirmishing continued until the 13th. On July 14 the Salvadoran army and air force attacked, seeking to imitate Israel's victory in its "six day war" of 1967. In contrast to that war, the Hondurans decisively won the air battle. The practical effect of the air war was small, however, consisting mainly of the destruction of some of El Salvador's oil reserves. On the ground, superior Salvadoran forces penetrated as much as 15 miles and occupied several towns near the border, but the hoped-for lightning push to capture the major Honduran cities never materialized. The Salvadoran offensive soon bogged down, due in part to shortages of supplies. Pressure from the United States and the OAS then produced a call to cease-fire on July 18, and the gunfire finally stopped on Sunday, July 20. At least 2000 people, most of them civilians, had been killed on both sides during the brief period of fighting. After explaining this estimate, Thomas Anderson comments that "On the whole, considering the pitch to which tempers had been raised, it is surprising that there were no wholesale massacres on either side."[15]

The imposed peace was not popular in El Salvador, where many people had dreamed of a decisive triumph. Napoleón Duarte says that some of the military were unwilling to leave Honduras, and even threatened to mutiny. Duarte helped organize a gigantic "victory" parade in the capital with a celebration at the national stadium to soothe patriotic feelings, and a major avenue in San Salvador was renamed "El Bulevar de los Héroes" in honor of the troops.[16]

After the trash from the parade and rally was cleared up, Salvadorans soon realized that in fact there had been no victory. Tens of thousands more people were returning to El Salvador as refugees owning nothing beyond what they could carry, and they added to already severe problems of poverty and unemployment. The social safety valve of emigration to Honduras was gone, and the border was closed to trade as well. The Central American Common Market, which had been a plus for the Salvadoran economy, became in reality only a memory. A few prominent individuals and the illegal Communist Party had opposed the war all along, the latter predicting through its front organization that armed conflict would hurt the common people of both countries and retard the solution of urgent social problems. That is just what happened. The situation facing the government, and in particular the Ministry of Agriculture, had become even more difficult than it was when Enrique Alvarez accepted the position of minister a few months earlier.

Nevertheless, in the short run President Sánchez Hernández was widely backed. Salvadorans with differing political opinions tended to rally around the government, especially when El Salvador was criticized internationally for being the aggressor in the armed conflict. The major opposition party, the Christian Democrats (PDC), had fully supported the war, although Napoleón Duarte would later charge that the president exploited the nationalistic mood for political purposes while ignoring the nation's fundamental problems.[17] In the non-presidential election of 1970 the ruling "conciliation party" (PCN) regained considerable lost ground — in the popular vote, in the number of seats it held in the National Assembly, and especially in controlling city governments. (In 1968 the PDC had elected mayors in 78 towns and cities, but their total fell in 1970 to only 8. They did narrowly retain city hall in the capital even though Duarte himself did not run for a fourth term.)

Failure to resolve the issues behind the war, in particular the boundary dispute between El Salvador and Honduras, resulted in smoldering hostility and occasional violence throughout the 1970s. In October 1980 a peace treaty was finally signed by the foreign ministers of the two nations. By then, however, El Salvador found itself deeply enmeshed in internal conflict and was well on the road to another war — the civil war which would prove far worse in every way than the 1969 *guerra de fútbol.*

Minister of Agriculture

The 1969 war and the return by year's end of some 100,000 dispossessed people from Honduras left the Salvadoran countryside in crisis conditions. These events also produced a moment when real change seemed possible. President Sánchez Hernández was riding a wave of popularity, and he had announced that serious reforms were now on the national agenda — administrative reform, educational reform, and, above all, agricultural reform. The president promised to back the plans being developed by his new agriculture minister Enrique Alvarez, and after the elections of 1970 Sanchez chose to interpret the government party's electoral gains as a mandate for meaningful change.

"The agrarian reform we seek for El Salvador will be an expression of the national will, so as to be humane, nationwide, democratic, productive, and permanent," Enrique Alvarez told the Junior Chamber of Commerce in October of that year. The transformation of a people is everyone's job, he said, and social progress is essential to maintaining the pace of economic progress. Enrique added a theme that he considered fundamental: "In working for this goal we must sacrifice some part of our interests, in order that the concessions of today provide our security for tomorrow."[18] At this stage of his life he hoped to persuade fellow landowners that New Deal–like measures to improve the lives of campesinos and workers would be an "insurance policy" that could head off a social explosion in the future.

In the same talk, Enrique explained that the reform process would not be improvised. It would take time, effort and study to create plans that would work. The government had created a commission on agrarian reform, he said, that would come up with concrete recommendations for new laws. While the commission was conducting its study, the ministry would reject any premature criticism or pressure. They would not offer partial answers that, for lack of adequate analysis, might turn out to be counter productive.

Enrique Alvarez, Minister of Agriculture, ca. 1970 (cooperative El Jobo).

This cautious attitude explains the agriculture department's very limited participation in the National Assembly's 1970 Congress. However, Enrique assured his audience, the ministry "will expose itself to the verdict of the Salvadoran people if the fruit of its work turns out to be too small, demagogic, or insubstantial."

The president had appointed the commission to which Enrique Alvarez referred in August, shortly after the end of the war. Enrique chaired it himself as minister of agriculture, and the members included several other ministers and undersecretaries from related departments. Their mission was to develop a comprehensive plan to transform Salvadoran agriculture and rural life. From the beginning Enrique understood that a real solution must go far beyond simply transferring the ownership of land. As he told the Junior Chamber in October, "the goal of a systematic agrarian reform should be to promote a better distribution of income and provide an opening for more social equality, which will guarantee the survival of a democratic system of government." He also emphasized that reforms would be designed to stimulate, not decrease, production. The problem was not just the distribution of land ownership, Enrique insisted. He explained that the agrarian reform would mean the integrated use of *all* of El Salvador's resources, especially human resources, in a close and productive relation with the land. Economic and social factors had to be developed together. The land would be used to produce wealth, but that wealth must contribute to the progress of the people.

One of Enrique Alvarez's early acts as minister was inviting Lino Osegueda to be his undersecretary. Osegueda was still director of the national agricultural school but he gave up that position to work full time in the MAG, and their collaboration seems to have gone well. "We worked together like brothers for many years," Lino says.[19] As well as colleagues they were friends, and Enrique became the godfather of several of Lino's children. (Enrique in fact had many godchildren, often the sons and daughters of colleagues or employees.) Around this time Enrique resigned as president of the cattlemen's association (AGES) to avoid possible conflicts of interest. (He had already left the coffee-growers' organization for the same reason.) He believed that the AGES should rely on dues from members much more than on government funds, and as minister he cut the association's subsidy—gaining the lasting resentment of some of the big ranchers.[20]

The agrarian reform commission and its planning process was only one part (although a vitally important one) of Enrique's job as minister, and many other reforms plus routine and even ceremonial functions were on his agenda as well. For example, the MAG's periodical *Agricultura en El Salvador* pictured Enrique Alvarez along with President Sánchez Hernández congratulating participants at the 10th Central American cattle exposition, held in San Salvador in April 1971. Of course there were many such events.

An essential part of the new team's work was internal reform—changing the methods of operation and the culture within the government institutions themselves. Lino Osegueda describes a striking example:

> We had the Instituto de Colonización Rural, a government institute created in the late 1930s. For about 30 years they had been buying land, and had small farmers working on the land. They were the worst exploiters of people we had! They used to exploit people, not help them. They owned more than 100,000 hectares of land in El Salvador, and most of that land was not transferred to the campesinos. Campesinos could rent or lease land to have the right to work a small parcel, but they were exploited.
>
> It [the ICR] was the worst bad guy! So Enrique appointed me a member of the board so we could change that. The first thing I did was look for the statistics. They didn't have them! There was very little information.... So

> first we tried to put the information together and see what was going on. That's when we found all these horrible problems. For instance, some people had been paying for the same parcel of land, as a lease or rent, for 30 years, and they had paid much more than the value of the land at that time. And they said they were helping the campesinos!
>
> So we said, "Let's wash the dirty clothes at home first." We started inside the government. We had a change of attitude, and began to legally transfer the land to the small farmers.[21]

Alvarez and Osegueda made positive changes in many areas of the MAG's work, and some of the results are summarized with pride in their last annual report issued during the Sánchez Hernández government.[22] During their time in office the production of basic food grains increased substantially, and El Salvador went from importing large amounts of corn to having a surplus for export. Imports of beans were reduced, and other crops followed that pattern. Production of the basic export crops—coffee, cotton and sugar cane—also increased. Agricultural research and education were strengthened, as was the extension service offering technical advice and aid to small and medium producers. Some 220 MAG professionals were sent abroad for advanced training, although their work was missed at home. These people were chosen for their ability and not their political connections, Osegueda says, and they made a real impact when they returned. The creation of the National Center for Agricultural Technology (CENTA) was one of the ministry's achievements. The system of agricultural credits underwent a "change of mentality" to place more importance on the social scope of projects than on the security of the loans. Enrique and Lino wrote of their satisfaction that the MAG had helped implement a minimum wage for workers in the coffee, cotton and sugar harvests—in spite of strong opposition. Lino says that during this period their work had good support from the U.S. Agency for International Development (AID), adding that "it was a different entity at that time than it is now."[23]

Probably the most important change put in place during this part of Enrique's service as minister was a project to improve both marginal lands and marginal lives; its concept was to combine infrastructure development with redistribution of land ownership. A general law passed late in 1970, followed by a more specific one two months later, created the nation's first "Irrigation and Drainage District" in a region called "the Zapotitán Valley" located in three southwestern states ("departments"). That region was a natural but challenging choice. The government had purchased a large estate there back in the 1930s, and beginning in 1943 had sold numerous blocks of 7 to 10 acres to campesino families. No attempt was made to treat the region as a unit or to accommodate its large variety of physical conditions, and there was little support available to the peasants living there. As a result, many of the small farms failed and their land was acquired by large owners. On the whole that earlier government project had been useless, illustrating that mere distribution of land was not in itself a viable reform strategy.[24]

The new District was much better organized, and the plans included necessary roads, drainage and irrigation canals, administration buildings, and a model farm. A key provision of the legislation was that no single person or legal body could own more 50 hectares of land within the district, while the minimum for any parcel was set at 2 hectares. (A hectare is 2.47 acres.) The MAG was to be in charge of administering all this.

ECA editorialized about the new law, asserting that although the technical aspects of the "Zapotitán" project were well founded, that was not the heart of the matter. The key was that the law put limitations on the private ownership of land, in the interest of social justice. The total area of the district was 4580 hectares (11,313 acres). A mere 2 percent of the 1076 farmers there held more than half of that land. One person owned one third of it, more than the total held by the 900 smallest farmers. That pattern was reflected on a larger scale in the whole country, *ECA* said, and it would violate social justice if a few large owners were to benefit excessively from the investment of public resources. The editorial added, "Minister Alvarez Córdova is correct in speaking of this law as an instrument of agrarian reform, encompassing not only an increase in productivity but also a better distribution of land ownership."[25]

Of course there was opposition to the project, starting, not surprisingly, with that one big landowner who belonged to one of the leading families among "the fourteen." A few years later at another moment when land reform was high on the nation's agenda, *ECA* looked back to 1970 and described what had happened:

> To implement the law the Irrigation District of Zapotitán was established. It covered an area of 4500 hectares, and 1500 of these were the property of Miguel Dueñas. Faced with such a powerful person President Sánchez Hernández tried to negotiate, since he recognized the wealth and influence of "the fourteen." The mentioned member of "the fourteen" agreed to a voluntary sale [with acceptable compensation] without going through the laborious process of expropriation, but when the government tried to formalize the deal it found that the entire 1500 hectares had been legally distributed in small parcels to his relatives and agents. The rich man kept his property but not his word.[26]

The opposition did not stop with Miguel Dueñas and the other 10 owners holding more land than the 50-hectare limit, for it was clear to all that fundamental issues were at stake. Speaking before a hostile, or at least skeptical, audience, Enrique gave an eloquent defense of the philosophy and particulars of the law. He told the National Farmers Association that measures such as this were essential for the future of the country. "What are we going to do, or what are our children going to do, when in thirty years El Salvador's people number not 3 million but 9 million inhabitants who will live and work on this soil?" he asked. "We are going to go on fighting for this [reform] because we believe the nation needs measures like this one."

President Sánchez Hernández continued to back his minister and the project, and in spite of the objections the law went into effect. Its practical success partly quieted the opponents—for the moment. In the ministry's report dated August 1973, Enrique and Lino expressed satisfaction that the physical plant at Zapotitán was up and running, and they looked forward soon to starting District No. 2, which had just been authorized by the National Assembly.

Enrique Alvarez never needed to be converted to the cause of a better life for El Salvador's campesinos for, as Tony Cabrales insists, "He was born with a big heart." But there was a kind of conversion all the same. It appears that Enrique took on the job of agrarian reform with the intention of organizing top-down changes to the system. He wanted reforms that would *benefit* the rural poor. His first interaction with liberation theology priest José Chencho Alas, the kidnapping victim from the 1970 Congress, illustrates what this meant. Father Alas approached the MAG with a modest request. Alas had organized an agricultural school in his parish of Suchitoto; there campesinos from the area were learning better farming and management techniques, along with some analysis of Salvadoran social and political reality. The people were organizing religious communities and farming cooperatives, and they were ready for technical steps to improve their agriculture and livestock. Fr. Alas asked the Ministry of Agriculture for the gift, or even the loan, of purebred bulls to improve the quality of the local cattle.

He found the minister unsympathetic. "Those campesinos wouldn't know what to do with pure-bred cattle," Enrique told him, and more important, providing that kind of help wasn't his job. He was polite, but he turned Alas away empty-handed. The idea that the campesinos should be empowered to control their own lives instead of being raised from above was still too radical — but that is exactly where Enrique Alvarez was headed. When the two met again three years later, Alas says, "he was a completely different person."

In a period of optimism when real progress appeared to be on track, Enrique Alvarez and Lino Osegueda submitted their June 30, 1971 annual report from the MAG to the Legislative Assembly. They wrote:

> We think one of the best achievements of this government in the field of agriculture and livestock is the notable increase in the production of basic grains, with the goal of satisfying the nutritional necessities of our growing population and creating surpluses for export. Moreover, we emphasize the importance of recognizing that the traditional agricultural policy must be replaced with a new one which has for its basic goals not only achieving more and better production, but also raising the incomes and the standard of living of the rural workers.[27]

At the time, that optimism seemed well justified. By January 1972 the reform commission had done its job, and the draft of a comprehensive agrarian reform was complete. "Not only the law," says Lino Osegueda, "but programs that should be conducted to implement the agrarian reform. We didn't even use the name 'agrarian reform'; we called it 'agrarian development'..."

Osegueda explained what happened next:

> The document was finished — the technical documents and the legal ones, the draft law. But it didn't give Sánchez Hernández enough time to publish and start implementation of the process, because it was about February 1972. [The president] called Enrique and said, "Enrique, we have been working on this for about two years now. But I don't want to publish the law when I am leaving the presidency in a few months. We are close to elections, and it would sound too political. I want to leave the high responsibility of beginning this process in the hands of the new president."[28]

Enrique Alvarez was disappointed, but he accepted the political necessity. President Sánchez privately explained the situation to the two major presidential candidates, and both of them assured him that if elected they would carry the program forward. So the delay seemed to be only a temporary setback, and Enrique and Lino still expected that their work would soon become part of El Salvador's reality.

Elections 1972

A new president was a certainly in 1972 since Fidel Sánchez Hernández could not succeed himself in office. His National Conciliation Party (PCN) was the official (government) party and the party of most of the military and the oligarchy, although it faced opposition on the right in both those sectors. It was also the party of Enrique Alvarez. For years, even while serving in the cabinet, Enrique had resisted joining that or any other party. But by 1971 "he had developed such strong leadership in the agricultural sector that the PCN started putting a lot of pressure on him to become a member," says Lino Osegueda. "He refused at first, but they even told him he could be one of the possible candidates for president in 1972!" Enrique didn't want that job and told them he'd accept on condition that he *not* be a candidate for the presidency.[29] He did serve on the party's central committee as its agricultural expert, but did not campaign publicly for the eventual ticket.

Was it conceivable that Enrique Alvarez or *any* civilian might have been nominated for president by the PCN? No civilian had served as president of El Salvador since 1931, and each military man holding that office had nominated another officer as his successor. Osegueda maintains that a civilian candidate was indeed possible in 1972. He says the leadership seriously considered two men, Enrique Alvarez and Reinaldo Galindo Pohl. After Enrique's emphatic refusal, President Sánchez Hernández proposed the candidacy to Galindo Pohl, with the approval of the other military officers in his cabinet. Galindo waited until almost the final minute before declining, and the nod then went quickly to Colonel Arturo Armando Molina who became the official candidate for the 1972 election.[30] Whether military or civilian, of course, the nominee was selected by a small group of insiders and there was no taint of democracy to the process.

The political fireworks were just beginning, however, since for the first time in many years the election offered a real choice with credible opposition candidates. The Christian Democrats formed an alliance with two smaller parties of the left to offer a coalition slate. (Their initial hope had been to include on one ticket all the opposition to the government, but two small rightist parties chose to run their own candidates.) The challengers adopted the name UNO ("One" in Spanish) for the campaign. Their vice-presidential nominee was Guillermo Manuel Ungo, the son of one of the PDC's founders but himself the leader of a small social democratic party. Of course UNO's candidate for president was El Salvador's most popular Christian Democrat, Enrique's old friend and teammate Napoleón Duarte.

The campaign was dirty. UNO had very little money and counted on enthusiastic volunteers plus Duarte's proven stump skills. UNO meetings were often harassed and threatened by the military, one campaign worker was murdered and others were arrested and badly beaten. Attempts were made to kill Duarte himself. He explains that the soldiers acted out of an ignorant but deeply ingrained anti-communism. One officer who detained Duarte had been among his students when he taught engineering courses at the military academy. "Look, I know you're a good man," this local commander told him. "I like you, I respect you. But you're keeping company with the Communists. Therefore you must be a Communist. I have no choice but to treat you as one."[31]

Despite these handicaps, Duarte and UNO won a plurality in the election. At least he and his supporters believed that he did, and few Salvadorans today doubt that UNO defeated the PCN in 1972. (Neither had an absolute majority due to the votes going to the two right-wing parties.) Duarte writes that "Once the polls closed, the radio and television began providing official results, which the Central Electoral Council (CCE) passed on only from those places where the government [the PCN] was winning. By 2:00 AM they could not find any results that didn't favor UNO. The broadcasts faded off the airways."[32] Other observers reported much the same thing.

Napoleón Duarte did not become president of El Salvador in 1972, for as the saying goes, "It's not who votes that counts, it's who counts the votes." Two days after the balloting the CCE announced that the official candidate, Colonel Molina, had won a narrow victory. Although there was proven fraud and ballot box stuffing, the Council nevertheless asserted that the true totals favored the government slate.[33]

Fr. Chencho Alas states in his memoir *Iglesia, Tierra y Lucha Campesina* that Vicente Vilanova, a lawyer who was head of the CCE at the time, later acknowledged the fraud in a conversation. According to Alas, Vilanova said that Molina had actually lost the election by a large margin:

> In order to avoid the exit of the military from power Vilanova himself had to forge an electoral fraud. After a phone call to Molina, he stopped the vote counting late in the night. The next day, as if by magic, Molina had moved ahead of the other candidates. Vilanova explained to me that Napoleón Duarte coming to power would have meant the entrance of Communists into the government. Duarte was the candidate favored by the people, including some of the military.[34]

Alas adds that Molina himself admitted to a meeting of El Salvador's bishops that his election had not been entirely legitimate.

In fact, with no absolute majority in the popular vote the National Assembly, which was controlled by the PCN, had the constitutional power to choose the next president and could have picked Col. Molina despite the results of the voting. Admitting that a plurality favored UNO and still appointing Molina, however, would have been contrary to precedent, embarrassed the government, and denied the PCN the appearance of legitimacy at home and abroad, so the claim that Molina had won was important. In any event, Col. Molina was quickly proclaimed president-elect by the Assembly.

The story was not quite finished. In two weeks further elections were to be held, this time for city governments and the legislature. The Electoral

Council, however, disqualified on technicalities the opposition candidates in the six largest departments, ensuring that the PCN could not lose its majority in the National Assembly. UNO adopted the only remaining legal strategy and urged its supporters to annul their votes. Duarte reports that the tactic worked in the capital San Salvador, where deliberately spoiled ballots were actually in the majority. The city's electoral council then followed the law and voided the election — but it didn't matter; the national government overruled the local authorities and declared the PCN the winner anyhow. Widespread popular disgust with this maneuver included, significantly, parts of the military.

A sector of the armed forces, led by Colonel Benjamín Mejía and other reform-minded officers, then attempted a coup on short notice. Early on March 25 Mejía's men captured President Sánchez Hernández and took over some key military posts in the capital. Napoleón Duarte was not involved in the planning, but when Mejía appealed for his help Duarte made a radio broadcast urging the people to erect barricades and support the rebels. In vain. The coup failed, Sánchez Hernández was freed and returned to office, and Duarte paid a high price for his brief efforts— he was dragged from the home of a Venezuelan diplomat, badly beaten, and thrown in prison. Hastily organized international pressure probably saved his life, and he was flown out of El Salvador to Guatemala. Other problematic figures, including Dr. Fabio Castillo and Colonel Mejía himself, followed him into enforced exile. President-elect Molina would be inaugurated on schedule.

And Enrique Alvarez? He left no written record of his thoughts during those days. Enrique remained a member of the PCN Central Committee although he took no part in the election campaign. One fact is inescapable. When the new president asked him to continue as minister of agriculture in the next government, Enrique agreed to serve.

Why did he accept that offer? Enrique's friends emphasize that strict honesty was a fundamental part of his character, and Colonel Molina had not won an honest election. Enrique undoubtedly agreed with much of the moderate reformist program advocated by his friend Napoleón Duarte, and he must have sympathized with Duarte's personal trials during the campaign and after the aborted coup. Nevertheless, Enrique joined Molina's government. Some of his friends suggest that he may have believed the PCN's claims of victory, that the fraud was not as clear at the time as it became later. A more likely explanation, with which others who knew him agree, is that achieving real agrarian reform was by this time Enrique's supreme purpose. Molina offered him strong assurances that the controversial policies carefully designed during the previous administration would be enacted into law, and there was no other way to move forward. Colonel

Molina *was* the incoming president, his party controlled the national legislature, and for the foreseeable future his government was the only hope for change; no other social force could push through the reforms.

Years later Enrique reportedly confirmed that this was indeed his motive. While he was living "underground" in the fall of 1980, he talked about this with a comrade. "Look," he said, "I never agreed with those military governments. When I served in the Molina government, it was basically because of the commitment to carry out the agrarian transformation."[35] In view of all that, Enrique Alvarez once again became El Salvador's Minister of Agriculture and Livestock.

President Molina and Cerrón Grande

Soon after assuming the presidency In August 1972, Col. Molina announced a major public project: the Lempa River would be dammed in the northern region known as Cerrón Grande. The dam's main purpose was to supply electricity to meet El Salvador's growing demand, and its construction would have the backing of international financial institutions including the World Bank. The country needed this project, the president said, because increased electrical capacity was essential if its industrialization was to advance.

At the same time, President Molina expressed concern for the human side of the great undertaking. He noted that ownership of the land in the zone to be affected was highly concentrated, and that much of that land was not being used productively. He had visited the area in person and had seen the miserable living conditions of the people there. Many of the campesinos, he said, were seasonal workers employed for only a few months of the year during harvest season, and their lives were precarious. The social evils that the president described, of course, were found not only in this zone but throughout the country, and his public recognition of these problems had radical implications.

Construction of the dam, Molina then promised, would be accompanied by a plan that would significantly benefit the medium and small farmers and all the campesinos of Cerrón Grande. The plan was to include these points: fair payment for lands to be flooded; help for farmers to relocate on other land of equal value which they could choose; organization of the campesinos into cooperatives with credit and technical aid available; construction of new housing in model villages; and a program of reforestation in surrounding areas. "The government will guarantee to all the residents of the zone that this plan will be promptly carried out," Molina concluded.[36]

To implement his program, on August 15 the president named a "Commission on Relocation and Integral Development of Cerrón Grande" which would be chaired by the nation's vice president, Dr. Enrique Mayorga Rivas. Among the Commission's members was the minister of agriculture, Enrique Alvarez; a smaller executive committee was to be headed by the architect Felix Osegueda Jiménez, one of Lino Osegueda's brothers.

The region affected by the dam included much of the parish of Father Chencho Alas who has recorded what happened in the memoir noted above. Briefly: the dam was built, and it continues in the 21st century to supply a significant part of El Salvador's electricity. In the end the plan to benefit the people largely failed, despite the expertise and honest efforts of some of the officials involved. Very low prices were offered as compensation for lost property, Alas says, and the U.S. firm hired to supervise construction of the dam showed little interest in the human side of the project and greatly underestimated the number of people affected. Fr. Alas and other priests in the area encouraged the campesinos to organize — not to oppose the dam itself whose construction appeared to be inevitable, but to defend their own interests during the relocation. A group of them visited President Molina in San Salvador to present their grievances, and as a result Molina came to the area to see for himself. He appeared to be affected by what he saw and heard, and after that visit the compensation offers improved. Encouraged, the campesinos continued to organize.

Soon after the president's visit the Commission on Relocation called for a general meeting with area residents, and it was held at the agriculture school founded by Fr. Alas. Among the officials present were Enrique Alvarez and Victor de Sola, the latter being president of the CEL, the government committee in charge of the entire dam building project. Some 400 campesinos showed up to argue their cause. One man in particular made a deep impression on Chencho Alas, and apparently also on Enrique. His name was Francisco Ortiz, and Alas describes him as "advanced in years, thin, blind in one eye, wearing hat and sandals and always dressed in white." Ortiz spoke up politely but in a way that was light years distant from the humble campesino manner of old:

> I wish to speak to Dr. Mayorga Rivas [the vice president and chair of the Commission] and also to Don Victor de Sola [the president of CEL]. Dr. Mayorga, I thank you for what you said about the importance of we campesinos for the nation; you are right. I have heard the same thing other times, such as during elections when you needed our votes. We are important to fill the urns, but afterwards we weren't important anymore to anyone.
>
> You told us on the radio that we were invited to visit any place in the

> country and see the lands that we liked, that these could be ours because we campesinos of Cerrón Grande are going to be privileged. We are going to sacrifice our small farms for the construction of the dam and we ought to be rewarded for our sacrifice. You know what we did, Dr. Mayorga? We rented a truck over there in San Juan on the other side of the Lempa, and we drove about 60 kilometers to La Cabaña, to your hacienda, Don Victor.
>
> Don Victor, you have some very nice land, all growing cane. We said to ourselves that this was going to be our land, according to that which Dr. Mayorga said. We were approaching the main house and out came your manager. We said to him, "We're here because these are going to be our lands; we have the promise of the government." We explained it to him. He was surprised and said to us, "Pardon, Señores, but these lands aren't for sale." Don Victor, since we have to sacrifice because you need energy, can't we then have some of your land?
>
> Don Victor, you are an intelligent and educated man, and so are all the others who have come to visit us. But I think—and I haven't had much schooling—that you are mistaken, that you are overlooking three things. First you ought to see if flooding these lands is necessary or if something else could be done. You ought to think about what will happen to us, the fate of thousands of us, because we are people and more important than a dam. And finally, have you thought about the consequences of this dam? Once the water rises, there will be millions of mosquitoes and other plagues, and who will they attack—you who live far away or us campesinos? But you didn't do these studies, because the only thing that interests you is to have more energy for your factories.[37]

Years later Chencho Alas encountered Enrique Alvarez in Washington D.C., when Enrique was president of the Democratic Revolutionary Front (Chapter 7). Both of them remembered that meeting, and Francisco Ortiz, very well. Alvarez told Alas that he had never known Enrique Mayorga to be so furious as on this occasion, and that for the first time he saw Victor de Sola shedding tears. They were tears of rage and shame.[38] For Enrique Alvarez, too, the meeting had been memorable. It may well have moved him another step away from seeing himself as a benefactor of the campesinos and toward understanding and supporting their right to a share of power.

The campesinos of Cerrón Grande impressed Enrique Alvarez and President Molina, but they did not gain much of what they sought. As the dam project advanced during the next few years, the more progressive officials within the project's bureaucracy lost ground, the landowners dug in their heels, and the needs of the poor received the lowest priority. Architect Osegueda resigned from the commission in frustration. The compensation for lost lands and homes was inadequate, and the replacement housing turned out to be badly located and unhealthy—just as Francisco Ortiz had predicted.

Campesino organizing around Suchitoto and nearby Aguilares continued all the same, under the leadership of the Federation of Christian Campesinos (FECCAS) and with the help of progressive priests such as the Alas brothers and the Jesuit Father Rutilio Grande — who would become in 1977 the first priest/martyr of the decade. The landowners' association FARO called these men communists and subversives. But many campesinos felt that their eyes were opened and vowed they would never return to the hopeless submission of the past. The government had promised to help them improve their lives. It was the failure of those promises that was truly subversive, helping to form recruits for the national rebellion that was already brewing.

The End of Agrarian Reform

Enrique Alvarez believed that President-elect Molina was sincere in promising to go forward with agrarian reform, and Molina's progressive program for the people of Cerrón Grande appeared to reinforce his private assurances. The MAG had formed concrete plans during the previous administration, and the ministry was ready and eager to move ahead. It could not happen overnight, but one year later there was cause for optimism. An *ECA* editorial entitled "El Salvador is moving" stated that although other problems and reforms were important, the agrarian reform was "truly transcendent" and would give the best measure of the government's intentions. At the end of August 1973, a "National Seminar on Agrarian Reform" was held for officers of the armed forces; this event let the public know that something important was happening. "The impression is that the government has seriously and radically confronted the process of agrarian reform," the *ECA* editorial stated. It suggested that UNO's strong showing in the 1972 election, plus the aborted coup which followed, had helped motivate the new president and the armed forces toward serious reform.[39]

Unfortunately these hopes were soon dashed. Lino Osegueda summarizes what happened during Enrique's time as Minister in that government:

> In 1972 Molina became the next president. He wanted to go forward with the project. But then since President Sánchez publicized the law, the large landholders adopted a selfish attitude. They would accept everything we mentioned *but* rural development. "We will not let them touch our land!" And they began to campaign. That campaign was not in the newspapers only, or in the radio, because they knew they were going to lose. There were more people in favor of the [reform] than against it. They began to work with members of Molina's cabinet, to convince Molina to postpone the publication of the law. And Molina did postpone it until October 1973, one more

year. And he told Enrique, "Give me a chance to know more about this. Let me travel around the country, let me expose myself to the campesinos and understand more about their needs. Then we will go forward with this, and it will have my full support."

Enrique didn't like that, but he accepted. One more year. He continued being Minister of Agriculture, and he asked me to continue also. And then what happened? October came; the man had changed his mind. It wasn't the same cabinet Sánchez Hernández had; some of the members of that cabinet didn't have the same kind of responsibility....

Molina had told Enrique, about July of 1973, OK, we'll do this and that and make some polishing of the law, and then I will present this law by the end of September. We [the PCN] still had a majority of the Congress, so he said we would approve this law by the middle of October. Enrique was very happy with that.

Then what happened? Early in October Enrique was in London, I was in Switzerland. Enrique was working with coffee; I was working with sugar. He finished his mission and went back to El Salvador. He was waiting for me to get back to give me the good news about the approval of the law. To my surprise I got a phone call while I was in Switzerland, and it said that Enrique Alvarez resigned today. He went to the presidential palace and Molina said, "We'd better not present this law; let's wait a little bit longer."

Enrique told him, "I can't wait. They are pulling out my hair, so forget it." When Enrique resigned so did the minister of finance, the minister of CONAPLAN, because they had been working with us for two years.[40]

Enrique Alvarez resigned as Minister of Agriculture on October 10, 1973. He was joined by the Minister of Economy, Salvador Sánchez Aguillón. Lino Osegueda, the undersecretary, resigned a couple of months later after "cleaning up the office."

This was a major blow for El Salvador—and for Enrique Alvarez. Lino says that Enrique moved the next week to his farm *El Jobo,* to a house that had been built for him there a year or two earlier. His disillusionment must have been great. Enrique used to say that "We who have the most need to share a little bit. That would be life insurance for this country, to avoid bloodshed." He was right, Osegueda says, but the most powerful men in El Salvador were not ready to listen. "I can tell you, now that so many years have gone by, a lot of the people who criticized him so much at that time have repented. When you talk to them now they'll say that Enrique was right. But we didn't have that vision at that time." Eleven years of civil war and some 80,000 dead were a high price to pay for that lack of vision.

Enrique's approach had something in common with the New Deal of Franklin Roosevelt. Some concessions and reforms had to be accepted by the privileged in order to relieve the pressure on the suffering majority, he said. These reforms were needed to save the system, not to destroy it. In both countries, many people of wealth could not accept that reality. If anyone in El Salvador could have convinced the great landowners, it would have been Enrique Alvarez. His own wealth, family connections, and excellent personal qualities gave him the best chance to persuade them to accept change. But most — not all — just couldn't see that far. Change, reform — that was "communism," and they would not yield one inch.

There was an interesting sequel. Despite his reluctance to take on the powerful opposition in 1973, President Molina did not give up altogether on agrarian reform. A law passed in 1974 provided some conditions under which unused land could be forcibly rented or even expropriated; another bill in 1975 created the Salvadoran Institute of Agrarian Transformation (ISTA) to manage government agrarian programs. Although these laws had no immediate impact, the landowners saw a future threat and fought them in the courts. Perhaps surprisingly, they did not win. But they had not yet pulled out all the stops.

In mid 1976 the Molina administration went a step further and got ready to use its new powers; it prepared to form the first "agrarian transformation zone" in the far eastern part of the country. This was a limited project, but it was on a much bigger scale than the "irrigation districts" and involved some 60,000 hectares (almost 150,000 acres) of relatively unproductive land devoted at that time mainly to cattle grazing and cotton growing. That region badly needed reform. Land ownership was highly concentrated there; five owners possessed three times as much land as 2500 small holders. Some two thirds of the people there were illiterate, half of them lacked access to clean water, and unemployment was over 50 percent. About 12,000 family farms of from 3 to 35 hectares were going to be created in the "transformation zone." The plan was an important but limited pilot project that did not touch the far more valuable coffee farms in the West.[41]

The project received strong support from a wide political spectrum. Opposition Christian Democrats in the National Assembly supported the reform even though it was a government project — and so, of course, did the PCN (government party) majority. Other opposition parties also backed the measure. Moderate and liberal NGOs were in favor, as was the Jesuit-run Universidad Centroamericana (the UCA) which devoted a special number of its journal *ECA* to the issue. Of course the oligarchy, through organizations such as the National Private Enterprise Association (ANEP), was passionately opposed, but President Molina insisted that the project would go forward. On July 1 in a major speech he declared to the nation that "Nothing and no one will make us retreat a single step in the agrarian transformation." Those who know him, the President asserted, were aware that "I only promise that which I am certain to be able to carry out." He added that his colleagues in the Armed Forces fully supported the reform project and would guarantee its fulfillment against any opposition. On September 15, Independence Day in El Salvador, the president repeated that "we will not take a single step backwards on the road toward national transformation."[42]

One month later, Molina and his government were in full retreat from those promises. They had not taken a "single step" backward, they had made a 180-degree turn. The National Assembly, still under PCN control, amended the law establishing ISTA and the reform project, leaving it a "transformation" in name only without power to carry out its purposes. "What happened?" asked Fr. Ignacio Ellacuría of the UCA in a bitter *ECA* editorial article entitled "A sus órdenes, mi capital."[43] There was no doubt that the administration wanted the project to go forward, he wrote, but as soon as the transformation was unveiled the ANEP and some satellite "ghost" organizations unleashed

> a campaign for which it is difficult to find precedents in the political history of El Salvador. Its most visible face was the daily pronouncements appearing with no regard for expense in the commercial press.... The less visible maneuvers ... used lies, calumny, threats, every possible tactic, against the authorities of the nation ... and in general against everyone who could be supposed to support social change.
>
> This offensive campaign should be called a *class struggle.*

Two of the government ministers most responsible for the transformation project resigned in protest at the government's defeat. These events were similar to what had happened in 1973, Ellacuría noted in the same editorial: "Then too it seemed as if the agrarian reform was about to begin, then too the military seemed to agree, then too the government pulled back, and then too the men who knew what had really happened resigned their positions."

But all was not lost, Ellacuría concluded. The campesino had been cheated once again, and no real structural change could be expected from any government that was allied with the oligarchy. Nevertheless, consciousness had been raised and popular organizing had to continue. "It is still the hour," he wrote, "to do everything possible so that there can never again be this scandalous, shameful and unjust *at your orders, my capital.*"[44]

How Things Work

The question remains, *how* did "capital" get its way? When so much of Salvadoran society wanted the reforms, when the need was so obvious, when they were endorsed by intellectuals and approved by the Church, when they had the full backing of the president, of the government, and (apparently) of the armed forces, just how did the interests of the far right prevail? Father José Inocencio Alas had asked another of the nation's presidents almost exactly that question a decade earlier, and he got a revealing answer.

The president was Colonel Julio Rivera (1962–67), the immediate predecessor of Sánchez Hernández. In the 1960s, before he moved to Suchitoto, Fr. Alas conducted "cursillos" (workshops) in Christianity for El Salvador's elite, and the president himself attended one of them. Alas taught the classes in religion, but he himself received a lesson about politics and power:

> Rivera knew that the real power resides in the oligarchy and in the U.S. Embassy, not in the military. Julio told me that himself in a conversation we had around midnight during the Workshop in Christianity that he attended. He saw the need to improve the lives of the people, especially the campesinos and the workers, the need for an agrarian reform.
>
> Pensively, he asked me, "Do you think that is possible?" I naively imagined that the president had total power, being above all the commander in chief of the army in a country like ours.
>
> The reality was different. Julio asked me, "And who would I depend on?" I replied, "On the military officers you can trust." "That's not possible," Julio explained. "Every officer has his price. Some cost ¢200,000, others ¢100,000; some can be bought by offering them a new Mercedes Benz, others something else. There are even officers who don't cost more than a bottle of whiskey. The corruption is too much. If I announced tonight that there was going to be an agrarian reform, tomorrow morning there would be a coup. It wouldn't bother Miguel Dueñas—the grandson of Francisco Dueñas who governed the country during the last century—to pay a million colones to overthrow a president of El Salvador.
>
> We aren't in control here; those who have the real power are a handful of rich men. Besides, you have to take into account the will of the U.S. ambassador. The Embassy is the second power, or maybe even the first.[45]

Was it really that clear, that easy? Perhaps the point is that President Rivera *believed* in the conditions he was describing. In any case there is no reason to think things were any better, or even very different, in 1976.

5

The El Jobo Years

Somos los que más tenemos los que más debemos preocuparnos en beneficio de los demás.

We who have the most must be most concerned for the welfare of others.

— *Enrique Alvarez Córdova*
(Inscribed on monument at El Jobo)

Shortly after leaving the government Enrique Alvarez moved to the country, to live on his farm "El Jobo" a few kilometers south of the provincial capital of Sonsonate. Now he could devote full time to developing the finca and leave the ranks of the "San Salvador farmers" as he rather scornfully called them. He already had a home at El Jobo, a modest but comfortable house built to his orders during his tenure as minister. It was designed by one of Lino Osegueda's brothers, both of whom were architects. Despite the hyperbole in the poem "The murder of the polo champion," this was the nearest thing to a "mansion" that Enrique himself ever owned.[1]

The farm consisted of two properties, El Jobo itself near Sonsonate and another, called "El Polvón," closer to the Pacific. The altitude is low and the climate is not suitable for coffee. As already explained, these lands came under Alvarez family control around 1953, first rented and later purchased by Enrique's father with his son's enthusiastic support. "El Jobo" was a sugarcane farm at that time, says Lino Osegueda:

> Enrique was helping his father; he started working with his father part time. He tried to move his father from sugar into cattle, what they called dual-purpose cattle. That took place because his father liked cattle as well. The father had cattle at another ranch near San Salvador, and also in the eastern part of the country, usually Brahmin and Creole, upgraded cattle. About 50% of the animals were used as dual purpose, milk and meat.[2]

Home of Enrique Alvarez at "El Jobo."

When the Alvarezes took over El Jobo, Enrique found the usual miserable conditions for the farm's workers and he began to do something about them. He was also supervising other Alvarez farms and tried to make changes at all of them. He talked to his father and they made improvements such as better food. They also built shelters for the coffee pickers—it gets cold at night on some of the farms a mile above sea level.

The situation at El Jobo was more complicated. Enrique wanted to develop the farm to produce dairy products and meat, gradually converting the acres then devoted to sugar cane whose price was falling. He was also ready to invest in breeding improved cattle and other kinds of modernization. The technical success of this project was indisputable. One glimpse into how it was done can be found in the article on intensive pasturing mentioned in chapter 3. Further research carried out at El Jobo about improving milk production appeared later in the agricultural literature.[3]

But from the first, says Lino Osegueda, there was something more. Enrique wanted to develop the farm technically, but he also wanted to develop the potential of its workers. According to Osegueda,

> He thought about their potential to become efficient at farm management, and said, "We have to care about our workers and provide them some kind

> of assistance. We owners are not the ones who are plowing the land and milking the cows. I have gone to the university, my dad knows a lot about financing, and these people know nothing about life." He started some kind of communication system with his workers. He wanted to involve them, not just give orders.

This theme would continue at El Jobo throughout Enrique's life, and beyond.

The Birth of a Cooperative

There were earlier modern-era attempts to develop cooperative farms in El Salvador. In 1954 the Instituto de Colonización Rural (ICR) selected two government-owned properties for conversion to "proportional-benefit farms," basically cooperatives with a community center that provided housing, schools, clinics and other advantages. The government paid for putting in the first crops and supplied an administrator. As described briefly by David Browning the project sounds excellent. But, Browning says, within two years it had failed and had become "a burden to the state and an absolute

El Sr. Enrique Alvarez Córdoba
(der.) y su consultor, el Ing.
Antonio Cabrales comentan los
progresos realizados en la alimen-
tación del ganado mediante la
intensa fertilización de pastizales
sembrados con pasto jaragua.

Enrique Alvarez and Antonio Cabrales at "El Jobo" (*Agriculture de las Américas*).

economic catastrophe." The most important reason seems to have been the inability of the co-ops' campesino members to adapt to a different mode of work:

> The government found it impossible to re-establish the structure of the land-holding village that had been abolished with such enthusiasm in the previous [19th] century. The primary cause of failure was the attitude of the subsistence cultivator: a cooperative project required changing the peasant's attitude away from a conservative self-reliant independence to a willingness to cooperate and be supervised. When the origins of these peasant attitudes are recalled, the failure to change them by a hastily conceived and poorly executed plan may be appreciated.[4]

In other words, peasant subsistence farmers were too individualistic to adapt easily to cooperative production. The opposite problem could be as bad or worse. *Colonos* and day laborers working on the large haciendas or as pickers during the harvests were trained in the "you're not paid to think, just do what you're told" style of labor management. For them, the problem was too little independence, not too much. In both cases, however, the worker was pushed into thinking of his own gains with little concern for any larger unit than his own family.

Of course Enrique Alvarez knew all this, and he was determined to avoid the pitfalls that had doomed earlier experiments. To begin with, the farm had to be prosperous. Lino Osegueda says that by 1973 production had gone downhill, but the decline soon reversed once El Jobo had Enrique's full attention and day-to-day supervision. At first he invested, spending thousands of dollars to bring high quality cows and bulls from the United States. In 1973 Osegueda became a formal (salaried) advisor to the farm and again they worked well together. Lino says that they "made changes, moved the office to the farm, trained the people." (The office had been in San Salvador. Enrique and Lino decided that "if the accountant doesn't like the smell of manure, we'd better look for another accountant!") In a couple of years production was up and the farm became highly profitable.

The first year that El Jobo brought in a big profit, Enrique asked Lino how he thought they should use the money. Lino suggested investing in feeding corrals and new storage silos. Yes—but what about the people? Enrique considered offering everyone a big year-end bonus, but he feared that many workers would squander that "free" money and he wanted to achieve something more permanent. The books were closed in March, and by June he had decided. $100,000 would go to a social fund, to be managed by a committee of workers for the benefit of all. Its purposes would include health care, help with education, sports and recreation, and a fund for short-term loans. This worked well, and (among other things) the El Jobo soccer team became the champs of the region. Enrique used to play! Lino told him he was "too old" (about 45) but he didn't listen. Another benefit of the social fund, for Enrique this time, was that the committee became a comfortable way for workers to make suggestions and get involved in how the farm should be run. For many, developing enough self-confidence to speak to the boss about what to do was a difficult process that took time.

A year later the same thing happened. The finca again turned a large profit, and they had the "problem" of how to use it. Of course for many farm owners this would have been no problem at all; investing for profit, often outside of El Salvador, plus jet set living easily took care of any surplus. But at El Jobo some different decisions had to be made, and that's when the cooperative was born. It was not a simple matter. The plan was that eventually the workers would become members and would take responsibility for managing the farm. This could not be done overnight, and the knowledge of previous failures signaled caution. A committee was formed to study the process and spread the word. Osegueda says that they started with four or five men—Antonio Longhares and several others, then five more, and so on until they had about twenty. Enrique asked them all to pass on the ideas to the workers they supervised. The first El Jobo cooperative was set up that year (1976). It had an Indian name, Yutathui, meaning roughly "dawn."

Lino Osegueda recalls one of those early co-op meetings. At the time El Jobo had about 70 permanent workers, he says.

> In the meeting we had about 40 or 45 attending. It was free; nobody was going to be hurt if they didn't come to the meeting. Enrique said, "I would like to organize a cooperative with you, and I will be honored to be a member. What do you think of this idea?" He thought the group was mature enough for him to say that.
>
> To his surprise about half of those at the meeting did not believe him, that the cooperative was going to be organized, or that if it was organized that it would benefit them. Enrique asked why, and I was surprised by the answer. They said that at the farm just across the highway they had organized a cooperative many years ago. They told the workers "part of the earnings will be yours, so you have to work harder." They worked harder—and they never got a penny out of it! Years later that cooperative was dismantled by the owner of the property. So they felt betrayed because they had been members of that. "How can you guarantee to us that it won't happen here?" they asked.
>
> Enrique said, "Well, I am not the same person as that guy across the street! If I offer this, I mean to commit myself. It is voluntary, and if we come up with a cooperative and some of you do not want to be members,

don't worry. Nobody is going to make you join; you can continue to work here...."[5]

Raúl Ernesto Chapitón has worked at El Jobo most of his adult life, and he too remembers the early meetings. The nearby owner who had initiated a cooperative was Hector Herrera. His intentions were honorable, Chapitón says, and he had

> much the same mentality as don Enrique. But those who managed his enterprise weren't very honest. The people believed in it, but when it came time for the payoff they'd been promised, it wasn't there. But not because of don Hector, it was those working for him. This had just happened and then came don Enrique with the same idea. Because of that experience, the people [at El Jobo] were hard to convince.

But Enrique persevered, and with the help of advisors including Lino Osegueda and Carlos Montoya he managed to convince some—"especially those of us who worked most closely with him," says Chapitón—that his plan was worth a try. Enrique's manner had changed a lot since his years in the government. Before that he just visited El Jobo and dealt with the manager and foremen. "The other people couldn't talk to him then," Chapitón recalls, but now he was very different. "He'd invite us to drink coffee at his house; he'd take us out to eat papusas on the weekend; he began to organize the soccer team here for the young guys—we were all still young then—OK, and volleyball too.... And he began little by little to win over the people."[6]

By the end of the year the first co-op was up and running, although it wasn't legally formalized until 1979. Raúl Chapitón and Antonio Longhares were among the founding members, and perhaps a third of the full time workers joined. Those who didn't join did not suffer financially; they got special bonuses paying nearly the same money that the members received from their shares. And the finca continued to succeed. Thirty-plus years later dairy items bearing the names "El Jobo" and "Yutathui" are being sold in most Salvadoran supermarkets. They are a bit more expensive than other brands—and are considered to be worth the difference.

Yutathui did not own or control the farm itself. It ran the "Despensa Familiar" which marketed El Jobo products and also supplied essentials for the farm's own people. Turning the whole enterprise into a cooperative was complicated and involved several stages. First, a corporation called "Atecosoz S.A." was set up under the control of four men: Enrique Alvarez, Lino Osegueda, Carlos Montoya (who was both a friend and their CPA), and a fourth partner named Mauricio Rodriguez. This company was going to acquire El Jobo itself with its lands, cattle and equipment, as well as other major properties that Enrique owned. The plan was that eventually Yutathui or a successor cooperative would buy El Jobo from Atecosoz, and the members of the former would then collectively own the finca where they lived and worked. They would have control on a one member, one vote basis. Enrique expected to remain as a member with one vote—but not as the boss.

One huge problem in doing all this came, as in the failed "proportional-benefit" farms, from the people at El Jobo themselves. Gaining their trust was only part of the process. Tony Cabrales recalls Enrique saying, more or less, "These guys, I have to do everything for them. I'm like a father to them, they don't make any decisions." Shafik Handal, a leftist leader who knew Enrique Alvarez in the 1970s, also commented that Enrique was troubled by the reactions of some of the workers who continued to have "an individualistic attitude, taking advantage of the situation so that others would work more while they themselves could do less and still gain more." Of course these problems were deeply embedded in the culture.

Education was the answer, but what kind of education? The project at El Jobo got a boost from the work that Father Chencho Alas and his brother Higenio Alas, also a priest, had been doing in their parishes near Suchitoto (north of San Salvador). Enrique Alvarez had been deeply impressed by the changed attitudes of the campesinos he met there during the Cerrón Grande process, and they might also have an effect on the people at El Jobo. Lino Osegueda recalls that Enrique sent several of his workers to visit the area and see how the campesinos of Suchitoto were benefiting from their organizations. The group stayed about 10 days, and then there was a return visit. Chencho Alas borrowed a truck and took 30 people to visit El Jobo. They spent the day, ate a good lunch and saw some of the farm's prize cattle and its fishpond. Father Alas talked to a group of the El Jobo workers about personal change, the need for education and respectful assertiveness. Still, probably the greatest impact came from meeting men like Francisco Ortiz, the campesino who "spoke truth to power" at the meeting with the Cerrón Grande Relocation Commission (Chapter 4).

Enrique Alvarez himself was not the same person as the minister who had refused to help the agriculture school in 1971, Alas says.[7] His consciousness had been raised too. Enrique must have rethought his refusal to help Alas's school with a quality bull, for now he was doing things just like that on a large scale! Antonio Longhares thinks Enrique's changed attitude got a push during that final year he served in President Molina's government:

> In the year with Molina there was a "mobile government" that went out in all parts of the country. Don Enrique really saw the needs of all the people.

> And then when he saw those needs, he'd go and help the communities by giving them a bull. That year, don Enrique gave about 60 bulls to different communities.... Don Enrique was a very special man![8]

There were many more meetings at the finca, Lino Osegueda explains, in order "to train the group to work together and to understand that if they want to move forward they have to develop some education and new abilities and skills. These were meetings before the co-op was organized, to help people be prepared." The process was not easy or quick, but it did succeed—where earlier efforts at cooperation had failed. As Enrique himself said, by 1980 nearly all the workers were cooperative members, and the workers were running the farm. El Jobo's production of milk and meat was, and is, impressive. But its human development is certainly the greatest triumph.

An Example

José Antonio Longhares Diaz has worked at El Jobo since 1970, and he began working for Enrique Alvarez even earlier then that, when he was only 16 years old. He says he became a close personal aide ("hombre de confianza") to "Don Enrique," who was Godfather for two of Longhares's children. When Enrique moved into his new house at the finca, the Longhares family moved into the one where he had been staying until then. Antonio was there during the whole process of building the cooperative and knows it from the ground up. Today he is one of the farm's top managers, and he talks about Enrique Alvarez with obvious emotion.

"We as a cooperative are proud of having been able to work with don Enrique," he says.[9] "Don Enrique was a person who was always helping someone, preparing someone. Look, one day he was getting ready for a trip outside the country and he said to me, 'Antonio, I'm going to leave this check that I've signed, and I want you to buy a transport vehicle for the business.' He gave it to me signed and without filling in the amount."

Longhares, surprised, asked what sort of vehicle they should buy. "I don't know," Enrique replied. "What make?" Again, Enrique wouldn't tell them what to do. "You have to analyze what the business needs most," he said. In the end, Longhares decided to buy something he thinks Enrique wouldn't have chosen, a Volkswagen pickup.

When Enrique returned, he asked Antonio if he had bought the vehicle, and of course he wanted to see it. "A Volkswagen," Enrique said, "why a Volkswagen? I never would have bought a Volkswagen, but tell me why you got that one." Longhares explained his reasons. "OK, that seems to make sense," Enrique replied,

> and that's really what I want. If I'd told you what to do, you'd have just done it as I said. Now you're learning. You might have made a mistake but first of all I made you think—you had to think about what we need, you all always have to think about what's best for the business. Today I'm here, but tomorrow you'll be on your own and you have to do your own thinking.

There were many times, Longhares says, when Enrique knew something might not go well but didn't say anything. He kept quiet, he said, to force the men at the farm to make decisions themselves. "If I'd told you, you never would have learned," Enrique would explain. "Although you made a mistake this time, now you really know how to do it, because that's how you learn things, by doing them." Antonio sees "a great truth" in this approach. "That's how don Enrique was in every way," he says. "He was a teacher, a father, a brother, a friend; he was always for the community. And he wanted that just as this community was doing well managing itself, there should be more communities that could share these benefits."

Enrique Reflects

In October of 1979 Enrique Alvarez left El Jobo for good. A coup d'etat staged by junior military officers deposed President Romero and promised national reforms, and Enrique was persuaded to join the new government (Chapter 6). He became deeply involved in El Salvador's tangled political movements, and never returned to live at his farm. Years later he gave an unusually reflective interview that was recorded in August 1980, in English, during a visit to the United States.[10] In this segment Enrique looks back on his service as Minister of Agriculture and on forming the cooperative at El Jobo.

> [Enrique Alvarez speaking] This has been a long process. Since I was very young I resented—and it hurt me—hearing from the people I moved around with—first of all, racism. This was very much a stress to me, hearing that we were different from the other people, that we were superior to the other people, and this I didn't agree with. So I started looking around to see how the rest of the people were.
>
> I used to do a lot of sports, and there I had a chance to meet people that belonged to another class. And this was very helpful, to understand how different the conditions that they lived in were from the conditions of my life. I started working, after I got back from school, in agriculture. Coffee, mainly. And there it was very clear to me that the people that were making us so rich lived in very poor conditions. So we started doing many things to improve, to change, those conditions, such as better houses, nurseries, schools, and so on.

But I found something which I think is the most important thing: that the more I did, the more people depended on me. And I don't think that's right. I don't think anybody should depend in that way on another person. So I started then reading and studying other systems, and I made a decision then that the people should be allowed to decide their own future. That they should take the decisions of what to do.

In 1969 I was asked to be part of the Sánchez government, and I accepted. And very shortly I found out that I had to make a decision — either to continue, as other Ministers of Agriculture have done, serving their class, or I would have to serve the majority of the people. I think it was just a matter of being honest without thinking of ideological reasons, that I took the decision to serve the majority of the people. We tried, and we did a few things to improve those conditions, such as salaries, better conditions for the majority of the people. And from the first moment we started doing that, we found that the same people that I was born with, the same people that I — the group, the class that I belonged to — opposed every single measure that we tried to do. Then I saw the power that this group had, and that they were not willing to share — not willing to give away an inch of the land, and not willing to share any part of the privileges that they had had for so long.

Then we talked about an agrarian reform, in 1969 — that it was a necessity and that it had to go through. We worked very hard on that, and we finished all the work by the end of the period of Sánchez. I was asked then by Molina to continue as the Minister of Agriculture, and I only put one condition, that I would continue *if* we would go through with an agrarian reform. I was told that we would do it, so I accepted. But after a year I discovered that they didn't want to do it, that they kept saying that we'll do it but this is not the moment, you know — all kinds of excuses. So I resigned then.

At that moment I had to make a decision what to do. I didn't want to join any political parties, because I wasn't very sure that they were doing the right thing. I didn't have much confidence in either the Christian Democratic or the Socialist Democratic party. So I decided that I was going to go through with an agrarian reform in the property that I owned, which is a cattle ranch where 100 people work permanently and of course we have about 500 people that depend on them. At that moment we made the decision that all profits from the ranch would be for the benefit of the people. This was in 1974.

We told the people what we wanted to do. We formed a group that would administer, would control that money, and that would decide what to do with it. At first, there were many doubts from the people. They didn't believe that this was true, and there wasn't much participation from the people. But we started working, and I think the most important thing was that they had never had the opportunity to discuss things and make decisions for themselves. They had always received orders: "Do this, do that, don't do this, don't do that." So it was hard at the beginning.

But after a while they started participating, and the first decisions that they took were, first, a health program —for the father, the mother and all the family. Completely free. Then they made a program for recreation—sports and trips to the seashore and so on. They also established a store where they could buy their main needs. They also established a loan program, which is very important. They were in the hands of a man that worked there at the property, that used to charge them 25% interest every two weeks. Every two weeks! So they never had the capacity to pay the loan, but they paid 5 bucks every two weeks; they got a loan of 20 bucks.

After a year and a half we decided we should give a legal form to this, and a cooperative was organized. But—and this is important—only 45 people decided to participate in the cooperative, out of the 100 people. We tried to figure out why it was, and the main reason, we found, was that this group that was conducting all this work, this social work, was considered [as if they were] part of me, because many of them were at a meeting level within the farm. So [the other workers] didn't consider them as part of themselves any more, they considered them as being part of the management. So not until all the people really participated in decisions—of all kinds, not only social but also in decisions about how to manage the property, how to decide on what salaries, etc.—not until that moment was there full participation by them all. At this moment 97 persons are part of the cooperative, there's only three people that don't want to belong—but they receive all the [same] benefits as anyone else. At this moment, since the 15th of October [the date of the 1979 coup] that I've been spending all my time on [political work], they are managing the property by themselves, and they are doing a wonderful job.

So I am convinced that the people have to participate in this. This is just an example, of course. They have the capacity; all they need is the opportunity to make decisions, which they never had the opportunity to do.

And maybe ... something very interesting in my opinion is some of the ideas that they have for solving future problems. They are not thinking individually any more. It is only natural that they did think that way, because the system had pushed them to that, being individuals, but [now] they are thinking about, like, the housing problem, the houses not being owned individually but being owned by the group, and things like that—which I think shows you how much they have developed.

And another very interesting thing is that out of 100 [co-op members] of many ages we have about 40 people that are going to school at night! We have a man 50 years old that is going to first grade. They have found the need to learn, in order to better their situation.

The 1977 Election

While the cooperative at El Jobo was coming together, elsewhere El Salvador was falling apart. The possibility of honest elections did not improve after 1972. The 1974 voting for city governments and national assembly delegates was again marked by fraud, even more blatant than it

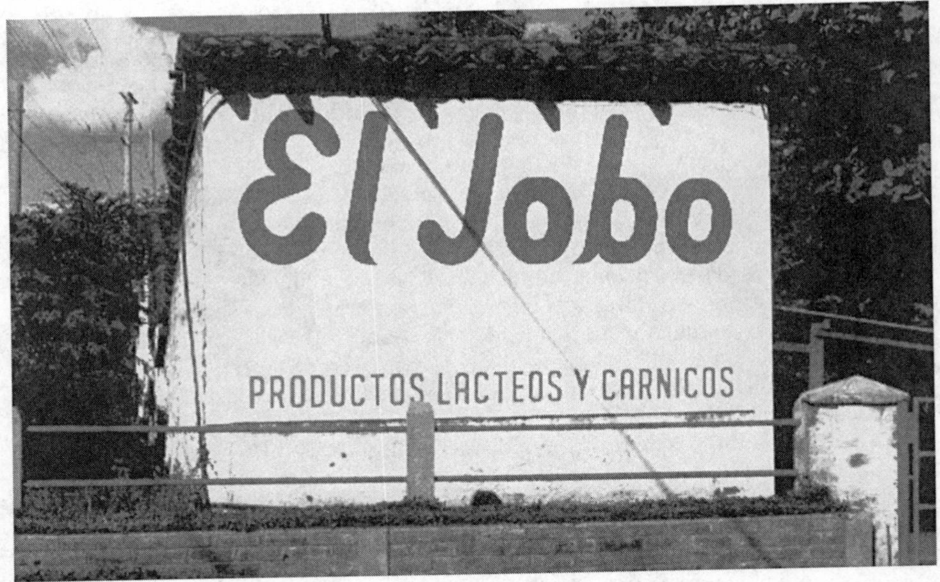

Main entrance to cooperative "El Jobo," Sonsonate, El Salvador.

had been two years before. (San Salvador, where the Christian Democrats easily won the race for mayor, was an exception.) The next time around, in 1976, the Central Electoral Council refused even to register the majority of the UNO (the opposition coalition) mayoral and legislative candidates. This was done "without legal reason" according to the PDC's José Antonio Morales Ehrlich, San Salvador's mayor from 1974 to 1976.[11] Faced with a prearranged defeat, UNO decided not to participate at all in the rigged election in order to deny it the appearance of legitimacy. (The outgoing Christian Democratic deputies in the national legislature nevertheless patriotically voted for the Molina government's "agrarian transformation zone," only to see it abandoned due to oligarchy pressure.) But the next year UNO decided that it would again contest the selection of El Salvador's president.

As before, the major party within UNO was the PDC. Napoleón Duarte wrote that "We had analyzed our problem as the armed forces' basic distrust of Christian Democrats. We felt the military officers might accept our election victory if they had confidence in the candidate. Therefore, he had to be one of their own."[12] UNO's presidential nomination thus went to a former colonel and Army commander during the 1969 war, Ernesto Claramount Rozeville. Morales Ehrlich became the candidate for vice president. Duarte, still exiled in Venezuela, campaigned for the ticket through recorded and written statements.

Duarte also visited Washington D.C. "to lobby for Democracy in Central America." He and other PDC leaders hoped that the newly-installed U.S. government of Jimmy Carter with its promises to support human rights would exert pressure for honest elections. Senator Ted Kennedy and Representative Tom Harkin listened to them sympathetically, but in those days the Carter administration had no time to spare for El Salvador's election woes. "The Salvadoran government could shoot up the university, persecute the Christian Democrats, eliminate peasant leaders, and steal elections without any outcry being raised in the United States," Duarte wrote bitterly. "There was no television coverage, no inquiring Congressional delegation."[13] But when the U.S. did focus much more attention on Central America a few years later, its influence was hardly benign.

The official party's (PCN) candidate in 1977 was General Carlos Humberto Romero, the minister of defense in Molina's government. He was an ominous choice. Romero had once been in charge of ORDEN and was responsible for instances of bloody repression during the 1970s. President Molina's record regarding agrarian reform suggests an inability to carry through on more or less good intentions, but the 1977 elections highlight a much darker side of his administration.

Polls convinced UNO activists that they would win an overwhelming victory, but what happened was quite different. Napoleón Duarte wrote that General Romero was elected "in the most blatant fraud that El Salvador has ever known." Stephen Webre's study comes to the same conclusion. "The fact that Romero 'won' the election," Webre writes,

> was less surprising to observers than the obviousness of official manipulation. Ballot boxes in some areas were reported already filled when the polls opened. Many UNO observers were arrested or otherwise bodily removed from their stations. Opposition representatives were present to certify the results from only 920 of the country's 3540 boxes, nearly half of them in the capital area. Observers noted that Claramount defeated Romero handily in these boxes, but received less than a third of the vote nationwide.[14]

A subsequent report from UNO added details of how the election was managed by the military. A radio network had linked the polling places to PCN headquarters, and the opposition was able to listen in and record many of those conversations. Ray Bonner described some of them:

> There were instructions to "put more sugar than coffee in the tank." "Sugar" was the code word for PCN votes, "coffee" for ballots for the opposition party UNO, and "tank" for ballot boxes. "The head of M-4 is buying the tamales" came a voice from one of the outlying provinces. "Tamales" was the code work for fraudulent votes. Another voice: "Well, about the worry we had

> about the little bird, the ten little birds, I have to tell you that they are here at our headquarters in this district.... I am giving them lessons." The code for opposition party poll watchers was "little birds." "Giving lessons" meant using force.[15]

The immediate aftermath of the PCN "victory" was horrifying, and the comparison with Beijing's Tiananmen Square massacre of June 4, 1989 is, in retrospect, inescapable. Tens of thousands of angry UNO supporters gathered in and around San Salvador's Plaza Libertad, vowing to stay until the fraudulent election was annulled. Colonel Claramount spoke to the crowd and promised to remain with them until their demand was met. Support groups organized food, and a sympathetic priest, Alfonso Navarro, said mass for the demonstrators. The protest went on for a week. Numbers rose and fell, peaking at perhaps 100,000 people according to Claramount. Thousands spent nights as well as days in the plaza, demanding an honest election. The demonstrators reportedly were careful to avoid provoking the soldiers and police who ringed the area, giving them no excuse to attack.

The night of February 27-28 the armed forces attacked anyway, with fire hoses, tear gas, and bullets. Officially 6 people were killed, but other observers, including Claramount himself, put the number at least ten times higher; there were many wounded as well. A report from the Unitarian Universalist Service Committee contains eyewitness accounts of totally gratuitous beatings, assaults and murders by the troops, and describes how more people were killed later in the morning.[16] Some 1500 to 2000 demonstrators took refuge in the nearby El Rosario church. Among them was Colonel Claramount, who later told U.S. reporter Tom Buckley what happened:

> At 3:30 AM several officers pushed their way into the church. Many of them were old friends of mine. They warned me that if I didn't surrender they would massacre everyone in the church. I could tell that they meant it. My son was with me and so was Bishop Rivera y Damas. I wasn't worried about myself, but I could see that I didn't have any choice.
>
> They told me I had to go with them to Santa Tecla. Rivera y Damas and the president of the Red Cross insisted in going with me. There several senior officers put a document in front of me and told me to sign it. It said that I had left the church voluntarily. I told them I hadn't, and that I wouldn't sign it. They said that if I didn't, they would kill my entire family. So I signed it.[17]

Buckley says Claramount was devastated that it was his "brother officers, comrades in arms, lifelong companions" who had done this to him and who threatened to kill his wife and children. Given a choice between arrest and exile, Claramount and his family left for Costa Rica.

Damián Alegría was a student at the time and had been with the demonstrators earlier that week. On the evening of February 27, however, he went home to sleep. Passing Plaza Libertad early the next morning he saw the traces of the massacre. "There was a military cordon around the plaza," Damián recalls. "There were no sounds, no loudspeakers. Inside the military circle you could see fire trucks, pumpers, spraying water to wash the blood off the pavement." He learned that when the soldiers attacked, many people ran to take refuge in El Rosario. They were cut off and couldn't leave the plaza or the church at that time. Police went behind the church and threw tear gas bombs into the interior, violating the sanctuary that the church had offered hoping to avoid a massacre. Many people ran out to escape the gas, were beaten by the troops, thrown into trucks and taken away.

That election, Alegría said, was the last opportunity to find a democratic way out of the crisis. After the fraud and the massacre many people, including Damián himself, were convinced that armed struggle was the only way for El Salvador to change.[18]

That massacre in Plaza Libertad gave the name to the Popular League of February 28 (known as LP-28), which was founded the next year as the above-ground mass organization associated with the fledgling guerrilla group ambitiously named "Revolutionary Army of the People" (ERP). The crime was also the last straw for the Communist Party, which until then had clung to its traditional nonviolent strategy of demonstrations and labor organizing. After February 28 the party decided to prepare for armed struggle. By the end of 1979 it had created the Armed Forces of Liberation (FAL), which later became one of the five military components of the FMNL guerrilla forces.

The Left, the Right, and the Church

The failed elections and accompanying repression were the visible tip of the iceberg. The governments of Sánchez Hernández and Molina, despite many promises and some good intentions, had not come through with the reforms that the country desperately needed. The economy was in decline after the better years of the 1960s and living standards were falling for many Salvadorans. The subsequent administration of General Carlos Romero (1977–1979) likewise had no solutions and even dispensed with the good intentions. As the election fiascoes of the 1970s showed, fundamental changes could not be achieved through electoral politics and organizing outside of the constitutional system took its place.

The first of the underground "political-military" (guerrilla) organizations was born in 1970. Salvador Cayetano Carpio (nom de guerre "Marcial"), then secretary general of the outlawed Communist Party (PCS), believed that the time had come to prepare for armed struggle and that the PCS should take the lead. Unable to convince the majority of his comrades, he led a small group out of the party to form the Popular Forces of Liberation (FPL). Two years later further disagreements within the PCS and disgust with that year's electoral fraud led to the birth of another armed group, the ERP. The ERP itself split a few years later over the importance of political as well as military organizing. One related and bitterly divisive issue was the murder of the revolutionary poet and writer Roque Dalton, apparently by political opponents within this organization. Dalton's supporters founded a militant party called the National Resistance (RN), with an armed wing that they named the Armed Forces of National Resistance (FARN). As noted, the remainder of the PCS contributed the FAL to the mix in 1977. By the end of the decade there were five distinct revolutionary armed forces.

Marcial was an exception among the leaders of this movement, both for his age (he was born around 1920) and for his working-class background. Most of the others were much younger, and many had been students or intellectuals from the urban areas. Some were middle class, some were radicalized Christians, others had been politically formed in the old left. All five groups began in the cities, and the development of guerrilla warfare in rural areas required that some hard lessons be learned.

The FPL and the other revolutionary groups, says T.S. Montgomery, "were from their inception more than armed bands. Each had a clear political line to which it held tenaciously. By the late 1970s that tenacity was impeding the process of unity that they all recognized would be necessary if they were to ever achieve victory."[19] But recognizing the need for unity and achieving it were two different things. The union — never a complete merger — of the five groups into the Farabundo Martí Front for National Liberation, the FMLN, was not achieved until the fall of 1980. By that time the larger groups had established areas of operation in different parts of the country — the FPL in Chalatenango and the ERP in Morazán, for example. Their ideological differences were largely suppressed during the war years, only to reemerge in the 1990s when the FMLN became a political party. But that's another story.[20]

During the 1970s another, perhaps more important, type of organizing was going on. This was political rather than military, and it involved tens of thousands of people. The "mass" or "popular" organizations operated above ground, more or less legally. Their tactics were those of political education and protest, including marches and demonstrations, strikes, and sometimes illegal but mainly nonviolent sit-ins in public buildings such as embassies and churches. All of these actions, legal or not, were met with deadly violence from the armed forces. It was these popular organizations even more than the armed guerrilla forces to which Robert White's description applies. White, who served as U.S. ambassador to El Salvador during 1980-81, told a congressional committee that they

> almost without exception began as associations of teachers, associations of labor unions, campesino unions, or parish organizations which were organized for the definite purpose of getting a schoolhouse up on the market road. When they tried to use their power of association to gain their ends, first they were warned, and then they were persecuted and tortured and shot.[21]

T. S. Montgomery gives much of the credit to the Catholic Church. "It is less well known," she writes, "that the church, at the parish level, spawned the mass popular organizations that in less than six years brought El Salvador to the brink of revolution."[22] This may be an overstatement, but there is a lot to it. To understand the connection, Montgomery says, it's necessary to study the parish of Suchitoto and the work of its priests, "los curas Alas."

Fr. Chencho Alas tells in his memoir how the United Popular Action Front (FAPU) was created.[23] "The proposal to create a mass front didn't just happen," he writes. "It was due to a process that developed in Suchitoto, with its starting point in evangelization conceived of as a commitment to the community and to our faith." More concretely, the immediate stimuli were the fraudulent election of 1974 and, before that, the struggle around the Cerrón Grande dam relocations. Shortly after the election there was a regular meeting of Celebrants of the Word, the group of lay pastors selected and trained to lead the many Christian Base Communities (CEBs) that the pastoral work of the Alas brothers had created. The group decided that they needed a broader organization to defend their interests with the government, so they approached leaders of the teachers' union ANDES which the campesinos had supported when it went on strike in 1972. Together they then sought contacts among workers and students. The police in Suchitoto were showing too much interest, so Fr. Alas arranged to use San Salvador's Basilica of the Sacred Heart for their first big meeting. It took place in the same large room where he had conducted those "Workshops in Christianity" for members of the elite a few years earlier.

That meeting was attended by at least 200 people, Alas writes, including campesinos, teachers, students and workers. The group chose the name, discussed objectives, and set up a structure for participation by member organizations. In the first months there were at least three campesino groups participating, one group of workers, three of students and ANDES itself representing the teachers. There were also representatives of socially committed clergy. A central committee was set up in which each organization had a voice. "Thus for the first time in Latin American history," writes Montgomery, "a popular mass organization came directly out of the evangelizing efforts of the Roman Catholic Church."

During 1974 and 1975 FAPU carried out campaigns and demonstrations for popular causes including women's' rights, but it was soon plagued by tensions among the member organizations which had varying priorities and strategies. Father Alas recalls that there were demonstrations in Suchitoto in which followers of the RN and of the FPL treated each other with hostility and even destroyed the propaganda of the other faction. "I had to ask myself whether the people's enemy number one was the oligarchy and the military or their own lack of unity," he wrote.

These differences led to yet another split and the founding of a new organization, the Popular Revolutionary Bloc (BPR). This schism was a disappointment for Chencho Alas, but in reality it meant change, not retreat, for the movement. By 1980 the Bloc had become the largest of what were by then five revolutionary mass organizations; the BPR alone had over 60,000 members. What remained of FAPU was taken over by members of the National Resistance who moved it in a somewhat different direction. Montgomery says that FAPU became known for "incisive analysis" and for its publications. "Through this work," she writes, "it exerted a profound impact on the development of a unified political program in 1980."

The third popular organization, the Popular League of February 28 (LP-28), was founded a year after the Plaza Libertad massacre by sympathizers of the ERP, who realized that their guerrilla organization needed a political mass front. Two others soon followed. By 1979, then, each of the five political-military organizations of the left was associated with a mass front group roughly sharing and promoting its political goals and strategy. When they managed to work together, these "popular organizations" spoke with a powerful voice for the interests of the workers and campesinos who made up their memberships. Like the armed groups they had difficulty in cooperating, but at the start of 1980, before the founding of the FMLN, the five did achieve a considerable degree of unity with the formation of the Revolutionary Coordination of the Masses (RCM, or the "Coordinadora"; see Chapter 7).

Underlying much of this was the radically new role of the Catholic Church, based on the "preferential option for the poor" declared at the 1968 bishops' conference in Medellín, Colombia. Some of the Salvadoran clergy, led by Archbishop Luis Chávez y González and of course including the Alas brothers, fully embraced the ideas of Vatican II and Medellín, although many others hung back. The Church's fundamental contribution was not explicitly political at all; it consisted of raising the consciousness of oppressed people and giving them a new sense of their own worth as children of God. In particular, participating in the "base communities" (CEBs) gave many campesinos their first experiences of leadership and organizing. All this led many to attempt to better their lot materially—for example by forming cooperatives to market farm produce and free themselves from exploitation by landowners and middlemen. In El Salvador such efforts, especially by campesinos, represented "subversion" and "communism" and brought down serious repression on the people and on the priests who had encouraged them to think.

On February 22, 1977, two days after the stolen presidential election, Oscar Arnulfo Romero y Galdámez became Archbishop of San Salvador, the highest office of the Catholic Church in the nation. His appointment was disappointing to progressive elements in the Church, for Romero had been no friend of liberation theology or of Medellín. He was chosen by the Vatican with the support of the Salvadoran elite in the belief that he was thoroughly conservative and would cause no problems between Church, government, and oligarchy. That belief was understandable. Romero was close to the conservative faction Opus Dei, had attacked "communist" teaching in the Church's schools and seminary, and had shown little sympathy for social activism by Church or clergy. He looked like a thoroughly safe choice.

The satisfaction of conservatives with their new archbishop was short lived, for almost at once Romero seemed to undergo a conversion of, so to speak, Biblical proportions. The apparent final straw was not the massacre of February 28, although that was related; rather, it was the murder on March 12 of a close friend. Father Rutilio Grande, a Jesuit, was the parish priest at Aguilares, a neighboring town of Suchitoto. He had been involved with the formation of many CEBs, and had encouraged the growth of the Christian Federation of Salvadoran Campesinos (FECCAS), active in labor organizing and strikes in the region. Landowners blamed the Church for these changes, and Fr. Grande was gunned down together with two campesino companions while on his way to offer a mass at his birthplace, the village of El Paisnal.

Romero's response was radical. He ordered the cancellation of all church services in the archdiocese with the exception of a single funeral mass to be held at the cathedral. All the priests and thousands of people came to celebrate, defying a national "state of emergency" declared a few days before. In his homily Romero denounced the murders and conditions behind them before the huge crowd. Holding this single mass had been a difficult decision for Romero, which he made, after much prayer and thought, against the virtual orders of the Papal Nuncio. Romero also declared that he would attend no official government functions until the murder of Fr. Grande was investigated and those guilty brought to trial. Since this did not happen, the archbishop was absent when General Romero (no relation) was sworn in as president in June. Such a symbol of Church/State division was without precedent in El Salvador. The conservative cleric had been transformed almost overnight into a prophet who would soon be known to the Salvadoran masses as "the voice of the voiceless."[24]

The 1970s was a decade of organizing; it was also a decade of ever-growing violence. The new role of (one part of) the Church made it a target. A month after the murder of Rutilio Grande another priest was killed by a military death squad; this was Fr. Alfonso Navarro who had said mass for the demonstrators in Plaza Libertad a few months earlier. These two murders were not the whole story. Ray Bonner reports that

> During the first five months of 1977 five priests were tortured, eight expelled, and six denied reentry after leaving the country. There were continual threats against priests along with bombings of their houses, the church radio station YSAX, and the Jesuit-run high school. In the summer of 1977 pamphlets circulated throughout the country: "Be a patriot! Kill a priest!"[25]

Persecution of the progressive Church was an obvious example, but violence took many forms. Police and National Guard units in rural areas, sometimes aided by members of ORDEN, killed peasants one by one and in groups—often on behalf of local landowners involved in labor or land tenure disputes. Aguilares, the former parish of Fr. Rutilio Grande, was put under a brutal military occupation, cynically code-named "Operation Rutilio," in order to wipe out the gains the people had achieved there. Penny Lernoux summarized what happened there: "Then the killing began. The armed forces and the police, using tanks, aircraft and tear gas, sealed off a 500 square mile area, and every house was searched. The exact death toll is not known, but Church sources estimate that 350 to 400 people were gunned down, most of them unarmed peasants."[26]

In the cities killings served to repress organizing or demonstrations, as in the Plaza Libertad massacre. An ugly example had occurred in 1975 when El Salvador was chosen to host the "Miss Universe" contest—twenty years after Maribel Arrieta so nearly won that title in Los Angeles. Over 2000 UES students marched to protest the misuse of some $30 million in public funds for the pageant while urgent social needs were unmet. The students were slaughtered by National Guard troops, who eyewitnesses said opened fire without provocation. Montgomery and Webre report that at least 37 students were killed while several dozen others were arrested and disappeared.[27]

In May 1979 a demonstration outside the cathedral in central San Salvador was fired on by police, killing 23 people. There were many such incidents. Torture of prisoners by the security forces was routine, and disappearance after arrest became more and more common late in the decade. Unofficial executions were conducted by "death squads" closely linked to the armed forces. The roots of these organizations led back to the 1960s and to U.S. "help" in setting up anti-communist intelligence and police organizations such as ORDEN. The repression would get even worse in the years to come.

Of course there was also growing violence from the armed groups of the left. Their initial purpose seems to have been amassing money to finance the coming armed struggle, and robberies and kidnapping for ransom were carried out with considerable success in the early 1970s. Several dozen well-known people were kidnapped and released after the payment of large sums; victims included Salvadorans from some of the wealthiest families as well as foreigners managing multinational businesses. (Among the former was Dr. Emilio Alvarez, brother of Mauricio Alvarez and a relative of Enrique.) Millions of dollars were raised by the guerrilla groups in this way, and much of that money went to purchase arms. Leftist violence also included out and out assassinations, such as the murder of a symbol of past repression, ex-president Osmín Aguirre. Killing of policemen, presumably in retaliation for acts of repression, became common as well.

In at least a dozen cases prominent kidnapping victims were later found dead. Some of these were undoubtedly decent people who had been doing constructive work. By all accounts, Roberto Poma was a rich young man with a social conscience, and like Enrique Alvarez he had attended the Hackley School in New York. In January 1977 Poma was kidnapped by the ERP. His captors did not intend to kill him, but Poma was wounded during the act and died a few days later. In April 1977 the FPL captured the foreign minister of Colonel Molina's government, Mauricio Borgonovo Pohl. The kidnappers did not want money for his freedom; instead they demanded the release of 37 political prisoners, plus air transport out of the country. Some of the 37 could not be found and may well have already been dead. In any case Molina refused to negotiate, and Borgonovo Pohl was assassinated on May 10.

Perhaps most notorious was the case of the ambassador of South Africa, Archibald Dunn. Captured on November 28, 1979 by members of the FPL, Dunn was held prisoner for nearly a year. For his release the FPL demanded publication of its political manifestos in major newspapers of El Salvador and South Africa, additional publications in many other countries, plus, eventually, $20 million. Eminent people including Archbishop Romero appealed for Dunn's life, and his family and friends were attempting to raise the ransom money in South Africa. But the FPL's demands could not be met in the time specified, and Ambassador Dunn was murdered on or around October 10, 1980.

These prominent victims received much public attention and sympathy, which they surely deserved, and the crimes were widely condemned.[28] On the other hand, the demonstrators murdered in the Plaza Libertad, the students shot down while protesting the Miss Universe pageant, or the campesinos killed at a place called Las Tres Calles while returning from a religious service, did not have their stories told in the media, their faces and names were not known, and the government did not denounce or investigate their deaths. But all these people were equally human, they far outnumbered the victims of the left, and their killers were acting in the service of the Salvadoran state and its backers.

A Visit to Cuba

Late in the 1970s, probably in 1978 or early 1979, Enrique Alvarez made an extended visit to Cuba. He had mentioned wanting to see "other systems" in action, and in particular wished to study Cuba's agricultural development, which might embody some of the changes Enrique sought for his own country.[29]

The trip was not illegal, but it was highly suspect in the anti-communist climate of El Salvador and had to be managed discreetly. Enrique received help from Shafik Handal, then the leader of the Salvadoran Communist Party (PCS). Handal explained in an interview that he and Enrique had been on friendly terms since 1973 when Enrique was still in the government. "It happened in an unexpected way," he said.

Returning from a trip abroad in 1973, Handal was arrested at the airport. "The police grabbed me and took me to the station of the customs police to torture me," he explained. "They took away my clothes, blindfolded me and were beginning to beat me. Then a messenger arrived from President Molina telling them to stop because he wanted to talk with me." Molina told Handal about the plans for agrarian reform that the administration was working out with Enrique Alvarez, with Salvador Sánchez Aguillón who was the minister of economy, and with the minister of planning.

"But that's another story," Handal says. "After that I struck up an acquaintance with Enrique...."

Shafik Handal knew that Enrique Alvarez was intensely concerned about social conditions in El Salvador. When Molina canceled the agrarian reform in 1973, Enrique resigned and soon decided that the way forward was to give an example. That's when he began the project of turning El Jobo into a cooperative, a process well advanced by the late 1970s. But he still wasn't very satisfied with the results, Handal says, and adds that "he was also under great pressure from the other landowners and businessmen of the region because he was such a bad example, as they saw it — a traitor to his class." Sure enough, workers at other enterprises started to demand something similar for themselves. Enrique was becoming disillusioned with the method he had chosen to try and reform the society, as he saw that it had no echo among others of that class. Besides that, he was not too happy with the reaction of the workers themselves at this time, because to a certain extent they still had an individualistic attitude of taking advantage of the situation, of waiting for others to work more and doing less themselves. These things worried him, Handal says.

"I used to visit him regularly at El Jobo," he continued. "I was living clandestinely, but I managed to get there." Handal says they had long talks, and asserts that he educated Enrique about aspects of Salvadoran history which are not taught in school and weren't well known. He loaned Enrique books in which, he says, Enrique "started to find the key to why the country is the way it is.... I began to give him Marxist literature too. Then one day he said to me, 'I'd like to see socialism; I want to go to Cuba. Because I want to see how it is, here in our own part of the world.' And he asked me to help organize a trip."

Enrique traveled via Panama, which had commercial air service to Cuba. He made contact with an official of the Cuban Embassy in Panama and they set up his visit. He went alone and stayed in Cuba for at least two weeks, perhaps somewhat longer. The Cuban authorities told him to go wherever he wanted and talk to anyone he liked, Handal says, and Enrique took full advantage. He went into the interior of the country and dropped in unannounced at schools, workplaces and private homes, and talked alone with people he met.

The trip also got a boost from sports. While visiting a cattle ranch, Enrique discovered that the manager was an old acquaintance, a former star with the Cuban basketball team. They had met when playing against each other back in the 1950s. The ranch was a leading establishment that carried out research in breeding and raising superior cattle, so the two had a lot more than basketball to discuss. Enrique spent time with this man, learning about cattle raising on the island and about Cuba's farm system in general. Handal says Enrique had access to data and plans for the future, not only in agriculture but in social development as well. He returned to El Salvador full of ideas and enthusiasm.

Shafik Handal explains that now Enrique better understood some of the problems with the workers at El Jobo. Such experiments often fail—although El Jobo did not fail!—because the system chokes them. The workers are immersed in the general psychology of each looking after his or her own advantage, and there aren't conditions that could encourage any different attitude. Alvarez told Handal that he saw that El Salvador needed an overall change in the system. It wasn't just an economic reform that was necessary; education and other things had to change too.

"He came back with his head full of this new perspective," Handal says, "and he wanted to tell the world!" Enrique was eager to go public with his new understanding and set the record straight about Cuba "because what they say here is slander." Handal says he worked hard to talk Enrique out of doing that. "You have an important role to play in this country," he told him, "and if you begin to talk positively about Cuba you'll be marginalized. Leave that to others." Finally Enrique accepted this advice, and spoke of his experiences among friends but not in public.

In private he was not secretive and talked about his trip on social occasions, so the fact that he had been to Cuba became rather widely known. Lino Osegueda describes Enrique's reaction to his visit as generally positive but much more guarded than it sounds in Handal's description.[30] Enrique was conscious that he did not see everything, Lino says, and he did not meet with any important figures of the opposition. His daily schedule was fixed and he traveled with a guide who also served as a "chaperon." Still, there is no doubt that he found much to admire and many ideas that he thought could be applied in El Salvador.

Although Enrique agreed to forego speaking out in public about Cuba, he felt he had to talk with his father. Shafik Handal warned him that it might not go well. "Look," he said, "sometimes class interests are even stronger than family love." But Enrique didn't listen. Handal says Enrique told him later how it went.

> Enrique went to his father's office in the bank and sat down in front of his desk and told him "I've been in Cuba and seen this and that...." At his first words the father began to shout at him: "That's not true! It's a lie!" "But Papa, it's me telling you this, your son. You know me...." "It's not true! All that is a lie!" "But Dad, that's what I saw...." Then the father got to his feet and told him, "I don't want to hear any more!" Enrique insisted, and his father was outraged, told him to get out of the office and said he didn't want to see him or hear from him any more. His father broke off relations with him; he threw him out.
>
> The next time I saw Enrique he said, "You were right. It's a very hard thing."

The Co-op at El Jobo

The co-op became a legal reality on March 12, 1979, with 28 or 29 members. This was a very happy day for Enrique Alvarez. The new entity was Yutathui, the farm's store and marketing organization. The plan was that Yutathui and the second group which was to own the property, called Aticosoz, would form a bridge to the third organization, the El Jobo society. "That was going to be the big one, the big umbrella, covering all kind of businesses, with the possibility to invest money here [at El Jobo] or elsewhere," explained Lino Osegueda. That never happened. Two of the four partners in Aticosoz died (Alvarez and Montoya were both murdered), making it impossible to carry out the plan. And with Enrique's death in November 1980, the fate of El Jobo itself became highly uncertain.

When Enrique was killed, the planned transfer of El Jobo's ownership had not taken place and he was still the legal owner. He died without a will. (There were reports that he had written one, but it was not found.) Enrique's property, therefore, reverted to his nearest relatives—which meant to Enrique's father, Enrique Alvarez Drews, from whom the son was estranged due to their political differences.

The El Jobo families were in a bad place. In addition to their grief at Enrique's death, they had to be concerned about their own futures and that of the farm. Antonio Cabrales explained that a delegation from El Jobo came to see him.[31] Tony telephoned Enrique's father who was then living in Guatemala. "What should the El Jobo people do now?" he asked. "Tell them not to worry," was the answer from Enrique Sr., "I will carry out the intentions of my son." And for the immediate future he authorized new banking arrangements so the farm could continue to operate.

Señor Alvarez Drews was a man of his word. He called a family meeting and found that not everyone agreed with his promise; some wanted to keep all the property in their own hands. But on one major point the father was unmovable: Enrique's wishes for El Jobo would be respected. The promise was kept. The legal process took years to complete, and that umbrella organization intended to control all of Enrique's properties was never formed. Nevertheless, today El Jobo is owned and managed—land, animals, and all—by the cooperative association of its workers. Lino Osegueda, as a trained and experienced agronomist, still consults with the management, but he doesn't give the orders. And it is there at El Jobo, of all El Salvador, that the memory of Enrique Alvarez is best preserved. A monument to him stands outside the farm office and proclaims the cooperative's promise: "Enrique, we will carry on!"

6

A Moment of Hope: The 1979 Coup

> Those who make peaceful revolution impossible make violent revolution inevitable.
>
> — *John Fitzgerald Kennedy (Assassinated 1963)*

Shortly after 8:00 AM on October 15, a nearly simultaneous uprising at the major Armed Forces installations overthrew the existing government. The coup was carried out by some 400 "young officers," who convinced most of their colleagues that the nation and the military institution could no longer tolerate "a regime of repression, corruption and ineptitude like that of President Romero."[1] There were less high-minded motives as well. A number of officers still resented the imposition of General Romero as president in 1977, which had restricted their own chance for advancement. Another factor was the triumph of the Nicaraguan revolution in July 1979, along with the complete defeat of the Nicaraguan National Guard. A change of leadership and some reform was more acceptable than risking a similar experience in El Salvador.

The Armed Forces—that is, the coup's spokesmen—issued a brief initial statement on October 15. After sketching the evils of the Romero regime, they promised to restore order, to create "the foundation and proper climate to establish a real and dynamic democracy," and to hold free elections at an unspecified time. The statement appealed to "the extremist forces of the right and the left" to end violence, since in the future "they can participate peacefully in the country's democratic process." All this was standard post-coup rhetoric and didn't inspire much enthusiasm. Two colonels, Jaime Abdul Gutiérrez and Adolfo Arnoldo Majano, were said to have been entrusted with the "command of the movement." Finally, a more comprehensive proclamation was promised for the near future that would include the names of the civilians slated to join the two colonels in a governing junta.

That next proclamation twelve hours later went much further than the first; it had some real substance. This statement began by accusing the previous government of corruption, incompetence and "violation of all human rights of the community." These problems, it said, "are the product of antiquated economic, social and political structures ... which do not offer the majority of inhabitants the minimal conditions for living as human beings." The new declaration, known as the *Proclama,* asserted that the governments of Colonel Molina and General Romero had come to power through massive electoral fraud and were subservient to the "conservative sectors, which have at all moments defended their ancestral privileges as dominating classes...." This was strong stuff; labor and campesino leaders, as well as several priests, had been killed for saying much the same thing.

"Therefore the armed forces, whose members have always been identified with the people [sic!], have decided ... to install a revolutionary government junta comprised for the most part of civilians of absolute honesty and competence," the *Proclama* continued. That junta would put an end to violence and corruption, dissolve ORDEN, provide a general amnesty for exiles and political prisoners, guarantee human rights, ensure the right to organize for all sectors of labor including campesinos and for all political parties, provide consumer protections, and (last but not least) implement a genuine agrarian reform. The junta would also guarantee the right of all citizens to housing, food, education and healthcare. That is an ambitious program for any nation, to say nothing of backward, repressed and poverty stricken El Salvador! Finally, the *Proclama* proposed "positive channeling" of foreign relations, including prompt restoration of ties with Honduras that had remained broken since the 1969 "soccer war."[2]

The military had governed El Salvador almost without interruption for 48 years, ruling in the interest of the landowning and business elites. It was to be expected that the coup's spokesmen would promise honest elections and a prompt return to civilian government. But they seemed to be implying something more surprising and profound, that the armed forces *were changing sides.* Instead of serving as the private police of the oligarchy, the military would become the guardians of justice and democracy. That was a big order! Not surprisingly, it was greeted with opposition from some and with hope from others—but above all with entirely understandable skepticism.

The first civilian to join the two colonels in the new junta was Román Mayorga Quirós, the Rector of the Universidad Centroamericana (the

UCA). Mayorga, who was trained as an engineer (he's an M.I.T. graduate), had helped to found the new Jesuit university in 1965 and is still the only layperson ever to serve as its head. Mayorga says he was doubtful at first, but became more hopeful after talking with some of the coup's organizers. "I set three conditions for me to participate in the junta," he explained much later.[3] "One was a cleanup of the army; I didn't want to be associated with criminals, assassins or torturers—but I didn't know who they were, except the very prominent ones like D'Aubuisson.... That was one of my conditions, that the people *they* knew (because we didn't know who they all were) to be bad should be expelled. They promised that."

Mayorga's second condition was that there should be a public statement committing the new government to important reforms; that became the *Proclama* described above. "I didn't write it," Mayorga says, "but I did approve it in the end."

"Third, at least one of the other civilians should come from the *Foro Popular*," he added. The Foro, organized only a month earlier, was a loose center-left coalition of 14 organizations opposed to the Romero regime; it included sectors of the Catholic Church, labor organizations, universities, political parties and some but not all of the popular organizations. (The largest of those, the Popular Revolutionary Bloc (BPR), was not a member of the Foro.) "So they said yes," Mayorga continued, "and I tried to get two from the Foro [onto the junta]. My candidates were Guillermo Ungo and Enrique Alvarez."

Guillermo Manuel Ungo was the leader a small social-democratic party called the National Revolutionary Movement (MNR) that belonged to the Foro, and he had been Napoleón Duarte's vice-presidential running mate in the stolen election of 1972. When Mayorga called him, Ungo said that he would accept a position on the junta if the Foro nominated him as a candidate. Then Mayorga tried to contact Alvarez, but wasn't able to get in touch with him. "It was very difficult for me to find Enrique," he said. "I think he was hiding! He knew what I wanted, and I think he didn't want to accept. He had been extremely disappointed with the military people. He felt they had broken their word; they had promised him a lot of things and didn't fulfill them."

In the meantime the military had contacted the private sector via the Chamber of Commerce and spoken to a politically moderate businessman who agreed to serve; this was Mario Andino, the head of the Salvadoran subsidiary of the U.S. firm Phelps-Dodge. Thus by the time the Foro presented its two candidates, Ungo and the prominent Christian Democrat José Antonio Morales Ehrlich, the fifth position on the junta had already been committed and only Ungo actually joined the new government.

The United States government warmly welcomed the coup and the new junta; they seemed to offer reform without revolution, which fit closely with declared U.S. aims. Washington's first official reaction on October 16 called the coup "encouraging" and its leaders "moderate." A State Department memo commented on the three civilian members of the new junta: "All are moderate, well-known to the Embassy, and friendly to the U.S. From the internal Salvadoran perspective, the *junta* membership offers good political balance. All in all, we could not have hoped for a better group."[4] The memo went on to assert that the new government would face challenges from the right and from the armed left, and it discussed the need for prompt U.S. support.

There was substantial truth in all this. However, overshadowing the good intentions of the three civilians on the junta was the question of who would control the armed forces. This crucial point was not discussed in the State Department memo or in official U.S. public statements, and U.S. Ambassador Frank Devine barely mentions it in his memoir about service in El Salvador.[5] This matter of control, or lack of it, would be critical in the junta's failure to achieve the laudable goals of the *Proclama*.

In practice U.S. support often favored the military establishment over the civilian government. Soon after the coup a trickle of military aid began arriving in El Salvador, followed by six advisors. The junta had not requested any military aid; Ambassador Devine had made the arrangements privately with Colonels Gutiérrez and Majano, and the civilians in the government did not know the military advisors were on the way until they actually arrived. The human rights bureau within the U.S. State Department had opposed this sort of aid, and so too did Archbishop Romero who soon warned that it would only be used for repression of the people. The Carter administration, by ignoring these highly plausible warnings, contributed to the failure of the junta and the slide toward civil war — presumably not the result the U.S. was seeking.

Of course it was widely suspected that the United States had organized the coup or at least helped it along; many Salvadorans, especially those on the left, felt certain this was true. The plotters undoubtedly had received private assurance of a positive U.S. response to their coup should they bring it off, but there seems to be no evidence of direct U.S. participation. Ambassador Devine insists that he and the Embassy staff "leaned over backward" to avoid giving any appearance of encouragement. "The young military never told me anything about talking to the United States," added Román Mayorga. "If anyone suggested that, as the far left did, they became infuriated. To my knowledge they didn't have any contact with the United States. But I can't say the same for Gutiérrez and the older military."[6] Still,

The First Junta. From the left, Col. Gutierrez, Mario Andino, Román Mayorga, Guillermo Ungo, and Col. Majano.

it is clear that the Embassy knew months ahead of time that a coup was on the way and that U.S. intelligence had continuing, up-to-date information on its progress. One well-placed informant keeping the CIA posted was none other than Col. Jaime Abdul Gutiérrez.[7]

Some Reactions

Archbishop Oscar Romero issued a positive but cautious statement the day after the coup. In this "pastoral call," Romero first gave thanks that the change of government was accomplished almost without bloodshed. He called upon the Salvadoran people to be prudent, to "watch and wait before judging and acting." "A violent and impatient attitude," he said, "would be as culpable and unjust as the oppression and repression in which our poor nation has been submerged." Romero reminded the Salvadoran upper class that the unjust defense of their privileges was one of the major causes of the crisis, and he urged them to listen to the voices of the poor and the demands of justice. The militants in the political parties and in the popular organizations were cautioned to show "political maturity, flexibility and capacity for dialog." Finally, the archbishop directed a few words to the members of the junta itself. He recognized in their messages "good will, clarity of ideas and a clear awareness of their responsibility." However, to deserve the confidence and collaboration of the people the government would have to show that these were not mere words but the genuine beginning of a new era. "For our part, as pastor of the Church," he said, "we are ready for dialog and cooperation with the new government. We make only one condition: that both, government and Church, be aware that their reason for existing is to serve the people, each one in its own sphere."[8] In other words, the junta's intentions are good and citizens should give it a chance to show what it can do.

Some Salvadorans saw the moment very differently, and sectors of both the left and the right were unwilling to heed the Archbishop's call. Many from the business and land-owning elites feared that the new government might actually try to implement the reforms promised in the *Proclama*. To prevent any such thing they marshaled support within the Armed Forces (journalist Ray Bonner says pointedly that "they began buying officers"[9]) and took much of their wealth out of the country, severely cramping the national economy. The two largest daily newspapers, both thoroughly right wing, unrelentingly attacked the junta and its reform program.

At the same time, much of the left considered the coup to have been counter-revolutionary, designed to preempt a popular insurrection like the one in Nicaragua. (The Communist Party, one of the more cautious actors on the left, supported the junta and several party members agreed to serve in the new government.) Most of the leftist organizations waited a few days before taking action, but the LP-28 and its political/military cousin the ERP did not hesitate. Hoping to seize the moment, they tried to spark a popular insurrection in several suburbs of the capital and even distributed weapons to citizens there. The new defense minister, without authorization from the junta and despite opposition from Colonel Majano, ordered the National Guard into action and the rebellions were quickly and violently crushed. The military also "settled" a number of long-standing labor disputes by attacking factories that had been occupied by striking workers. According to the Salvadoran Human Rights Commission, more than 100 people were killed by the armed forces in the first week after the coup, hardly a promising sign of a "new" military.

"What effect did the October 15 coup have on your lives?" two writers later asked Javier, half of a revolutionary couple whose wife Eugenia was killed in 1981. His answer was that of many on the left. "I'd say there weren't any major repercussions," he replied.

> ... if you recall, the FPL [Popular Liberation Forces, the guerrilla organization to which the couple belonged] was the only organization which insisted at that time that the October 15 coup was a maneuver of U.S. imperialism, a different card played to deepen its counter-revolutionary strategy. Neither our organization nor the two of us in particular had any special expectations for the coup or for what might come out of it.
>
> The BPR [the mass organization allied with the FPL] was asserting the same thing. We said that it was necessary to continue the struggle, to unmask the imperialist maneuver.... it was important that the people under-

> stood that it was just a maneuver. All our efforts were devoted to this, in contrast to the ideas of other revolutionary organizations at this point. Later experience demonstrated that the analyses and plans of our organization were correct.[10]

In the same spirit, ERP leader Ana Guadalupe Martínez argued with Archbishop Romero about giving the junta a chance. During a meeting in November 1979, she firmly asserted her organization's total lack of confidence in the new government. When Romero asked why, she answered, "Above all, because this change came about without the participation of the people, who have been organizing for a long time." Despite the archbishop's plea, the ERP would not give the junta more time to demonstrate its good intentions. She says that Romero was sobered by news she brought about massacres in rural areas committed by the "new" military forces. The two parted amiably.[11]

These attitudes from the left may to some extent have been self-fulfilling prophecies. Junta member Román Mayorga and others believe that the hostility and militant attitude of the left toward the post-coup government reinforced the hard-liners in the armed forces and seriously weakened the junta, contributing to its inability to control the military and the eventual failure of its program for peaceful reform.

On October 22 Archbishop Romero met with members of the LP-28 and found them "intransigent." He offered to promote a dialog with the new government, but the delegation thought it would prove useless since the junta "was nothing more than an obstacle to the process of popular insurrection." "I tried to make them understand," Romero wrote in his diary, "but they were very stubborn."[12] He may have accomplished more than he realized since the LP-28 and other popular organizations soon declared a truce and suspended militant actions, waiting to see how the announced reforms would turn out. The BPR occupied two government ministries on October 25, taking a number of hostages including the ministers of labor, economy, and planning who happened to be meeting there.[13] Fortunately this incident was resolved peacefully a few days later, and BPR leader Juan Chacón explicitly offered the junta a 30-day respite from protests. He promised renewed militancy, however, if by the end of November it could not show progress toward fulfilling the promises of the *proclama*.

The emergence of Colonel Gutiérrez as a spokesman for the coup and his presence on the junta should have provided early warning that fundamental reforms would not come easily. His record was not promising. Ray Bonner tells of evidence that Gutiérrez had been involved in high-level corruption while serving as manager of ANTEL (the state communications system),[14] and nothing in his past suggested any commitment to reform.

In August Gutiérrez had inserted himself into the group of younger officers preparing the coup, partly by playing on fears that he might betray their plans if excluded. Through devious political maneuvering Gutiérrez then displaced Lt. Colonel René Guerra y Guerra to become one of the two military members of the future junta. (Guerra, a far more progressive officer, had been one of the original organizers of the coup.) In the first hours after the coup Gutiérrez somehow managed, without the knowledge or consent of Majano, Guerra or the other leaders, to install his friend Col. Guillermo García in the key post of minister of defense. Another hard-liner, Col. Nicolás Carranza, then became vice-minister; both men, like Gutiérrez himself, were CIA "assets."[15] García and Carranza in turn appointed senior, right wing colleagues to crucial command posts around the country. They also managed to release a number of officers, starting with President/General Romero, whom the reformers had wanted to put on trial. (General Romero flew to exile in Guatemala the afternoon of the coup.) Some of the worst human-rights offenders (including Roberto D'Aubuisson) and the most corrupt officers were removed from the armed forces, but there were no trials. As Bonner says, "There was a housecleaning, but it missed most of the dirt."[16]

An immediate problem for the junta was the fate of political prisoners and the hundreds of "disappeared"—that is, people arrested and never seen again—from the Romero years and even earlier. Releasing those prisoners and accounting for the disappeared was a specific promise of the coup organizers, but it was not easy to follow through. Román Mayorga told a committee of mothers that he had no idea where most of the prisoners were. "I pray they are still alive," he said, "but I just don't know." Mayorga promised that the new government would do its utmost to find them, and on October 26 the Junta created a Special Investigating Commission charged with finding the missing persons or at least learning what had happened to them. It would also try to locate clandestine prisons and graveyards. The members of the Commission had impeccable credentials and undoubtedly did their best, but the military did not cooperate and only a few prisoners were found alive. Some bodies of the disappeared were located and identified but it was impossible to clarify the circumstances of their murders. This failure cost the junta credibility with the popular movements, even though the task was not within its power to carry out.

Permitting the return of exiles, another promise of the *Proclama*, was much simpler. For example, lawyer and teacher Rubén Zamora immediately returned from two years of enforced absence to take a key cabinet position in the post-coup government. During the fall of 1979 three men associated with the disputed elections of 1972 and 1977 — José Napoleón Duarte, Col. Benjamín Mejía and Col. Ernesto Claramount — also came home to El Salvador. One of the three, Duarte, was destined for an important and controversial role in the years to come. His return on October 25 was itself dramatic. Duarte was met by "several thousand" supporters at Ilopango Airport, and tens of thousands more people were on the streets and in Plaza Libertad as he entered San Salvador. He has given a graphic account of street battles and an attempt by "the left" to kill him during the trip into the city. Journalist Jorge Pinto Jr. says, in contrast, that the Plaza was filled with demonstrators for another cause — they were mothers and supporters of the disappeared — and that Duarte was not well received when he tried to speak there. All accounts agree that the scene was one of some violence and a great deal of confusion.[17]

A few weeks later things were becoming all too clear. There is a story that one day Colonel Majano and another officer called on Monsignor Romero to request a statement of support for the Junta at a difficult moment. Romero replied that what they said sounded reasonable, but there was something about the government that he didn't like.

"What is that, Monsignor?" Majano asked anxiously.

"It is that from the beginning you have named as Minister of Defense, and still keep on after two months, an officer as repressive as Colonel José Guillermo García," Romero said.

At that the second officer drew himself up. "Listen," he announced, "*I* am Colonel García!"

"I know," replied Romero, "that's why I said what I did. I like to speak with people directly face to face."[18]

Once Again, Agrarian Reform

The Junta's membership was named on October 17, but the cabinet (aside from defense) was still to be appointed and a week of intense maneuvering and negotiations ensued. The result was a highly diverse administration that included members of former opposition parties, more or less progressive businessmen, and unaffiliated individuals with a reputation for honesty and capacity. *ECA* called it a cabinet "de lujo," in effect "the best and the brightest."[19] But this very heterogeneity would cause serious problems in practice, and so would the two important social sectors that had been omitted: the conservative oligarchy and the popular (mass) organizations of the working class. Despite these contradictions there *was* hope in the early days that El Salvador could change without war, and many people of good will felt they had to give it their best shot.

Enrique Alvarez was the obvious choice to serve again as Minister of Agriculture. Although widely supported for the job, he had mixed feelings about accepting. On one hand, his hopes and hard work for an agricultural reform under two military administrations had failed to produce tangible results; two presidents had promised that reforms would be enacted, and both had failed to come through. On the other hand, the good intentions of Mayorga and some of the others could not be doubted. Monsignor Romero, as a friend and spiritual advisor, suggested that it was a moral obligation to try once again. And Alvarez was nominated and supported for the position by the Unión Comunal Salvadoreña (UCS), the country's largest campesino organization.[20]

After hesitating, Enrique agreed to accept the position. Román Mayorga recalls him saying, more or less, "Look, I'm very disappointed with these people, I don't trust them and I don't think we should trust them ... but in this case, I think we might as well try. It's the last chance to do something peacefully." A year later, speaking in English at a meeting in the United States, he himself explained it this way:

> Let me tell you that when I was asked to belong to that government after the 15th of October, I had many, many doubts. I didn't want to, and I said I was not going to accept. But I was under pressure from many of the peasant groups. They visited me the day before I accepted, asking me to accept. I was also visited by many labor union leaders, and I was called by Monsignor Romero asking me to accept in order to give this last try of peaceful ways to achieve those structural changes. So with those many doubts I accepted, but with — I mean, I was not very certain that this could be done.[21]

He was the final minister to join the new government.

Despite his misgivings, Enrique Alvarez set to work again to give reform the best chance to succeed. Ten days after the coup, Alvarez and Undersecretary Jorge Villacorto sent an open letter to the employees of their department. Its theme was the historical moment, when a break with the past was necessary and possible. The department's work would be based on the Armed Forces' declaration, they said, which promised "a profound change" in the existing political and legal system. The key points needed to achieve this change were a reform of land ownership, organization of the campesinos, emphasis on food production aiming at self-sufficiency, assistance to the export sector, and the restructuring of production by means of technology and irrigation with the goal of diversifying exports and increasing their value. The MAG would open a dialog with the popular organizations and ensure that "those who never have had access to the means of communication" would have a voice in the reforms to come. The two officials finally declared that they "would not rest until they achieved a total break with the past, a process of genuine democracy, and a new politics based on liberty and social justice."[22] It was an ambitious declaration — and, as its authors well knew, it laid out a program far easier to state than to accomplish.

The reform program went public early in December when the junta issued Decree 43, "freezing" the ownership of large agricultural properties. Any person or organization owning in total above 100 hectares of land, anywhere in El Salvador, was prohibited from selling, transferring, or mortgaging it until the future Law of Agrarian Reform should come into force. Holdings of between 50 and 100 hectares could be transferred, but only with the approval of ISTA. Owners of less than 50 hectares in all were not affected.

An approving editorial in *ECA* explained the reasons for the measure.[23] "To understand why this is necessary," the journal contended, "we have to go back to the time of the First National Congress on Agrarian Reform in 1970.... For the first time, there was open, semi-official questioning of the structure of land-holding in El Salvador and its inhuman consequences for our people." Although the Congress had called for radical change, the government of Gen. Sánchez Hernández opted for a more cautious approach and decided to test the political (and literal) waters by creating Irrigation Districts, within which a single owner could hold no more than 50 hectares. The editorial reminded *ECA's* readers that in the first such district (Zapotitán) one large owner had maneuvered to preserve his property through timely distribution of small parcels of land to family and employees (Chapter 4). This and similar experiences "were taken into account in 1973 by Agriculture Minister Enrique Alvarez Córdova when he was preparing an agricultural reform project for the nation," *ECA* continued. Alvarez had urged then that the first step should be a law freezing land transactions, to prevent the frauds and evasions that had happened earlier when reforms were proposed. But the oligarchy would have none of it, and pressured President Molina to scrap the measure. At this point Alvarez resigned from the government, joined by two other ministers. These past experiences "reinforce, justify, and legitimate" the need for Decree 43, *ECA* stated. But the journal warned in conclusion that "the mere existence of the Decree will have no significance" unless it is rigorously enforced.

Archbishop Romero had been disappointed by the junta's accomplishments so far, but he was enthusiastic about Decree 43 and the promise of agrarian reform. One of his senior seminary students was highly skeptical.

"But the Minister of Agriculture is a very honorable man," Romero argued. "Yes he is, but he's not in charge," the seminarian replied. "It's the rich guys who really give the orders, especially when the land is at stake.... This government talks about reforms, but then the blows fly. Just look how bad the repression is in all those places where they say they're going to make their agrarian reform." Talking with groups of campesinos in the following days, Romero found that many of them felt the same way. The National Guard had recently massacred over 20 people including children, and what reforms could they expect from a government which tolerated things like that?[24]

The people's doubts and *ECA*'s warning were justified, especially since the reform had almost failed before it began. On December 2 the San Salvador press reported rumors that three ministers, including Enrique Alvarez, had submitted their resignations from the Cabinet but were being urged to continue in their posts. A few days later, U.S. Ambassador Devine wrote to Washington about what had happened.[25] In the case of the agriculture ministry the trouble arose, Devine reported, because Alvarez made the "tactical error of announcing to a group of campesinos about two weeks earlier that the junta was on the verge of introducing a new law to freeze land transactions ... as a prelude to introducing the long-awaited agrarian reform law." According to the Embassy's source, Alvarez "jumped the gun" by announcing the law before it had been fully approved.

But that was not the real problem. The fact was that Defense Minister García had sidetracked the freeze decree. Saying that he wanted to clear it with the Armed Forces Council (COPEFA), García instead sent the draft decree to the Supreme Court. The court then issued an opinion that the freeze was of dubious constitutionality. Ray Bonner comments that García's action was "not only a delaying tactic but also highly improper," since the Court might later be called upon to rule on the same measure.[26] Apparently Enrique Alvarez thought the whole reform project was in danger of slipping away, and he threatened to resign immediately unless the junta supported him and passed the proposed law. Decree 43 was then issued and reform had won—for the moment. But the military leadership had made clear their limits: this far, and no farther.

On December 11, Enrique Alvarez addressed the nation by television and radio.[27] "The agrarian reform is the most important, transcendental step," he told his listeners, "for changing the structures which have permitted and institutionalized the injustice in our country." To take this step was not just the opinion of one minister; it was "the unalterable decision of the junta, the cabinet, the armed forces, and, of course, the Salvadoran people who have insisted on it through their popular organizations." He stated his conviction that the agrarian reform "will be the crucial test for the current government and for the armed forces to show whether they are, or are not, on the side of the people."

"Ten years ago," Enrique went on, "to speak of agrarian reform would have meant prison or exile." But now, he said, it is the stated policy of all the political parties, and the popular organizations are demanding that the reform should go forward. He reminded his listeners that agriculture is vitally important to El Salvador, the basis of its wealth — and that it is principally the campesinos who produce this wealth. "It is a contradiction that those people who produce, those who feed us, those who contribute significantly to the wealth of El Salvador — I repeat, it is a contradiction that they are the ones who suffer most from the injustices which exist in our country" the minister continued.

Enrique presented some figures illustrating the conditions of rural life: Two thirds of campesino women give birth without specialized medical help. Infant mortality is 60 per 1000. Of every 100 children, 73 are undernourished. Only 37 percent of campesino families have access to pure drinking water. Half the rural population is illiterate. More than 250,000 families live in one room, although the average family size is between 5 and 6 people. "No one can agree with these conditions!" he said, and assured the public that the "military youth" in their October 15 *Proclama,* together with the governing Junta, had committed themselves to a process of agrarian reform that would change the structures leading to such injustice.

But what do we actually *mean* by "agrarian reform?" Enrique asked rhetorically. It has many aspects, but the most important is the ownership of the land. He explained just how concentrated that ownership was: About 0.7 percent of landowners held 40 percent of the land — and that was the best land, the land producing profitable export crops like coffee, sugar and cotton. The rest of the land, less fertile, that belonging to the great majority of farmers, produced the food for the Salvadoran people. Who would benefit from the reforms? *First of all* it would benefit the campesinos, he said, but not the campesinos alone. Once the rural workers begin to achieve decent salaries a significant internal market will develop in the nation, and commerce and industry will flourish too. "That means," said the minister, "that the agrarian reform process is going to benefit and favor all Salvadorans."

"The agricultural reform process, as we said, is going to take place *with* and *for* the campesinos," Alvarez continued. "That's why since the first day when we took charge of the Ministry of Agriculture we made it clear that we would support *campesino organizing* ... in all kinds of organizations, including cooperatives, labor unions, community organizations, and whatever else the people decide." This government will take that step, to authorize forming labor unions among the farm workers, in just a few days, Enrique promised. We believe that only with a rural population "organized, prepared and trained" will the agrarian reform have a real chance to help those for whom it is intended, he said.

The process would take place by stages, and the first stage had already begun with Decree 43, freezing the ownership of large land holdings. Enrique explained the necessity for this freeze, adding that it would only affect some 2000 owners—the 0.7 percent with over 100 hectares (250 acres) each. He then announced that the government had that day taken a second step seeking to control inflation. He explained that their goal was to control the prices of basic foods, but not at the expense of the (mostly small) farmers who produce them. Therefore the junta had approved a two-pronged law: it automatically extended all rental contracts for farmlands, but at the same time it fixed maximum rents, depending on the type of land and crops grown but generally well below the going rates. "These measures will benefit all those who sow and cultivate rented land, and that includes small, medium and large farmers," he asserted.

All these measures, Enrique told his listeners, were temporary, to last only until the comprehensive Law of Agrarian Reform was in place. His ministry would soon present a draft of that law, and he explained some of the principles on which it would be based. It would affect the whole country; that is, it would not exclude coffee, cotton or sugarcane lands as some had suggested. "An agrarian reform of that type would be a sham," Enrique asserted, "since we would be "reforming" precisely the majority sector whom the State was intending to support, and leaving untouched the large landowner who, and we should say this clearly, *is* going to be affected by a process of agrarian reform, in order to benefit all the others."

"On the other hand," Enrique continued, "the agrarian reform which we envision will *not* mean just giving a piece of land to each campesino; that is not the solution to our problem." Such a policy, he said, would only be "institutionalizing poverty." He explained that the government intended to preserve the existing efficient economic units and to maintain production, but the benefit of that production would be distributed among all those who worked to create it; that is, it would be "for the great majority of the campesinos."

In concluding Enrique spoke of general themes affecting social justice:

> Recently ... it has been said, with great vehemence, that what the country needs is peace and order; that the violence should stop. I am not in favor of violence. On the contrary, I am against it. But I am against every type of violence, and the truth is that this country and a majority of its people have lived in a system of violence. ... We believe that before talking of peace,

before talking of order, we must talk of justice. We cannot talk about peace and order while injustice is the rule for rural Salvadorans and for many other sectors of our people.

There is talk of the "silent majority." We think the only silent majority that has existed in El Salvador is precisely the campesinos, who have been silent for centuries. But we see that this is a *moment of hope,* hope that the current government is going to change the situation that has prevailed for so long. That is why we believe that the campesinos have stopped being silent and are going to defend their rights, which have been denied for so much time. That means that they will defend the process of agrarian reform that this government has undertaken.

MUY BUENAS NOCHES, y MUCHAS GRACIAS.

Reform at the Crossroads

This speech was the high-water mark for the first junta and for the third and final term of service of Enrique Alvarez as minister of agriculture. By December 11 when he gave the speech, reform was nearly dead in the water and the government's fate was sealed — if indeed it had ever had a chance. The biggest issue — there were others— was whether or not the junta controlled the armed forces. As time went by it became crystal clear that it did not.

The worst aspect of the situation was that state violence and repression had *increased* sharply since President Romero's ouster. The aggressive military actions immediately following the October coup might be discounted, since the new government needed time to organize itself and take charge, and the opposition similarly needed time to rethink its position. For much of November while the organizations of the left maintained a truce, there were indeed fewer deadly confrontations and political killings. But early December was much worse than any corresponding period under the Romero government. These generalities are reflected in the numbers of civilians killed by state forces: around 50 per month from July to September, 159 in October, 10 in November, and 281 in December.[28] After the November truce ran out popular protests and demonstrations increased, and even completely peaceful manifestations were often met with lethal violence from the army and the so-called "security" forces.

"We couldn't agree with the military on how to deal with opponents," said Román Mayorga. "The civilian government wanted to establish some kind of dialog, to have a lot of patience and try to incorporate the guerrilla movements into the political process.... The military didn't want to do that. They just wanted to kill them."

Dr. Rubén Zamora, who served as Minister of the Presidency in the post-coup cabinet, agrees. "The main problem with the first junta was not its lack of coherence," he said.

> In fact it was *not* very coherent; we could concede that point. But the main problem was that the military continued to be the dominant power. They continued to rule this country and they continued to kill people. Unless we solved that problem, it didn't matter how coherent we became.[29]

Why did Mayorga, Ungo and the civilians in the cabinet ever think they had a chance? It seems they were counting heavily on the younger officers who carried out the coup and issued the *Proclama.* The civilians were right about the good intentions of Colonels Majano, Guerra y Guerra and some others, who had meant what they said about reform. But the "military youth" could not deliver the internal changes needed to keep the armed forces on a new track. In fact, they had lost their grip on the situation soon after the coup became a reality. "We did trust Majano, that he was in control," Mayorga recalled. "But he wasn't. He was a good man, in my opinion, but he didn't have enough following in the military to consolidate the power of the younger people, and they were pushed aside."

The "Permanent Council of the Armed Forces" (COPEFA), established soon after the coup, should have been a key tool for the military reformers. This council had 26 elected representatives from all the major units, and it was supposed to serve as a review board by means of which the younger, reform-minded officers could ensure that the military remained faithful to the goals of the *Proclama.* But the very existence of such a council was highly threatening to the traditional command structure, and senior officers immediately set to work to subvert it. By December 18 they had succeeded. "We have managed to control COPEFA and convert it into a consultative, administrative organ, so that it will no longer be attacking my orders as Minister of Defense," Colonel García declared privately.[30] Apparently the civilians in the government did not fully realize what had happened.

To make matters worse, the United States undermined the junta's control of the armed forces, which was tenuous at best. In November the Carter administration sent a "defense survey team" to assess the situation in El Salvador. Neither the U.S. authorities nor the two colonels on the junta bothered to inform Ungo or Mayorga, much less ask the junta's permission. U.S. military aid and training were then reinstated at a low level with the rationale of "professionalizing" the security forces and improving their capability for non-lethal crowd control. The amount of this aid was small but it had a symbolic effect; it was announced just one day after the military had massacred at least 24 people during a demonstration in the capital. Archbishop Romero protested, saying that aid to the armed forces would only increase repression. But hardliners in the Salvadoran military leadership saw that they had powerful allies in Washington, and they must have judged the civilian government to be increasingly irrelevant.

An obvious question is *why* the U.S. government, which had welcomed the coup and the new junta with its program of reforms, gave it so little support during the fall of 1979. Raymond Bonner thinks that the first junta probably could have been saved if the Carter administration had acted decisively:

> ... if, for example, it had insisted on the implementation of the land reform in November or December instead of a few months later; if it had made clear to the Salvadoran military that aid was dependent on submitting to civilian control; if it had insisted on a thorough purge of all the officers closely linked to the violence; if it had reached out to Ungo, Mayorga, Andino and the moderate military officers. But it did none of those things; indeed, in some cases it did the opposite.[31]

Bad information from San Salvador was partly responsible. For example, the CIA station chief reported that Majano, Mayorga and Ungo were *leftists*, a distortion which was red meat for the cold warriors in Washington. (The next U.S. Ambassador, Robert White, described that CIA man as having an "incorrigible bent to the right" and got him removed.) Embassy cables consistently exaggerated the guerrilla threat, Bonner says, and Ambassador Devine represented the viewpoint of the wealthy and conservative classes more than that of the junta and the *foro popular*. All this strengthened the hardline, Cold War faction within the Carter administration, and the United States did not take the steps that might have helped the junta survive and carry out its program.

Crisis of Power

The government crisis came to a head shortly before Christmas. "On December 23 we were going to have a party at the presidential palace," recalled Rubén Zamora, who explained that as coordinator of the cabinet he had invited all the ministers and vice-ministers to come. That same day the senior officers of the armed forces had a meeting. "We were supposed to meet with the junta," Zamora recalls, " and afterwards have an evaluation and then go on with the party." But when they sat down, the Minister of Defense (Col. García) approached and said that the senior officers wanted to have a common meeting with the cabinet and the junta. The civilians naturally agreed. That meeting, Zamora says, was the beginning of the end:

> In this meeting the ministers started to talk about the situation, and I remember that Enrique Alvarez was one of those most outspoken. He pointed out that repression in the country was on the increase again. He also stated that the reforms that we were committed to implement were being slowed down, and that the army was an obstacle to implementing these reforms. It wasn't only Enrique; other members of the cabinet were also speaking out.

A big argument developed between the civilian members of the cabinet and the officers. Colonel Vides Casanova, who later became Minister of Defense — he was at that time head of the National Guard — made a strong speech. Zamora recalls that he told the ministers that "You are there because we put you there, we the military did the whole thing and we can get rid of you any time." That ended the meeting, and the ministers went on to their party. But, Zamora says, "the party was no longer a party; it was another meeting where members of the cabinet were saying we couldn't continue like that. From that moment there was a group of the civilian ministers— more or less the democratic progressive element of the government — and we started to develop our opposition."

> At the beginning the attitude was to resign, that this was the end. But then after discussion the idea became to challenge the military. And from that group came the decision to talk to the young officers and ask them for clear definitions of the role of the junta, the commitment to reform, democratization, etc. In that document Enrique participated a lot.[32]

The result of these talks was that on December 28 thirty-three ministers, vice-ministers, Supreme Court justices and other high government officials, Enrique Alvarez among them, sent a message to the Armed Forces by way of COPEFA. It had elements of an ultimatum but also resembled a plea for help, and it was published in the newspapers and read on TV by Rubén Zamora.[33] They were participating in the current government, the officials stated, because they felt they had to try everything possible to obtain a peaceful and democratic solution for the national crisis. They were there too because they believed that the group of young officers could put the power of the military behind fulfilling the promises of the *Proclama* which they themselves had issued. That *Proclama* was in essence directed toward eliminating the power of the oligarchy. Of course that would not be easy since it would represent an historic change for the nation. But the group of officials said that they had faith that it could be done, based on the participation of the people and of the "young, progressive officers who were not corrupted nor stained with the people's blood."

The officials said they had presented to the junta their worries that things were not going well — that basic decisions were very slow in coming, that a clear anti-oligarchy line was not being expressed, and that the coercive power of the state was directed only against the popular organizations. They asserted that the fundamental cause of these problems was a progressive shift that had taken place in the military leadership — *derechización,* a move to the right. The current high command was not the same one that had committed itself to the new political project back in October. The minister and vice-minister of defense and some post commanders were exercising power over the heads of the junta and in contradiction to the original principles of the military youth. This shift of power had moved the political process to the right and strengthened the oligarchy in its resistance to necessary changes and reforms. The country was returning to the bad days before the pro-reform coup of October 15.

By means of COPEFA, therefore, the ministers and officials were presenting to the Armed Forces the measures they considered urgently necessary. There were seven points. The junta must be effectively in control of the armed forces, with the political leadership exercised through COPEFA, and this must be explained to the nation by TV, radio and the press. The statement should recommit the armed forces to the principles of the *Proclama* and make it clear that the power of the oligarchy was the chief enemy of reform. The interventions of the military in labor disputes must stop and new rules of conduct had to be defined. The junta should be reduced to four members, namely Mayorga, Ungo, and the two colonels. The government and COPEFA must begin an urgent dialog with the popular organizations. These were the main points, and to carry them out the group suggested regular meetings between COPEFA and various government ministries.

The ministers' letter closed with the warning that in spite of all their efforts, a disastrous civil war was a threatening possibility. Therefore it was urgently necessary that the government modify its course and return to the principles of the *Proclama.* And so — finally the ultimatum — the ministers would be waiting on December 30 at 3:00 in the Ministry of Agriculture to hear COPEFA's reply to the points of their letter. "Our future participation as functionaries of this government will depend on a clear reply and acceptance," they said. At the very end came a beautiful piece of wishful thinking. "We send you fraternal and revolutionary greetings," wrote the ministers and justices, "with the firm hope that 1980 will be glorious for the people and for the Armed Forces, since it will be known in Salvadoran history as the year when the alliance between the people and its armed forces became a reality." The letter was signed by 32 men and one woman, all of them high officials of the "revolutionary" government.

The End of the First Junta

The string had not quite run out, and Monsignor Romero hoped that the reform process begun with the coup and *Proclama* could still be saved. On December 31 he met in the morning with the "young military" of COPEFA, warning them of grave risks and urging a solution to the confrontation with the government civilians. (COPEFA had not yet replied to the cabinet's letter despite the request for an answer on December 30.) Later that day he talked with the Minister of Health, Dr. Roberto Badía, who suggested that the Church convene a meeting between the two sides to the conflict. When Romero proposed this to Gutiérrez, the colonel offered to bring along the officers of the high command as well. The archbishop agreed to this, provided they came "with sincere intentions of holding a dialog with the civilians." The meeting was set for the morning of January 2.

Archbishop Romero described that meeting in his diary.[34] The civilians arrived promptly at the appointed time, 9:30 in the morning. The military officers arrived late and in a resentful mood, saying they hadn't understood it was to be a meeting with civilian officials and they didn't want to talk with them. Romero told them he had clearly stated that the meeting would be with the civilians, and he insisted they must have a dialog "for the sake of the people." Finally Gutiérrez said he was willing to talk, and business got underway around 11:00.

"A very frank dialog opened up between the military and the civilians," Romero wrote, "although one got the impression that the civilians didn't want to believe the officers' promises ... in favor of the *Proclama*, which the government had promised to defend." The archbishop summed up, urging mutual respect, communication and cooperation. "It seemed that a cordial atmosphere was achieved," he noted, "and the tone on parting was very different from that at the beginning. But unfortunately while we were leaving, the reply from COPEFA was coming over the radio." The junta was planning to meet at 3:00 PM to receive that reply, and instead it was being broadcast and not forwarded directly to the government — which had to send for a copy. "These things re-aggravated the situation and provoked the first resignations of some ministers," the archbishop concluded sadly, "and the others will no doubt follow."

Román Mayorga felt that there was no longer any hope for the first junta. He and Ungo were clear that they had to resign, but they waited until after the meeting out of respect for Monsignor Romero. "We were sure that our conditions were not going to be met," he said. "We knew there were already negotiations to form a new government, because the answer was going to be 'no.'" The two presented their resignations from the junta the next day.

In fact, COPEFA's reply had dashed the hopes of all but the most stubborn optimists. Despite respectful bows toward the *Proclama* and assurances of the military's commitment to reform, the Council's answer to the cabinet and officials was clearly negative.[35] First, COPEFA asserted that its primary loyalty was to the Armed Forces as an institution, and that its purpose was to maintain the unity of all the armed elements. It would guard against "extremist" attempts to deflect the Armed Forces from their legitimate mission and would prevent persons or groups outside the Armed Forces from intervening in their internal functioning. COPEFA rejected a "political" role and stated that the junta must communicate with the armed forces through the Minister of Defense. It asserted, in not very diplomatic terms, that if the government had trouble in carrying out the reforms it was the fault of the officials themselves and that delays were due to their "lack of real motivation [for reform], inefficiency, or allowing personal or group interests to prevail over the public interest." The armed forces, the reply claimed, had never intervened in labor disputes but had simply carried out their responsibility to maintain law and order.

"Finally, this reply to the document presented to us," COPEFA continued, "demonstrates categorically the unbreakable unity of the Armed Forces.... We assert that the consequences which could derive from the assertions of the document in question are not our responsibility, and that an intransigent attitude could produce unpredictable results and endanger ... all possibilities for achieving social peace...."

"This response was absolutely unacceptable to us," said Rubén Zamora,

> and so then came the discussion of resignation. The whole cabinet agreed—without the junta; they were not involved [in the discussion] although some of the members were in agreement with us, like Guillermo Ungo and Román Mayorga. Then we decided to resign. I spent a lot of time with Enrique; we sort of engineered a lot of the things that were done.

But Enrique Alvarez didn't wait for Archbishop Romero's meeting. He had bitter memories of trusting the good intentions of the military, and perhaps he was just tired and frustrated. On December 31, Enrique, as Minister of Agriculture, and Salvador Samayoa, Minister of Education, together with two undersecretaries and the president of a state bank, presented their "irrevocable" resignations from the government. Their letter stands as an epitaph for the first junta of October 1979:

> We accepted our positions, although not without doubts, with a certain conviction that an important sector within the Armed Forces was firmly committed to supporting, against its tradition, a political project of gen-

uine benefit to the people ... the project set forth in the *Proclama* of October 15.

By now the course of events has clearly demonstrated the contrary. The struggle of the people has been repressed, contrary to the principles of the *Proclama*.... The military and political power has been shifting toward persons and positions clearly repressive and anti-popular.

The Minister of Defense and his aides, and certain military commanders, are exercising power — as stated in the document presented by the Cabinet to COPEFA on December 28 — over the head of the governing Junta and contrary to the democratic aspirations of our people.

Once more the democratic sectors of the nation are being used and deceived. The most reactionary part of the oligarchy has been strengthened and has again imposed the historically false concept of carrying out 'reforms' with repression — a thesis that in practice always means lots of repression and very little reform.

All our efforts as public officials have been obstructed by the vast power of the oligarchy and by the military scheme that has been put into operation.... The situation has become intolerable for all of us who do not wish to be instruments of the economic, political and social domination that sectors of the oligarchy plan to continue to exercise over all our people.

The answer which the oligarchy and the Armed Forces have given to the Cabinet's document consists of virulent accusations and threats against the signers.... In these circumstances we consider that time has run out for the possibility of implementing in the nation political solutions such as that which, with much effort and good faith, we have been working toward since October 15. We feel it would be a betrayal of the people to continue collaborating with a government that responds more and more, without our being able to prevent it, to positions contrary to the public interest.

We see now that this political project was from the beginning a maneuver against the people. Even so we do not regret having been part of the government, trying with all our efforts and capacity to make things turn out differently. But we would have to regret it all our lives if we continued to take part now that everything is clear. Perhaps some of us— military and civilian — have been ingenuous from the start. We are not prepared to be dishonest at the finish.

... This is perhaps the best thing that we can leave our country: the strengthening of the Popular Movement by the increased conviction as to the historical correctness of its political positions.

In conclusion, we testify to the admirable generosity, spirit of sacrifice, and skillful labor of the majority of our companions in the Cabinet and the government Junta. But it is time to recognize that our project was not able to find the way to a different outcome for the national crisis. Now, without any doubt, the people will know what they have to do.[36]

Enrique later explained to the press that the outcome had been almost inevitable and justified his initial reluctance to join the government:

> And very shortly we confirmed our doubts, that [reform through the junta] was not possible, that the army was only saying that it wanted changes, that they wanted to keep the power for themselves, and also we shortly found out that many people that were in the government, representing what is called private enterprise, were there in order that changes could not be pushed through, not to support them but to oppose them. So we resigned, and I confirmed my position that only a government with popular support, with popular participation through their organizations, could really do the things that the country had been needing for so long.[37]

The rest of the cabinet and the other signers of the appeal to COPEFA now knew what they had to do. A press conference had been called at the Ministry of Agriculture, but the reporters, Salvadoran and foreign, had to wait while the cabinet finished meeting with two members of the junta, Colonel Majano and Guillermo Ungo. When Majano left at last, Rubén Zamora explained what had happened and Victoria de Avilés read the group's joint letter of resignation. Junta members Ungo and Mayorga followed suit by resigning the next day. Their own letter was addressed "To the Salvadoran People and to the Armed Forces"; it expressed "solidarity" with the officials who had already left the government and announced their own "irrevocable resignations" as members of the Revolutionary Governing Junta.

The hopes of October had now grown very dim. The first junta was finished. But the bloody year 1980 had barely begun.

7

From Reform to Revolution: The FDR

> 1980 will be the year of liberation for El Salvador!
>
> — *Enrique Alvarez Córdova*

As 1980 began El Salvador was without a government, but that would not last long. Even before the end of the first junta, the armed forces had been negotiating with leading Christian Democrats about forming a new military/civilian government; those discussions were a factor in the military's willingness to reject the junta's December 28 ultimatum. Rubén Zamora, who was himself at that time an influential member of the Christian Democratic Party, explains that when the civilians in the first junta and its cabinet resigned, there was a big discussion inside the PDC. One side proposed to join the government, hoping to make a clear agreement with the military about power sharing. Their argument was that the first junta had failed, the country needed clear leadership, and only an alliance between the Christian Democrats and the armed forces could provide that leadership. That was the policy of the U.S. government as well, Zamora says. The other position inside the party — the one that Zamora endorsed — believed that since all the democratic forces together had not been able to beg power from the military it was unlikely the PDC alone could have any greater success. This faction wanted to refuse any deal with the military, join with all the other democratic forces and establish a clear position. *Then* they would negotiate with the military — not just the Christian Democrats but the whole democratic camp. "That was the big discussion inside the party at the beginning of January," he says.

> But the party came to a sort of compromise; until there was a convention, we had to be part of the government. In other words, we [the progressive

> faction] lost. But we did gain the point that there should be discussion with the armed forces to state what was going to follow. That's why the second junta came about, between the PDC and the armed forces.[1]

As Zamora says, the Christian Democratic Party sought and received promises of cooperation from the military as the price of its collaboration. U.S. officials played an important role in bringing the two sides together. The State Department believed that the military/PDC alliance offered the best hope for achieving its goal of stability and moderate reform without the participation of the left. Assistant Secretary of State William Bowdler reportedly "thought the PDC was the only salvation." But although the armed forces and the PDC needed each other, their attitudes were tinged with strong suspicion based on two decades of conflictive history and agreement did not come easily. Deputy Assistant Secretary James Cheek engaged in a sort of "shuttle diplomacy" between PDC leaders and the high command, emphasizing to the officers that the United States would not provide major aid to a purely military government, while stressing to the Christian Democrats their "historic responsibility" to lead the nation toward democracy.[2]

In the end it was agreed that several officers and officials would be replaced, that human rights would be respected, and in general that the armed forces would obey the government's orders; that was supposed to be the basis for the second junta. None of those promises would be kept. Repeatedly the Christian Democrats in the government would protest some new abuse, the military command would agree to make changes but would stall and fail to carry them out, and the civilians would back down and do nothing.

Some people of undoubted good will were prepared to give the reorganized junta a chance, still hoping that worse bloodshed could be avoided. Among them, for the time being, was Archbishop Oscar Romero. Another was Dr. Héctor Dada Hirezi who had served as minister of foreign relations in the cabinet of the first junta and had resigned together with Enrique Alvarez and the other civilians; he now joined the five-man second junta. Dada and the archbishop talked by telephone on Sunday, January 6. Dada wanted to discuss a "tragedy" in Chalatenango, where he had heard there were more than 70 dead. Romero replied that he knew only of the four victims he had reported in his homily that day, but he would try to stay informed about this and other similar situations "which cast doubt on the good will of the government. I wished them success," Romero wrote in his diary, "and assured [Dada] that we would pray that the country might find a solution in the choice it had just made, that of calling on the Christian Democracy to help the government resolve this crisis."[3] Hector Dada must have had conflicting feelings about his own choice, and he would continue only two months on the second junta before resigning once again. Romero's hopes would not last long either, and by February his Sunday homilies were stating his belief that the junta offered no solution to the suffering of the Salvadoran people. In early January, however, both of them wanted to give the new government a chance.

Another Christian Democrat joining the new government was José Antonio Morales Erlich, who had succeeded Napoleón Duarte as the mayor of San Salvador and was the party's vice-presidential candidate in 1977. Colonels Majano and Gutiérrez continued as members, while the third civilian was a little-known physician and political independent, Dr. José Ramón Avalos. Rubén Zamora himself did not join the government "because he did not agree with that policy," although he continued for the time being as a member of the PDC.

Enrique Alvarez was having none of all this; he'd heard promises from the military too many times already. In addition he was angry with the PDC for negotiating with the armed forces' leadership behind the back of the civilians in the previous government. "He was such a good man," one of his colleagues commented. "He never wanted power. But he would get so mad—the time I saw him maddest was with people who were playing a double game, the Christian Democrats. When we were planning our resignation back in December, we met at the Ministry of Agriculture, in Quique's office, and we were being taped by the military! When he found that out he was so mad!"[4]

On January 12 Alvarez, joined by a dozen other former government officials, published a strong denunciation of the path that the Christian Democrats had chosen. In their "Analysis of the current political situation, so that the Salvadoran people can decide," the ex-officials declared that:

> The condition of misery and exploitation in which the Salvadoran people are living is well known, and so are the efforts and struggles both spontaneous and organized with which it is being met, in spite of the systematic repression of the people by the so-called security forces.[5]
>
> The militancy of the popular sectors, the intransigence of the oligarchy, and the anti-patriotic attitude of the reactionary elements of the armed forces, have led the country to the edge of civil war.
>
> With patriotic determination, good faith, and the determination to achieve the structural changes necessary for peace, we accepted positions in the cabinet and other institutions of the previous government, within a political scheme which would minimize the human cost of those changes and which required the armed forces to break with their past and to clearly support the reforms. Time has shown us that the correlation of forces within the Armed Forces has turned against its progressive elements.

> The honest officers have been shoved aside; the proposed reform laws have been delayed or compromised under corrupting pressures from the oligarchy. Moreover, continuing the traditional pattern the security forces have kept up the repression against the people and its organizations. It is not, then, a "Cabinet crisis," it is a crisis of the national political system.
>
> In the face of this crisis, we are fully convinced that time has run out for the possibility of implementing reformist solutions in alliance with the current leadership of the Armed Forces which is controlled by pro-oligarchy elements, and even more so if there is no genuine popular participation. For all these reasons, on the second or third of this month we irrevocably resigned from our positions in the government.
>
> At this moment, we feel we must declare to the Salvadoran people and to international public opinion our denunciation and repudiation of the leadership of the CHRISTIAN DEMOCRATIC PARTY (PDC) for having entered into a coalition with those sectors of the Armed Forces influenced by the oligarchy and by imperialism, in order to fill the vacuum of the resignations. This irresponsible attitude has put the PDC and its honest activists in clear opposition to the interests of the people.
>
> Their position looks even worse if we recall that the officials who resigned, among whom were several from the PDC, unanimously agreed at the beginning of our meetings in late December — a position which was explicitly reaffirmed on the 31— that any discussion with the Armed Forces would have to be held with the entire group. In spite of this reaffirmation of collective dialogue, the PDC now informs us that since December 31 it has had conversations with elements of the high command of the Armed Forces in order to begin negotiations leading to the formation of a new government — in contradiction with its previous position and even while the answer of COPEFA was still pending since it was only January 2 at the time.
>
> Finally, we wish to reiterate our conviction that, under the current circumstances and since the conditions mentioned above still persist, any possibility to establish a democratic regime with real social justice requires as a fundamental element, the participation and leadership of the people with their popular democratic organizations, and genuine confrontation with the oligarchy and its allies as their principal enemy.[6]

Clear enough! The *proclama* of October 15 was dead, and continued attempts to work with the current military leadership were hopeless. Enrique Alvarez had now broken for good with the politics of his old friend Napoleón Duarte. But then what, concretely, was to be done?

Enter MIPTES

Working with the second junta was out of the question for Enrique, but he did not return to El Jobo to live as a private citizen. Instead he stayed on in the capital, living in the apartment he'd taken while serving as minister with the previous government, and set to work on a new project. It was called MIPTES, the acronym for "Independent Movement of Professionals and Technicians of El Salvador."

MIPTES began with a handful of people who came together to talk about their roles in regard to the national crisis. Enrique was chosen president of the fledgling organization, and Mauricio Silva, an engineer with business training, became vice president. There were meetings at the two universities (the national and the UCA) and in private homes. Silva recalls that "One of the favorite places to meet was at the house of Manuel Sevilla because it had two entrances. Well, it had one entrance and one way out in the back where we thought we could escape if we were attacked. That [situation] made us all very nervous; we were not at all used to all those things ... but we had to learn pretty fast."[7]

He adds that MIPTES even met once in the home of Enrique's parents, in the upper class district Colonia Escalón. They didn't know about it, he says, and surely the father, at least, would have strongly disapproved. Silva had not been to the house before, and he was struck by the lifestyle that it represented. "There was a huge table, wood, sort of like from the knights of the British court," he recalls. The others were impressed too, but probably not with thoughts of Arthurian legend.

Not only was this sort of organizing dangerous, but Quique Alvarez was the prime target. Mauricio Silva says that he was well aware of it.

> When we came into government [with the first junta], they had already bought bulletproof vehicles for many members of the cabinet. And since planning [Silva's ministry] was the first one in the list in ranking, we got the bulletproof cars first. So I got mine before Quique. When we resigned, someone was with us and they told Quique, "Especially you—you have to be very careful." And I said, "Quique, why don't you take my car?" And being as humble as he was, he accepted. That's one of the few times I have seen that from Quique. He was conscious since then, the first days of January 1980, of how much his life was in danger.[8]

Francisco Altshul joined MIPTES a little later, "in the second round." MIPTES was very unusual for El Salvador, he says, because people traditionally think of workers or teachers forming trade unions, but never an association of professionals and technicians who came together around general political perspectives rather than strictly professional ones. Altshul recalls how the members of MIPTES saw their role:

> I think it was very important because at that moment the expectations were that it would be only a short time before there would be a new government,

> and demonstrating that there was an ample group of qualified people willing to support this political project was key. One of the things the conservatives had always used here was that if there would be a government of the left, what would they know? I mean, they are poor peasants and workers, almost illiterate, and what do they know about how to rule, how to govern? So to give this image — not just an image but to show that you indeed have a lot of very capable people supporting the political project of the left — was very important. That was the political importance of MIPTES.[9]

Concretely, MIPTES began work to prepare a platform for the new government that its members saw coming. They drew up the basic guidelines for new economic and social policies, which of course included plans to complete the aborted reforms of the first junta. Both Silva and Altshul stress that they, and Enrique Alvarez, expected the existing Christian Democratic/military government to fall quickly, and they all believed that the opposition needed to be ready to step in. "The failure of the first junta," says Altshul, "was ... the proof that we had reached a point of no return. It seemed that with that opportunity closed, there was no other way ... than to go into this revolution." A military victory of the armed left — which at that time consisted of several growing but distinct armed groups, not yet organized into the FMLN — seemed necessary and inevitable.

Many of their colleagues found the situation confusing and the idea of war hard to swallow. "Most of us in that group ... were kind of lost," says Mauricio Silva. "We hated and couldn't accept that war was inevitable. Quique accepted it, through his actions. Quique saw very clearly that what that implied was supporting the FMLN."[10]

"How could we collaborate?" Silva continued. "Either with the [coming] war, or in supporting the opposition to what was going on? By that time [the government] was clearly an U.S. project, with the military and everything. The best way we could collaborate was with our prestige. This idea came very much from 'el grupo de los doce' [the group of twelve] in Nicaragua.... So now the [Salvadoran left] wanted and needed something like that, and that was the idea of MIPTES."

The best-known member of Los Doce was the author Sergio Ramírez, later to be the vice-president of revolutionary Nicaragua. The group formed after an unsuccessful Sandinista offensive in October 1977. Several prominent men including Ramírez had agreed to be part of a provisional government that would declare itself as soon as the rebel forces had reached some of their objectives and were holding enough territory within Nicaragua. The offensive failed, largely through poor coordination between different groups of attackers. The would-be government members knew they could not return home and resume their normal lives; instead, they declared their continuing revolutionary commitment in a public manifesto backing the Sandinista Front. Sergio Ramírez writes that this "caused uneasiness and commotion in Nicaragua because of the caliber of the signers. Business executives, priests, international officials—supporting guerrillas! And Somoza ordered that we be prosecuted on charges of sedition, terrorism, disturbing the peace, defending crime and conspiring to commit it."[11] The group did later return to Nicaragua in a political challenge to the Somoza regime and was received with great popular acclaim in the streets of Managua. After the 1979 triumph several members of Los Doce assumed important roles in the revolutionary government.

The Nicaraguan example, then, was a model for both parts of MIPTES's dual purpose: to bolster the opposition to the existing government and to plan for the revolutionary one that would replace it. The success of the insurrection in Nicaragua, however, proved only that a popular revolution *could* win. For Enrique Alvarez and other Salvadorans who now saw no way to work for peaceful change, that translated into faith that *their* revolution *would* win, and in a relatively short time. The decade of civil war and the blood bath to come were not part of their calculations.

The Government and the Popular Opposition

Napoleón Duarte has described how the second junta with its new civilian/military alliance was formed in spite of great internal contradictions. "Following Zamora's plan, the Christian Democratic Party laid down a series of conditions under which we would agree to participate in the government," Duarte wrote later; he listed these conditions as restructuring of the junta, civilian control of all the armed forces, and an agreed timetable for implementing the agrarian and economic reforms promised in the *Proclama* of October 15. "In the Army's mind," he continued, "the issue was whether our political plan would help them to defeat the leftist guerrillas or handicap the Army by our insistence on applying the law and respecting human rights. In every discussion they asked, 'Are you willing to fight the guerrillas?' It was a clash of two mentalities."[12] The contradiction was never resolved, but the two sides needed each other and decided to go ahead. On January 9 the armed forces "published their promises to implement reforms, bring forth a democracy and respect human rights."[13] The PDC then confirmed its decision to enter the government, with Héctor Dada and Antonio Morales Erlich as its members on the reconstituted junta.

Duarte felt that the Party should call a "meeting of the people" to explain its position and ask for their support. Duarte, PDC veteran Julio

Adolfo Rey Prendes who was then the mayor of San Salvador, and others attempted to organize a public demonstration. It was scheduled for mid February and a good deal of preparation went into the event; moreover, Duarte had been a charismatic public figure in the past. Nevertheless, the demonstration was a total failure. "Instead of twenty thousand people, five hundred showed up," Duarte wrote, adding accurately, "That was how our junta period began — with the image of a government that no one seemed to want."[14]

Meanwhile, on January 22 the popular movement had successfully mobilized a huge group of supporters in the same capital city. The contrast with the PDC demonstration spoke volumes about the will of the Salvadoran masses, but Napoleón Duarte and the party leaders, to say nothing of the military and the United States government, did not seem to be listening.

"As its first joint action and first POPULAR CELEBRATION of the recently achieved unity, the Coordinating Commission called the Salvadoran people to a GREAT DEMONSTRATION OF UNITY on January 22. That demonstration proved the enormous support of our people for the various popular organizations...."[15] The *Coordinadora* called, and the people came. Napoleón Duarte says there were "over 100,000." Other sources put the figure much higher and somewhere around 200,000 may be a reasonable guess. The demonstrators filled more than 20 blocks of the broad Alameda Roosevelt, from the statue of the Savior of the World on the western side of the capital to the central plaza opposite the cathedral and the national palace. "There were columns of state employees, organized slum dwellers, factory workers, electricians, teachers, and, endlessly, the farm workers and peasants who had slipped through the roadblocks to enter the capital before dawn."[16] Nothing on this scale had been seen before in El Salvador's history, and it would not happen again.

The march and the *Coordinadora* itself had been organized in a hurry, for it was only 11 days earlier that the four major popular organizations had announced a new level of unity.[17] With a ceremony and press conference at the national university they launched the *Coordinadora Revolucionaria de Masas* (CRM) and called for the overthrow of the existing regime in El Salvador. The *Coordinadora* promised to work for a future democratic government dedicated to fundamental reforms and to ending forever the power of the oligarchy. Tommie Sue Montgomery reported that when El Salvador's flag was carried across the stage during the ceremony, a woman shouted, "The flag is not the property of the oligarchy!" Everyone then sang the national anthem.[18] To celebrate its unity and demonstrate its strength, the new coalition called for a grand march on January 22 — the anniversary of the disastrous 1932 rebellion that had been organized in part by Farabundo Martí.

The government and the Right tried to derail the march before it began. Roberto D'Aubuissón's newly formed "Broad National Front" (FAN), an alliance of right-wing military, business and oligarchy elements, had filled the media with warnings of a "communist" plot and threats of violence against the marchers. Bus companies announced a work stoppage to discourage travel from outside San Salvador. A number of labor unionists were arrested while heading for the capital. On the eve of the march, the death squad "White Warriors' Union" fired mortars and machine guns into areas of the national university campus where people were assembling to take part the next day. There was an intimidating presence of helicopters overhead and armored vehicles on the streets. On the morning of the 22nd two small planes dumped insecticide (malathion, according to FAPU) on streets along the route, and the planes returned later in the day to spray more of the stuff directly on large groups of marchers. As Armstrong and Shenk comment, for many of the campesinos at the demonstration this was nothing new. "Their bosses regularly carried out spraying missions over the fieldworkers' heads. Why shouldn't they now try to exterminate rebellion as if it were merely a larger breed of pest?"[19]

There was worse on the way. By about 1:00 PM demonstrators were filling the central plaza and streets of the capital, while others far to the west had hardly begun to move. Suddenly soldiers began to fire on the crowd from the National Palace (facing the plaza) and the roofs of surrounding buildings. Some demonstrators tried to return fire with pistols, but were not able to defend the mass of marchers who scattered as best they could into side streets and sought refuge in nearby churches. Officially 21 people were killed and 120 wounded, but the Salvadoran Human Rights Commission and other independent observers put the figures three times higher.

The violence of the day, and much more repression soon to come, distracted attention from the two great lessons of January 22. First, the civilian, basically non-violent, opposition to the existing political and social system had overwhelming popular support. And second, the narrow political opening of earlier years was now tightly closed. Since manifesting opposition peacefully in public would be met with slaughter, the *Coordinadora* could not continue organizing public assemblies and would have to turn to new strategies such as the future general strikes. This realization would further unify the armed opposition and accelerate the formation of effective guerrilla forces. The situation illustrated once again JFK's (and Marti's) dictum that "Those who make peaceful revolution impossible make violent revolution inevitable."

Monsignor Romero

Archbishop Oscar Arnulfo Romero (Wheater/Maryknoll Missioners).

"But where is all this going to lead us?" This was Archbishop Romero's worry when he saw the advance of the popular movement and the weakness of the government. If the Left's dream of an insurrection and overthrow of the junta came to pass, it might well produce something like the revolutionary process underway in Nicaragua. "Very well then," Romero concluded, "I must go and see how things are in Nicaragua!" César Jerez spoke with Sandinista leaders Daniel Ortega and Miguel D'Escoto about the proposed visit, and he found them eager to receive the Archbishop and show him what the revolution was doing. Jerez reported that the Nicaraguans would consider the visit an honor and that Romero could see whatever he wanted.[20] But the trip never took place.

More and more, El Salvador's best "newspaper" was the Archbishop's Sunday morning sermon. It was his custom to report and denounce crimes and abuses by the armed forces and the death squads, and also abuses by the guerrillas and the left, as part of his weekly homilies. These masses, held in the Cathedral or in the San Salvador Basilica if the former was "occupied" by protesters, were extremely well attended. They were also broadcast by the Church radio station YSAX, so the messages were widely heard. Reporters told that walking through San Salvador's central market the homily could be followed easily, since every stall had a radio and every radio was tuned to the same broadcast.

On January 6, one of the items Romero listed, not mentioned in the regular press, was that the home of ex–Minister Enrique Alvarez had been shot into with a machine gun. Colonel Guerra y Guerra was attacked more directly. Guerra, one of the original "young military" who planned the October coup, had served as undersecretary of the interior in the first junta's government and was the only military officer to join its civilians in resigning. In his homily Romero commented that "it was without doubt for this reason that he was marked for revenge, and they machine gunned his car but miraculously he escaped unhurt." Both attacks made it into the press on January 8 only when they were denounced in a communiqué from the BPR.[21]

In March the archbishop had a private meeting with members of

MIPTES. He wrote in his diary that this organization, which by then had some 150 members, had found its place in the people's movement. "Without supporting a political party," Romero wrote, "they want to be a center of illumination and of progress in the political process of the country." Romero found much common purpose and thought between MIPTES and the Church and they ended promising each other mutual support, each in its own sphere.[22]

As in October, Monsignor Romero began the year prepared to give the reorganized junta a chance to prove itself. Desperately hoping for a nonviolent solution to El Salvador's crisis he prayed and worked for reconciliation and tolerance, even while each Sunday he denounced acts of violence by all sides of the conflict. But as the weeks passed, the killing escalated and the nation became more and more polarized; correspondingly Romero's hopes for peaceful progress through the junta grew dim. He rejected the claim that the left was the basic problem. Instead of "the left," Romero insisted, one should speak of "the side of the people," whose mass organizations would have to form a big part of any true political solution.

In his homily of February 17, the archbishop declared that the junta was not serving the cause of the people, and he denounced the presence of the Christian Democrats in the militarized government:

> It has become more clear this week that neither the junta nor the Christian Democrats are governing this country. They are merely lending the appearance of doing so at national and international levels. The February 12 massacre against the MERS [high-school student organization] demonstrators, and the bloody eviction of the occupiers at the headquarters of the Christian Democrats, show clearly that they are not the ones who govern but that it is the most repressive sector of the Armed Forces and the security organizations....
>
> It has also become clear that the current government lacks popular support; it is based only on the Armed Forces and the support of some foreign powers. This is another serious responsibility for the Christian Democracy: that its presence in the government, joining with private political and economic interests, is leading countries such as Venezuela and the United States to back a choice which claims to be anti-oligarchy but which in reality is against the people.

Romero then read aloud a letter he proposed sending to U.S. President Jimmy Carter. It was greeted with prolonged applause. In the letter the Archbishop appealed to Carter as a fellow Christian and as a declared defender of human rights, and he made a specific request:

> I am very concerned by the news [from the press] that the government of the United States is planning to further El Salvador's arms race by sending

military equipment and advisers to "train three Salvadoran battalions in logistics, communications, and intelligence." If this information from the newspapers is correct, instead of favoring greater justice and peace in El Salvador, your government's contribution will undoubtedly sharpen the injustice and the repression inflicted on the organized people, whose struggle has often been for respect for their most basic human rights.

The present government junta and, especially, the armed forces and security forces have unfortunately not demonstrated their capacity to resolve in practice the nation's serious political and structural problems. For the most part, they have resorted to repressive violence, producing a total of deaths and injuries much greater than under the previous military regime, whose systematic violation of human rights was reported by the Inter American Commission on Human Rights.

The brutal way the security forces recently evicted and murdered the occupiers of the headquarters of the Christian Democratic Party, even though the junta and the party apparently did not authorize the operation, is an indication that the junta and the Christian Democrats do not govern the country, but that political power is in the hands of unscrupulous military officers who know only how to repress the people and favor the interests of the Salvadoran oligarchy....

For these reasons ... I ask you, if you truly want to defend human rights:

Forbid that this military aid be given to the Salvadoran government.

Guarantee that your government will not intervene directly or indirectly, with military, economic, diplomatic, or other pressures, in determining the destiny of the Salvadoran people....

In these moments we are living through a grave economic and political crisis in our country, but it is certain that increasingly the people are waking up and organizing and have begun to prepare themselves to manage and be responsible for the future of El Salvador, as the only ones capable of surmounting the crisis....

It would be unjust and deplorable for foreign powers to intervene and frustrate the Salvadoran people, to repress them and keep them from deciding autonomously the economic and political course that our nation should follow....

I hope that your religious sentiments and your feelings for the defense of human rights will move you to accept my petition, thus avoiding greater bloodshed in this suffering country....

Yours sincerely, Oscar A. Romero (Archbishop)[23]

The Carter administration, however, thought it knew better than the archbishop what El Salvador needed — or else it simply had different priorities.[24] On March 14, newly appointed ambassador Robert White personally delivered the U.S. government's reply. Romero respected White as a man with genuine concern for human rights who wished to help the Salvadoran people. "He recognizes the errors committed by his country in Latin America, and plans to work to show a different face of North America,"

Romero wrote in his diary.[25] But the answer White brought from U.S. Secretary of State Cyrus Vance rejected the archbishop's plea. The $5.7 million in military aid was on the way, a small installment on the flood that was soon to follow. This was only "non-lethal" aid and training, Vance's letter stressed, intended to make the security forces more "professional" by improving their mobility and communications.

The archbishop told White that he accepted the good intentions of Vance and the U.S. government, but that the Salvadoran Ministry of Defense would be in charge of the aid. The same ministry was in charge of the security forces, and who could guarantee that this aid wouldn't be used to intensify their repression?

"They tried to explain that it was aid to help the people," Romero added in an interview with a Venezuelan newspaper. "Did you believe them, Monsignor?" the journalist asked. "No," the archbishop replied. "I suggested that they should direct their aid to other purposes, because aid for repression would not be aid for the Salvadoran people." Other comments during this interview show the evolution of Romero's thought under the impact of the Salvadoran reality of 1980.

Q. To you, Monsignor, what does the right represent?
A. The right stands precisely for social injustice, and it is never just to maintain a rightist line.

Q. And the left?
A. I don't call them the forces of the left, but rather "forces of the people," and their violence can be considered the fruit of this social injustice. What they call "the left" is the people....

Q. Say something more, Monsignor, about the Christian Democrats.
A. It is a grave risk for the PDC to participate in a government that, while it has good intentions about enacting structural reforms, is carrying out such tremendous repression. In this sense, the PDC is complicit in the wrong against the people.... I want to make it very clear to you journalists, that ... yes, the Christian Democrats are there [in the government] and so are the reforms, but all the people are getting out of this is terrible repression.

Q. Monsignor, why do you believe the government is so repressive?
A. The only explanation is if its intention is to destroy the organization of the people....

Q. Monsignor, what do you think is going to happen?
A. If we are rational and use our higher capacities we can resolve all this quickly and peacefully. But if we stick to the polarization of forces, the spiral of violence will keep growing and explode into something worse. So the role of the Church must be mediation and the call for reconciliation.

Q. And if the Church fails in this purpose?
A. Then we would have the case of an insurrection that the Church would accept, when all the peaceful means have been exhausted.

"It still cannot be said that this is a civil war," Romero concluded. "I only know that we are in danger, but there is still time."[26]

Repression

"Repression" was a common word in the El Salvador of 1980. What did it really mean? A North American perhaps thinks of press censorship, of arbitrary dismissal from employment, even of the jailing of vocal dissidents—something like the McCarthy period in the United States of the 1950s. All those things happened, but that was not what repression meant to Salvadorans. It meant torture and violent death. The shots fired at the huge popular march on January 22 are one example—the U.S. Kent State killings of 1970 multiplied by orders of magnitude. The murder in March of Archbishop Romero was another. The slaughter under the "reformist" juntas utterly eclipsed the killings carried out by the infamous pre-coup regime of General Romero.

In 1980 some 12,000 Salvadorans met violent deaths, most of them at the hands of the government's armed forces. (The U.S. State Department conservatively estimated "only" 9000 dead.) Few of these people died during any armed combat; the great majority were simply murdered. There were fewer killings in the winter and early spring, but the pace accelerated enough to push the average up to one thousand per month for the year. Here are five examples illustrating different patterns of murder. Each was multiplied many times over.[27]

Disappearance

Two students of law, Francisco Arnulfo Ventura and José Humberto Mejía, were among the thousands who took part in the great protest march on January 22. About 2:30 PM, after the demonstration was broken up by gunfire, the two were walking back to the national university. As they passed the entrance of the United States Embassy a few blocks south of the campus, members of the National Guard stopped the pair and took them into the Embassy's parking lot. There Ventura and Mejía were turned over to a group of men in civilian clothes who had arrived in a private car. They were forced into the trunk of the car, driven away, and never seen again.

Relatives of the missing men and the university student organization AGEUS promptly began looking for them. They talked with U.S. Embassy personnel, who admitted witnessing the arrest of the two students but insisted that the Marines on duty there had only watched and not participated. In spite of this testimony, the commander of the National Guard, Colonel Eugenio Vides Casanova, denied any involvement by the Guard and obstructed the attempt to investigate the disappearances.

The Procurator General of El Salvador at this time was Dr. Mario Zamora Rivas, Rubén's older brother and also a prominent Christian Democrat.[28] He began a judicial proceeding on behalf of the two students, and on February 22 the Supreme Court ordered an investigation. The court-ordered process came to an abrupt end when Zamora himself was murdered a few days afterwards.

Three months later, a "death squad" calling itself the Secret Anti-Communist Army published a list of supposed enemies. The list included the names of people already known to be dead such as Mario Zamora and Monsignor Romero, along with many others whom the terrorists wanted to threaten or intimidate. On the list were the names Francisco Arnulfo Ventura and José Hunberto Mejía. At the end was this exhortation: "...help us to eliminate all these traitors and communist criminals. The *patria* will be grateful."[29]

Targeted Assassination

Dr. Mario Zamora, like his brother Rubén, was influential in the "progressive" wing of the Christian Democratic Party. He was critical of the party's alliance with the military, argued that the Armed Forces were not fulfilling their January commitments, and he had begun to explore dialogue with the left. For these and similar acts, ex-major Roberto D'Aubuisson publicly accused Zamora and other PDC leaders of being traitors, communists, and members of guerrilla groups. Zamora replied with a legal action for defamation, saying it was his duty as a public official to respond to false charges.

On the evening of February 22, Mario Zamora and his wife were entertaining half a dozen guests. As the party was breaking up around midnight, six armed men invaded their home and ordered everyone to lie on the floor. Zamora's wife Aronette Díaz recognized a policeman among the intruders; the rest wore masks. Their leader asked for Zamora, who identified himself in order to protect his guests. The gunmen then took him into a bathroom and shot him in the head.

Zamora's murder was never judicially investigated, although a member of the government stated privately that within two days the junta knew that Nicolás Carranza, the undersecretary of defense, was involved in the crime.[30] The military's General Staff did an internal investigation and learned who the organizers had been, then it covered up the information to protect the killers. A decade later, the Truth Commission found "sufficient evidence" to conclude that the murder was planned and committed by the intelligence unit of one of the state security forces, without explicit orders from the High Command.

Mutilation and Torture

In one respect Mario Zamora was fortunate: his death was swift, and his family and friends were spared. Most of the victims of kidnapping and murder were not that lucky.

The young sociologist Roberto Castellanos and his wife Annette Matthiessen had been kidnapped by members of the National Police on February 24. Roberto worked with Socorro Juridico, the legal defense team of the Archdiocese, and was active in left-wing politics. Annette had been a teacher in Denmark and was studying at the UCA. A friend wrote:

> I didn't want to believe it: they had assassinated Roberto and his wife. He was a great friend of mine, like a brother — we played and grew up together. ... He had returned from abroad a little while ago to live in his native country. He came with his wife Annette, a Danish girl as blond as could be, who didn't even speak Spanish yet.
>
> A death squad disappeared the two of them, and after some days of very anxious looking, their bodies were found by accident. A friend of the family went to the beach, and the gardener told her that he had seen near there a blond girl being buried. It was Annette. The two bodies were destroyed by tortures; they had cut off her breasts....[31]

The couple were buried on March 9 after a morning mass celebrated by Monsignor Romero in the San Salvador Basilica.[32] At 5 PM that same day, Romero returned to the Basilica for the funeral of Mario Zamora.

Killing of Peasant Leaders

On March 6 the junta announced that the long-awaited agrarian reform was at hand (more on this later). To begin with, it said, all estates larger than 1250 acres would be expropriated and turned into peasant cooperatives to be run by their workers. Troops were sent to the largest farms to implement the changeover, and on the same day a state of siege was declared throughout El Salvador.

To many campesinos the reform sounded too good to be true. It was. The Army's purpose was counterinsurgency, not social justice, and it proceeded to implement "reform with repression." A technician working with ISTA, the government agency charged with implementing the reform, explained how they did it on one finca:

> The troops came and told the workers the land was theirs now. They could elect their own leaders and run it themselves. The peasants couldn't believe their ears, but they held elections that very night. The next morning the troops came back and I watched as they shot every one of the elected leaders.[33]

This was not an isolated example but part of a pattern; the killings witnessed by the ISTA worker were one case among many. Ten days after the reform began Amnesty International issued a report condemning its military implementation. During this period refugees flowed into San Salvador to seek shelter with the archdiocese, coming largely from the very areas whose people were supposedly benefiting from the agrarian reform.

Indiscriminate mass killing

In El Salvador, massacres of civilians were not accidents of combat or unavoidable "collateral damage." They were deliberate acts of terrorism by the Salvadoran army and "security" forces. The slaughter at the Rio Sumpul was neither the first, nor the last, nor the worst of these. But it illustrates clearly why reformers such as Enrique Alvarez believed that peaceful means to achieve change had been exhausted and that armed struggle was the only way left.

The "summary of the case" from the *Report* of the Truth Commission:

> On May 14, 1980, contingents of the Military Detachment No. 1, of the National Guard, and of the paramilitary National Democratic Organization (ORDEN), deliberately killed not less than 300 non-combatants, including women and children, who were attempting to cross the Sumpul River near the hamlet of Las Arades in the department of Chalatenango in order to escape to Honduras. The massacre was possible thanks to the cooperation of the Honduran Armed Forces, who prevented the Salvadorans from passing.
>
> The Salvadoran military operation had begun the day before as an anti-guerrilla sweep. The troops left from various points and were converging on Las Aradas, which is located on the bank of the Sumpul River. During the operation there were various encounters with the guerrillas.
>
> There is ample evidence that the government forces committed acts of violence against the population during their advance, and this caused the

> flight of numerous people, many of whom gathered in the mentioned hamlet, which consisted of a dozen houses.
>
> The soldiers attacked the hamlet with artillery and fire from two helicopters. The inhabitants and the people displaced by the operation then tried to cross the Sumpul to take refuge in Honduras. The Honduran soldiers stationed on the opposite bank of the river refused to let them come to shore, and they were killed by the Salvadoran troops, who deliberately opened fire on them.[34]

As bad as that sounds, it probably understates the reality. According to eyewitness testimony, the victims numbered over 600. A report signed by the bishop and all the priests of the neighboring Honduran diocese described the scene with brutal details. After telling how Honduran soldiers cordoned off the border and warned the Salvadorans by loudspeaker that crossing was forbidden, the Church report continues:

> On the opposite bank at about seven in the morning ... the massacre began. At least two helicopters, the Salvadoran National Guard, soldiers, and the paramilitary organization ORDEN began firing at the defenseless people. Women tortured before the final coup de grace, nursing babies thrown into the air for target practice, were some of the incidents of the criminal slaughter. Salvadorans who crossed the river were returned by Honduran soldiers to the area of the massacre....
>
> At least 600 unburied corpses were prey for dogs and buzzards for several days. Others were lost in the waters of the river. A Honduran fisherman found the bodies of five little children in his fish trap. Rio Sumpul became contaminated from the village of Santa Lucía on down.[35]

The massacre was promptly described in the Honduran press, and the *London Times* summarized the clergy's report when it was published in June. In El Salvador the report was reprinted in *ECA* along with a bitter commentary on the events.[36] Nevertheless Honduran authorities and El Salvador's defense minister, Colonel García, denied that anything had happened. The major U.S. news media ignored the Sumpul river killings, and so did the State Department's country reports on human rights for 1980. In October, junta member Napoleón Duarte acknowledged to a Canadian publication that "an action" had taken place in which some 300 people died, but he insisted that all of them were "communist guerrillas." In February 1981, however, the British press reported at length on the massacre, including horrifying stories from survivors.[37] Ten years later the Truth Commission found clear proof that the hundreds of victims who had been deliberately massacred were indeed unarmed civilians, as contemporary reports had stated. In recent years, the massacre has been confirmed by excavation of bodies and forensic analysis.

"The concept of repression is relative," Minister of Defense Colonel José Guillermo García later told Christopher Dickey of *The Washington Post* (July 1, 1980): "When there is disorder, you try to put order. The reaction has to be strong." Judging by its actions rather than its words, the United States government did not disagree with García's conception of "order."

"Reform" and the Third Junta

In the meantime, the junta had again reorganized. On March 3 Héctor Dada resigned, less than two months after he had joined the government. His reasons echoed the themes of Romero's plea to President Carter:

> We have not been able to stop the repression, and those who commit repressive acts contemptuous of the authority of the Junta remain untouched.... The promised dialog with the popular organizations has not happened, and the possibility of achieving reforms with the backing of the people is receding beyond reach....
>
> In a note that I have already sent to the Christian Democratic Party, I have stated at length the reasons why I cannot continue to represent that political body at the highest level of government.... I feel obliged to present my irrevocable resignation from the position with which this honorable Junta entrusted me, in the conviction that thus I will best serve the true interests of the Salvadoran people.

Archbishop Romero read Dada's letter of resignation during his homily on March 9. Dada was slandered by members of his own party, who portrayed his resignation as the result of personal weakness rather than a rational political choice. He left the country almost immediately, after receiving all-too-credible death threats.[38]

Several things now happened at almost the same time. On March 6 the junta, responding to strong U.S. pressure, announced that the long-delayed agricultural and banking reforms would begin at last. That same day it declared a state of siege throughout the nation. The armed forces began to implement the agricultural reform, sending units to a number of large farms to inform managers and workers that the farm was now owned by the state. Three days later the Christian Democrats held a crucial party convention to reconsider their role in the government.

The agricultural reform was designed to have three phases. As noted, the first phase that began on March 6 nationalized all farms larger than 500 hectares (1250 acres); the owners were compensated with 20 to 30-year government bonds. There were 238 farms in this group, and they made up around 15 percent of El Salvador's arable land, being largely devoted to cotton or cattle production. These farms were formally converted overnight into government-owned cooperatives, to be managed by their workers.[39] Phase II would have affected some 2000 farms of intermediate size, including most of the productive coffee fincas. This phase was "postponed," and in fact never implemented at all, a crucial omission in the program. Finally, phase III was expected to benefit some 150,000 rural families. This was the so-called "land to the tiller" program modeled on earlier U.S. projects in Vietnam; it was supposed to instantly make the renters of small farm plots into owners by providing them with titles to the land they worked. (The farmers had to make payments for 30 years to receive formal ownership papers, however.) It began to take effect at the end of April. The United States was strongly involved in all this, working through AID and AIFLD. Some U.S. experts were convinced that the reforms would convert many campesinos from government opponents to supporters and undercut the strength of guerrilla movements in the countryside.[40]

At the same time, the government moved to implement the two other major reforms that had been promised back in October: nationalization of the banks and nationalization of the exportation of coffee, cotton, and sugar. These steps were essential for a real reform of El Salvador's economic inequality. "But," Ray Bonner says, "they languished almost from the day they were announced, receiving only tepid support from the Carter administration and staunch opposition from Reagan." According to an UCA study, the nationalizations "failed to bring important improvements in the economic lives of the intended beneficiaries and generated profits for the very class of wealthy individuals who were supposed to have shouldered the burdens of the economic changes."[41]

The convention of the PDC on March 9 produced a Pyrrhic victory for the party's right wing. The move to withdraw from the government was defeated, and the majority of the delegates—who by some accounts were "hand-picked by José Napoleón Duarte and his supporters"—selected Duarte to replace Héctor Dada on the junta.[42] Col. Majano representing the "young military," the Christian Democratic ministers in the government, and junta member Morales Erlich all opposed Duarte's election but were in the minority. In the end, most of the party's left wing walked out of the convention and resigned from the PDC soon afterwards. Their statement, issued the next day, asserted that "the maintenance of repression, and complacency in the face of foreign [i.e. U.S.] interventionist plans, constitute the gravest accusations of behavior absolutely contradictory with the posture our Party has maintained throughout twenty years of struggle on behalf of the Salvadoran people." The governmental process would become "neither democratic nor Christian" under these conditions, the dissidents charged.[43] Nearly all who left the PDC then joined in forming the rival MPSC (Popular Social Christian Movement) that before long would incorporate with the rest of the opposition into the Democratic Revolutionary Front. The new (third) junta was born even more divided and isolated than its predecessor.

On March 26, three more cabinet officials resigned from the government. Two were the ministers of economy and of education; the third was Jorge Villacorta, who had been Enrique's undersecretary of agriculture in the first junta and held the same office with the second. Villacorta's statement clearly describes the reality which official propaganda obscured:

> After March 6, I participated directly in the process of the take-over of the properties of persons who owned more that 1250 acres of land in El Salvador....
>
> In my opinion, this agrarian reform law, so essential to El Salvador in resolving the basic problems of our society, has been rendered completely useless by the climate of political violence in which it has been promulgated.... None of [the law's] objectives have been achieved, nor can it be predicted that they can be achieved, due to the repressive action that the very government is carrying out with its security forces and the army.
>
> I resigned from my position on March 26 because I believed that it was useless to continue in a government not only incapable of putting an end to the violence, but a government which itself is generating the political violence through repression. My remaining in the government was related to compliance with the agreements of 9 January [between the PDC and the military], but these agreements have not been kept. The repressive process has not been stopped. That is an indispensable condition for moving ahead with political reform. Further, the popular sectors have not been incorporated into the provisions of the reform....
>
> There exists clear evidence that during March, while I served as subsecretary, recently elected directors of the agricultural enterprises were killed by gunfire. In the first days of the reform, to cite one case, five directors and two presidents of the new peasant management organizations were killed ... every day this repressive process has become stronger. Recently, in one of the large estates taken over by the agrarian reform, uniformed members of the security forces accompanied by a masked person brought together all the workers. The masked person pointed out the directors of the self-management group and then these individuals were shot in front of their co-workers.
>
> ... likewise, several technicians of the Ministry of Agriculture and the Institute of Agrarian Transformation, who are advisors and co-managers in these properties, have fallen victim to the repression.
>
> These bloody acts have been carried out by uniformed men of the National Guard and Treasury Police, accompanied by civilians of ORDEN, all heavily armed....

> Within this framework of reform with repression, it is impossible to implement and complete an agrarian reform program....
>
> My resignation was based on the fact that it is impossible for the agrarian reform to gain popular participation. On the contrary, what one saw was that day-to-day government increasingly distanced itself from the people and established a closer relationship with rightist sectors, whose criminal action is strengthened and stimulated by the complacency of the security forces.[44]

Romero's Last Homily

On March 23 Monsignor gave his last and best-known Sunday homily. The previous week had been eventful. The Coordinadora had called a general strike, which was largely successful in paralyzing economic activity and showed once again that the left enjoyed a high level of public support. In the United States, former ambassador to El Salvador Murat Williams had publicly declared his solidarity with Romero's letter to President Carter. An U.S. religious delegation had arrived in San Salvador to study the condition of human rights; its members were present for the mass in the Basilica and Romero welcomed them in his homily. The radio station of the archdiocese, YSAX, was finally back on the air, just in time to broadcast the Sunday services. The transmitter and antenna had been bombed a few weeks earlier, and a technical crew had made Herculean efforts to restore this powerful voice to the embattled Church.

It had also been a week of terrible repression. The archbishop listed the victims of each day's crimes. Last Saturday, March 15 saw "one of the strongest and most painful military operations in the rural areas. ... Many houses burned and looted, and, what is never lacking, many cadavers. At the lake they killed the family consisting of Ernesto Naves, [his wife] Audelia Mejía de Naves and their children Martín and Hilda of 13 and 7 years, as well as 11 other campesinos." Romero named three campesinos murdered on Sunday by ORDEN. Monday was a day "of tremendous violence" when at least 50 people died. And so through the week, day after day. A campesino named Augustín Sánchez, who had been captured by 15 soldiers and turned over to the Policía de Hacienda, was found alive, barely, but able to give an account of the horrendous torture he had undergone. The last incident on the archbishop's list took place the day before. At 1:15 in the afternoon a unit of the National Police raided the campus of the Catholic University (the UCA). "They came in shooting," Romero said, "and a student whom they found studying mathematics, Manuel Orantes Guillen, was murdered." A number of other students had been arrested and disappeared.

Some of the blame belongs to the government, Romero said, which had wanted to put an end to these horrors but proved unable. "Without roots in the people no government can be effective," he declared. Then came his famous peroration:

> I want to make a special call to the men of the army, and especially to the ranks of the National Guard, of the Police, and of the barracks. Brothers, you are of our own people, you are killing your own campesino brothers, and above an order to kill which a man gives, there must prevail the law of God which says DO NOT KILL.... No soldier is obliged to obey an order contrary to the law of God....
>
> In the name of God, then, and in the name of this suffering people whose laments cry out to heaven more strongly every day, I ask you, I plead with you, I ORDER YOU in the name of God, STOP THE REPRESSION![45]

The archbishop had received many threats, and they sounded more and more serious as his identification with the popular cause became clearer. Roberto D'Aubuisson had called Romero dangerous and a communist in one of his television broadcasts, and the people whom he so labeled were marked for death. Going beyond words, two weeks earlier a large charge of dynamite had been placed in the Basilica when the archbishop was scheduled to celebrate mass in memory of Mario Zamora. Somehow it failed to explode. If it had gone off, said a police official, it could have taken down the entire building.[46] Colonel García, the defense minister, had offered Romero an armored car and military bodyguards but the archbishop refused the offer, saying that he could not accept them while his people had no protection. "Why don't you give security to the families of the disappeared, of the dead, of the prisoners?" he asked. García reportedly left in a rage.[47]

Antonio Cabrales recalls one day that winter when he was talking in his office with Quique Alvarez. The phone rang, and the caller asked whether Enrique Alvarez was there. Tony said, "Enrique, it's for you," and then asked, "Who's speaking?" "Monsignor Romero," was the answer. "They were very much, in some way, in communication with each other. I'll never forget that!" That call was Romero's way to say goodbye, Cabrales thought later.[48]

Romero knew his time was short. He told reporters from the Mexico City daily *Excelsior,* "Yes, I have often been threatened with death, but I must say that as a Christian I do not believe in death without resurrection. If they kill me, I will live again in the Salvadoran people.... A bishop will die, but the Church of God, which is the people, will never perish."[49]

On the very day after his call to the troops to obey conscience rather than military orders, the threats were carried out. The archbishop did not live in a palace or official residence, but in a few simple rooms at a hospital maintained by nuns for incurable cancer patients. There, in the hospital's chapel, he planned to celebrate a mass in memory of Señora Sara Meardi de Pinto, the mother of Jorge Pinto Jr., on the first anniversary of her death. (See Chapter 3. Yes, El Salvador is a small world!) The mass was scheduled for 6:00 PM on March 24 and had been widely advertised in the press. The archbishop's sermon began with these words:

> Because of the manifold relationship I have had with the editor of the newspaper *El Independiente*, I am able to share to some extent his feelings on the anniversary of his mother's death. Above all I can appreciate her noble spirit, how she put all of her educated upbringing, all her graciousness, at the service of a cause that is so important now—our people's true liberation.

As Monsignor Romero reached the end of his homily and called for prayer, the shot rang out that ended his life. He was rushed to a nearby emergency room but died within minutes. According to a nun who accompanied Romero to the hospital, his last words were "May God forgive them."[50]

Despite international attention, repeated government promises, and ample evidence, no one was ever arrested for Romero's murder.

A Few Reactions

Nidia Diaz: I don't believe there was a single guerrilla in El Salvador who did not cry for him. Me included. On that day, we all lost.[51]

Leoncio Pichinte: We of the FDR [see below] were in a clandestine meeting: Juan Chacón, Quique Alvarez, all of us.... That's when we got the news. And I'm not embarrassed to say that all of us shed tears. We couldn't analyze; we couldn't get into our heads how anyone could eliminate like that such a wonderful man. If we had given the call that day, there would have been a popular insurrection! But we were not ready.[52]

Alirio Ramírez Amaya (judge appointed to investigate the murder): Monsignor Romero was killed by a professional assassin who was obeying the orders of General Medrano and of Major D'Aubuisson, both [former officers] of the Salvadoran army.[53]

The Commission on the Truth: Ex-major Roberto D'Aubuisson gave the order to assassinate the archbishop, and gave precise instructions to members of his own security group, acting as a "death squad," to organize and supervise carrying out the execution.[54]

Marisa D'Aubuisson (sister of Roberto): Everything implicated Roberto in that crime. I wanted to disappear, to evaporate, that day. For me it has been a permanent trauma to bear this name and be of the same blood as someone who did such an awful thing against the Salvadoran people. From the first moment and to this day I am convinced that man who was my brother is the one responsible for the assassination of Monsignor.[55]

MIPTES: He, who was the voice of the voiceless, presented an image which we wish to take for our own — that of God cursing Cain for the murder of his brother. Together with Monsignor we insist that any reform that is undertaken will be sterile if it is stained by the blood of the people....[56]

John Bushnell (U.S. State Department): We do not think at this point that the event [Romero's murder] should cause us to deviate from the course which we have embarked on in the government. [The "course" was to send the military aid that the archbishop had opposed, and they did not alter their schedule by even one day.][57]

Funeral

The funeral of Archbishop Romero was a triumph and a tragedy. "More than 30,000"[58] mourners jammed San Salvador's central plaza facing the cathedral; the crowd spilled over into surrounding blocks. Among many foreign observers, Rev. Jorge Lara-Braud was there representing the U.S. National Council of Churches. He later described what happened:

> The plaza was jammed with the archbishop's flock — mostly poor people on whose behalf his voice had been so compelling.... I saw an orderly column of some 500 enter the plaza, marching 8 abreast behind banners that identified them as representatives of the huge coalition of popular organizations called "La Coordinadora Revolucionaria de Masas." These were the famous "leftists" one reads about, whom the archbishop loved and sometimes rebuked. The crowds in the plaza cheered....
>
> As the mass continued, Cardinal Corripio paid tribute to the martyred archbishop. Just as he was paraphrasing an oft-heard teaching of Archbishop Romero ... he was stunned, as were we all, by the thunderous detonation of a bomb.
>
> The explosion occurred at the far corner of the National Palace.... I saw leaping fire and thick fuming smoke as if the pavement were aflame. The crowd stampeded away from the palace. There was the immediate sound of some return gunfire....[59]

There are conflicting reports of how the violence began and who was responsible. The junta, supported by U.S. Ambassador White, immediately blamed the left, claiming that all the armed forces were confined to their barracks. Most of the international observers and many Salvadoran witnesses testified that they saw snipers in uniform shooting from the National Palace and other buildings. In any event, once again a popular assembly of the people resulted in disaster — dozens of people died, many of them crushed in the panic, and hundreds were injured. The masses who had loved their archbishop could not bid him farewell in peace.

The Frente Democrático Revolucionario

On April 18 Enrique Alvarez returned to center stage — literally. At 10:50 AM, the Executive Committee of the newly formed *Frente Democrático Revolucionario* (FDR), or Democratic Revolutionary Front, entered the auditorium of the University of El Salvador Law School to the cheers of some 5000 supporters. The seven committee members took places on the platform and their new President, standing in the center behind a long table, gave a short speech accepting responsibility to lead the revolutionary movement. "This event is another sign of the maturity of the forces that compose the Front," he said. "These forces, setting aside sectarianism, intolerance, dogmatism, and real but secondary differences, are uniting around a common project where the two great currents, the revolutionary and the democratic, merge."[60] The president was Enrique Alvarez Córdova.

Enrique entered the FDR as the leader and representative of MIPTES, and he was chosen to be the FDR's president for his personal qualities, not because of his political base. Still, MIPTES fit well into the larger pattern of opposition evolving in 1980. On April 2 it joined in forming a coalition of civic organizations, some of which had been part of the now-inactive *Foro Popular* that had figured in the first junta of 1979. This alliance was called the *Frente Democrático.* A State Department telegram described the FD as "a 'popular front' type organization which backs [the] program of insurgent Coordinadora de las Masas [the CRM], but is designed to attract broader, more moderate segments of domestic and international support."[61] Along with MIPTES the new coalition included the dissident Christian Democrats who had left that party in March, plus several labor unions and federations, university students, and the smaller political parties of the left. The national university and the UCA, as well as an organization representing small businesses, were included as "observers."

Enrique Alvarez was the "spokesman" of the Democratic Front. According to the embassy telegram, Enrique said the purpose of the FD "was to 'support and enrich' the CRM's program 'which the great majority of the

Founding the Frente Democrático Revolucionario: Enrique Alvarez at the center (El Independiente).

Salvadoran people support,' and to call on all 'popular, democratic, and progressive domestic forces' to join the Front with their 'revolutionary' (CRM) colleagues. It would also appeal to foreign governments to support the Salvadoran people's struggle." But the FD proved to be short lived as an independent organization, for it quickly merged with the Coordinadora to form the *Frente Democrático Revolucionario,* the FDR.[62] This powerful coalition included virtually all the civilian left that opposed the junta, including the popular organizations that in turn had links to the growing guerrilla forces. Without explicitly making the claim, the FDR formed the basis for a new, democratic government of El Salvador.

The U.S. Embassy sent John Glassman to observe the FDR's founding ceremony on April 18. A telegram based on his report notes without further explanation that the ceremony was "interrupted briefly" by a "firefight between [a] military unit and leftists and buzzing of university by air force plane."(!) The new front, the embassy telegram continues, "will be directed by an executive council led by Enrique Alvarez Córdova, president, a liberal man of wealth and several times Salvadoran minister of agriculture, representing [MIPTES]." The six other council members, two of whom would die with Enrique in seven months, represented the four popular organizations making up the CRM, plus the "popular tendency" (dissident)

Christian Democrats and the Social Democratic Party MNR. "According to Front President Alvarez," the embassy telegram continued, "the creation of the revolutionary-democratic front will lead to the 'liberation' of El Salvador this year."[63] An article in *Excelsior* quotes Enrique more dramatically: "The year 1979 was the time of liberation for Nicaragua, and 1980 will be the year of liberation for El Salvador!"[64]

In addition to the groups represented on the executive council, six major labor organizations signed the founding document of the FDR and accepted its statement of principles, as did the association of university students. Also signing as "observers" were Engineer Félix Ulloa, the rector of the national university, and a representative of the UCA on behalf of the Jesuit fathers. Former UNO presidential candidate Col. Ernesto Claramount, widely considered to have been robbed of the electoral victory in 1977, "declared his approval and requested entry as head of the recently founded Movimiento de Acción Democrática Revolucionaria."[65]

And what was the document these groups signed? The "First Declaration of the Democratic Revolutionary Front" resembles in spirit the (North) American Declaration of Independence, which undoubtedly provided some of its inspiration. Like the Declaration, the FDR statement begins with a list of troubles and grievances. It notes first that El Salvador found itself in a "profound economic, social, and political crisis" as a result of its dependent capitalist economy, which concentrated all the power in a small group of families. The great majority of the population was obliged to live in misery. The people had asked for change through their democratic organizations, but the oligarchy responded with demagoguery and with repression — that had reached a scale and level of cruelty not seen in El Salvador since 1932. The people could not stand for this any longer, and were organizing to struggle for change.

For all these reasons, the declaration continues, the signers agree to form the Democratic Revolutionary Front to advance their struggle for liberation and to construct a new society that will be just and humane, free from corruption and the continual exploitation of human beings, a society based on human rights. After naming the initial signers, the document defines its national objectives: "to mobilize and incorporate into the liberation process all the honest, genuinely representative sectors of our people, joining to support the platform of the Democratic Revolutionary Government" as defined earlier by the Coordinadora. The goals "at the international level" were to seek the understanding and support of the "democratic peoples and governments of the world" for El Salvador's effort to build a new society. At the same time, the FDR would denounce the backing of the United States for the military/Christian Democratic junta, and it would organize international opposition to the military intervention that the U.S. was planning. Finally, the document calls on all organizations and sectors of Salvadoran society to join the Front, so that the social and human costs of the coming revolution could be minimized.[66]

Like the *Proclama* of October 1979, this was ambitious! Since October the situation in El Salvador had become highly polarized. The coup's "young military" reformers had been betrayed from within the ranks of their own institution, but the FDR's main enemies were external. They were the oligarchy, the military leadership, and its civilian allies in the government—the Salvadoran Right whose partial divergence of interests did not mean that any of its competing factions formed a democratic "center." But the most tenacious and strongest enemy of all would be that looming foreign intervention clearly foreseen by Archbishop Romero—the power of the United States.

Captured by the Police

For Enrique Alvarez, becoming president of the FDR had immediate personal consequences. His long-time friend and co-worker Lino Osegueda says he hadn't been aware of Enrique's growing involvement with the "people of the left":

> Finally they came up with a new idea and convinced him to be president of the FDR. It was a big surprise for all of us, even to me, and I was like a brother to him. I got mad, came running to him. He was waiting for the storm. Enrique said he hadn't said anything because he didn't want to involve any members of the farm [El Jobo] in the FDR. He gave his reasons for joining. He said, "We went a century backwards when they stopped the agrarian reform. I feel empty from a human point of view; I'm making money but that's not enough. I want to do something for this country. That's why I joined. I am not so convinced of all their ideas, but instead of criticizing them, if I am inside maybe I can help them find other ways of doing the work."[67]

El Jobo's lack of involvement with the left was not enough to keep it from danger; in El Salvador at that time guilt by association was often sufficient for a death sentence (see chapter 9). But Enrique's efforts to separate the finca and its people from the nation's political storms helped to make the survival of the farm, and of Osegueda himself, possible.

Another close friend, Tony Cabrales, was also shocked. "I went to his house to see him that night." Tony recalls. "He had just accepted becoming the president of the FDR. It had just come out in the paper. 'Jesus Christ,'

I said, 'how did you accept that?'" Enrique replied, "Well, you've got to be decisive. You're either white or black."[68]

On April 21 Enrique was arrested at a police roadblock. As usual there were conflicting reports about what happened. A U.S. embassy telegram sent that day to Washington says that he was "kidnapped" between 10 and 11 AM on the road to Sonsonate. Ambassador White was told that junta members Duarte and Gutiérrez were "consulting closely on the case" and were "deeply concerned" with the impact it would have. "They believe," White's telegram continues, "with no proof so far, that he has been taken by right-wing terrorists who may kill him, provoking a gravely adverse reaction domestically and internationally."[69]

Mauricio Silva tells of his own involvement in the matter:

> And then one day I was at home, and I received this call from Quique. "I am here at the police in Santa Tecla and I've been captured." ... Quique probably called me because we were working together very closely, but also because I lived in Santa Tecla. And that was all he said: "I just wanted to let you know, to take the actions that are needed." So I immediately called Monsignor Urioste. The only thing he said was to ask me, "Are you sure?" I said "Yes, Monsignor, because Quique called me." (They let him make one call.) So he told me to stay home and said he'd call me back with instructions.
>
> About one or two hours later — it felt like eternity — he called back. And he said, "Mauricio, I just talked with Morales Ehrlich and he promised me that they are going to release Quique to you. But only to you. So go to the police and pick up Quique." ... I think that after that Quique was never out in the open like he was up to that point, like I was.[70]

Silva adds a personal note about this incident, saying that he had three children by that time and his wife was (understandably!) very nervous about the family's safety. Mauricio used to reassure her by saying "Before they do something to me, they'll do something to Quique." When they did capture Enrique, he says, the immediate reaction of his wife was "You're next!"

A second embassy telegram the next day reported the new cover story, saying that Enrique Alvarez "was arrested by the National Police for illegal possession of weapons and subsequently released, according to press reports attributed to official sources." Robert White added a telling comment. "Incident is another illustration of how little knowledge or control the JRG [junta], particularly its civilian sector, has of the actions of the security forces. As reported [yesterday], junta members several hours after the story of the Alvarez 'kidnapping' broke, still did not know he had been arrested. Even Cols. Gutiérrez and García were uninformed."[71] White also pointed out that there was no general police effort at gun control, an observation undercutting the "illegal weapons" rationale for the arrest and supporting the obvious supposition that it was a political act—and a warning.

On April 22, a brief front-page article in a leading San Salvador daily gave the official story of Enrique's detention, and even included a photo of the "ex-minister of agriculture." The FDR was not mentioned, and indeed in the mainstream media the Frente hardly existed. The same paper had noted the founding of the FDR with a page 4 photo of the executive committee and a bare-bones announcement of the Frente's formation, but with no description of what it was all about. The organization's program and reasons for existence were never described.[72]

The arrest may have been meant as a warning, but Enrique Alvarez was not intimidated. At a news conference two days later he showed that his purpose had not changed:

> I am going to answer a question here in public that is often asked me: Why did I resign? Why have I changed?...
>
> My participation in previous governments was due to my belief that I could help those governments make the changes that our society needs, but I found out that those in power, those sectors which have had control of the government for years, do not wish to have the least amount of changes in our society for the benefit of other sectors.
>
> As representative of the Independent Movement of Professionals and Technicians [MIPTES], I have reached the conclusion that only a government that results from the triumph of the people's struggle, as the Revolutionary Coordinating Board of the Masses [CRM] has suggested and which the FDR accepts and supports, can make possible the new society for which we are all hoping.

Jorge Pinto Jr.: El Independiente

The editor of *El Independiente* had come a long way from the brash young man who denounced Enrique Alvarez and his *Arco Iris* teammates as homosexuals back in 1957—and was punched out by Enrique for his pains. So had the paper itself. *El Independiente* was now one of very few public voices raised in El Salvador against the repression and crimes of the system and calling for fundamental change. Its daily editions gave readers a totally different picture of Salvadoran reality from that found in the pages of *La Prensa Gráfica* and *El Diario de Hoy.* Readers of those larger papers were informed that there was a great deal of violence in the country, some of it committed by "subversives" and some due to "unknown actors," while the authorities were trying to bring about order and progress. *El Independiente,* on the other hand, provided accounts of repression by the police, massacres by the armed forces, acts and manifestos of rebellion and news of international reactions. It showed that a revolution was in the making.[73]

Of course taking that stance had its price. Early on March 13 bombs were exploded in the offices of *El Independiente* and, at the same time, in the office of the Salvadoran Commission on Human Rights. (The two were located close together, and Pinto was a member of the Commission.) The paper did not miss an issue, and Pinto expressed his determination to continue: "Censorship might quiet our voice, but dynamite only makes it stronger." In his next Sunday homily Monsignor Romero quoted this phrase with admiration as he reported the bombings. In fact there was much worse in store for *El Independiente* and its staff. On July 2 the *Washington Post* published a photo of Pinto's car riddled by bullet holes after an assassination attempt from which he miraculously escaped unharmed. The U.S. human rights organization Americas Watch reported the paper's subsequent fate:

> In 1980 the premises of *El Independiente* were repeatedly bombed and fired upon; in one incident, a fourteen-year-old newsboy was shot dead while standing in a doorway. Jorge Pinto, the editor, was the target of three assassination attempts in the course of two months alone. On January 15, 1981, army tanks and trucks surrounded the newspaper offices and occupied Pinto's home. Several days later, eight employees of *El Independiente* were arrested. The newspaper closed permanently that month.[74]

On April 17, the front page of *El Independiente* carried four stories, none of which were reported in the major dailies. The headlines: Militants of the LP-28 testify about torture; Massacre of railroad passengers [by the National Guard and Treasury Police]; Nicaraguan journalists denounce brutal repression in El Salvador; and finally, The Democratic Revolutionary Front is formed. This last—founding of the FDR—was barely mentioned by the major papers but extensively covered in *El Independiente*, which called it "an event of capital importance." The subhead "A great man for a great Front" led to the announcement that Enrique Alvarez Córdova, "the ex-minister of Agriculture and Livestock and one of the political figures most widely recognized by the Salvadoran people," was expected to be named president of the FDR.

The new Frente continued to be front-page news in *El Independiente* for several days. Much of page 1 on April 19 was given to a photo of the *directiva* of the FDR, with Enrique prominent in the picture and quoted in its caption. *Frente Democrático Revolucionario: Revolución y Democracia* was the headline. Another photo shows Enrique in an earnest face-to-face discussion with Jorge Pinto himself, something both would probably have found difficult to imagine in 1957. Pinto later recalled their conversation:

"Now I understand you. You must have gone through all that I am experiencing now." (This referred to the 'aristocratic' origin of both of us.) These were the first words of Quique Alvarez, president of the FDR, when he came to visit me in the offices of *El Independiente*....

Enrique had really hoped that I would join the FDR by means of MIPTES. I explained to him that my struggle was in journalism, and that I believed in the power of the word. That I had inherited from my father and my grandfather their zealous independence, but that in no way was I neutral or apart from the struggle of my people. I felt linked with that man by understanding his search for the truth and the common well being, and his desire to contribute and to serve. Although we were connected by the fact that his sister was married to my first cousin, one might have thought that there would be an unbridgeable ideological distance. But when he put himself in that trench, different from mine but for the same cause, a true brotherhood was sealed, much more solid than that of family.[75]

It was evidently a bond capable of erasing, or at least overriding, past conflicts in the light of shared hopes for the future of their country. A number of Enrique's long-time friends wondered how he could appear on friendly terms with Pinto after the pain of the 1957 scandal—but by 1980 their de facto political alliance had become far more important than past quarrels.

Enrique Alvarez on the Junta's Agrarian Reform[76]

El Independiente published a long interview with Enrique devoted largely to his critique of the junta's reforms.[77] "There is no foundation to all the propaganda claiming that the agrarian reforms aim to change the structures of an unjust society," he began. "The big coffee growers have not been hurt at all, since the amount of land which the agrarian reform lets them hold is enough to maintain the economic strength of the coffee oligarchy—from which nothing has been taken away."

(Jorge Pinto) Is the current agricultural reform really designed to help the campesinos?

(Alvarez) I personally believe that the project being carried out by the current government is an act of desperation. The government is trying to obtain some popular support, especially from campesinos, since it can't claim to be based on any sort of consensus. The agricultural reform, in my opinion, will not help the campesinos and it is going to be impossible to carry out. First, because it doesn't have the support of the campesinos, the sector which it claims to benefit, since as everyone knows [the government] is killing campesinos every day. It is very difficult for rural people to believe that this action is in their favor when the same people who claim to be helping them are killing them.

(Pinto) Is the FDR, under your leadership, preparing some plans for agrarian reform that would be implemented at the time of taking power?

(Alvarez) I am in the FDR as the representative of MIPTES. This movement now has some 250 members who are professionals in many different fields such as psychology, sociology, journalism, engineering, medicine and law, and naturally all these compañeros are working on different projects. This work started when the group was founded last February. But now that MIPTES forms part of the Frente, all these efforts are going to be at the disposition of the FDR. We have many works in progress and others already completed which will be at the service of the Frente, so that it and the organizations that comprise it can discuss them. This material will be ready for the moment in which there is a change, the moment of taking power.

That is the fundamental objective of the FDR—to prepare for taking power and to know what to do and be ready after having assumed power. We are working; we have lots of material—material that was prepared earlier and brought up to date, and especially material that is going to be useful for all the groups making up the Democratic Front. There will be laws that are not imposed from above but laws that count on the participation and approval of the Salvadoran people, and an agrarian reform that embodies the aspirations of the campesinos expressed through their organizations.

(Pinto) Much could be said about Enrique Alvarez Córdova, and very few Salvadorans, of whatever social class, would disagree about the noble principles and the honesty of this man.

(Alvarez) Another reason I believe that this law is not going to favor the campesinos is that it says that lands will be purchased from the current owners at prices that they declared in 1976 and 1977. Prior to that, the government allowed reevaluations of those lands for tax purposes. Since they have been talking about agricultural reform for ten years, [the owners] saw that it was coming sooner or later—and the government allowed them to reappraise their land without any penalty. The majority of those lands now carry unreasonably high prices. By all this I mean to say that these lands, at the price which the state is going to pay for them and which the campesino who is going to acquire them will have to repay according to the law, will have a highly unrealistic cost.... The campesinos, if they ever receive these lands, will not be able to pay for them.

Another thing: we have already seen that irregular things have been happening in many of the properties that have been occupied by the state. The army has stolen the cattle and the crops. There has been repression against the campesinos themselves. Those who were thought to be organized have been shot. They [the military] are setting up the cooperatives, putting in as directors people they think they can control. I have been informed that in many cases these directors are members of ORDEN. We all know the kind of people who formed that organization.

There is another important reason why this project is going to fail, and that's the lack of the necessary administrative and technical knowledge. On one hand there has been a great exodus of agricultural technicians who could have been leading or advising this process. On the other hand, we all know there was corruption in the earlier operations of the Institute of Agrarian Transformation when it was buying properties. The corrupt people are the ones who remain in these institutions; the honest and capable personnel are gone, and so the technical and administrative capacity needed to run the system isn't there. Besides the lack of technical capacity, they don't have the administrative skill to carry the process forward. That's the basis for concluding that this process is not going to favor the campesinos, and that like all the rest it is going to be stuck halfway there.

I am convinced this is true — not only in the case of the agrarian reform but all around. The government still has not been able to form a cabinet, and I have reliable information that this week there will be more resignations in the cabinet and among key people in various ministries. This will show that the government is alone, that it definitely doesn't have popular support and still less the support of the middle layers, the technicians and professionals, who are abandoning the ship because they think it is sinking.

(Pinto) Does the project that is being implemented now have any relation to the plan that was presented during the first junta when you were the minister of agriculture?

(Alvarez) No. In the first place, we never actually presented a plan for agricultural reform, although we did have one ready. We didn't present it because we came to see that in reality we weren't there to carry out such plans, but only to say that we were going to do them and then not actually do anything. There were many people within the government itself who acted as a brake in order that things wouldn't get done. We recognized this situation and decided not to push the project any more, because we saw we wouldn't have any chance that it would be approved. But in any case, that project is complete; it is a draft law available to any government that wants to implement a genuine reform, one that would radically change the ownership of the land and put that land at the service of those who work it.

As I said, we didn't actually present our project for land reform. But the current project of the government is very, very different from the one that we in the first junta had prepared. We consider that our program was more radical, that it really could have modified the land ownership, the production system or the cultivation.

I want to give an example to show that this [reform] is not affecting the coffee oligarchy, which is the greatest concentration of wealth — the people who own the largest coffee-producing lands, the same ones who own the banks, the agroexports and the industries. According to the census of 1971 only about 1% of the coffee properties would be affected by the current law, and that's only if they implement phase II of the project. At this moment all these properties are intact.

> Now, we consider that a property of 180 hectares of coffee land, with an adequate productivity of 40 quintals per hectare, should give a total production of around 7000 quintals of coffee. At current prices and current production costs this would produce 570,000 colones of profit; that is, more than $200,000 profit per year. So as you see, with a property of 180 hectares the coffee oligarchy is not being harmed at all.

Of course other members of that oligarchy disagreed. Their long-standing distrust of the Christian Democrats, plus the actual impact of the reforms, led some of the wealthiest Salvadorans to label the junta and its U.S. sponsors as leftists, even communists, since they were bringing about changes in the traditional pattern of rural life. In reality the military and the United States were far more interested in counterinsurgency than in social justice. Some of the top officers, moreover, were seeking to join the ruling class in their own right rather than continuing to serve as its paid subordinates. There *were* divergent interests among these groups— but they were differences between the right and the extreme right. The "center" in Salvadoran politics had died with Monsignor Romero.

8

Traveling for the Cause

> Enrique's popularity was due to his tenacious struggle for the agrarian reform, because of which he had incurred the enmity of his own family....
>
> — *Jorge Pinto Jr.*

"The junta is being sustained exclusively by the United States," Enrique Alvarez was quoted on June 4 in a story datelined Mexico City. "U.S. intervention is a fact, and it must stop. Peace can only exist in Central America if El Salvador is allowed to determine its own destiny." Enrique contradicted the U.S. government's repeated assertion that the governing junta represented the political center, trapped between extremes to its right and left. "The positions of the junta and the extreme right coincide more and more," he told the press. "There are really only two forces in El Salvador — the left that represents the great majority of the people, and the alliance of the government with the right."[1]

Alvarez was leading one of the FDR delegations — there were four in all — which planned to cover much of Latin America, Western Europe, and North America in order to explain Salvadoran reality, discourage aid to the junta, and seek political and financial support for the revolutionary cause. He told the press that 23 countries in all were slated for visits by FDR representatives. The Frente team had arrived in Mexico in mid–May. Already FDR leaders including Enrique had met with Gustavo Carvajal Moreno, the president of the PRI (Partido de la Revolución Institucional), the long-time Mexican governing party. Carvajal Moreno responded by calling for his country to break relations with the Salvadoran governing junta. The PRI would turn out to be one of the FDR's best foreign allies, and the Frente's headquarters in exile would remain in the Mexican capital until the end of the civil war.

A few days earlier members of the FDR group had spoken with press and public in San José, Costa Rica. Guillermo Ungo characterized what the

FDR wanted to do: "Our future regime will be national and democratic, and its program, although not socialist, is anti-oligarchic and anti-imperialist," Ungo said. Enrique Alvarez explained that it was too late for a peaceful political outcome in El Salvador and that the country was already in a state of war. "The only way out is armed struggle," he said. Delegation member Juan Chacón added, "We can seize power without the participation of foreign forces." The support the FDR wanted was not military, the group agreed. Salvadorans would settle matters among themselves—if other countries could be persuaded or pressured not to intervene on the side of the junta. Reportedly when Enrique Alvarez finished speaking to a public meeting held in a San José movie theater, the cheers, chants and applause continued for ten minutes.[2]

The picture that Alvarez and the other FDR leaders presented to the press and public was diametrically opposed to the Carter administration's description of the situation. Privately, however, U.S. officials on the scene in El Salvador agreed with most of the FDR's assessment. In October, just one year after the coup, Robert White cabled Washington that "Plainly put, the military have the power; no government can exist without their approval." At the same time Richard Oulahan, the AIFLD director in El Salvador, wrote, "Government here operates with no real popular support." As for the claim that Duarte and the government represented the "center," Oulahan stated that "In the past several months, Duarte and company have sided with the conservative military ... the conservative officials who look to a military solution are very much in control."[3] That was the reality which the United States officially denied and which the FDR wanted the world to know: the situation was polarized, there was no center, and the U.S. was solidly aligned with the right.

Majano and D'Aubuisson

In the meantime events in El Salvador had clarified the concentration of power within the government and armed forces. Since the October coup, Colonel Adolfo Majano had been the military reformers' man in government. A member of all three juntas, he should have counterbalanced, or even dominated, the right-wing influence of Gutiérrez and García and given the progressive younger officers not only a voice but also a powerful arm. Majano had support among the troops at a number of bases including two important ones in San Salvador, and he was nominally the commander in chief of the armed forces. In the first post-coup months he had accomplished little toward consolidating a new, more progressive military, and in

December the rightist takeover of COPEFA demonstrated the weakness of the "young military" within the institution.[4] Early in 1980, however, Majano became more active in challenging the military right. By April he had a new ally in U.S. Ambassador Robert White, who reportedly hoped to "rebuild the army around Majano" as part of a strategy to fortify a political center that could avert both civil war and a leftist takeover of the government.[5]

During the same period Roberto D'Aubuisson had grown steadily in importance among the shadowy forces of the ultra-right. A major at the time of the 1979 coup, D'Aubuisson had been deputy director of the military intelligence unit ANSESAL. He already had an evil reputation as a torturer and killer, and was forced by the new junta to retire from the armed forces.[6] He maintained many influential allies, however, and had access to ANSESAL's files which contained dossiers on perceived government opponents including leading Christian Democrats, labor organizers, priests, etc. These files were invaluable for D'Aubuisson's new career as a death-squad organizer, working in collaboration with wealthy individuals of the extreme right and former colleagues among the armed forces. His most notorious "success" in this field, one among many, was the assassination of Archbishop Romero. He also helped organize and lead the "Broad National Front" (FAN), supposedly a mass organization of the right and a counterpart to the genuine popular organizations and their Coordinadora. (The FAN's formation was announced in Washington, not in San Salvador.) The FAN took over the tasks of the ostensibly disbanded ORDEN, from which it differed in little more than name. Human rights organizations accused the FAN of organizing hundreds of murders of alleged opponents, and U.S. officials privately conceded the truth of these charges.[7]

In late April D'Aubuisson returned to El Salvador, hoping to lead a right-wing coup that he had been organizing from abroad. To prepare the ground he had circulated among military installations a video that, among other things, absurdly accused Colonel Majano and junta member Morales Ehrlich of being Communists.[8] Informed of the plot Majano confronted García and Carranza with his information, but they refused to move against the conspirators. Majano, with uncharacteristic decisiveness, then acted on his own. On May 8 troops from the First Brigade descended on Finca San Luis near Santa Tecla, some ten miles from the capital. There they arrested two dozen conspirators, including civilians and active-duty officers—and Roberto D'Aubuisson.

Robert White described the results of the raid:

> D'Aubuisson was holding a meeting to launch a coup. A few of Majano's boys went there, bluffed their way past the guards, broke in and caught

> them. [The conspirators] had a little bit of warning so they destroyed some of the stuff [evidence]. Among the things they captured were these diaries, and Majano gave them to me. I sent them to Washington. I said, "If you get on the ball here, we can take this thing [the conspiracy] apart." All the names, the nicknames, and that kind of thing were all there. But of course I got no help at all.[9]

White calls the diaries a "Mafia-type notebook," and says they had details of the plans for Archbishop Romero's assassination along with other death-squad operations. There were records of payoffs to National Police officers and of arms purchases, including guns with silencers and other special equipment, plus documents incriminating right-wing landowners and businessmen in the coup plotting. Majano's men also found propaganda flyers attacking U.S. policies such as the land reform, and urging support for a coup. There were ample grounds to put D'Aubuisson and most of the others on trial for treason and murder.

The immediate result was a dangerous crisis for Majano and the junta. The prisoners were taken to the First Brigade headquarters, where some officers wanted to have them shot for treason. The PDC leadership, after an all-night meeting, decided to back Majano in calling for trials and the removal of García and Carranza from the Ministry of Defense. On the other side, officers of the Third Brigade and other units threatened to attack the First Brigade and the Presidential Palace if the prisoners were not released; First Brigade commanders replied that if attacked they would kill their captives. A right-wing crowd picketed the residence of U.S. Ambassador Robert White until dispersed by Marine guards with tear gas. (White favored prosecution of the plotters, but the United States took no active part in the dispute.) After a series of threats, counter threats and negotiations, D'Aubuisson and the other non-active duty prisoners were remanded for a preliminary hearing before a military judge — who, after reportedly consulting with García, ordered their release because of "insufficient evidence."[10]

This outcome was a disaster for the reformers within the military and the government. A "senior diplomat" in San Salvador (presumably Ambassador White) told the *Washington Post* that the release of D'Aubuisson was "a case of lunacy. This is about as foolish a move as possible. It plays right into the hands of the ultra left, which says the government is run by right-wingers anyway.... This is very bad."[11] Majano was then voted out as military commander-in-chief by a narrow majority of the officer corps, to be replaced by Gutiérrez. His decline would continue, and within a few months Majano's influence was totally ended. In December he was forced into exile after narrowly escaping assassination. The Christian Democrats in the government once again protested but did nothing, and lost much of whatever remained of their credibility.

Meanwhile the evil star of ex-major Roberto D'Aubuisson rose higher. Less than a month after the arrests he was back in Washington, hosted by the American Legion and giving a public press conference under the aegis of the American Security Council. There he characteristically accused U.S. Ambassador White of communist sympathies and urged strong U.S. backing for the Salvadoran military. The State Department told the press it had canceled D'Aubuisson's visa, but he apparently had no difficulty in openly entering the United States where he was able to "hide out" at the capital's Hyatt-Regency Hotel. He also found time to confer with ultra-right members of the U.S. Congress before returning to Central America on July 2. There, according to one U.S. source, he would "probably be having drinks with the High Command."[12]

The consolidation of hard-line control within the government and the armed forces had its counterpart on the left. Political, non-violent tactics, such as January's huge demonstration and the two short general strikes in February and June, had not been able to change or dislodge the junta. A murderous repression was coming down, not hitting the elusive armed opposition but targeting the visible, civilian activists of the mass movement. One result was that the armed groups of the left accelerated their preparations for actual war. On May 22 the four main "political/military organizations" formed a Unified Revolutionary Directorate (DRU), setting aside substantial differences to move toward a joint command structure. The ERP, isolated since the murder of Roque Dalton, now rejoined the other guerrilla forces. A true unified command was still distant, but a big step forward had been taken. The collective military opposition became the FMLN (Farabundo Martí Front for National Liberation) in October.

Travels for the FDR

The work of the Frente Democrático Revolucionario, in contrast, was entirely civilian and political, and its leaders turned now toward international diplomacy. Panama and Costa Rica were important potential allies for the FDR. Both countries had given vital help to the Nicaraguan opposition in its struggle against the Somoza dictatorship. Moreover, some of the weapons intended for the Sandinistas had been left behind in Costa Rica and were coveted by the Salvadoran guerrillas. The FDR delegations were not seeking arms in the summer of 1980, but they knew that the sympathy of the two governments would be important links in their chain of support. These two countries were the only ones in Central America on the Frente's schedule. Guatemala and Honduras were under hostile military control and offered no openings, while the positive reaction of revolutionary Nicaragua was already assured.

There was another reason for the travels of the FDR leaders: to protect their lives. Inside El Salvador they were all in danger. Surveillance had been stepped up after the FDR's founding ceremony at the university, and Enrique Alvarez began to be followed wherever he went. It seemed to be only a matter of time until the first assassination. Leaving the country or going underground were the alternatives for survival.

Alvarez and his companions were enthusiastically received in Costa Rica on June 2. According to Armstrong and Shenk, Enrique spoke to a "tumultuous crowd" at a cinema near San José, telling them that

> The Salvadoran people have had to take up arms to end the conditions we have been subjected to for the last fifty years— by military governments, by the oligarchy and by U.S. imperialism. The people have risen in arms to say "Enough!" and to take power in the only way they leave us, the way of armed struggle.
>
> One of the obligations that our delegation has is to ask the nations of the world to keep hands off El Salvador.... We also ask the solidarity of the peoples of the world to support the just struggle of the Salvadoran people. We ask for understanding of our cause and help to prevent the direct and massive intervention of U.S. imperialism.

The crowd responded with cheers and chants including *¡Si Nicaragua venció, El Salvador vencerá!* (Nicaragua has won and El Salvador will win!) that went on for ten minutes.[13]

"The FDR started to operate with a series of trips abroad," says Rubén Zamora. They set up a base in Mexico, organized several groups and prepared themselves for taking the FDR's case to the world. Zamora accompanied Enrique Alvarez on some of the trips. From Mexico, he says, people went first to Europe, where the groups divided. Enrique Alvarez, Hector Silva, Napoleón Rodríguez Ruíz, and Rafael Menjívar (who had been the chancellor of the national university) went to the northern countries including Sweden and Norway, while Zamora and others visited France and Italy. Then after Europe they were ready for the United States.[14]

The United States was the most important mission, and of course Enrique Alvarez led the FDR delegation visiting this country. They tried to touch all the bases. There were meetings with members of Congress and with the administration. There were formal press conferences, and chances to speak to the public in churches, schools and universities. There were private meetings with sympathizers and organizers. The FDR leaders took part in conferences such as "Theology in the Americas" held in Detroit (more below). Two other FDR representatives, Hector Silva (Mauricio's brother and later the first post-war FMLN mayor of San Salvador) and Rafael Guidos Vejar, talked to officials in the Canadian foreign ministry and gave interviews in that country, including one with *MacLean's magazine*.[15] Alvarez, Ungo, and Zamora visited the United Nations in New York to see what could be done there. And some of them found time to take in a baseball game in Philadelphia.

One friendly contact close to the Washington establishment was Murat Williams, a former U.S. Ambassador to El Salvador. "He was quite a gentleman—from Virginia, I think," recalls Mauricio Silva.

> He knew Quique, and he invited us to this club. At that time women weren't allowed; it was a very elite club. And he invited Quique there, for breakfast.... He was the only one that Williams was sure of, that had a clear image ... and it probably was because of the class that we came from.... So it was Quique and me that went to that breakfast. I still have those images, of the *gentleman* that Quique was. That was an environment that he knew very well, that he could manage very well.... Quique knew that environment.[16]

Williams wanted Enrique to explain the meaning of the FDR's project. His own experience in El Salvador had been many years in the past, and the situation seemed to have turned upside down. Were the year-end resignations of the government just a cabinet crisis, as described in the U.S. media? Was the FDR a communist plot? What was behind the whole thing? "It was very confusing having the Christian Democrats, having Duarte, supporting the government," Mauricio Silva noted, recalling that during Williams' tenure as ambassador the newly organized Christian Democrats had been part of the left-of-center opposition. "That was very confusing, something that history has to settle with Duarte," Silva said. "Anyhow, that was the objective of the breakfast, for [Williams] to understand what was happening in El Salvador from someone he trusted who was in the opposition."

Ambassador Williams later gave his own recollection of this meeting during an interview in the film *The Houses Are Full of Smoke*:

> Enrique was determined that change must come in El Salvador to the old structure, that it couldn't last. I saw him in Washington, took him out to lunch. Enrique had so much to say that I thought really he ought to go to the State Department. He went back to El Salvador to talk about elections, talk about peace, talk about whatever he could talk about—and there he was seized by people in uniform, taken off, tortured, mutilated, and murdered. He and five colleagues.

Mauricio Silva added that he has been back to Washington often. "After this period," he says, "I worked for the World Bank for 10 years, and always when I go to that corner — it's only one block away from the bank — when I go there I always think of Quique ... all the ghosts around those times."[17]

Toward the end of the trip, Enrique summed it all up during an interview in Chicago. "For the past few months," he said,

> the Democratic Revolutionary Front has been on a diplomatic offensive. We are trying to alert the governments and peoples of different countries to what the real situation is in our country, to denounce the intervention of the U.S. government, and to warn of the possibility of a more direct and massive intervention, possibly by a multinational force or even U.S. marines. We want the United States to stay out of our country, to recognize that we have the right and capacity to solve our own problems, and to respect the self-determination of our country.[18]

To Mauricio Silva all these experiences underscore what a key figure Enrique Alvarez had become for El Salvador. Enrique was chosen president of the FDR for his personal qualities, not his political base, and he was the right choice for the job, Silva said. "Quique was a mentor for us, now that I think about it," he added.

A Press Conference in Washington[19]

The conference took place during the last week of July 1980. Enrique Alvarez took the lead, and he opened the session with a resume of the reasons for the Salvadoran revolution and for the existence of the Democratic Revolutionary Front. The other FDR representatives were Rubén Zamora, Mauricio Silva, Guillermo Ungo, and Salvador Arias. None of them had mastered the technique of the "sound bite," and the session had the spirit of a college seminar.

> (Alvarez) Good morning, ladies and gentlemen; we're very pleased that you are here this morning. We would like to talk to you about the situation in our country, and about the Democratic Revolutionary Front. We want this to be a very informal, but on the other hand a very serious, talk.
>
> What's happening in our country? As I said a minute ago, it's hard to believe that [such] things could happen in 1980. I hope you'll forgive me for my English — even though I went to school here I don't practice it very often so I probably will make many mistakes.
>
> The people of our country are right now struggling for their liberation. The cause of this struggle is the conditions to which the majority of our

Enrique Alvarez, press conference, Washington, D.C., 1980 (Sandoval/ Maryknoll Missioners).

people have been submitted for the past 50 years, conditions that in many ways it is very difficult to realize that they could happen in this century. Just to give a few examples: the peasants, who are 60% of our population, are not allowed by law to get together [to organize]. The mortality in the countryside is such that 120 children out of a thousand die before they are a year old. Illiteracy is up close to 50% altogether in the country, and it's higher in the countryside. Unemployment is very, very high, and at this moment the situation is even worse than it has been in past years; unemployment at this moment—we don't know exactly the figure but it's way up high. Usually 50% of the people in the countryside have work only during three months; that's when the coffee, cotton, and sugar harvests coincide, and that's when we have *full* employment—for only three months of the year, November, December, and January. The rest of the year unemployment goes up at certain times to 40 or 50 percent. We are considered, together with Bangladesh, as one of the countries belonging to the "hunger belt."

These conditions on one side, and on the other side we have less than 2000 families which own about 40% of the land, which receive about 50% of the national income, which own also banks, industry—all the productive means are owned by a very few people. So we have on one hand a very small minority that owns almost everything, and on the other side we have the large majority of the country who live in very, very tough conditions. This is really the cause of what's happening in El Salvador.

On the political aspect, we have had parties, democratic parties, which have been working for quite a few years to make the changes that the country needs, and have participated in elections which all have ended up in frauds. All of us here have participated in government before. Some belonged to political parties; others participated in former governments, trying to make the changes that the country needed. We always have found that the dominating class in El Salvador has not been willing to give an inch of what it holds.

On the other hand, we have had parties, political groups, who have been on the political ground for about 10 years, who decided that elections was not the way to obtain power; that the way was to do it by arms. At this time in the struggle, and after participating as I said in different ways trying to obtain power in order to change the structures of the country, we all coincide now that only a government with popular support can make these changes.

This is the way the Democratic Revolutionary Front gets together. We really think that we represent the majority of our people. We have in the Democratic Revolutionary Front two political parties, the MNR that belongs to the International Socialist Movement, we have the MPSC, which is the dissidents of the Democratic Christian Party, we have the group of technicians and intellectuals— there are three of us here that represent this group that has between 450 and 500 technicians. This is a group [MIPTES] that was organized late January of this year, and many of the people that belong have participated in different ways in governments; most of them now are, or were, teaching in the universities of El Salvador. We also have all the five groups, the popular revolutionary groups—I don't know if you're acquainted with all of them, but all the popular revolutionary groups are in the Front. We have the two most important universities, the national university and the Catholic university. We have the four most important trade unions. We have other independent trade unions, namely the textile industry union and the social security labor union. And we have some student associations, university and schools, and we have a private enterprise group, mainly small and medium sized groups that own transportation. This is the way the Democratic Revolutionary Front is formed. And as I said it comes out into the political picture of the country as a result of all the failures that we have had trying to make the changes that the country needs.

Right now the situation in our country is as follows: There is really no center in this political situation. The government is on the extreme right, coinciding more and more every day with the more extreme people on the right. On the other hand we have all the popular, democratic and revolutionary forces, together fighting to take power in order to do the things that our people need, to get out of the situation they have been in for the past years.

It's important to say that in the Front there is really a democracy — within the Front. Many people have said that the democratic sectors of the front are overpowered, and we are only putting some cosmetics to this thing. That is not true. We realize that the revolutionary and popular groups are more [numerous] in the Front, but in the executive committee of the front, which is the top of the Front, all decisions are taken by consensus. All of the groups that form the front maintain their own personality, their own principles, so there is really a discussion of the activities of the front in a democratic way.

I was saying that the country is ruled now by a government — it's a military government. The few Christian Democrats that are still in the government don't really represent the Christian Democratic Party. Most of their leaders and most of the bases are leaving this party and are forming the party that Rubén [Zamora] represents right here. The people that really rule the country are the military; they have been doing so for 50 years. And of course they have no popular support whatsoever, they have only the support of the government of the United States, the government of Venezuela and the government of Guatemala in some ways. The only way to stay in power, they think, is through one of the worst repressions we ever had in our country, which can only be compared to the repression we had in 1932 when 30,000 people were killed at that time.

Here you have [reliable] news, that they are killing—it's hard to have figures, but we think that they are killing between 20 and 30 people a day, mainly peasants and, of course, they are also killing leaders of the popular and revolutionary movements, they have killed leaders of the democratic movements, they have killed priests, and the repression is selective and massive. You have heard recently—we denounced this the first days of June—the killing of between 500 and 600 people trying to cross the border with Honduras. [This was the Sumpul River massacre; see chapter 7.] It was said that we were exaggerating when we denounced that in Mexico at the time; now it's been proven, and it's been denounced by the bishops of Honduras after an investigation of what happened there. This is happening all the time. The Church has been persecuted. You have heard how Archbishop Romero was killed. You know that the University of El Salvador has been taken over, that a Catholic school also was taken over, and this is happening every day.

Another important thing is that our population is not informed at all of what is happening in the country or outside the country. We, the Democratic Revolutionary Front, have been working for almost two months in the diplomatic campaign and the people in our country don't know what is going on outside. And of course the information inside is also distorted. This is very important because the only news that the people get is what the government gives, and according to them nothing is going wrong in the country; there are just a few leftists that are trying to make trouble for the government. This is important because many of the things that we denounce, we are asked to have proofs for them. We are very serious about what we denounce, but we think that the people who should prove all the things are the press people. But you know that the press people have also had a very tough time in the country? They have killed press people; they have taken their equipment, they have taken their material away, and some of them are not even allowed to go in the country at this moment.

So the situation is that way. We want to assure you that the information we give has been confirmed as far as it can be confirmed. We may make a mistake in a figure or so, but the communication is very difficult. We cannot go into the country; we appear, all of us, on a death list that has been published, and most of us have been persecuted. A few of us have been in jail more than once now, and so it is very difficult for us to go into the country by legitimate ways.

This will be a very brief presentation. We are willing to answer all the questions you wish to ask; we want to make sure you have all the information you need to write your stories. We think you can help us very much, because we believe that the people of this country don't participate in the policy that the [U.S.] government has in order to help the [Salvadoran] government in many ways—financially, politically, and especially with equipment, arms, which are being used really to massacre our people.

Question: The State Department says that they support the junta because of the reforms they are making. What are your criticisms or objections to these reforms? What specifically do you find wrong with them?

(Alvarez) They [the junta] have talked a lot about two reforms, the financial reform and the agrarian reform. The financial reform ... well, let's put it this way. When the agreement [between] the Christian Democratic party [and the military] was made after the first version of the government failed in the first days of January, they made an agreement with a list of all the reforms they were going to do. There was a list of 10 reforms. The two main ones were those two, and also the exports, the coffee, sugar. Right now they have passed the financial reform. The way they have done it is that they are going to buy a percentage, some 50 or so percent, of the stock that the bankers own. These are banks that were in a very, very difficult position, mainly because of the flight of capital that we've had for the past two years. In October we had a report from the time of the government of Romero: $1,500 million gone out of the country. By now we figure it is over two billion. So the banks were in a very difficult position, and the people, the stockholders.... I mean the banks have been capitalized really by the reform. On the other hand, the people that are running those banks are almost the same. The owners are not in the banks any more running them, but everything else has been kept. So we think that the power of this group is still there, and there has been no real change in the economic power that this group holds.

It's very important to repeat that when in October we were trying to do these three things, we had lists of the people that were going to be affected in the land reform, the people that would be affected in the export of coffee, and the people that would be affected in the bank reform, and almost the three lists were identical. The same people were in the three lists.

Another member of the FDR group then commented further about the financial reform. His main point was that the banks had been largely decapitalized before the "reform," so that the stock purchase by the government became more nearly a bailout for the owners than a true move toward reform.

(Alvarez) Before going to the land reform: It was agreed at first to nationalize the banks, the savings and loans associations and the insurance companies. They decided to only nationalize the banks. To give you an example in what sort of situation they were, in the 10 weeks that we were in the government after the 15th of October, the central bank had given the savings and loans associations over 50 million colones so that they could respond to the people that were withdrawing their savings. I think we were ready—and Mauricio [Silva] knows better than I—we were ready in a couple of weeks to take over all the savings and loans associations because they could not stand one more day. But they let them—they didn't nationalize them. Another measure is that they announced that they are only going to nationalize the banking system and they will leave out the insurance companies.

On the land reform, they decided that they would do this in two periods. First they would affect the properties that were over 500 hectares, and in the second period they would affect properties over 150 hectares. Right now they have announced that they are not going to carry through the second part; they are only going to go through with the first part of the agrarian reform.

It is true that they have taken a few of the big properties in the coastal area, properties that were mainly producing cotton, sugar cane, and some cattle. It is true that they have taken them over; the army has taken these properties over. But it is also true that the coffee plantations, which are the heart of this economic class that has ruled the country, have not been touched at all. I think there have been only one or two properties that have been taken over in coffee. Most of the coffee [properties] that would be affected would be in the second part of the reform.... So it is not true that the reform was aimed to take away the power of this group, the coffee—like you press people have called them quite a while ago, the landlords of the coffee—they have not been touched whatsoever.

Another thing that is very important is that instead of being a social and economic agrarian reform, this has become a political and military reform. They have done this in order to try to get the support of the peasants, who are supposed to be the beneficiaries of this reform. But what they have succeeded in doing is having military groups spread all over the nation. These groups are repressing the people, and we see the incredible thing that the people are running away from the areas where supposedly the agrarian reform is going through.

Another member of the delegation (probably Guillermo Ungo) spoke to this point:

The reforms are not for the people; they are a tool of repression. The military is using the agrarian reform for greater control of the peasants. For example, the undersecretary of agriculture, the main person responsible for implementing the reform, resigned in April, some three weeks after the reform was announced. He said he couldn't go on participating in that government because the same military that was talking about reform was killing the peasants, and they were killing exactly those who were appointed as directors of the coops formed in the agrarian sector. This undersecretary was Jorge Villacorta. He said that he knows of a case where one day the board of directors of a coop was elected by the peasants. In the early morning next day, the National Guard came to that farm, put all the peasants together, and then one man with a mask over his face went around and pointed out all the men elected. Then in front of all the others, the Guard shot and killed all these directors.

This is what is happening with the agrarian reform in El Salvador. Not only peasants but even technicians of the [government] Agrarian Reform Institute were killed by the security forces. How can you carry on an agrarian reform if you are at the same time killing the same peasants who are supposed to be the beneficiaries of the reform?... This is very clear in El Salvador because at the same time the reform was being implemented, thousands of peasants began flowing out of the countryside where the reform took place and going to towns, because the repression was increasing so much in the countryside.

Enrique Alvarez again:

We believe that without the U.S. government support, the [Salvadoran] government could not be the government any more. That it is only in power due to the support — political, financial and military support — that it is getting from the U.S. government. Another indication of that is that they haven't been able to form a cabinet since January. They've had so many people resigning, at the level of ministers, of undersecretaries, at the level of technicians ... another problem with the agrarian reform is that they don't have the technicians they need to go through with it. On top of what Guillermo [Ungo] said, they don't have the technical people to really go through with it. So we believe that the U.S. government support is the only support that maintains that government in power right now.

Rubén Zamora:

We want to be very clear about this point. In El Salvador we have tried for many years different ways to achieve peace and democracy. We have tried to work through elections, but the result was fraud. The wishes of the people were never respected by the military governments. We have tried through an alliance with the military after October 15 to achieve democracy by pacific means. This too failed because the civilian part of the government had no control at all over the military. We were talking about dialog in El Salvador. We were talking about reconciliation among all the Salvadorans, and at the same time the military was killing the same people we were trying to dialog with. Now we say — all the forces inside the Democratic Revolutionary Front — the only way left to the Salvadoran people is armed struggle. We don't want the killing in El Salvador. We would prefer a different way to achieve peace. But all the alternatives have been closed by the military, with the support of the US government....

A member of the press then put the obvious question: "What do you think the United States *should* do?" Rubén Zamora answered for the FDR:

We are asking everybody to take their hands off! We are able to set up a democratic and revolutionary government. We want the U.S. to stop military aid; we want everybody to stop. We, the Salvadoran people, want to straighten things out and install a new government....

At the State Department: Dialogue of the Deaf

On July 25, Enrique Alvarez led the FDR delegation to a meeting at the Department of State. There the Salvadorans talked with William Bowdler, the assistant secretary of state for Latin America, who was accompanied by James Cheek and John Blacken. The other Salvadorans present were Guillermo Ungo, Rubén Zamora, and Mauricio Silva. Silva says that the meeting was difficult to arrange, and adds, "it was only because of Bob White, the U.S. ambassador here, that we got it." He heard later that White told the State officials, "You have to listen to them. These guys are the only thing that is viable, and it's your only contact [with the opposition] that you can admit to having."[20] So finally the meeting took place, and lasted for almost two hours.

Silva's description of the conversation was succinct. "They lost an opportunity. They tried to convince us to separate ourselves from the FMLN—what is now the FMLN. That was their whole message." Rubén Zamora says he remembers almost word for word what Bowdler said. Bowdler made it absolutely clear that he was (reluctantly) meeting with the FDR but would *never* meet with the FMLN since they were taking up arms against the government. "He made a big distinction," Zamora recalls. "His point was that

> it is true that we [the U.S.] have some very nasty people in our camp. But it is also true that you have allies who are very nasty people as well. What I propose, Bowdler said, is that we will get rid of our nasty people, but you have to break with your nasty allies. Then we are going to put together all the moderate people like you from both camps to produce a process of democratization.
>
> What was the immediate response from all the FDR people? You are proposing to us *treason.* And besides it was impossible to do that, the situation was too polarized.... The only way out, to negotiations, was to make the junta and the U.S. realize that they had to negotiate with *all* of the other camp, or there would be no way forward. The United States had to negotiate with the FMLN....[21]

A State Department account elaborates on this version but does not contradict it.[22] Bowdler began the meeting, the telegram reports, by declaring that the United States wanted a moderate, democratic, nonviolent solution that would respect human rights, etc. He said he was sure the FDR delegates shared these goals—unlike the extremes of left and right who sought to impose their views by force. The U.S. "had twice used our influence to block rightist coup attempts," he said, while it also "deplored the violence and terrorism" of the armed left. The Secretary added, "We support the JRG's [junta's] efforts to pacify the country, but are unalterably opposed to indiscriminate use of violence by the security forces."

According to the State Department, Alvarez replied that the FDR was "a strategic alliance representing the great majority of the Salvadoran people." He reviewed the past futile attempts to gain reforms through the political process or by alliance with the military, including the coup of October 15. "But from the first days," he said, "it was clear that the military high command was not disposed to make the changes it proclaimed. Repression actually increased to a level much worse than under General Romero.... With no alternative, violence has therefore been imposed on the people and through the people on the FDR." He told the State Department team that the existing junta was not a political "center" and that the United States could not create one. In reality, he said, the Salvadoran government was moving closer to the extreme right every day, and only U.S. support kept it afloat.

"Alvarez said that the FDR is supporting the revolutionary process," the report continued, and it quoted Enrique directly as saying "We are not giving one face to you and another to our allies." He said that the FDR wanted "the cost in human terms of achieving the new government to be as low as possible," and that it hoped for the support of the U.S. government in bringing that about.

There was a discussion of the U.S. military intervention, but it focused on a side issue rather than the basic question. Bowdler and Cheek scolded the FDR people for making exaggerated claims about U.S. bases and arms shipments, claims that Ungo and Silva admitted were based on "reports" they could not at that time substantiate. Of course all the statements in those reports and much, much more would come to pass in the very near future, so this debate seems inconsequential, especially in retrospect.

The U.S. officials apparently did not respond directly to the FDR request that military aid should be stopped. Enrique reported, however, that the people from State told the FDR group that "the USA could not stay neutral while 'other countries' were also involved." This presumably referred to U.S. claims that Cuba was aiding the revolutionaries, a charge the Salvadorans denied. Silva says the State Department group also emphasized the violent acts of the armed opposition in El Salvador and urged Alvarez, Ungo and the others to distance themselves from "a left dominated by violent extremists." But Bowdler and his companions did not acknowledge the far greater violence of the armed forces that the United States was supporting. Of course the outcome of the meeting was foreordained — neither side conceded anything of substance to the position of the other.

A consistent theme of U.S. spokesmen was that civilians such as

Alvarez, Ungo, and Zamora represented mere democratic camouflage for "extremists" of the armed left, and that if the Salvadoran junta were to fall the FDR civilians would be swept away in favor of a hard-line Marxist government backed by the rebels' guns. Enrique and his colleagues denied this as well, arguing that the FDR and the FMLN (the guerrillas) needed each other and would be able to work together. Significantly, U.S. government statements never noted the obvious parallel—that the U.S.-backed Christian Democrats were providing only a thin civilian facade for a government where the real power rested with the military high command. Nor did U.S. spokespeople ever suggest that Duarte and his Christian Democratic colleagues in the junta should "distance themselves" from the "violent extremists" of the armed forces and the far right—something just as impossible as the U.S. call for the FDR and the FMLN to separate.

From the State Department's telegram: "At the *conclusion* of the meeting, Bowdler said that he met with all Salvadoran factions on an off-the-record, private basis" (emphasis added), and he asked that the conversation be considered confidential. The Salvadorans did not accept this belated request, and insisted they were free to discuss the meeting in general terms.

In addition to their visit to State, the FDR group talked with several members of Congress. Mauricio Silva first of all mentioned Senator Ted Kennedy. That meeting went "very well," he said, far better than the one with the administration team: "He was a lot more clever than they were, he had a better perspective." The group met with others, including some Republicans. "They were also good, in the sense of not seeing us as the devil. [But] we met with a lot of people who had that position, that you guys are the devil—communist plotters, or at least stupids who were being used.... That position was the most common," Silva said.[23] Unfortunately the climate would grow even colder when the Reagan administration took over in 1981.

"Theology in the Americas"

Enrique Alvarez and his FDR comrades could not change the thrust of United States policy, any more than had Monsignor Romero's pleas and his death. But the FDR spokesmen made good use of their chances to speak to the American people. This work bore fruit in the U.S. movement against the war policies of soon-to-be president Ronald Reagan, a movement based in large part in the churches and religious people of North America.

Detroit was an important stop on the odyssey of Enrique Alvarez. There in the first week of August some 600 men and women met for the second conference on "Theology in the Americas." It was "a historic milestone for the Christian left in the United States," says the introduction to the published conference proceedings. "This gathering signified the extent to which theologies of liberation and resistance are becoming more and more a living reality and presence in this country." A vital example of liberation, repression and resistance was the "Statement from El Salvador" by Enrique Alvarez.[24]

Enrique began with a few words in Spanish, presenting "un cordial y fraternal y revolucionario saludo" from the Salvadoran people. Then he told in brief the story of his people's struggle against misery and oppression, how Salvadorans had tried elections and labor organizing but found the cards stacked against them so that they could not win.

> I'll give you just a few, a very few examples of the conditions that the majority of our country live in. We have the highest malnutrition index in all of Latin America; we're even higher than Haiti now. Almost half of our population does not know how to read or write. One hundred twenty children out of a thousand that are born are dead before they're a year old. On the other hand, we have a very few families— not fourteen, but less than two thousand families— that own more than forty percent of the best land, the main resource in our country, and that receive fifty percent of the national income. This is the situation, the cause why at this moment our people are struggling with arms in their hands in order to succeed, in order to find their final liberation.

Summarizing the events of the last year. Enrique explained how, despite their doubts, he and others had joined the government after the October 15 coup: "We participated because we thought it was the last peaceful chance to achieve power, to make structural changes," he said. But it didn't work.

> In the first few days of January we all resigned, and this process of unity that had started in the 1960s really took very rapid steps in our country. First, the military and political groups [of the opposition] got together, then all the popular and mass organizations got together, the Democratic Front was formed, and in the first week of April these two forces— the democratic and the revolutionary forces— got together and formed the Democratic Revolutionary Front. We are the expression of the majority of the people. We have in the Front two political parties, we have the four largest and most important trade union federations in the country, we have all five mass organizations, we have the National and Catholic Universities, we have the movement of technicians, we have independent labor — the great majority of the people.
>
> On the other hand we have a government that is supported by the army (of course it includes a very few Christian Democratic leaders too) and that

> exists because of the support of the U.S. government—a government that has started an extermination war, a war to destroy not only the leaders of the popular and revolutionary movement but also the leaders of the democratic movement. The worst expression of that repression is the killing of our Bishop Oscar Romero who, I think, made very clear what the actual intentions of the government were.

Enrique talked about the State Department's image of a centrist government, besieged from both the right and the left. "This center is not real," he said. "There are only two forces fighting in our country: on the one side the great majority of the people, and on the other side the army and the oligarchy trying to destroy them." But as the FDR delegation traveled around the world it had found understanding and solidarity from churches, trade unions, political parties—and even governments. The Mexican foreign minister, for example, compared the situation in El Salvador with that of Nicaragua one year ago. (In the near future Mexico and France would offer official recognition to the FDR/FMLN.) The Socialist International stated that the FDR was the real representative of the people and called on the U.S. government "to revise their policy because it is only causing more bloodshed."

Enrique then added something "very personal." He told the conference that he had gone to school in the United States, "around New York." The FDR group had visited Brooklyn, the Bowery, and the Bronx a week earlier, and they were appalled by the evidence of social decay that they saw there. "It's hard to believe that in this country—the biggest power in the world—conditions like that still remain. We think you need a revolution here too," he said.

In concluding, Enrique told the delegates one thing more. "We have found in this country that the media are completely closed," he said. "We have had many press conferences, many interviews, but very little printing, hardly any. So it is very important for you to tell this message...." This led to a final plea for solidarity:

> We would also like you to pressure your government.... We think they realize that their alternative is not viable, but they will not allow "another Nicaragua." I think they have no right to say that. We agree that the example of Nicaragua has inspired our struggle. All we ask of Nicaragua is that they consolidate their struggle; we do not ask for any aid. And all we ask of the United States is that they stay away. We only ask that which Bishop Romero asked the president in his letter: do not support the current government because all the aid you send is being used to kill our people.
>
> And all we ask of you is that you be the voice of our people. Thank you.

"The voice of the voiceless"—that was one name for Monsignor Romero. Now something similar was to be the task of the North American religious left and its secular allies. Many tried. But the United States government did not respond to their call.

"*We Are Fighting for a Just Cause*"

This is the conclusion of Enrique's 1980 interview explaining his work and thinking (see chapter 5).

> ... I could say that I am convinced that the system that we have in our country has not solved any problems; on the contrary, it has contributed to creating them. And that the [wealthy] minority of the people are better off right now than they were 20 years ago, but the great majority of the people are poorer and getting poorer every day. So I think a radical change is needed, and that's why, after leaving the government the second of January this year, I decided that it was the moment to really fight, to really struggle with the people, and that the moment has been reached — that we could see we could achieve this change in a very short period.
>
> So that's what I'm doing there, and I don't think that the class you are from determines how you form your political ways. On the contrary, I think belonging to that [wealthy] class helped me a great deal to find out how much injustice there was, and I am convinced right now that things have to change.

At this point the interviewer mentioned the murder of Mario Zamora as an example of the repression against people working for change in El Salvador. What was it like to stay on and keep working in the face of such personal danger? he asked. Enrique's reply began with a comment about the failure of the first junta of 1979, which he had joined reluctantly in the belief that it was the last hope for peaceful change. He was, he said, not at all sure the reformist project could succeed:

> Very shortly we confirmed our doubts that it was not possible, that the army was only saying that it wanted changes, that they wanted to keep the power for themselves. And also we shortly found out that many people that were in government, representing what is called private enterprise, were there in order that changes could not be pushed through — not to support them but to oppose them. So we resigned, and I confirmed my position that only a government with popular support, with popular participation through their organizations, could really do the things that the country had been needing for so long.
>
> When I took this decision I realized all the risks that I would have, but — and this is very important — these six or seven months that I've been really working full time for this, I have found out something that is very beautiful, I would say. You forget about everything else. You don't care about

your own safety, you don't care about pleasures, you don't care about anything else. You're just completely absorbed by this kind of work. And I think this means, this reflects, that we are fighting for a just cause, and that when you are doing that you forget about the other things that don't really have any value at all; they are just part of the system that we have here.

So I am not worried about it [personal danger]. I am conscious of it, but I am even thinking right now about going back to the country if my presence there is needed.

I think it is very important for me to tell you that now that I know well some of the leaders of these [revolutionary] groups, I have found the kind of persons that they are. Many people have the idea that they are just a group of young fellows that are very happy with a machine gun, but they don't realize the quality, the human quality, that those people have. I am so impressed with these people, and I am convinced that because we are fighting a just struggle, and because our people have those kind of leaders, this struggle will not fail.

Mexico Again

In mid August, soon after the Detroit conference, Alvarez and his FDR companions returned to Mexico City where their organization would have its headquarters in exile for the next decade. There was important work to be done there and Enrique met with influential Mexicans and other foreigners, as well as his Salvadoran colleagues. It was also in Mexico that he first met several leaders of the armed revolution, the soon-to-be FMLN. Among them was long-time revolutionary Salvador Cayetano Carpio (Marcial), former secretary-general of the Salvadoran Communist Party and now the leader of the FPL. Other old friends and acquaintances turned up in Mexico City around this time. One of them was Jorge Pinto Jr., who described their meeting in his political autobiography *El Grito del Más Pequeño:*

On September 5 the president of the Democratic Revolutionary Front, Enrique Alvarez Córdova, invited us to have dinner in the Hotel Saratoga of Mexico City. There he was called "Señor Montoya." Staying in that hotel was Juan Chacón, also a member of the Executive Committee of the FDR.

Teresita [Pinto's wife] was familiar with Quique Alvarez's "little agrarian reform" at his finca El Jobo. She had seen a ray of hope and faith in the faces of his campesinos. Enrique's popularity was due to his tenacious struggle for the agrarian reform, because of which he had incurred the enmity of his own family since he had been undersecretary of agriculture in the government of Sánchez Hernández and then the minister in the governments of Sánchez Hernández again and then of Molina. He occupied the post of secretary of agriculture once more during the first Junta of 1979.

Quique Alvarez had great faith and enthusiasm in the development of

> events. At some point he got up and went to get a clipping from the Mexican newspaper *Uno Más Uno* in which Adolfo Gilly analyzed the latest strike. Enrique and Gilly had become good friends. I asked him about his old friendship with Duarte and he answered me with a mini-poem of Roque Dalton: "Never forget that the least fascist among the fascists are still fascists."[25]

In fact there had been not one but two general strikes in El Salvador during the foreign tour of the FDR leaders, and Gilly wrote about both of them. The first strike had been a nearly total success for the opposition. It paralyzed the economic life of the nation for two days, June 24 and 25, and once again demonstrated powerful support for the Frente. The armed forces patrolled the streets during the strike, but, remarkably, there were almost no casualties on either side. Gilly described it euphorically as successfully "continuing *the preparation of the masses for the insurrection*" (emphasis in the original).[26]

In contrast, the strike to which Pinto was referring, which took place from August 13 to 15, was a mixed bag for the FDR. Participation was far less complete than it had been in June, and the junta, echoed by the United States government and media, was quick to declare this strike a total failure.[27] Gilly's *Uno Más Uno* article analyzed events differently, taking into account the massive military repression aimed against the strike plus numerous guerrilla actions away from the capital made possible by the concentration of government forces in San Salvador. His conclusion was that "far from being a success for the junta," the three days of the strike were "one more proof" of the growing strength of the revolutionary movement.

There was important work to be done from the FDR's Mexican base, but Enrique Alvarez was not content. "It became clear to me that Enrique was becoming sort of desperate," recalls Rubén Zamora. "That kind of life, doing political work, diplomatic work, was not for him. He became more and more uncomfortable with the whole thing, and he started to talk about returning to the country."

Zamora says there were two groups among the FDR people in Mexico. There were those — he mentioned Guillermo Ungo and himself — who could not go back to El Salvador, or who could at most return clandestinely, "otherwise you would be killed the next day." But others, including Enrique, believed they could go back. Enrique pointed out that he was a member of an elite family, that he was not associated with any radical party, etc. The leadership debated the issue at length. Zamora says he told Enrique not to think of returning, that he'd be killed in spite of those factors. But all the same he started to think of going back. Again according to Ruben Zamora, "It seemed that his desire to be in the country, to work there, to do the kind of work that he was used to, with the common people, with the peasants, that sort of thing, started to eat at his reason until he was absolutely convinced that he could go back to the country. And he did."[28]

There were political reasons, and there were personal reasons. Enrique *wanted* to return to El Salvador. His strongest political base was there — the farmworkers, the campesinos. His friends agree that Enrique had a remarkable affinity and sympathy with the rural people of his country that went beyond politics, and he was deeply moved by the continuing reports of atrocities against them. He felt strongly that he could not lead the movement from a safe exile; he had to be present, and to let it be known that he was present. He was actually well aware that his family background would not provide safety, but he may have overestimated the ability of the armed groups to protect him. For whatever combination of reasons, he longed to return. It was officially a group decision, but Enrique's determination finally persuaded his FDR colleagues to approve the inevitable. In October, Enrique Alvarez was back in El Salvador.

9

Into the Fire

> You don't care about your own safety, you don't care about pleasures, you don't care about anything else. You're completely absorbed by this kind of work. And I think this means that we are fighting for a just cause.
>
> — *Enrique Alvarez Córdova*

According to Mexican journalist Adolfo Gilly, Enrique Alvarez returned to his country on October 6, 1980 and immediately took up the work and leadership of the Frente Democrático Revolucionario. Enrique entered El Salvador clandestinely and in disguise. Gilly "asks himself whether under the disguise there didn't shine forth that aristocratic air which he carried and which might have betrayed him to an alert observer at the checkpoints which he undoubtedly had to pass." But Gilly also suggests that Enrique knew how to adopt a certain attitude of the countryman, which wouldn't fool the campesinos but many times could get him by the guards at the roadblocks.[1]

Certainly there was still important work to be done abroad for the FDR, and Enrique Alvarez with his background and sophistication would have been well equipped to do it. "Was he more useful for those tasks than returning to the internal front within El Salvador?" Gilly asks, and speculates that although his return was a collective decision of the leadership, Enrique's own desire to be inside the country may have tipped the balance. Others who knew him say the same thing.

There is no question that Enrique wanted to come home. Salvador Sánchez Cerén was a revolutionary leader who knew Enrique during the last two months of his life. He says Enrique considered himself "in exile" living in Mexico. His return was a decision of the party directorate, yes, but he himself was pushing hard for that decision. "It implied a serious risk," says Sánchez Cerén,

> to come [to El Salvador] to do semi-public work, because of the changes that had taken place with the Junta, where the military had again taken control of the Revolutionary Junta and had begun a series of massacres....
>
> It was a goal of the Right to eliminate him, to kill him. But it was in the framework of our preparations for the offensive of [January] 1981, which included the idea of taking over the government, and it was important that Enrique be here, have a presence here, since he was the man who was going to head that government.[2]

An old friend of Enrique and the Alvarez family, Coralia Godoy, confirms that he badly wanted to return. After his death she asked Guillermo Ungo why they (the FDR directorate) had let him come back to El Salvador. "You couldn't stop him," Ungo replied. She recalls asking Enrique himself why he took the risk. He and the others of the FDR "had to be visible and present in the country, so that people know that we're here and what we're after and that it's not communism," he said. Coralia Godoy believes that "He had democratic ideals, he wanted justice in the country. He wasn't a politician, he really wasn't. He was just an idealist working for his country. And he gave his life for his country."[3]

El Jobo Under Attack

At 5:00 PM on October 9, 1980, the Salvadoran armed forces invaded El Jobo. Men of the National Guard and the Army arrived with plenty of firepower on display although they encountered no resistance. Soldiers spread out over the farm, looking for weapons, signs of guerrilla activity, or any other evidence of "subversion." Enrique Alvarez, whether still in Mexico or in hiding somewhere in El Salvador, was not there. Lino Oseguéda, however, was at El Jobo that afternoon. He was ordered at gunpoint to stand against the wall and not move, which he did for two hours. The officers in charge of the raid had a list with 12 or 13 names, and soon all but one of these men, and others as well, had been captured and taken away.

Some of the invaders had doubts about what they were doing. Soldiers from nearby Sonsonate had been to El Jobo before, to play soccer against the finca's team and to buy the excellent farm products sold at the cooperative store. Some even had friends among the workers. One junior officer tried to explain to his superiors that this was all a mistake, that El Jobo was not subversive. He was told to "shut up and obey orders." The leaders had "intelligence." An informer had told them that El Jobo was a guerrilla base, and had given them the names of alleged subversives operating there. That report was very nearly a death warrant for the arrested men.

Lino Osegueda's name was not on the list, and after two hours he was allowed to leave. Lino says he made the fastest trip of his life to San Salvador, where he began trying to contact people with influence. The men who had been arrested were not guerrillas; they were farm workers, including some of the cooperative's managers whom Enrique had trained and encouraged. They were going to die at 4:00 AM, Osegueda had been told, and the situation was desperate.[4]

This was not an idle threat. The officer in charge of the raid on El Jobo was a captain named Figueroa Morales. Three years later soldiers from the "Jaguar Battalion" raided Las Hojas, another cooperative in the same department (Sonsonate). The soldiers had a list of alleged subversives that time too, and they picked out 16 men with the help of masked civilian informers. The sixteen campesinos were taken away and killed in cold blood shortly afterwards. In command of that massacre was the same man, Captain Figueroa Morales.[5]

In the case of El Jobo, fortunately, Osegueda's efforts were successful. He managed to convince some sufficiently influential people and the execution orders were canceled. There was a catch. One man named on the list had not been found at El Jobo; that was Antonio Longhares, one of the top managers of the farm. He missed the raid since he was in Sonsonate that afternoon visiting a friend and picking up his wife at her business. Longhares was especially important because the military's "intelligence report" stated that he had been trained in Cuba and Russia — places where in reality, of course, he had never been.

An officer whom Longhares knew from soccer sent word that he must report to the army post at 7:00 the next morning; the situation was "serious." He went, but was told to come back later. In the meantime men of the National Guard had been seeking him at El Jobo, threatening to take his wife and children if he couldn't be found. Knowing the reputation of the Guard, Longhares returned instead to the army base hoping to get help from the officer he knew. He was in luck, and eventually he was confronted there with the accuser.

"It was one of the many times that I have seen that God exists and had not abandoned me," he says, "because that man, in front of all the officers and people there, looked at me and said 'It isn't true. All that on the tape is false.'" The Guard had beaten and threatened him, the informer said, and made him say those things, but they weren't true. Even with that confession some of the military weren't convinced that Longhares was innocent, but they let him go.

Longhares had had to make a tough choice, for that call to appear and demonstrate his innocence could well have been a death trap. But failing to appear might have endangered the others, who were supposed to be released that morning as a result of Osegueda's intervention. Antonio decided that he had to go. This time it turned out well, and all the El Jobo prisoners were released unharmed.[6]

Two details illustrate the ambiguity that events in El Salvador often presented. One of the people Lino Osegueda contacted—Lino knew him through family connections—and who helped save the lives of the El Jobo men was Colonel Eugenio Vides Casanova, the commander of the National Guard. There is no question whatever that the Guard committed many horrible atrocities against civilians during his tenure in command. One of those was the rape and murder of four religious women, three nuns and a lay missioner, all U.S. citizens, a couple of months after the El Jobo raid.[7] Two decades later Vides Casanova and Colonel Guillermo García, who had been the minister of defense since the coup of October 1979, were defendants in two civil suits brought in Florida during 2001 and 2002. The first suit accused the pair of responsibility for the murders of the four women; the second was about the brutal torture of three Salvadoran civilians—who survived the war and were able to bring the charges themselves. Vides Casanova and García were acquitted in the first suit, on the questionable ground that they were not always informed or in control of what their subordinates did. They were convicted in the second case, and face a damage award of $55 million.

Lino Osegueda, recalling Vides Casanova's help when El Jobo was attacked, thinks the first jury got it right. But the very fact that Vides Casanova was able to intervene positively in the El Jobo case suggests that he had the power to prevent other abuses as well—and failed to do so. Napoleón Duarte wrote that "Vides Casanova's influence was disproportionate to his rank. He was like a barometer of the armed forces. When he moved in one direction, the others followed."[8] The Commission on the Truth concluded that at least he knew of the crime against the four women and participated in covering up the National Guard's responsibility, while García was blamed for failing to carry out any real investigation.[9] García, as minister of defense, arguably had become the most powerful man in El Salvador by the end of 1980.[10]

The second postscript to the El Jobo raid is that the informer, the false witness who perhaps unwillingly caused the near tragedy, was informally—that is, with no sort of judicial proceeding—killed shortly afterwards.

A Near Miss

About 11:00 PM on the night of the El Jobo invasion—while the dozen workers were still held prisoner unsure whether they were to live or die—

a powerful explosion partially destroyed the San Salvador house in which Lino Osegueda and his family were living. They were all sleeping in the rear of the house when the bomb went off. It was placed in front near the street, and the family escaped serious injury although Lino was wounded slightly in the hand by flying glass. A chair where he had sitting shortly before the blast was riddled, and Lino would surely have been killed if he'd still been there. After the explosion he rushed out barefoot to see what had happened, and doesn't understand why his feet weren't cut by the thousands of glass fragments littering the floors.

Within a few minutes of the bombing a police car arrived. Osegueda says he didn't know if they were coming to help — or if they had arrived to finish the job in case there were survivors. Fortunately the patrol was not related to the attackers; it had simply happened to be nearby when the bomb went off, and the police were helpful.

That house belonged to Enrique Alvarez. It was the central one of three which were properties of the Alvarez family, located on a side street near the famous statue "The Savior of the World," a major San Salvador landmark. Lino was in the process of buying the house from Enrique, and he thinks the bomb was aimed more at the FDR's president than at himself. The crime, like so many others, was never solved or even investigated.[11]

Bombings like this one were almost common in El Salvador that year. Opposition newspapers, the campus of the UCA, and the radio station of the archdiocese which broadcast the Sunday homilies of Monsignor Romero, all were bombed repeatedly. Private houses were also targets. Seventeen sticks of dynamite destroyed the home of Mauricio Silva the day after he and his family had left it. The home of Ana del Carmen Alvarez was also bombed in the summer of 1980 — "because I was working here in the university [the UCA], and because I am friends with people who joined the guerrilla." No one was hurt because she and her family weren't sleeping in their own house that night. But the matter would hardly end there, she explained. "If you are bombed like that, and if you escape by a miracle, there are only two things you can do. Either you go underground, or you leave the country. In my case, I had children, I had my mother, I had grandchildren, one of whom depended on me directly, so I preferred to go into exile. And so on May 5 of 1980 I left for Costa Rica."[12]

Still, Lino Osegueda neither left nor went underground. (Unlike the cases mentioned above, Osegueda himself may not have been the intended target in the attack on his house.) The house was too badly damaged to be habitable, and Lino and his family found temporary lodgings elsewhere. An elderly man from a nearby neighborhood offered to watch the property while it remained vacant. A couple of weeks after the bombing this watchman called the Oseguedas' new home with a report. A man and woman had come by the house and asked him how to contact the family, and after hesitating he gave them the phone number. The man, he said, looked like a "cowboy"—a big mustache, cowboy boots and a wide brimmed hat.

Soon afterward the woman from this odd couple called to ask if Lino and his family were all right. Told they were, she then offered to rent the wrecked house and undertake the repairs! Who would make such an offer? Lino Osegueda believes that the "cowboy" must have been Enrique Alvarez.

There was a sequel. In January 1981 after the murders of the FDR leaders, presumably this same woman was killed during a police raid on a house elsewhere in San Salvador; she was said to have belonged to the FMLN. Officials then reported finding Enrique Alvarez's passport and "cedula" (domestic ID card) in that house, both bearing the false name Eduardo Arce Cardona (initials EAC) but clearly identifiable as his. The FDR promptly issued a statement equating this report with a confession that the police themselves were Enrique's murderers! They pointed out that the fake cedula would have been useless unless Enrique carried it with him, adding that his comrades knew that he did just that. Thus his documents, which were not found with his body, must have been taken by the killers. This bulletin was published in *El Independiente,* with a supporting editorial by Jorge Pinto Jr.[13]

Apart from this ambiguous contact, Lino Osegueda did not hear from Enrique after his return from Mexico. Lino thinks news of the bombing of the house and the danger to the Osegueda family may have reached Enrique and been among the concerns which made him eager to return to El Salvador that autumn. Of course if Adolfo Gilly's timing for Enrique's arrival is correct he was already in the country when the bombing occurred. There is no independent confirmation of that date.

A Secret Visit[14]

In October the daily press announced that Enrique Alvarez, along with Juan Chacón and other FDR leaders, had returned to El Salvador. Soon afterward Antonio Longhares had a visit from the young man, a former El Jobo worker, who had been looking after Enrique's apartment in San Salvador.

"Listen Antonio," he said, "I need to find out if you'd like to see don Enrique." "Yes, of course," Longhares replied, "but where is he?"

"I can't tell you that," was the answer. "I want to tell you that he's in the country and he wants to talk with you. But he said to find out first if you feel like meeting him, he doesn't want to force you into anything. If you want to do it, we'll make an agreement right now and I'll take you when the day comes."

Longhares said he'd go. The plan was that he would take the bus to San Salvador and wait to be picked up at a certain place and time. Once the messenger had left, however, Antonio had serious misgivings. He well knew that any contact with the left, including Enrique Alvarez, could mean serious trouble and, he says, he was thinking of his family — his wife and two children. He talked it over with her later that day, and asked whether she thought he should go.

"You've always said that don Enrique was like the father you never had, that you lacked," she replied. "Don Enrique has been a very special person for you, and not just you but also for me and the children. It's true that there'll be some risk, but he is running big risks too. The main thing is to ask God and have faith that nothing bad will happen. So as far as we are concerned, I give you my blessing to go."

It was a Wednesday when the young man had arrived and Longhares said he'd make the trip; he agreed that on Saturday he would be in the capital's western bus station at one o'clock. Antonio knew that he was under surveillance by agents of the army, who often had cars parked near the farm to watch who came and went. To escape their observation he got a ride to Sonsonate, not using his own car, and entered the shop his wife kept in the town. He stayed out of sight until a local bus arrived, took it to the station, and got on and off three or four different busses until finally staying on the one headed for San Salvador.

Antonio had been told to just walk around the terminal when he arrived and he'd be contacted; he didn't know who he would be meeting. Suddenly someone said to him "Compa, compa.... Get in, we've come to pick you up." It was a great risk, Antonio says, "because I didn't know if they were from the army or the guerrilla." But he got into their vehicle, and they took him to a certain place there in San Salvador.

There was the young man — Pablo — who'd been the messenger. He asked if there had been any problems; Antonio said no. They talked a bit until Pablo said "It's two o'clock. Let's go." "And we began to walk," says Antonio, "we crossed two streets and came to a vehicle, and Pablo said 'This one is going to take us.' So we got in, and they said 'Please close your eyes; don't open them.' And they put something on my eyes so I couldn't."

The driver made many turns and succeeded in getting Longhares totally lost. Finally they told him he could look, and they all entered a house somewhere in the city. He saw a girl ironing clothes, and another young woman cutting some cloth with a child sitting nearby. At the end of the courtyard there was a screen, and Enrique Alvarez came out to greet him when he heard Antonio's voice.

They talked about their problems, and Enrique told something of what he'd done abroad and of how he wanted to return. "Look," he said, "this isn't easy—but it's got to be done because there are a lot of people who need us, a great many people."

"But you've never been a man of violence," Antonio said.

"I'm still not a man of violence," Enrique replied, "and that's just why I'm here. I could have gone on working in the country where I was, but I came because I felt that the people here weren't doing what needs to be done. It's not by violence that we're going to win, and that's why I've come back."

The two talked of their families, and of events at El Jobo. Antonio told about the army raid on the farm and about threats from the guerrillas as well. Enrique reassured him about that and said nothing would happen. Then he asked Antonio what he was going to do.

The near disaster with the military had occurred a short time ago. Longhares remembers replying, "Look don Enrique, I don't know. My mother has been badly worried by all this. My sister who's living in the United States found out and wants me to come there. She'll send us the tickets and everything, and I already have a visa. Maybe it's better that we go and live in the United States."

Enrique replied,

> You know something? I've never asked you to do anything ... but today I'm going to. I'm here because I believe in this, I believe that we have to fight to defend all the poor who have such great needs, and because the country needs change. That's why I'm here. But if you leave the country, that's going to make problems for us. If you leave, El Jobo is going to have problems. I have confidence in you, and I know that you mean a lot for the people there. That's why I want to ask you from my heart that you don't go.
>
> You've come because things at El Jobo are still going the way we've always wanted. You know the projects we have planned for El Jobo. You, and Lino Osegueda, and Dr. Rodriguez—you're the people who understand. As long as that team works together, El Jobo will keep going. But otherwise things are going to fall apart, and it will hurt a lot if this work and all my efforts are lost. But if you all keep on there, it will stay strong the way I've hoped. Even if I'm not there, if you all are there things can go forward.
>
> El Jobo ought to be an example for the whole community, those that are nearby and even the whole country. You must keep on with all that we've planned—and one day there will be more El Jobos in this country. You should help other people to learn how to make cooperatives work. The people will need that; help them! You know the society we live in, all the things the people need. You are the ones who have to help these people move forward.

> So there is something I want to ask. I want you to promise me that you won't leave El Jobo, that you'll always be there.

Longhares gave Enrique that promise. "I told him 'yes,'" he said. "And in spite of all the time that's passed, for me it's as if all this happened yesterday. It hurts to remember these things. I know that here in El Jobo there have been times we didn't do so well, when we ought to have worked better. Don Enrique deserved all that, and a lot more." He paused. "Sorry but it's not easy to talk. I have a knot in my throat."

> So much time has gone by. But I think don Enrique would have helped this country. He was a person with great social feeling, and he was capable of giving away what he had to help others. There were so many examples.... He was a practical, everyday person but with such a big heart, very noble, a very special person. So many things he did to help the people who were most in need....
>
> He wanted to help people get ahead and improve their lives. There are a lot of people here [at El Jobo] who were pretty badly off, and this business has helped us get on.

"Semi-Clandestine" Life

Enrique Alvarez could not think of living normally in El Salvador. He entered a "semi-clandestine" existence, which means that he took many precautions although he also made carefully selected appearances in public. He of course did not return to his apartment to sleep, and spent his nights with different friends or in "safe houses" maintained by the guerrilla groups. One temporary refuge was the home of the Godoy sisters. "He came here to stay for 3 or 4 days," says Coralia Godoy. "He was semi-clandestine. We asked my mother and she said yes. She loved Quique very much. His life was in danger but she was happy to have him come here. I asked him about his family and his friends. He told me his father wouldn't talk to him. His mother and his sister were more or less against him too."[15]

His longest stay in one place during this period was two weeks or so spent in a safe house belonging to the Popular Liberation Forces (FPL), one of the five guerrilla groups. He shared this time with Salvador Sánchez Cerén, who had left his open life and was living fully underground. The two weeks were used for planning the work of the FDR and deciding where and how Enrique would move around, live, and appear in the country. Enrique must also have been involved during that time in negotiating the unified command for the armed opposition; on October 10 the Farabundo

Martí Front for National Liberation (FMLN) was officially created. (One missing group, the National Resistance (RN), joined the FMLN a month later.) Certainly during those weeks the participation of Enrique Alvarez was essential in working out the future relationship which the military FMLN would have with the civilian FDR.

There was still time for conversation, and Alvarez shared experiences from his years in the government and from the work at El Jobo. Sánchez Cerén was impressed by Enrique's dedication to agrarian reform and his feeling for the lives of campesinos. He had tried hard to raise the consciousness of his own class, of the landowners, Enrique said. He had tried to show them that there were better ways to do things: to produce, yes, but so that the workers didn't need to live in misery. But all he got was rejection.

Sánchez Cerén's wife and children were living in the house too; she would go out to do the shopping while the two men remained out of sight. Salvador and his wife were surprised at how easily Enrique Alvarez adapted to this style of living. Often Enrique did the cooking—while she was out of the house doing errands, he prepared the meal for them all. There were other details. The house had tubs and containers that had to be filled with water when it was available, because the supply frequently failed; Enrique did that too. Salvador says, "I couldn't get over how a person with his background, coming from an oligarchy family with so many resources, would do all that. We didn't see any difference between his style and ours.... His way of living agreed with what he thought, what he believed."[16]

Enrique Alvarez was present when the FDR leadership paid tribute to Felix Antonio Ulloa, the rector of the University of El Salvador who was murdered on October 29. Ulloa had been elected rector in 1979. Late in June of 1980 the army occupied the UES campus in San Salvador, as well as its eastern and western branches, in a bloody operation that resembled a wartime invasion of enemy territory except that here the "enemy" didn't shoot back. Some fifty students and teachers were killed, however, and the campus was looted. (Napoleón Duarte, to his discredit, publicly approved of this crime.) Ulloa and much of the university faculty were trying to continue classes "in exile" at various places around the city. Jorge Pinto Jr. and his paper *El Independiente* paid front-page tribute to this man, shot by plainclothes terrorists in the center of the capital. Pinto wrote that

> I arrived late for the funeral mass in the cathedral. Teresita [Pinto's wife] was waiting for me there. I came at the moment when the leaders of the FDR were giving a last tribute to Engineer Ulloa. There was Quique Alvarez. I could see Juan Chacón. The people in the temple were nervous. A few minutes before, the cathedral had been surrounded by a cordon of National Guards....[17]

Adolfo Gilly described the scene in these words:

> ... the entire directorate of the FDR within El Salvador, headed by Enrique Alvarez, presented itself publicly in the cathedral to pay homage to the remains of the fallen university leader. The working class people, the Salvadorans present there, stared at Enrique surprised by that audacious move, and immediately took it in; some cried, they say, because they understood. There Alvarez Córdova must have felt that he was truly carrying out his role before his people.[18]

Ulloa's funeral was one of Enrique's few public appearances during his two months back in El Salvador. Another was a press conference in late October, rather surprisingly reported (with a photo) in *El Diario de Hoy*. Enrique and four other FDR directors explained their rejection of an offer by the Salvadoran Episcopal Conference to "mediate" between the FDR and the junta. The group of bishops included extreme rightists and reflected the strong division within the Church hierarchy that had tormented Oscar Romero during his tenure as archbishop. Such a group could not mediate in good faith, the FDR believed, although a direct dialog with the government might be possible. Jorge Pinto had expressed the same view in *El Independiente* a day earlier.

Enrique Alvarez and Juan Chacón gave an interview on November 10 to the Mexican paper *Uno Más Uno*. Enrique thanked the Mexican government for its support and looked for even more solidarity with the cause of the FDR. Discussing reported divisions within the Salvadoran armed forces, Alvarez repeated a call to the officers and men of the military "to join the ranks of the revolution, an invitation which remains open." Alvarez and Chacón also spoke of the provisional revolutionary government that they hoped would soon be proclaimed in El Salvador. Its constitution was being debated at that moment, Enrique said. He added, "One thing which is certain is that when the time arrives, we will inaugurate that government here in this country and not from exile."[19]

With hindsight, the location of this interview was an evil omen. It was held at the Externado de San José, the site of the fatal last meeting of the FDR directors less than three weeks later.

Pieces of a Life

The life of any human being is hugely complicated. No person can be captured whole simply by accounts of his or her public actions, career history, or even of hobbies, family, and friends. Enrique Alvarez was far more than this historical outline can contain. There are bits and pieces of his life that do not easily find a logical place in a political portrait, but that do help to form a picture of the man. In no particular order, here are a few more of those pieces.

- Enrique, the child of a coffee empire, did not much like to drink coffee. He took a cup on occasion, but preferred chocolate.
- Anna María López was more than ten years younger than Enrique. Their families were acquainted and lived not far apart; Enrique's uncle Roberto was her godfather. Despite that, Anna María and Enrique first met while she was working at the Alvarez family's Banco Capitalizador in the 1960s. She already knew Ernesto Alvarez from school; he was close to her own age. She saw Enrique at Ernesto's parties as well as more formally at the bank, and eventually they became close friends. Anna María is the source for several of the following glimpses.
- He was different from the other bank directors, she says. For example, when they'd have an office Christmas party the other directors would look in, stay a little while, perhaps give some award to an outstanding employee, and then they'd leave. All very formal. Enrique wasn't like that. He'd stay and participate in the party — he'd talk to people and make them feel that they really knew each other. He stood out that way.
- Enrique was godfather to at least 28 children. Often his employees asked him to be godfather to their children, and he never refused. One Christmas Enrique asked Anna María to help him wrap presents for his godchildren, and she was stunned at how many there were. On Christmas day he would go around and visit all their families and bring presents to the children.
- Enrique preferred *El Diario de Hoy* to the other major daily newspaper, *La Prensa Gráfica*. The former was a straightforward right-wing paper that didn't pretend to be anything else, while with the other one "you never knew where you stood." With *El Diario de Hoy* you did know where you stood! It was right out there and attacked everything he was trying to do. (Anna María López)
- He didn't drink much; this was very unusual for men in his situation. Enrique would take a little, but Anna María always felt safe if he drove her home from a party. He did smoke — Lucky Strike cigarettes in the early days. He also liked to play poker with a circle of friends. He loved music, and was a big fan of the Beatles. He kept up with the pop music scene, and would ask, "Did you hear [this or that group]?" Yes, he had a sense of humor too, although he didn't show it much at his parents' home. There he tended to be very formal.

- Enrique personally rejected violence and always sought political or agreed solutions to problems—although in the end he believed that armed struggle was necessary to achieve social change. Still, he liked guns and even had a collection of them. One day as threats were becoming more and more commonplace, he said lightly to Anna María, "Well, I guess I'd better buy a machine gun." She replied, "Oh don't do that, you wouldn't even know how to use it." "Don't be so sure," Enrique replied. (Anna María López and Ernesto Alvarez)
- "I'm from a village where there's a coffee finca belonging to the Alvarez family, the finca Colombia.... One of my brothers worked there as a carpenter, another worked as a clerk, and they told me that when Enrique came there he talked with everybody and didn't make any distinctions.... Of course he used to be well known as a basketball player, and when I met him personally I told him that I'd admired him as an athlete. He was famous! 'And besides,' I said, 'I knew about you through my brothers. They worked at your father's hacienda, and they told me that when you came there to the finca you'd always come and greet them, something that nobody else did, and they saw this difference.'" (Salvador Sánchez Cerén)
- "I worked for the Alvarez family as a driver, from 1971 to 1980.... Quique never looked at us just as workers, he always saw us as people. That made us feel very good, to know that although he was so rich he related to poorer folks that way. Actually they all treated us very well, at least during the time I was with them; all the Alvarez family were good people. But there was a difference between Enrique and Carmen Elena and Ernesto. They were more typical in their relation with their workers and friends; they made a separation. But Quique never separated the workers from the other people." (Salvador Núñez)
- Once in the middle 1970s Enrique took cattle from El Jobo to show at an international fair in San Salvador, where they won several prizes. At the fair he was congratulated and asked what was the reason El Jobo had such excellent cattle. Enrique replied, "The congratulations shouldn't be for me, because the cattle we have are due to the efforts of our workers. If you want to have cattle like those we have in El Jobo, you have to pay good salaries to your workers!" (Salvador Núñez)
- Enrique was fond of pupusas, a very common Salvadoran food made from tortillas stuffed with beans, sausage or cheese. Once when the FDR directors were meeting at a school in the capital, they sent someone out to buy food for lunch. All he could find were pupusas (which are more often eaten for supper than for lunch), and he brought some back to the meeting. Juan José Martel, one of the directors, remembers seeing Quique Alvarez Córdova sitting there on a school chair. He put his briefcase on his

lap, spread a handkerchief over it like a tablecloth, and began to eat pupusas "with almost aristocratic elegance." Martel commented to another comrade, "Look at Quique eating." "Yes," the other replied, "as if he were seated in the best gourmet French restaurant!" But he really did love pupusas. (Juan José Martel)

- Enrique had firm opinions, but he wasn't dogmatic. He was able to be flexible, and he helped others find points of agreement and reach compromises when they were deadlocked. That quality was one of the reasons he was chosen to be president of the FDR. When the leadership was planning the public act for founding the Democratic Revolutionary Front, someone proposed that the event should begin with singing the national anthem. Others objected; they felt the national anthem did not represent the whole nation; that it was the hymn of the wealthy classes. They wanted instead to sing the "March of Solidarity" which was the true hymn of the working class, of the campesinos, of the humble people of the country. And everyone got into a debate that seemed to have no way out. Quique made the suggestion that we sing both, first the national anthem and then the hymn to solidarity, and that was how it turned out. That seems obvious now, but in the atmosphere of that time it was a difficult decision. His facility with situations like that was why we all agreed that Quique Alvarez should be president of the FDR. (Juan José Martel)
- "It was during this period that they murdered a good friend of his, Carlos Montoya; he was a CPA who helped Enrique manage some of his affairs. When they killed Carlos I went to his funeral, and I can't forget the image of Enrique carrying Carlos's coffin.... He was a man of great sensitivity, great compassion, with a Christian and human sense that was extremely important in his daily life...." (Monsignor Ricardo Urioste)

The Election of Ronald Reagan

The situation in El Salvador worsened measurably after November 4, with the news that Ronald Reagan would soon replace Jimmy Carter as president of the United States. Most of El Salvador's elite rejoiced at the election's outcome. Some 250 upper class Salvadorans attending an election night party at Hotel Presidente greeted the news of Carter's early concession with a "wild and enthusiastic celebration," Ray Bonner reported, and added that "In the posh residential neighborhoods of Escalón and San Benito, homeowners stepped onto manicured lawns and squeezed off a few rounds from their automatic rifles to register their joy."[20]

To the far right, the election of Reagan meant the end of "interference" with their bloody struggle against rebellion and change. The United States would no longer insist on measures such as the land reform, and they thought there would be no more U.S. protests, however tepid, against human rights abuses. The right believed that U.S. support was now assured for any measures they chose to use against the leftist opposition. Aid, including military aid, would flow in the name of "stopping communism" with few or no restrictive conditions.

Of course what the right hoped for, many others feared. During his November 10 interview, Enrique Alvarez declared that the Reagan administration would not be able to stop El Salvador's revolution, although he saw trouble ahead. "Our own process, our struggle, our internal advances, are the elements which will bring the triumph of our revolution," he said, "although we know that Reagan is going to stimulate the fascist elements not only here but in the whole region."[21] Salvadoran Archbishop Arturo Rivera y Damas also warned that "right-wing fanatics, inside and outside the Government, may now feel openly encouraged to increase repression." As an example, a week after the U.S. election two bodies turned up in San Miguel with signs hung around their necks. The message: "With Ronald Reagan, the miscreants and guerrillas of Central America and El Salvador will be finished."[22]

This common expectation about future U.S. policy proved to be entirely correct. Terror was no stranger to El Salvador, but after Reagan's victory it took on new dimensions. Within one month of the election two internationally notorious crimes were committed, the murder of the civilian opposition leaders including Enrique Alvarez, and the rape and murder of the four North American churchwomen. The United States collectively shook its head in disapproval, and did nothing. The day following the FDR murders, aides of president-elect Reagan "were promising right-wing Salvadorans combat equipment and announcing, in the words of Jeane Kirkpatrick, that they would 'have no problem with a little terror.'"[23]

The disappearance in December of a young U.S. journalist, and the deliberate murder a month later of two more U.S. citizens, official advisors to the Junta/U.S. agrarian reform program, together with the Salvadoran official who headed that program, likewise caused no wavering of U.S. support for the Salvadoran junta and military.[24] Three of these crimes were among the cases studied by the Truth Commission, and all three were known at the time to be the work of government armed forces.

Writing in the *New York Times* on November 30, Alan Riding clearly connected the rise in terrorism with the outcome of the U.S. election:

> The assassination of six opposition leaders in San Salvador this week is apparently part of a right-wing offensive throughout Central America aimed

at dealing a severe blow to the left before President-elect Ronald Reagan reaches the White House.

Although conservative businessmen, politicians, and military officers in the region welcomed Mr. Reagan's election as marking the end of Washington's human rights campaign, they have reportedly decided that the best time to strike at liberals and leftists is in the final weeks of the Carter administration....

The clearest bid for power by rightists has come in El Salvador....[25]

U.S. Ambassador Robert White later wrote about the murder of the four women, in an article bitterly critical of the directions in which the Reagan team had taken U.S. policy. This paragraph gives the essentials:

> The new message from Washington seemed to be that the United States would look the other way when the military used murder as a political weapon. This, the Salvadorans learned, would apply even when the victims were United States citizens of the "wrong" sort. Secretary of State Alexander M. Haig sought to play down the December 2, 1980 murder of four American missionary women in El Salvador. Although our Embassy reported unequivocally that the women were deliberately killed by the Salvadoran military, Haig responded to a Congressional inquiry with the fiction that the women might have been killed while running a roadblock. Mrs. Kirkpatrick followed Haig's lead by falsely describing the women as "political activists." The exact opposite was true. These women, as I personally know, rejected any political role and saw themselves only as servants to the poor. But to some minds, identifying with the poor is the same as identifying with revolution.[26]

Finally, Ray Bonner reported another kind of right-wing intransigence, also related to the U.S. election. Ambassador White had hoped to use military aid as a "carrot" to move the Salvadoran armed forces toward reform. In October, Bonner says,

> White promised Defense Minister García two helicopters in exchange for the dismissal of Colonel Francisco Morán, the head of the Treasury Police, widely considered the most brutal of the security forces. García agreed but never delivered, stalling until Reagan promised aid, and the helicopters came without any conditions being set.[27]

November 27: Kidnapping and Murder

The Report of the Truth Commission gives a bare bones outline of the basic facts. It records that on this date six men — Enrique Alvarez Córdova,

Juan Chacón, Enrique Escobar Barrera, Manual de Jesús Franco Ramírez, Humberto Mendoza, and Doroteo Hernández, whom it identifies as directors of the Democratic Revolutionary Front (FDR)—were "abducted, tortured, and, after a short period in captivity, murdered, in San Salvador." The report describes the condition of their bodies, notably the number and location of bullet wounds and the presence of "signs of strangulation"; in the case of Enrique Alvarez, "the corpse showed that he was struck by twelve bullets."

The Truth Commission's report states that "The kidnapping was carried out during the morning at the colegio [school] Externado de San José by a large number of heavily armed men." The Commission added this sad commentary on conditions in El Salvador:

> The climate of violence and insecurity prevailing in the country at the time was such that, had it not been for who the victims were, the place and time of the abduction, and type of operation and the public outrage it caused, it would have been just one more in the long list of abuses that were occurring at the time.

The Jesuit-run Externado de San José is located on a central avenue of San Salvador, just a few blocks south of the 1980 location of the U.S. Embassy. Enrique Alvarez had attended the school as a boy, and in the 1950s he often coached its basketball team. The campus is quite extensive and includes some half-dozen buildings plus athletic fields and a swimming pool. In 1980 a main building, no longer standing,[28] housed the rectory and other administrative offices of the Externado plus the headquarters of the legal aid organization Socorro Jurídico. That fall the FDR directors, Enrique among them, sometimes met in Socorro's offices on the school grounds.

Socorro Jurídico (the name means simply "legal aid") was formed in 1975 by twelve Catholic lawyers, in order to provide legal assistance to the poor. In June 1977, a few months after assuming the role of Archbishop, Oscar Romero officially recognized it as the institution of the archdiocese responsible for the legal defense of human rights in El Salvador. Its mission included careful documentation of abuses, and the cases denounced by Monsignor Romero in his Sunday homilies were first investigated and verified by Socorro Jurídico. Naturally such an organization was a special target for police spying and persecution. Moreover, the Externado could provide very little security for its campus, and on the morning of November 27 there was only one unarmed porter controlling the main entrance. Nevertheless, that is where the FDR leadership had arranged to meet that day.

The Truth Commission described what happened:

> The operation was carried out between 9:30 and 11:00 AM. Initially an unspecified number of men seized the porter, took him some 500 meters from the entrance and radioed to other people that they could go in.
>
> They opened the gate and let in a number of vehicles carrying people who were heavily armed with machine guns and G3 rifles. (Those rifles were the regulation weapon of the security forces at that time, having been used during the 1969 war with Honduras.) The group went swiftly to the central entrance of the main building, and placed people against the wall, ordering them to lie on the ground and close their eyes. Members of the group also stationed themselves at the entrances to the school and dealt in similar fashion with anyone who approached. ...

The men who entered the Externado were dressed in civilian clothes, although at least one of them was recognized as an agent of the national police. After taking control of the administration building and the people inside, they singled out Alvarez, Chacón and the four others, hit them and tied their hands behind their backs, then shoved them into their five vehicles and drove off. They took some two dozen other temporary hostages as well.

There were conflicting reports about the presence of uniformed troops outside the school. The government and the armed forces high command initially denied their presence, and indeed insisted that they deplored the crime and that there was no participation by any of their men. Many witnesses, however, established beyond doubt that uniformed soldiers from the treasury police and other security forces, possibly as many as 200 of them, had surrounded the school before the invasion took place. An U.S. Embassy political officer interviewed an eyewitness who described the kidnappers as "a few 'commando type' national policemen and a great many more men dressed in civilian garb." He added that some of their vehicles were recognizable military vehicles without license plates. Interestingly, this same man when questioned by the police told them he had not seen any uniformed personnel among the invaders.[29]

The Truth Commission's report notes that it would have been extremely difficult to carry out the kidnappings without the cooperation of the police and other armed forces, and states that there is "substantial evidence" that the treasury police provided external security for the crime. The Commission also found that

> It is not possible to determine precisely which public security force carried out these criminal operations. Nevertheless, the Commission considers that there is sufficient evidence to indicate that State bodies were jointly responsible for this action, which violated international human rights law.

For some hours the fate of the kidnapped men was uncertain. There were initial press reports of their "capture" (arrest) by official forces, which together with the open participation of government troops in the operation offered hope that the police might acknowledge the arrests and bring the men before a tribunal. With this in mind, other FDR activists and supporters began planning campaigns to demand their leaders' release. Ambassador White called the foreign ministry and was told that the men were in custody and would be handed over to the judicial branch for trial.[30] That same evening, however, a telephone call to local newspapers, allegedly from the "Maximiliano Hernández Martínez anti–Communist Brigade," claimed responsibility for the murder of the six and told where the bodies of four of them could be found. The deaths of the other two—Alvarez and Franco—were confirmed a few hours later. The anonymous caller also threatened with death all "communist priests" and other "traitors to the fatherland."

The kidnappers did not make a clean sweep of the Frente's directorate; they sprang their trap a little too early and several latecomers escaped. One former FDR director who survived that day, and survived the war, is Juan José Martel. Martel explained that the meeting was originally scheduled for a safe house belonging to one of the popular organizations; ironically, it was moved to the Externado because of security problems with the house. They did take certain minimal security measures, he said, because they knew in advance that the government had a plan to assassinate the directors of the FDR. "But none of us were clandestine," Martel continued. We were public figures, known. The executive committee of the FDR organized press conferences and none of us were living underground. That's why the precautions were minimum."[31]

One of those minimal security measures was that the directors didn't arrive simultaneously for any meeting or event. On November 27 the nine participants planned to arrive in groups of three with an hour's separation. José Martel was in the last group. He was going to the meeting by car, he says:

> When I was heading toward the Externado de San José, I knew that the previous group had arrived an hour or so before, and the first group would have gotten there much earlier. As I approached the Externado, moving from east to west along 25th street, I saw the military encirclement. In fact there were two circles, an outer one and an inner circle which was much tighter. The men in uniform were a mixture of national police and treasury police. As I was passing the first circle I saw the heavy military presence and managed luckily to detect the presence of the second circle from which it would be very hard to escape. I took advantage of a side street that led to what is now Juan Pablo II [avenue] and managed to evade the line of troops—because at that moment I saw that they were surrounding the Externado de San José where the comrades were meeting. I thought about what to do and decided to head for the Commission on Human Rights....

The other two men in the third and final group also escaped the death trap for similar reasons. Those in the first two groups were killed later that same day.

The capture and murder of the FDR's executive committee was a carefully planned operation, says José Martel. "Using the government intelligence apparatus they knew when and where we were meeting." In fact, the U.S. Embassy learned that one of Juan Chacón's bodyguards was an informer who had betrayed the plans for the meeting to the police. "The only thing they didn't know was that we would not all arrive at the same hour," Martel continued. "If they had known that they would have put the operation back a few hours and captured all of us, killed all of us." In interviews at the time Martel simply stated that he was late for the meeting, since he didn't want to reveal the security precaution of staggered arrivals, which was still in use.

"I remember," Martel added,

> that in the previous directors meeting, which was held at my house, we were talking informally while we ate lunch. Quique Alvarez said, "Look, some very hard times are coming." We began to talk about the [FMLN] offensive. "But," he said, "we are going to win. I don't know who is going to survive and who isn't, but those who do survive will have the obligation to tell this story, of the struggle we are making." "You're very pessimistic to be talking about death," said Leoncio Pichinte. "We're all going to survive, we are going to see the victory of the Salvadoran people and we'll be together in Plaza Libertad on the day of the victory. If we write the story we'll write it together!"
>
> We didn't know that a few days later five of the comrades at that table would be dead.

What Was It About?

Three questions seem inescapable. What were the reasons for that meeting of the FDR directors? Who were the "intellectual authors"[32] of the plan to murder them? And finally, what were their motives for committing it?

These questions are easier to ask than to answer. Juan José Martel explained that one purpose for the meeting was to learn about the problems of certain marginalized sectors of society. Indeed, one of the victims, Doroteo Hernández, was the leader of an association of slum dwellers. He was at the meeting to discuss the needs of the people in his organization, and was not a member of the FDR directorate. (He was taken and killed anyway.) Another, larger, reason for the meeting, Martel continued, was to continue working on a future negotiating proposal to try and avert the civil war which they all saw coming.

Other sources mention that the FDR was planning a press conference "in which they intended to denounce before world and local public opinion the war of extermination which the ruling military/Christian Democratic regime has launched against the Salvadoran people." (The quote is from Socorro Jurídico[33]; Pinto, Gilly, and others reported this as well.) There were also speculations that the FDR planned to announce some substantial initiative toward a negotiated settlement of the crisis. A telegram from the U.S. Embassy mentions a report that the FDR intended to declare its willingness in principle to accept mediation.[34] Another account states that the FDR directors were going to hold the conference at the Cathedral in the presence of Church officials, adding that the difficulty in assembling that group accounted for their fatal delay in leaving the Externado.

"You know what I never got information about?" asks Lino Osegueda: "*What he was going to say in that press conference!* I knew Enrique," Osegueda continued,

> and he *prepared* for a speech or a conference. He always wrote an outline of what he was going to say, what he was going to do. It might be only one page or two pages, but he developed the ideas he was going to talk about. So I thought, if they've got him, I don't know who has that paper. He didn't like to improvise; he always thought and knew well what he was going to say.[35]

The military officers who actually made the decision and gave the orders to kill have never been identified. Of course there was no real investigation by government authorities; the members of the high command did not investigate themselves or accuse each other. But neither was there an investigation by the left. Martel says that after the murders "the situation in the country became so difficult and violent that there was no possibility of starting any serious investigation to determine the intellectual authors." However, it is clear that those authors included some, if not all, of the top commanders of the "security" forces. Roberto D'Aubuisson may well have been involved since he was believed to be behind the "Maximiliano Hernández Martínez" death squad (which was composed of elements of the armed forces), but he could not have been the sole or even the main organizer of an operation of this magnitude.

As to the motives behind the crime it is only possible to speculate. Presumably its immediate and obvious consequences were foreseen and desired by the plotters. One of those consequences was closing off any remaining possibility of negotiations between the government and the left and bringing the armed confrontation closer. "It is worthwhile remembering," says the Truth Commission's report, "that on the day of the crime Foreign Minister Fidel Chávez Mena was in Washington D.C. at the General Assembly of the Organization of American States (OAS), talking with sectors of the Church and the opposition to seek a negotiated solution to the crisis." After the FDR killings the chances for such a solution became nearly zero. "Who am I going to talk to now?" asked U.S. Ambassador Robert White.

Napoleón Duarte and Colonel Majano were also out of the country at the time of the murders. In any case it is impossible to believe that Duarte was personally involved in them. He and Enrique Alvarez had been good friends in the past, and his expressed grief seems to have been sincere. As Robert White wrote after talking with him, "Duarte's sadness was not only for the death of men he had known and respected; their removal was a serious setback for the cause of a negotiated peace."[36] But that setback was presumably something the "intellectual authors" of the murders wanted to achieve.

The military plotters may have had an additional motive, to provoke the left into an unplanned reaction that would provide the excuse for a major crackdown. Pinto wrote that "The desired unorganized popular uprising, hoped for by the repressive forces so they could repeat the feat of 1932, did not happen." Juan José Martel elaborated this point:

> ... the government was trying to achieve a political objective. They knew that the FMLN was preparing an offensive and they knew that the FMLN needed some weeks more to prepare. They were looking for ways to abort that offensive and one of them was to assassinate the directors of the FDR. Not because we were involved in the military operation with which we had nothing to do, but in order to provoke the FMLN into launching the offensive immediately. That way they could precipitate an offensive with a lower level of organization and preparation, and they'd be able to break it up at the beginning. But in spite of everything, we acted with great prudence.[37]

Of course removing able and charismatic leaders of the opposition probably seemed attractive in and of itself to some in the military and the right. There was also the general motive for any act of terrorism, to frighten other potential opponents into passivity. Finally, and especially in view of the savagery with which Enrique and the others were killed, pure, irrational hatred must have motivated some of the murderers quite apart from any calculations of political advantage.

The Funerals, and Some Reactions

The FDR directors were not laid peacefully to rest after their violent deaths. On November 28 the San Salvador cathedral was damaged by a car bomb, which exploded near the entrance where the coffins of five of the victims were on display. According to the *New York Times,* "The force of the blast ripped out the front of the church and sent the caskets of the leftists flying through the cathedral. The body of one of the leftists was badly mutilated by the explosion, witnesses said."[38] At least five people were seriously hurt by the bombing for which the "Maximiliano Hernández Martínez" death squad again claimed credit.

Tony Cabrales described his own reactions on learning of Enrique's death:

> His father called me up from Guatemala — he was living in Guatemala then. The situation here was terrible! The only reason I was here — I'd sent my family away, but I never left. Why? Because everything that I had really worked hard for was here, and I couldn't just leave everything....
>
> So his father called me up and said, "Tony, go and see Duarte and tell him that we'd like to get the body out." So I called the presidential house, Duarte received me immediately; he gave me a big hug and said, "Tony, you can't imagine ... you can't imagine how sorry I am. I told him many times not to get so involved, so radical. But he just wouldn't understand." I said, "Well look, I'm here with a special plea from the family. They want to see if they can get the body out so they can have a burial." "Tell them I'll help them in everything I can," Duarte said.
>
> Later I called his father and told him. But then the extremist groups took him, and you couldn't take him away from them, you see. I remember I was the only one of his family, the only one of his friends, who had the guts.... I went down to the center of town.
>
> That particular day, after killing those people, you could just feel the atmosphere. You could cut it, it was so heavy. And I said, "I'm going to go see him, I have to see him. Unless I do I won't really believe it...."
>
> So I found out where he was and I went down there. I was in this morgue right down in the center, and the guys from El Jobo saw me and said "Come here!" And they were pulling out Chacón's coffin and Enrique's and putting them in a car. And they said, "It's too late, go to the cathedral because that's where they're taking them. So I told my driver, "Look, I don't want to arrive there in this big bullet-proof car...."
>
> Anyway I went there walking, about five blocks... I went over there and they were pulling them out of the car. And the boys from El Jobo called me and said "Over here!" Right out on the street, right out on the steps of the cathedral they opened the coffin. And I did see that it was him, without a doubt. He was all bruised, and his arm was just completely mangled. But you couldn't see otherwise, his face was intact.... They closed the top again and then put it in the cathedral.
>
> Five minutes later a bomb went off! Luckily I didn't go up the steps, I stayed down — and the bomb went off. It broke the coffin and knocked it over, they said, splintered it. So I just very rapidly walked down the street,

> got in the car and left.... Then the groups took him to another funeral home and they changed him into another coffin. I wanted to go back, but....[39]

Antonio Longhares thought Enrique's body belonged at El Jobo. He and others from the farm wanted to take it there, but that proved impossible. He finally saw the body at the Cathedral. "It was very sad having to see him like that," he says. "I would have preferred remembering him as he was. Don Enrique lives in our hearts—perhaps not everyone's because many here [at El Jobo] didn't know him, but in the hearts of all of us who did know him, who know who he was and what he did for each of us...."[40]

The actual funeral for the slain men took place on December 3, without violence despite the tension of the preceding days. The ceremony was concelebrated by 10 priests—six Salvadorans, two Canadians, a Belgian and one from the United States. The *New York Times* reported some 1500 in attendance, and added that Duarte considered this relatively small number to indicate lack of support for the left. Others stressed the climate of fear and intimidation and the heavy military and police presence in the streets, which undoubtedly kept many genuine mourners away from the funeral. An article in the *London Times* mentioned that a mile-long march from the cathedral to a western cemetery had been canceled at the last minute to avoid a confrontation with government troops.

Jorge Pinto Jr. wrote:

> Teresita and I went to the Cathedral. That half-built edifice, which had been witness to the homilies of Mons. Romero and to the Salvadoran revolutionary process, was surrounded by guerrillas. Hours earlier the colleagues of Quique Alvarez had refused to deliver the body to his family, stating that it belonged to the revolution for which he had given his life....
>
> The body of Quique Alvarez was horrifying, because the sons of bitches had taken out their fury on him: Beside the tortures they had inflicted, they had put out his eyes. His body, totally disfigured and yellowish, seemed to say that the only way to deal with the army was with another army. That the fair play of the conferences in Externado San José would be buried when they buried the bodies which symbolized the cowardice of the murderers, incapable of dealing with an armed enemy but cruel with disarmed people like Quique Alvarez, with his pure principles, his honesty, his stature—"that surprising combination of quiet passion for the revolution and the manners of the wealthy class which must have first surprised and then attracted more than one high level person who talked with him" (Adolfo Gilly).
>
> ... the murdered men were buried in the Cathedral itself, to avoid the violence of the army attacking the funeral procession the way the people were attacked when they came to say farewell to Monsignor Romero.[41]

The burial in the Cathedral was intended as a temporary measure to avoid trouble. Later, a few years after the war, the remains of all the FDR men except Enrique Alvarez were removed and reburied in San Salvador's general cemetery. The Alvarez family could have recovered Enrique's body at that time, but they decided to allow it to remain in the Cathedral crypt. It is still there at the time of writing — in the newly renovated Cathedral, not far from the tomb of Monsignor Romero. Enrique Alvarez is the only layperson buried there among two dozen or so bishops, nuns, and other figures of the Church. An ornate chandelier hangs overhead, a gift from a member of the Alvarez family.

There is no doubt that U.S. Ambassador White was disturbed and angered by the murders. White visited the Externado to offer condolences and condemn the crime. "If this slaughter doesn't stop," he said, "if those guilty of this crime are not brought to justice, it will be another serious, perhaps irreversible, setback for the cause of peace and justice in this country."[42] A similar statement was issued by the State Department in Washington, which expressed regret while carefully not blaming the Salvadoran government or armed forces in any way. Soon less equivocal messages of condolence and solidarity, some including direct condemnations of the forces behind the crime, were appearing in El Salvador and in the press around the world.

Many Salvadoran military officers, however, were clearly happy about the murder of the FDR leaders. Declassified State Department documents from early December state that "most" officers were "highly pleased" and believe that other leaders "should be eliminated in a similar fashion whenever possible." These feelings were expressed in a meeting on November 28 in the presence of the minister and subsecretary of defense, Colonels García and Carranza, both of whom "indicated that they supported this line of thinking." All the officers present "accepted as a fact that the military services were responsible for the assassination of the six FDR leaders." The (name censored) author of one telegram adds that there is another large group of officers "who reject this type of barbarism and want to participate in a professional military." A related document confirms the participation of the National Police in the kidnapping and murders, and states that such operations "were carried out by security forces without informing the junta and without regard for possible political ramifications."

At the same time, many of the officers who applauded the FDR murders hoped to participate in another coup d'etat. A third Embassy telegram reports that a member of the government junta (name censored but presumably Gutiérrez) spoke of the desire of this group to remove the junta and install a military government headed by National Guard director Eugenio

Vides Casanova. They would then be free to carry out an unrestricted "dirty war" against the left and the popular movements, the source continued, adding that the only thing holding them back was Vides Casanova's refusal to participate. Of course U.S. policy was strongly opposed to such a coup, as it had been all along. In this case the incoming Reagan team was in agreement, and warned against a coup even while promising vastly increased military aid. Probably for a combination of these reasons there was no coup; instead, there was a reorganization of the junta which had almost the same effect. Napoleón Duarte was named "president of the junta," but with no real power over the armed forces. Colonel Gutiérrez took second place on the junta; he, and not Duarte, became the military commander in chief. Colonel Majano was dismissed from the government and soon forced to leave El Salvador for good. And García continued as minister of defense.

Along with these negative developments, one moving positive reaction must be remembered. Enrique Alvarez had been separated from all of his immediate family both by distance and by their different political and social beliefs. His alienation from his father was nearly complete, and they had not met or talked for many months. Yet when Tony Cabrales spoke with Sr. Alvarez Drews at the request of the El Jobo cooperative members, his answer was immediate. "Tell them not to worry," Sr. Alvarez said to Tony, "I will carry out the intentions of my son." He kept that promise—with, Antonio Longhares believes, the strong support of Enrique's mother. It took time and many legal formalities, but with the aid of the family El Jobo did become the workers' cooperative of which Enrique dreamed.[43] It is a going concern today, with products for sale in stores throughout El Salvador. Near the farm's office there is a modest monument to the founder with this pledge from the coop's workers: "Enrique, we will persevere!"

"To Walk Like a Poor Man Among the Poor"

The poet Quijada Urías got it right; that seems to be the final word. Adolfo Gilly wrote that when Enrique Alvarez returned to El Salvador that October, he also crossed a frontier in his personal life. The frontier

> was that which separates a leader and man of politics who is on the side of the people from a leader who shares the life of the people and is recognized by the workers as one of their own....
>
> In spite of having known him for only a few months,... I am sure he was one of those who didn't ally himself with the revolution, but who one day joined it with everything he had. He was won over by the legitimate ambition to fulfill a role and to be useful in the history of his country, El Salvador,

> and by the conviction that there was no other road for that nation than that of revolution.

But deeply rooted in his character was an ideal of justice, Gilly concludes, which when it exists in a person always finds its outlet in their conduct.[44]

Bishop Medardo Gómez wrote that Enrique Alvarez was counted among the poor, because "despite being a millionaire he was a convert, a person of understanding, a person of service ready to give and to share."[45]

"There are very few human beings who cut the ground from under their own feet when they are already getting old," wrote María López Vigil in her beautiful testimonial tribute to Archbishop Oscar Romero.[46] Romero broke that "law of history," she says. He was "converted" at the age of 60 years. As he rose to a high position, he came ever nearer to the people and to reality. "In that eleventh hour he chose to open himself to compassion and to put his life at risk. And he lost his life. This does not happen to many," she wrote. But another to whom just this did happen was Enrique Alvarez Córdova. Except for the 10-year difference in their ages, López Vigil's words fit him exactly. And some of the people who contributed "pieces" to her portrait of Romero have helped with this book as well.

Monument at El Jobo

Juan José Martel had similar thoughts during

that meeting where the FDR directors were eating pupusas. "Look," he said to another comrade,

> "I'm thinking of something. You and I are in this struggle because we come from a social sector of very poor people. And really we're defending that sector of society not only as representatives but because we were born into it. But Quique Alvarez Córdova was born in a golden cradle, born with money ... and here he is with us eating this fine food!" There he was, and we were all wrapped up in a sort of love for this man who had left behind practically everything that he had to dedicate himself to a cause to which he gave his peace and ease, gave his wealth, and in the end even gave his life.[47]

Finally, Antonio Longhares, a man from a different class background who was Enrique's employee, coworker and friend, spoke about what Enrique Alvarez had given to the people of El Jobo. They inherited the material things at the farm, he says: the land, the buildings, the animals. But their spiritual legacy was most important.

> The greatest patrimony he left us is the sentiment, the ideology of helping others. That's the patrimony of always being ready to work for those who have the greatest needs. That's the reason for the slogan there [on Enrique's monument], 'We who have the most are the ones who most need to sacrifice for those who have nothing.' ... I believe that the best inheritance don Enrique left us is what we have within, in our soul, our heart and our mind. That's what I really want to say about don Enrique.[48]

Epilogue

Quique, camarada, ¡tu muerte será vengada!
(chanted at demonstrations)

The assassination of the FDR leaders ended the last hope of avoiding all-out armed conflict. In the United States the killings were denounced by the government and in the press, but not for long. Less than a week later, the horrible rape and murder by Salvadoran soldiers of four women — Jean Donovan, Dorothy Kazel, Ita Ford, and Maura Clarke — deprived the FDR crime of the limited public attention it had received. The four were religious — three nuns and a lay missionary — working with the poor and war victims; to the military, this made them "subversives." After the murders of these U.S. citizens Washington suspended aid to the Salvadoran armed forces and demanded clarification of the crime — but instead of an investigation, there was a high level cover up. Six weeks later, while Jimmy Carter was still in the White House, the aid was restored. Years later the gunmen, enlisted soldiers, were identified, tried, and spent a few years in prison, but the higher officers who gave the orders were never charged.[1]

By January 1981 the civil war was fully underway with the FMLN's ill-named "final offensive." Clearly the rebel commanders hoped to follow the Nicaraguan example by presenting the incoming Reagan administration with an irreversible revolutionary victory. The offensive was premature and did not succeed in bringing down the government, but neither was it a clear defeat for the rebels as the junta and the United States claimed. The FMLN was able to reorganize and rethink its strategy, and by the summer of that year was making substantial gains in rural areas of the country.

The Reagan team came into office with the intention of using El Salvador to demonstrate an easy victory over what it called "international communism." Ambassador White was replaced and forced out of the Foreign Service. The administration then issued "Special Report no. 80" entitled

"Communist Interference in El Salvador," intended to justify the coming U.S. intervention. The shoddy analysis and twisted conclusions of this highly publicized "white paper" were soon exposed in major U.S. media, but the policy decisions did not change. Robert White summarized the situation in the *New York Times:*

> The Reagan Administration, on taking office, called the Salvadoran revolution "a textbook case of indirect armed aggression by Communist powers" against a Latin American state. It is nothing of the sort. The revolution is home grown, and—as revolutions do—it got its arms and support wherever it could. One might, however, describe the Administration's approach to Central America as a textbook case of boldness, ignorance and ideological certitude combining to weaken the region's defenses against Communist penetration.

Unfortunately that would remain an accurate description of U.S. policy as long as Ronald Reagan was in office.[2]

Of course there really was enormous foreign intervention in El Salvador and the region, and almost all of it came from the United States. Beginning in 1981, the U.S. poured military and economic aid into El Salvador; the total would eventually reach some $6 billion—almost $1000 for each man, woman and child in the country. The armed forces were greatly expanded, trained and equipped with new weapons, and advised by U.S. officers and NCOs. The Salvadoran military had proved on its own to be capable of extreme brutality against civilians; the Sumpul River massacre was the worst example through 1980 (chapter 7). The U.S. training and weaponry, however, made things even worse. In December 1981 the "Atlacatl Battalion" committed an atrocity of historic proportions by murdering more than one thousand unarmed and defenseless women, children, and old people in and around the village called "El Mozote" in Morazán department. The killers were an elite unit recently trained and equipped by the United States, and the Atlacatl's commanding officer, Col. Domingo Monterrosa, was a favorite of the U.S. advisors. This time the lies and cover-up were orchestrated from Washington.[3]

The same year saw the end of any opposition press in El Salvador, as both *El Independiente* and *La Crónica* were bombed and shot out of existence. The U.S. government, which vehemently denounced government censorship of the anti–Sandinista paper *La Prensa* in Nicaragua, did not seem to notice the extinction of media freedom in El Salvador.

A summary of the war years is outside the scope of this book; T. S. Montgomery's second edition (really a second book) is an excellent source. It appears highly likely that without the U.S. intervention the FMLN would have gained the military advantage and been able to force a settlement in a relatively short time. The United States was able to prevent that outcome, but it could not produce victory for the government without the direct use of U.S. armed forces, a policy that would have had unacceptable political costs at home and abroad. After a decade of fighting and destruction in which about one percent of the Salvadoran people were killed and a fifth of them driven into foreign exile, the conflict was admitted to be in stalemate. With the end of the Cold War and the breakup of the Soviet Union, and with George H. W. Bush in place of Ronald Reagan in the White House, the United States government changed course. It was now prepared to accept a negotiated settlement to the war, an outcome far short of the military victory that it had been seeking. With the help of the United Nations, a peace agreement was signed on January 16, 1992 that ended the decade-long civil war and set the stage for political struggle instead.

The peace treaty was regarded as generally fair by both sides and by most outsiders. With some overstatement, U.N. Secretary General Boutros-Ghali called it "a revolution achieved by negotiations." The agreement has been carried through in large part—but not completely. The Salvadoran armed forces have been greatly reduced in size and removed from internal police duties, and special units such as the Atlacatl were abolished. The repressive "security" forces have been eliminated as agreed and replaced with a new national civilian police (the PNC). A disarmed FMLN is now the nation's leading opposition political party, and it controls the governments of the largest cities including the capital. The FMLN also has the largest single-party bloc in the national Assembly, although it is short of a majority. Election returns seem to be honestly counted, an important change from prewar years and one that holds out the possibility of reform through the ballot.

On the negative side, the majority of Salvadorans were desperately poor before the war, and they still are. ARENA, the party founded by death-squad terrorist Roberto D'Aubuisson, has held the presidency since 1989. (D'Aubuisson himself and Napoleón Duarte both died of cancer, in 1988 and 1991 respectively.) The successive ARENA governments have failed to improve the people's condition and have followed economic policies considered mistaken even by many members of the business class. The end of the war brought the sudden demobilization of thousands of combatants from both sides, and with the lack of jobs and opportunities for them in civilian life the crime rate skyrocketed beyond the ability of the new civilian police to control. For some years surveys showed that Salvadorans considered common crime, especially violent crime, to be the nation's worst problem.[4] For a small fraction of what the United States spent on the war,

FDR poster "Vivan los Heroes" (T.S. Montgomery).

it could have helped avert this situation by financing a "GI bill of rights" for the ex-combatants. Unfortunately no such positive step was taken.

There are hopeful signs as well as problems. Many refugees have returned to El Salvador and begun new lives. Some have founded villages, such as Ciudad Romero in Usulután and Segundo Montes in Morazán, which are surviving and growing. (The latter is named for one of the Jesuit professors at the UCA who were murdered in 1989 by the army.[5]) Social and political conflicts are often fierce, but today strikes and demonstrations are not met with massacres, and people arrested by the police no longer disappear or turn up at body dumps. It is possible to struggle for change openly by means of organizing (even in the rural areas), strikes, elections, and other relatively peaceful means, and thousands of Salvadorans are doing just that with energy and faith.

El Salvador still badly needs agrarian reform. But in Sonsonate, the farm cooperative "El Jobo" carries on and continues to show anyone who is watching that "another world is possible."

Appendix: Letter from the FDR[1]

[Enrique Alvarez Córdova, President]

TO THE GOVERNMENTS OF THE WORLD

At a time when international solidarity is a determining factor in the triumph of the national liberation movements of the world, and when the people of many countries are fighting to achieve independence, peace, justice and liberty, we bring you greetings in the name of the Salvadoran people and their organic and political expression, the Democratic Revolutionary Front of El Salvador (FDR).

Our people have suffered for decades the political oppression of military dictatorships which have denied them their most elemental rights as citizens. This oppression has been established on an oligarchic exploitation model and has been the cause of the hunger and misery that the majority of our people live with.

Therefore, for many years the organizations and political parties that make up the FDR have made use of all the non-violent methods available to end this situation. They have tried participating in elections and the response has been fraud and repression. They have attempted to organize unions and exercise the right to strike and the answer has been unfruitful negotiations and more repression. The attack on opposition ideas, especially in the universities and other educational institutions, has become more widespread and intensified. Finally, the religious persecution that exists was demonstrated most dramatically and bloodily by the assassination of the highest official of the Salvadoran Catholic Church, Archbishop Oscar A. Romero, precisely because he had become "the voice of those who have no voice."

In the light of this situation, in which the dictatorship has closed all democratic channels for popular expression, major sectors of the people have been forming military and mass political organizations in order to fight back against the violence perpetrated by the military governments. These organizations also constitute a way of creating a power capable of overthrowing the forces of the oligarchy in order to create a new society.

The process of popular struggle has culminated in the organic unification of all the democratic and revolutionary organizations to form a broad united front in order to overthrow the dictatorship and install a new government. The Democratic Revolutionary Front (FDR) is the manifestation of this desire for unified struggle and the expression of the most deeply felt aspirations of all the Salvadoran people. All of the organizations that make up the FDR completely agree that the only viable alternative for our country is to politically and militarily transform the present power structure and implement a democratic revolutionary government.

The FDR has committed itself before the Salvadoran people and before all free people of the world to create and develop a national government that is both anti-oligarchic and anti-imperialist and whose policy is based on: the broadest pluralistic participation of the people in the management of the government, the strict respect of human rights, the principle of self-determination and equal status for all nations and the principle of non-alignment. A mixed economy that protects small and medium-sized businesses will be formed to replace the economic power of the oligarchy and new regulations will be established concerning foreign investments that will take the national interest more into account.

The current alternative, implemented by the military government with the determined aid of the reactionary forces of the U.S. government, is lacking in any social base and only manages to sustain itself through the repression of the civil population and the popular organizations. In practice, this repressive policy amounts to no less than genocide. Therefore, the "reforms" that have been decreed haven't favored the people but rather have become methods of political and military control in the slaughter that is being carried out by what amounts to an occupying army. Thousands of peasants and small-town dwellers have seen the necessity to abandon their homes and flee to the cities or neighboring countries in order to save their lives in the face of the terror unleashed by the army. This has created a serious refugee problem whose dimensions continue to expand.

In the face of this extermination policy, the people have responded by augmenting their struggle through continued actions on the part of the worker and peasant movement. The people have also responded by strengthening the popular army and its militias, which carry out armed actions throughout the territory of El Salvador. These actions are aimed at being the final blows to a government that is steadily collapsing day by day.

The present Christian Democratic/military Junta is not only the object of the massive repudiation of the Salvadoran people, but also of other peoples of the continent and of the democratic and progressive governments of the world that have offered solidarity and recognition to the FDR. The dictatorship that oppresses our people has only been able to find support from governments of the United States, Venezuela, Israel, and military dictatorships of the continent. These governments, within the framework of an incorrect and aggressive policy of "national security," have revived elements of the cold war in order to justify their aid to the bloodiest dictatorship in Salvadoran history.

The millions in military aid that the U.S. government gives to the Junta, its open as well as covert participation through unconditional alliances, and the constant threat of direct military intervention in El Salvador, are all elements that form a policy of aggression against a small nation that is struggling for self-determination. We are sure that the intervention on the parts of the U.S., Venezuelan, and Israeli governments will not succeed in destroying the democratic-revolutionary movement. It does, however, constitute a threat to the peace of the region and denies to the Salvadoran people the right to independence that the United Nations Charter recognizes as the right of all peoples.

We know that your government is humanitarian and has a policy that is respectful of human rights, against imperialist interventionism, and in favor of the people's right to self-determination. Therefore, in the name of the human principles consecrated by the United Nations, and in the face of the suffering and struggle of all the Salvadoran people, we ask your enlightened government to give us the following support:

1. Denounce the human rights violations that are being systematically practiced by the military forces in El Salvador and demand respect for human rights through international solidarity.
2. Inform the world's conscience of the grave problem constituted by the thousands of refugees and take international action to alleviate their suffering.
3. Condemn the military and political intervention of the U.S. government and its allies, and demand respect for national independence.
4. Condemn the present government junta for its repressive, anti-human, and anti-popular policy.
5. Recognize the FDR as the authentic expression of the Salvadoran people and as the only alternative to achieve peace and the just development of Salvadoran society.

The Salvadoran people did not look for war; it was imposed on them.

The Salvadoran people love life and love freedom and therefore want to reduce the social cost of the just war that will free them.

The Salvadoran people have earned the right to forge their own destiny.

We trust in the cause of our people, which is the cause of all Central America and of all the free people and governments of the world. It deserves the broadest understanding and solidarity possible from your people and your government.

CON LA UNIDAD HACIA LA VICTORIA

Enrique Alvarez Córdova

Notes

Preface

1. The story of the "fourteen families" is widely known, but its exact origin is hard to pin down. One account which seems credible was given by the Salvadoran banker Luis Escalante Arce in his book *Sacrificios Humanos Contra Derechos Humanos,* pages 223–225: "A certain minister of economy during the presidential period 1950–1956 approached a reporter from *Time* magazine at the inauguration of a hotel in San Salvador. With a noted alcoholic euphoria, the minister declared that just as France had been managed by 80 families, so El Salvador was run by its fourteen.... The myth of the fourteen [families] has been repeated in many countries, evidence of the widespread readership of the magazine *Time.*"

Sr. Escalente speculates on the strange choice of the number 14 and comments that 20 would have been a more common and plausible figure. Webre in his book on the Christian Democratic Party mentions 23 surnames which "any list would necessarily include"; "Alvarez" is among them.

2. Bonner, *Weakness and Deceit,* page 100. This book mentions Enrique Alvarez in many places. Bonner also published an informative obituary article in the *New York Times* shortly after Enrique's death: "In El Salvador, the Unmaking of an Oligarch," December 14, 1980.

3. The "eye of the needle" verse has been explained and interpreted in many ways. There are two "technical" explanations, which have been confirmed to me by a colleague who is a biblical scholar. One states that in the Aramaic text of the gospel the word "camel" is not found; instead the corresponding term means "cable" or "rope." The second explanation is that the "eye of the needle" itself refers to a narrow gate in the walls of Jerusalem through which an actual camel might squeeze with difficulty, especially if it were unloaded. Other explanations such as that of Bishop Gómez (see the following note) rely on reinterpretation of what is meant by "a rich man."

While these theories appear seem to be inconsistent making it difficult to adopt more than one of them, they all have the same effect: the verse means that although it is *difficult* for a wealthy person to "enter the kingdom of heaven," it is not absolutely impossible.

4. Medardo Ernesto Gómez, *Latinoamerica: Testimonio de Vida y Esperanza,* pages 287–288.

5. Monsignor Urioste told me this during an interview in 1996 in San Salvador. He has said much the same thing to others and it has been widely quoted.

6. See for example Claribel Alegría, *No me agarran viva* (bibliography).

Prologue

1. Frank McNeil, *War and Peace in Central America,* page 107.

2. These communiqués were published in the Salvadoran daily press on November 28 and 29, 1980. All three were reprinted in the journal *Estudios Centroamericanos (ECA),* no. 386 (December 1980), along with statements issued about the same date from death-squad leader Roberto D'Aubuisson, from the Democratic Revolutionary Front, and from the newly-unified guerrilla front, the FMLN.

3. *Duarte: My Story,* page 107.

4. *NYT* Sunday magazine, July 18, 1982.

5. November 30, 1980, page 1.

6. *Estudios Centroamericanos (ECA),* March 1993, page 210. This issue reprints the text of the Commission's report, which is also available from the U.N. and elsewhere.

Chapter 1

1. No bullet holes were in sight in 1995 for the hotel has been remodeled — and renamed; it used to be the Sheraton. On January 4, 1981 José Rodolfo Viera, the head of the Salvadoran agrarian reform institute, was lunching there with two U.S. advisors. All three were shot and killed at their restaurant table by Salvadoran soldiers. The shooters, two enlisted men, were eventually convicted and sentenced to prison, only to be freed by an amnesty in 1987. The identity of the officers who ordered the murders is well known but they have never been put on trial.

2. It is customary for the father's name to appear before the mother's; thus Alvarez was Emilio's father's surname and Lalinde his mother's name — that is, the surname of *her* father. "Emilio Alvarez Lalinde" would be called "Señor Alvarez" (or Doctor Alvarez), not Señor Lalinde. On marriage, a woman usually keeps her name but adds "de [husband's surname]."

3. From the *Diccionario Histórico Enciclopédico de la República de El Salvador,* Miguel Angel García, vol. 1, quoted in *Los Alvarez: Recuerdos de una Familia.*

4. *Los Alvarez,* especially "Memorias de Carlos Alvarez Angel," written in 1951.

5. *Los Alvarez,* page 5. "Pacho" is a common nickname for Francisco.

6. Some newspaper accounts credit Emilio and Jaime with originating coffee planting on that volcano; other stories suggest that coffee cultivation there began earlier and the brothers expanded and improved the production.

7. The eldest was Carlos, who later wrote "Memorias de Carlos Alvarez Angel" from which much of this family history is derived. "Memorias" states that Rafael joined the Liberal forces in 1882, but 1884 is more likely since historical references place the rebellion in 1884–85.

8. In "Memorias" Carlos says he has no recollection of this part of the journey. Since La Libertad is on the Pacific the family had to cross the Isthmus, or else go around Cape Horn which would have been far longer in time as well as distance. The Panama Canal was only a dream at this time but the Panama railroad was in operation, and that was probably their route. This is speculation, however.

9. "Memorias," page 51.

10. See José F. Figeac, *Recordatorio Histórico de la República de El Salvador* (San Salvador, 1934). This account at least acquits Carlos Ezeta of conspiring to murder his predecessor, stating that General Menéndez, sword in hand, was rushing out of his house to confront the pro–Ezeta uprising when he suffered a fatal heart attack.

11. Roque Dalton, *Miguel Mármol,* pages 60–63. This book is an oral history of the life of a revolutionary, as recorded by Dalton in the 1960s. Mármol lived to the age of 87 despite (among other things) facing a firing squad during the great massacre of 1932, and he is an invaluable witness to history as seen from below.

12. "Memorias," page 61.

13. The name *Izote* doesn't appear in English dictionaries. A dictionary published in Barcelona (which I purchased in Mexico) says that it is a garden plant of the Yucca family, reaching four meters in height and with white flowers. It is found in Central America and Mexico, and is the "national flower" of El Salvador.

14. Roque Dalton's satirical sketch "Fin de siècle" comments on this orchestra and its director. See *Las Historias Prohibidas del Pulgarcito, pages* 75–78. The orchestra has also been called "La Banda de los Supremos Poderes."

15. In November 1944 *The National Geographic Magazine* offered an impressive description and many photos of El Molino (pages 575–608). The article's author, Luis Marden, notes that "The Alvarez family, proprietors of El Molino, includes seven members of the National Geographic Society." Marden views Salvadoran society through rose-colored glasses.

16. Carlos Alvarez, "Memorias," page 130. Julia Angel died in 1926.

17. The Liberal/Conservative rivalry was common to the whole of Central America. For an accessible general history of the region including the struggles over unification, see Woodward, *Central America: A Nation Divided,* chapters 4–6.

18. After a failed attempt in Mexico, Walker and a group of American mercenary soldiers intervened in Nicaragua in 1855 to aid the Liberal side in that country's civil conflicts. They enjoyed initial success, and Walker even made himself president of Nicaragua where among other "reforms" he legalized slavery, hoping to gain Southern support for Nicaragua's annexation to the United States. Soon, however, Walker incurred the enmity of Cornelius Vanderbilt whose interests he threatened; in addition, the specter of Yankee imperialism induced all the Central American republics to send forces to resist Walker's occupation. He was driven out of Nicaragua in 1857. Walker kept on trying, but he returned to the region once too often and was executed in Honduras in 1860. See for example A.H.Z. Carr, *The World and William Walker* [New York: Harper & Row, 1963]. A feature film about these adventures, *Walker,* appeared in 1987 with Ed Harris in the title role.

19. Quoted in David Browning, *El Salvador: Landscape and Society*, page 208.

20. See note 1 of the Preface.

21. *Bohemia Libre*, June 25, 1961, pages 29 and 67. (Reproduced in *Los Alvarez*, page 395.) *Bohemia Libre* was published by Cuban exiles in Caracas, Venezuela beginning in 1960. It was intended to continue the popular weekly magazine *Bohemia* which had been published in Cuba since 1908, and if possible to supplant the latter which continued to be published in Havana after the revolution. Anti-communism in general, and opposition to the Cuban revolution in particular, were dominant themes in *Bohemia Libre* which is reported to have been financed by the C.I.A.

22. Interview with Mauricio Alvarez Geoffroy, San Salvador, March 1999.

23. Claribel Alegría, private communication.

24. Fr. José Inocencio Alas, *Iglesia, Tierra y Lucha Campesina*, pages 59–60.

25. During his two years in office (he was murdered in 1913) President Araujo introduced a number of other progressive measures such as worker's compensation for farm laborers and the abolition of debtors' prison. Miguel Mármol described the National Guard this way: "In the beginning it played a magnificent role in cleaning up society, it was on the front lines in the nationwide fight against delinquency... It was during the time of the Meléndez-Quiñónez dynasty [1913–1927] that the government bestowed on the National Guard the character it still has today, that of a terrorist, criminal body that represses political activity" (op. cit., page 65). For more on the role of the *Guardia Nacional* see Tom Buckley, *Violent Neighbors*, page 125.

26. Claribel Alegría and Darwin Flakoll, *Ashes of Izalco*, page 93. Alegría is a Salvadoran who grew up in Santa Ana; Flakoll, her husband and translator, is a North American. The date of the imaginary conversation was November 1931. According to a communication from the author, "don Jaime" who owns the landscape through which Frank and Eduardo are traveling is modeled on Carlos Alvarez.

27. T. P. Anderson, *Matanza*, page 24.

28. Paige, "Coffee and Power in El Salvador," page 29.

Chapter 2

1. Interview with Antonio Cabrales, San Salvador, 1996.

2. Anderson, *Matanza*, page 22. Much of the information in this chapter about the events of 1931–32 is derived from this excellent study. Miguel Mármol's oral history memoir gives a perspective from the left as does the biography of Communist leader Farabundo Martí by Jorge Arias Gómez; both Mármol and Martí were leaders in organizing the rebellion. Recent work, especially Erick Ching's investigation in the archives of the Comintern, helps us better understand the tragedy of 1932. Finally, two fictional accounts describe parts of the uprising and it's aftermath: Alegría and Flakoll in *Ashes of Izalco*, and Benitez in *Bitter Grounds*.

3. Roque Dalton, *Miguel Mármol*, page 223.

4. Quoted in *Matanza*, pages 113–114.

5. *Matanza*, page 36.

6. Masferrer, "El Mínimum Vital," *Ensayos*, pages 61–83.

7. Figures from *Diario Latino*, January 15, 1931, quoted in *Matanza*, page 69.

8. Hernández Martínez is commonly referred to as "General Martínez" rather than the more usual "General Hernández," reportedly because his parents were not married and the father did not officially give his name to the son.

9. Figures from Arias Gómez, *Farabundo Martí* (second edition), page 214.

10. The coup was supposedly planned by a group of junior officers and NCOs. Anderson explains that "At the close of the coup, the young men who had ostensibly planned it had given away to more experienced officers. The real leaders of the junta were now two colonels..." and behind them stood a leading banker. (See *Matanza*, chapter 4, especially *pages* 86–87.) These comments, written around 1970 in reference to 1931, foreshadow events of 1979 with remarkable accuracy.

11. It is natural to ask whether Martínez was involved in plotting the coup from which he so promptly benefited. The evidence is inconclusive but suggests that he did not take a direct part, although he undoubtedly knew in general terms that a coup was being planned. Araujo, however, stated in an interview in 1968 that he had always believed that Martínez led the conspiracy against him. (See *Matanza*, chapter 4, and Arias Gómez, *Farabundo Martí*, chapter 16.)

12. Arias Gomez, *Farabundo Martí*, pages 23, 26.

13. ibid, pages 29 and 27.

14. See Anderson, *Matanza*, pages 51–52, for an account of that meeting and more about Martí's several exiles.

15. Arias Gomez, *Farabundo Martí*, pages 132–133. The author credits the story of the air raid and the famous quote to a conversation with Miguel Mármol.

16. Their contact was through the "Secretariat of the Caribbean," which had its headquarters in New York. (Anderson, *Matanza*, page 42.)
17. These numbers are from Erik Ching (see note 21 below) who states that the maximum of 400 members was reached in late 1931.
18. Dalton, *Miguel Mármol*, pages 215–217.
19. Anderson, *Matanza*, page 109.
20. Dalton, *Miguel Mármol*, page 229.
21. This synthesis of events is largely based on the cited accounts of Anderson, Mármol and Arias Gómez. Recently Erik Ching has made interesting contributions using material not available to Anderson. Ching visited Moscow in 1994 and was able to study Comintern files relating to El Salvador including periodic reports on activities from the PCS. See his articles cited in the bibliography and a summary published in the Salvadoran press: "Por qué fracasó la rebellión del 32?" (*El Diario de Hoy*, February 21, 1999, historical supplement pages 8 and 9.) His principal finding was roughly that the Salvadoran Communist Party was a factor but not the prime mover of the rebellion, which was largely an "autonomous movement of the western campesinos." The article also describes some of the internal weaknesses of the Party.
22. Dalton, *Miguel Mármol*, pages 241–242.
23. *Matanza*, pages 175–176.
24. Alegría and Flakoll in *Ashes of Izalco* present a novelized, but not fictitious, account of parts of the rebellion and of the *matanza*, describing graphically how troops massacred hundreds of peasants assembled in the central square of one of the rebellious villages. Another fictional account of the 1932 events and of subsequent decades of Salvadoran history is the panoramic novel by Sandra Benítez, *Bitter Grounds* (see bibliography).
25. *Matanza*, page 176.
26. A recent (1998) study by Ching and Tilley "challenges the widely held belief" that the *matanza* "marked the demise of Indian ethnic identity." The authors show that the percentage of Indians in the population remained steady for some time, and even that their basic social institutions survived.
27. *Miguel Mármol*, pages 304–305.
28. Quoted in Sandra Boschetto-Sandoval and Marcía Phillips McGowan, editors, *Claribel Alegría and Central American Literature*, Ohio University Center for International Studies, Latin American Series No. 21, 1994, page 229. A short section from *Ashes of Izalco* was included in Chapter 1; see note 26 of that chapter. The novel's hero "Frank" was a witness to the rebellion and subsequent massacre of Indian campesinos in and near the town of Izalco.
29. *Matanza*, page 205.
30. Anderson, *The War of the Dispossessed*, page 25.
31. Interview with Coralia Godoy and Ana María Godoy, San Salvador, 1996. The sisters were neighbors and friends of Enrique Alvarez since early childhood.
32. Quoted in Pinto, *El Grito del Más Pequeño*, page 294.
33. Cabrales, *op cit*. Other family friends also mentioned this story.
34. Interview with Coralia and Ana María Godoy, *op cit*.
35. Letters to the author from Haven Whiteside and Alan Bell, Hackley School class of 1948.
36. *The Hilltop*, Hackley School Yearbook, 1948. The distinctions such as "Best Dresser," etc., were each awarded to two boys in the senior class.
37. Letter from Freeman Day, Jr., Hackley class of 1948.
38. Telephone conversation with Jerry Nolan, April 1997; letter from F.R. Schroeder Jr., May 1997; conversation with Jerry Nolan, April 2000.
39. *Los Alvarez*, page 438.
40. Interview with Mr. and Mrs. Edgar, 1997.
41. Leon Pierce, telephone conversation, June 2000.
42. As a freshman Enrique failed precalculus mathematics, but (from the author's point of view) he partially redeemed himself as a sophomore with a B in elementary statistics.
43. Letter from Carl Fleming, June 2000.
44. Patricia Parkman, *Nonviolent Insurrection in El Salvador*, page 44.
45. William Khrem, *Democracies and Tyrannies*, page 15. (English edition.)
46. Dalton, *Miguel Mármol*, page 419.
47. One of those arrested was Enrique's uncle Roberto Alvarez Drews. An editorial lamenting Roberto's death appeared in *El Diario de Hoy* on March 23, 1957. It states that he took a strong part in the rebellion, was jailed after the failure of the military coup, and was mistreated in prison with lasting damage to his health. The editorial adds that Roberto was nevertheless among the organizers of the subsequent general strike which led to the ouster of Martínez.
48. Interview in Guatemalan press, May 12, 1944, quoted in Parkman, *Nonviolent Insurrection*, page 80. It cannot be forgotten that Martínez had no difficulty accepting and ordering the mass killing of women and children in 1932.

Chapter 3

1. Letter from Hotel Plaza-Athenee, Paris, to Enrique Restrepo in San Salvador (hand written in Spanish), copy courtesy of Sr. Restrepo.

2. Interview with Ana del Carmen Alvarez (no relation) at the UCA, November 1996.

3. Interview with Coralia and Ana Maria Godoy, December 1996.

4. Interview with Antonio Cabrales, San Salvador, December 1996.

5. Interview with Mauricio Alvarez Geoffroy, San Salvador, March 1999. It was Mauricio who gave me a copy of the family history *Los Alvarez,* which he, together with his brother Emilio Alvarez, compiled for the 1995 family reunion. This history, and in particular the memoir by their grandfather Carlos Alvarez Angel, is the basis for much of chapter 1 of this book.

6. *New York Times,* July 24, 1955.

7. This comment, including the emphasis, is from an email sent me by Maribel's Los Angeles classmate Joy Bartula Wyse.

8. This was not Maribel's fault, for the script was pretty silly. The film is described in Emilio García Riera, *Historia Documental del Cine Mexicano* (Universidad de Guadalajara, Mexico, 1993), volume 8, pages 138–140, which includes a photo of Maribel in her role.

9. From "Pensando en Nicaragua" by Ignacio Briones Torres, 9/23/99, posted on the internet.

10. Interview with Antonio Cabrales, San Salvador, November 1997.

11. Interview with Lino Osegueda, San Salvador, November 1997.

12. Interview with Ernesto Alvarez, New York, May 1999.

13. *Duarte: My Story,* pages 42–43. Duarte played with and coached the Arco Iris team which was several times the national champion, and later in the 1950s he also helped coach the Salvadoran national team. El Salvador won the Central American championship in 1959, but of course was never the champion of all Latin America.

14. Interview with Rolando Duarte, San Salvador, November 2000.

15. Cabrales, op. cit.

16. Rafael Ruiz Izaguirre, *La Conexión Gringa,* page 80. Dr. Ruiz told me that he had talked with several surviving members of the Arco Iris team while writing the novel.

17. Cabrales, op. cit.

18. *El Diario de Hoy,* San Salvador, September 15, 1955, page 22.

19. *La Prensa Gráfica,* September 22, 1955, page 15. The Salvadoran team tied Guatemala for second place behind Panama, but since the Salvadoran players were not able to stay for an extra game to break the tie, the runner-up position was awarded to Guatemala.

20. *XI Campeonato Centroamericano de polo,* program, March 20–25, 1966, San Salvador. This program includes a brief history of polo in El Salvador, including a resume of the ten previous tournaments. (Courtesy of Mauricio Alvarez.)

21. Cabrales, op cit. The annual tournaments were not the only occasions for polo. For example in 1957 Enrique played with the team from "Club de Equitación y Polo" which on March 4 defeated "Elgin" from Guatemala by 10 to 3. Enrique scored 3 goals, and his cousin Jaime Alvarez scored one as well.

22. Cabrales, op. cit.

23. For example, on March 23 *La Prensa Gráfica* published an editorial headed "Irresponsible Youth." It spoke entirely in generalities, lamenting that "youths of good families" brought shame on their parents, etc. The editorial mentioned drunken driving as one of the evils involved, but there were no names and no mention of any form of sex.

24. *ECA* 1957, pages 503, 542 and 563. The Jesuit Universidad Centroamericana (UCA) was founded in 1966 and soon took over as the publisher of *ECA.* From that time the politics of the journal changed, and it would no longer celebrate right-wing victories such as the CIA coup that overthrew the elected government of Guatemala in 1954.

25. *La Conexión Gringa,* page 80–81.

26. Antonio Cabrales interview, note 4. Cabrales could have included the fourth person present, Jorge Pinto Jr., as another who would contribute to his country's history. Rolando Duarte (note 14) told me that Enrique also fought the captain of the Buitres team, but he didn't give details.

27. In my second conversation with Tony Cabrales, I mentioned having talked with a number of Enrique's Hackley School classmates. Tony asked me whether any of them had mentioned anything about homosexuality, and I assured him that they had not. Tony then told me that he had been Enrique's sports and locker-room companion over many years and had never seen anything detectably gay in his behaviour. Rolando Duarte, who also was Enrique's companion in sports, said much the same thing.

28. Jorge Pinto, *El Grito del Más Pequeño,* page 23. This book is my main source for the account of Pinto's youth up to 1957, but it does not mention the scandal or its aftermath.

29. The capucha is a rubber hood covering the victim's head and closed tightly around the

neck to bring on asphixiation. Often it was filled with lime or some other noxious substance. This torture method was described in painful detail in 1952 by the radical labor leader (later an FMLN commander) Salvador Cayetano Carpio from personal experience; see his *Secuestro y capucha en un país del 'mundo libre,'* San Salvador (UCA Editores), 1979.

30. Unfortunately I have seen only a few issues of the paper. A complete file is hard to find, and apparently no library in El Salvador retains back volumes of *El Independiente*. Having copies in one's home during the late 1970s and 1980s would have been extremely dangerous in case of a search.

31. *El Machete* seems to have been an occasional back-page section of *El Independiente* in its early years, devoted to muck-raking and sensation of a less substantial nature than the main paper. I have not been able to see the critical issue but it was described to me by someone who did see it.

32. *El Grito del Más Pequeño,* page 290.

33. The name refers to a kind of tree which grew near the farm. The farm includes another property called "El Polvón" some 20 miles away, which also forms part of the cooperative.

34. Interview with Lino Osegueda at El Jobo near Sonsonate, December 1996.

35. Cabrales interview, note 4.

36. Rollie Henkes, "Pastoreo Intensivo." *Agricultura de las Americas,* January, 1970, pages 20–23 plus the cover.

37. Interview, San Salvador, December 1999, in the offices of "Industrias Víctor."

38. The 2004 winner, Carlos Avalos, was born in 1980 a few months before the death of Enrique Alvarez.

39. Interview with Orlando Mungía, New York, January 1997. I met him through an amazing coincidence. I had telephoned the offices of NACLA in New York to ask about material in their files relating to Enrique Alvarez. A couple of days later I received a fax from the person there who had talked with me. "I couldn't find much about Alvarez in the files," he said, "but our UPS guy remembers him very well!" The "UPS guy" was Orlando Mungía.

40. Tony Cabrales first mentioned this incident to me. The story as told here is from my interview with Víctor Villeda in December 1999.

41. This was probably a small piece of land on the coast near Acajutla. El Jobo and the companion farm "El Polvón" are between Sonsonate and the port of Acajutla, but neither is near the coast.

42. Interview with Antonio Cabrales, San Salvador, December 1996.

43. Taped interview (English) with Enrique Alvarez from 1980; see note 10, Chapter 5.

44. Lino Osegueda, 1996, op. cit.

45. Interview with Damián Alegría, San Salvador, March 1999.

46. Enrique Alvarez, op cit.

47. Much of this summary is based on Russell, *El Salvador in Crisis*, chapter 4. The quote is on page 43. Another helpful source is Baloyra, *El Salvador in Transition*, chapter 3.

48. Russell, ibid.

49. "Human rights in Nicaragua, Guatemala, and El Salvador: Implications for U.S. policy," U.S. House of Representatives committee hearings, June 8 and 9, 1976, pages 31-34. This oral testimony is followed by Dr. Castillo's written statement on pages 35–49 with many details of police and National Guard abuses since 1960.

Castillo testified that while he was a member of the short-lived junta, he was visited by the U.S. chargé d'affaires accompanied by a wealthy and conservative Salvadoran, Ricardo Quiñones. The official told Castillo that "the U.S. Embassy did not agree with the holding of a free election and that he supposed that [the junta's members] were not talking seriously." The Embassy would agree to an election with two candidates that it had previously approved, he added. Castillo says he rejected this "advice" whereupon "Mr. Quiñonez, unable to contain his anger, turned to the chargé d'affaires and said: 'You see, they are Communists. We have to go ahead.'"

On another occasion the chargé "with no courtesy whatever" said to Castillo (who was also minister of education), "I guess you don't really want to go ahead with those plans to teach the people how to read and educate them." Castillo replied that they did intend to go ahead. It's possible that the U.S. objected to the planned literacy campaign because it resembled the one carried out in Cuba after the revolution there.

Dr. Castillo's testimony on this matter concludes that "The participation of U.S. diplomatic and military representatives [in the January coup] was at that time evident and open."

50. *Duarte: My Story*, chapter 2. The authoritative account of the PDC's early years is Webre, *José Napoleón Duarte and the Christian Democratic Party in Salvadoran Politics, 1960–1972.*

51. The PAR had been an opposition party of the moderate right. An internal struggle in 1964 produced a split, and the winning faction, which took control of the party's name and organization, gave it a new, leftist orientation. It was this "new" party that nominated Castillo.

52. In 1939 or 1940 Nicaraguan dictator

Anastasio Somoza García made a state visit to Washington. When he left, President Franklin Roosevelt is said to have commented, "He's a son of a bitch, but he's our son of a bitch!" Chele Medrano was our terrorist in El Salvador.

53. The main source for these paragraphs is Allan Nairn's 1984 article "Behind the Death Squads"; another useful account can be found in Pearce, *Promised Land*, chapter 3. Medrano himself boasted of his role on camera in a film entitled *The Houses are Full of Smoke*.

54. Inocensio Alas, *Iglesia, Tierra y Lucha Campesina: Suchitoto, El Salvador, 1968–1977*, page 134. The chapter contains more details about the founding of ORDEN and how it functioned, including its responsibility for the 1970 kidnapping and near murder of Alas himself.

Chapter 4

1. *Witness to War*, page 247.

2. See chapter 1. Many works of both fiction and nonfiction describe and sometimes explain the often-miserable living conditions of Salvadoran campesinos. Chapters 1 and 2 of Pearce, *Promised Land*, offer a good summary.

3. *La Universidad*, January-February 1970, year 95 of publication. This entire issue is devoted to the Agrarian Reform Congress and contains the texts of papers presented there.

4. Quoted in White, *El Salvador*, page 212.

5. *La Universidad*, Jan/Feb 1970, page 3 (Introduction).

6. Ibid, pages 7–15, "Situación Agraria en El Salvador" (paper presented by UES).

7. Ibid, pages 20–21, "On the injustice of the present form of land holding" by Mons. Dr. Ricardo Urioste and David Alvarado of the Curia Metropolitana.

8. In the United States the president's cabinet is organized into "departments" which are headed by "secretaries." The corresponding term in Spanish is *ministerio* or ministry, and the chief, of course, is called the "minister." Curiously, in El Salvador (at least) the minister's highest-ranking subordinate is called the *subsecretario* or undersecretary. I have used the English terms ministry and (cabinet) department interchangably, but the reader should note that *departamento* in El Salvador is the word for the 14 provinces or states into which the nation's territory is divided.

9. The kidnapping is described briefly by Montgomery (1982), pages 97–98, and in much greater detail by Father Alas himself in chapter 6 of his memoir *Iglesia, Tierra y Lucha Campesina*. The latter also discusses the Agrarian Reform Congress at some length.

10. Interview with Lino Osegueda, San Salvador, August 2002.

11. Interview with Lino Osegueda, December 1996.

12. Ibid.

13. For background and a description of the war see Thomas Anderson, *The War of the Dispossessed*.

14. After the visiting players were treated to sleepless nights in each other's capitals due to "serenades" by street crowds, and the referees had received credible threats against their continued good health, each team won on its home field—the Hondurans by 1–0 in Tegucigalpa and the Salvadorans 3–0 in San Salvador. Fans attending these games from the rival nation were harassed as well, and tempers ran high. The deciding third match was wisely played on neutral territory in Mexico City, and El Salvador won it by a score of 3–2 on June 26. In September, after the war, El Salvador's team beat Haiti and succeeded in qualifying for the World Cup to be held in Mexico in 1970. Once there, however, the Salvadorans lost all three games of the opening round to Belgium, Mexico, and the USSR, and went home disappointed after having yielded 9 goals and scored none.

15. *The War of the Disposessed*, pages 126–127. Other casualty estimates are higher. The school textbook *Historia de El Salvador*, for example, suggests that the dead from the war numbered some 4000 (vol. II, page 228).

16. *Duarte: My Story*, pages 65–66.

17. Ibid, page 66. To U.S. citizens all this should sound very familiar.

18. Quoted in *La Prensa Gráfica*, October 16, 1969, page 23.

19. Interview with Lino Osegueda, December 1996. (As the father of three boys, I can testify that brothers do not always get along without friction.)

20. Lino Osegueda interview, August 2002. Osegueda explained that the subsidy was used to pay the salaries of staff who were often the wives or daughters of wealthy growers, which Enrique considered unjustified. Some members of the association considered him a 'traitor' for this action.

21. Interview with Lino Osegueda, San Salvador, November 1997.

22. Report of the Ministry of Agriculture (MAG) for July 1, 1971 to June 30, 1972.

23. Lino Osegueda, op. cit.

24. The laws were Decrees 153 and 214, dated 11/11/70 and 1/20/71 respectively. "Zapotitán" was located in the departments of Sonsonate, La Libertad, and Santa Ana. For a

description of the region and previous land distribution efforts there, see Browning, *El Salvador: Landscape and Society*, pages 277–280.

25. "Ley de Avenamiento y Riego," *ECA*, October/November 1970, pages 529–531.

26. "La congelación de tierras y la reforma agraria," *ECA*, December 1979, pages 1079–1081.

27. Report of the Ministry of Agriculture (MAG) for July 1, 1970 to June 30, 1971, page 1.

28. Interview with Lino Osegueda, San Salvador, August 2002.

29. Interview with Lino Osegueda, San Salvador, November 1997.

30. This is Lino Osegueda's account. In *The War of the Disposessed*, Anderson says in contrast that "the ruling clique of army officers ... denied Galindo Pohl the nomination [of the PCN] for the presidency in the contest of 1972, preferring to stick with a military man" (page 142).

31. *Duarte: My Story*, pages 73–74. "The military officers always suspected anyone advocating change of being a Communist," Duarte continues. "To them, Franklin D. Roosevelt or Mahatma Gandhi would have been a Communist." Duarte complains that he was frequently called a Communist by the Right, while in reality he always "opposed the Communist philosophy and presented a democratic alternative." The paradox disappears when we realize that, for the Salvadoran ruling class, advocating social change was the *definition* of "communism"; no connection with the Soviet Union or even with socialist ideas was necessary. Peasant cooperatives, for example, and Archbishop Romero's concern for human rights, were "communist" in this sense. Of course this attitude was not confined to El Salvador.

32. Ibid, page 75.

33. I recall wondering when I first learned about this episode how the Salvadoran people must have felt when they had a president imposed on them who was not legitimately elected. Since November 2000, of course, I know.

34. Alas, op cit, page 165.

35. Interview with Salvador Sánchez Serén, San Salvador, November 2000.

36. Speech of Col. Armando Molina announcing the Cerrón Grande project, August 14, 1972, quoted in Alas, *Iglesia, Tierra y Lucha Campesina*, pages 172–174.

37. Alas, op cit, pages 186–187.

38. Op cit., page 188. Also private communication from Inocencio Alas.

39. *ECA*, September 1973, pages 553–555.

40. Interview with Lino Osegueda, San Salvador, November 1997.

41. These figures from the Salvadoran government were quoted by Fr. Ignacio Ellacuría in an article in the special issue of *ECA*. The article was reprinted in *Veinte años de historia en El Salvador (1969–1989), Escritos politicos, I*, pages 587–627. (San Salvador: UCA Editores, 1993). The figures cited are on page 597.

42. Quoted in *Veinte años de historia en El Salvador (1969–1989)*, page 652.

43. Reprinted in *Veinte años de historia en El Salvador (1969–1989)*, pages 649–656. Note that the title of this article differs by only one letter from the more common Spanish phrase "A sus órdenes, mi capitán." Publication of the article resulted in reprisals against the university, including loss of government funds and five bomb explosions on the campus. Fr. Ellacuría was the rector of the UCA in 1989 when he was murdered, along with five fellow priests/professors plus their housekeeper and her teenage daughter, by an elite, U.S. trained unit of the Salvadoran army.

44. Propaganda, capital flight and litigation were among the tactics the oligarchy used to defeat the pilot reform project, but there may have been more. Tommie Sue Montgomery was told by an unnamed but presumably credible informant that Defense Minister and future president Carlos Humberto Romero threatened President Molina with a coup if the "transformation" went forward. At this point, Molina surrendered. (*Revolution in El Savador: Origins and Evolution*, page 90.)

45. José Inocencio Alas, *Iglesia, Tierra y Lucha Campesina*, page 77. President Rivera's suggestion of Miguel Dueñas as one hypothetical coup plotter came several years before the same man's unethical behavior in the case of the Zapotitán irrigation district.

Chapter 5

1. During a telephone conversation in November 2000, poet Alfonso Quijada Urías confirmed the obvious, that his poem was indeed written about Enrique Alvarez. I told him that Ernesto Alvarez, to whom I had shown the poem, said that in fact Enrique did not own any yachts, nor did he have "mansions" other than the houses at El Jobo and in San Salvador. "It's poetic license!" was Quijada's response. And Enrique *was* an excellent polo player.

2. Interview with Lino Osegueda, December 1996, at the finca El Jobo near Sonsonate.

3. For the former, see *Agricultura de las Américas*, January 1970, pages 20–23 (cited in Chapter 3, note 36). A paper by Ortiz Martínez

and Miguel Angel entitled "Study of productivity in a dairy herd managed intensively in the tropics" describes work done at El Jobo during 1974 to 1979 (University of San Carlos, Guatemala, faculty of veterinary medicine, USAC/INCAP, 1981.) In addition, Enrique Alvarez and Lino Osegueda were among the multiple authors of a study presented at the 14th Annual Conference on Livestock and Poultry held at the University of Florida in Gainesville (1980).

4. Browning, *El Salvador: Landscape and Society*, pages 281–282.

5. Interview with Lino Osegueda, San Salvador, August 2002.

6. Interview with Raúl Chapitón at El Jobo (near Sonsonate), August 2002.

7. Telephone interview with Inocencio Alas, July 1998. I subsequently spoke with Fr. Alas several more times by telephone and in person, and I was able to read his book in manuscript before it was published.

8. Interview with Antonio Longhares, El Jobo, August 2002.

9. Ibid.

10. This interview was recorded in 1980 by journalist Eugene Palumbo, and came to me courtesy of Sr. José Simán when I spoke with him in December 1996 at his office in San Salvador. I am grateful to Mr. Palumbo for permitting its use here.

11. Morales Ehrlich, testimony in "The recent presidential elections in El Salvador: Implications for U.S. foreign policy," U.S. House of Representatives committee hearings, March 9 and 17, 1977.

12. *Duarte: My Story*, page 88.

13. Ibid, page 91.

14. Webre, *José Napoleón Duarte and the Christian Democratic Party...*, page 197.

15. Bonner, *Weakness and Deceit*, pages 34–35. The UNO report on which Bonner's account is partly based was appended to the Congressional hearings cited in note 11 above.

16. The report can be found in "Religious persecution in El Salvador," U.S. House of Representatives committee hearings, July 21 and 29, 1977, pages 55–59.

17. Buckley, *Violent Neighbors*, pages 142–143.

18. Interview with Damián Alegría, March 1999, San Salvador.

19. Montgomery, *Revolution in El Salvador: Origins and Evolution*, page 121. Her book provides a much fuller picture of the revolutionary process than the sketch in this section. Another good source is Bonner's *Weakness and Deceit*, chapter 6.

20. See for example Montgomery, *Revolution in El Salvador: From Civil Strife to Civil Peace*.

21. Quoted in Bonner, *Weakness and Deceit*, page 88.

22. Montgomery, *Revolution in El Salvador: Origins and Evolution*. The quote is on page 115, but see chapters 4 and 5 of this book for a much fuller picture.

23. Alas, *Iglesia, Tierra y Lucha Campesina*, chapter 12.

24. A moving account of Romero's "conversion" was written by Fr. Chencho Alas and forms chapter 15 in *Iglesia, Tierra y Lucha Campesina*. Of course the archbishop's transformation was not instantaneous although it may have looked that way to others; experiences with Salvadoran reality had been changing his thinking over a period of years. A great many books and articles describe Romero's life and ministry; my favorite is that of Maria López Vigil (see bibliography).

25. *Weakness and Deceit*, page 66.

26. *Cry of the People*, page 62.

27. *Revolution in El Salvador: Origins and Evolution*, page 89; *José Napoleón Duarte and the Christian Democratic Party*, page 189.

28. Details of these and many other cases of kidnapping and assasination by the left can be found in Escalante Arce, *Sacrificios Humanos Contra Derechos Humanos*. Repression and murder by the government and the right do not appear in this account.

29. Several people mentioned to me having heard that Enrique visited Cuba. This section is based largely on an interview with Shafik Handal, the former leader of the Communist Party of El Salvador. The PCS was a relatively conservative organization on the Left, and it was the last of five to form an armed force and join the FMLN in 1980. The interview took place in March 1999 in San Salvador and all quotes not otherwise attributed are from this conversation.

30. Interview in San Salvador, Aug. 2002.

31. Interview, San Salvador, Nov. 1999.

Chapter 6

1. Editorial in *Estudios Centroamericanos (ECA)*, October/November 1979.

2. The *Proclama* was reprinted in *ECA*, Op. cit., pages 1017–1018.

3. Interview with Román Mayorga, Washington, D.C., December 1997. Other comments in this chapter attributed to Mayorga were made during this interview.

4. U.S. Department of State internal memo, 10/18/1979.

5. Devine, *El Salvador: Embassy Under Attack*.

6. After careful study, William Stanley thinks the U.S. was not involved in actually planning the coup (*The Protection Racket State*, page 144). Ray Bonner and others earlier expressed the same opinion. Still, the possibility of CIA participation through its known allies within the Salvadoran military cannot be ruled out.

7. Stanley, *The Protection Racket State*, pages 137 and 280.

8. *Monseñor Oscar Arnulfo Romero: su diario*, pages 301–303.

9. Bonner, *Weakness and Deceit*, page 157.

10. Alegría and Flakoll, *No me agarran viva*, pages 96–97.

11. Ana Guadalupe Martínez tells of this meeting with the archbishop in *Piezas para un Retrato*, pages 328–330. Later she changed her mind to some extent. "Less than a month passed and all the civilians in whom he [Romero] had so much confidence resigned from the government," she wrote. "This confirmed Monsignor's interpretation and contradicted our black and white analysis. In fact, in that project [the junta] there were people with good intentions who, when they couldn't do anything more, had the courage to resign."

"The 'old man' had it right," we said. "This affair of the coup and the junta wasn't just a movie with the good guys and the bad guys!"

12. *Romero: su diario*, page 310.

13. Among the hostages the Minister of Labor, Gabriel Gallegos Valdés, was a member of the Communist Party while the Minister of Economy, Manuel Enrique Hinds, was from the private business sector.

14. *Weakness and Deceit*, page 152.

15. Montgomery (1995), page 282, note 76.

16. *Weakness and Deceit*, chapter 7.

17. *Duarte: My Story*, pages 100–102; *El Grito del Más Pequeño*, page 248.

18. Maria López Vigil, *Piezas para un Retrato* , pages 333–334.

19. September/October 1979, page 1005. *ECA*'s enthusiasm was no doubt enhanced by the many links between the new government and the Universidad Centroamericana.

20. UCS head José Rodolfo Viera commented a few days later that the UCS thought it had three friends in the new cabinet, starting with Enrique Alvarez. The other two were undersecretary of agriculture Jorge Villacorta, who had been a link between the UCS and the Christian Democratic party, and Alberto Harth Déneke, the Minister of Planning. (Declassified State Dept. telegram, October 25, 1979.) Viera noted that in addition to his work for agricultural reforms, Alvarez had opposed the 1973 expulsion of the AIFLD. In fact, in his earlier years as Minister Enrique had been more than willing to cooperate with AIFLD and with USAID in working for agricultural reforms.

21. This paragraph is from the interview recorded in 1980 by Eugene Palumbo; see Chapter 5, note 10.

22. The letter was reprinted in *ECA*, October/November, 1979.

23. "La congelación de tierras y la reforma agraria," December 1979, pages 1079–1081.

24. *Piezas para un Retrato*, pages 334–335.

25. U.S. Embassy telegram to State Department, Dec. 7, 1979.

26. Bonner, *Weakness and Deceit*, page 161. The question of "constitutionality" was an ongoing source of conflict. The progressives within the government maintained that the Constitution had been suspended by the coup and was not in force, while conservatives used Constitutional arguments to oppose the major reforms promised in the *Proclama*.

27. The text of this speech was reprinted in *ECA*, December 1979, pages 1116–1118.

28. From the San Salvador Archdioces, Secretariat for Social Communication, quoted in Stanley (1996), page 166.

29. This and subsequent quotes are from an interview with the author in June, 1996.

30. Quoted in Stanley (1996), page 154.

31. *Weakness and Deceit*, page 164–167. The quote is from page 164.

32. Zamora interview, note 29.

33. *ECA*, January/February 1980, pages 117–118.

34. *Romero: su diario*, pages 372–374.

35. *ECA*, Jan/Feb 1980, pages 119–120.

36. Ibid, pages 120–121.

37. Interview; see note 21.

Chapter 7

1. Interview with Rubén Zamora, Stanford CA, June 1996.

2. Stanley, *The Protection Racket State*, page 183.

3. *Romero: su diario*, page 378.

4. Interview with Mauricio Silva, San Salvador, March 1999.

5. The Salvadoran "security" forces were the National Guard, the National Police and the Treasury Police (Policía de Hacienda). Although these were separate from the regular military (Army, Navy, Air Force), all were under the same (military) high command and were really more military organizations than police. The security forces were smaller than the regular army and had some "elite" features such as higher pay and voluntary service. They

were considered to be more brutal and arbitrary in dealing with civilian populations. In many cases it appears that the security forces carried out operations against civilians without the agreement or even the knowledge of the Army leadership (to say nothing of the civilian side of the government).

6. Mauricio Silva gave me a copy of the "Analysis" in the form of a mimeographed leaflet.

7. Interview with Mauricio Silva, op. cit. Manuel Sevilla had been the undersecretary for income in the first junta's cabinet and was part of the progressive group in that government. Silva was also in that government, as undersecretary of planning.

8. ibid.

9. Interview with Francisco Altschul, March 1999, San Salvador.

10. Silva, op cit. He then commented that the FMLN as such was not yet formed in early 1980, but the groups which would later make it up were growing.

11. Sergio Ramírez, *Adios Muchachos,* page 127. In contrast to Los Doce, MIPTES did not feature prominent writers or cultural figures; instead it emphasized expertise in practical fields such as economics and agriculture.

12. *Duarte: My Story,* pages 107–110. There is contradictory testimony as to whether this was really "Zamora's plan," but the basic position seems clear.

13. The armed forces' statement was published in *ECA,* Jan. 1980, pages 132–133.

14. Duarte, op. cit., page 111. In telling the story Duarte omits the date of the failed Christian Democratic rally, but suggests that it came before the huge popular demonstration on January 22. "When the Left saw our failure, they seized the moment," he wrote. In reality, the PDC's planned rally was an unwise attempt to catch up with the opposition.

15. *Pueblo,* the weekly bulletin of FAPU, late January 1980, page 1. The emphasis (capitalization) is in the original.

16. Armstrong and Shenk, page 135.

17. The four organizations joining to form the *Coordinadora* were the People's Revolutionary Bloc (BPR, or the *Bloque*), the National Democratic Union (UDN), the 28 of February People's Leagues (LP-28), and the United People's Action Front (FAPU). The general secretary of the BPR, a young man (23) from a campesino background named Juan Chacón, was perhaps the most colorful and best known of their leaders. His father, a Delegate of the Word in Chalatenango, had been horribly murdered by the National Guard in 1977.

18. *Revolution in El Salvador* (1st edition), page 128.

19. Armstrong and Shenk, page 134.

20. *Piezas para un Retrato,* pages 360–361.

21. *Romero: su diario,* page 378.

22. ibid., page 458.

23. The Feb. 17 homily is reprinted in *La voz de los sin voz* (Spanish edition); the passage quoted about weakness of the junta is on page 262 and the letter to President Carter follows immediately after it. The English edition *Voice of the Voiceless* contains the letter but not the rest of the homily.

24. Of course not everyone within the U.S. government agreed with sending military aid. The archbishop's letter was reportedly received with "jubilation" by the human rights bureau in the State Department, but their view of the situation did not prevail. For an interesting description of the internal U.S. politics around El Salvador policy, see Bonner, *Weakness and Deceit,* chapter 8.

25. Romero, *Su Diario,* page 460. White's appointment was strongly opposed, and his confirmation delayed, by ultra-right Senator Jesse Helms. White was removed soon after the Reagan administration took office.

26. *La voz de los sin voz,* pages 435–439. This interview with *El Diario de Caracas,* which was published in that city on March 19, was not included in the English version entitled *Voice of the Voiceless.*

27. General descriptions of the state of human rights in El Salvador can be found in the reports by Americas Watch and the ACLU, by Amnesty International, by EPICA, and by the post-war Commission on the Truth, all listed in the Bibliography. Americas Watch and Amnesty International also published a series of shorter updates during the 1980s. See also U.S. Congressional Hearings on this subject.

28. The title of this position is sometimes translated "attorney general," but that gives an inaccurate impression. The U.S. counterpart of that Salvadoran position is not a prosecutor but a sort of chief public defender. That was Mario Zamora's job, a responsible government post but not one involving policy-making choices.

29. This account is from the *Report* of the Commission on the Truth, pages 248–250.

30. Tommie Sue Montgomery, *Revolution in El Salvador* (first edition), page 167.

31. Testimony of Margarita Herrera, *Piezas para un Retrato,* pages 365–366.

32. The Basilica of the Sacred Heart is a large temple on the outskirts of San Salvador in the direction of Santa Tecla. Romero held services there when the cathedral was "occupied" by protest groups as often happened in 1980.

33. Interview quoted in *NACLA Report on the Americas,* July/August 1980, page 17.

34. Report of the Commission on the Truth, pages 265–268.

35. Quoted in *Report on Human Rights in El Salvador*, pages 168–169.

36. London, *The Times*, June 25, 1980, page 8. In the same edition *The Times* editorialized against further support for the government: "Time to Change Horses in El Salvador," page 17. The mainstream U.S. press never followed suit — it would have meant opposing U.S. government policy. The statement by 38 members of the Honduran clergy describing the massacre was published in *ECA* (June 1980, pages 635–636), accompanied as noted by a "commentary" (pages 597–598).

37. On February 22, 1981, *The Sunday Times* of London published a detailed account of "A massacre that 'never happened,'" including interviews with survivors and with a Catholic priest from Brooklyn, Father Earl Gallagher, who was on the scene the day after the killings while bodies still covered the riverbanks. The same sources were available to the U.S. media, but it did not choose to report these events.

The Sumpul River massacre is vividly pictured in Sandra Benítez's novel *The Weight of All Things*.

38. Dada's resignation statement was quoted by Monsignor Romero in his March 9 homily (*La voz de los sin voz*, page 387) and was published by the Mexican daily *Excelsior*. It can also be found in *ECA* (March/April, 1980, pages 377–378) along with other documents relating to the controversy within the Christian Democratic Party. See also Montgomery, *Revolution in El Salvador* (first edition), chapter 6, for an excellent account of the changing political scene and of U.S. policy. The slander against Héctor Dada is described there on page 217, note 16.

39. The number of farms affected by phase I of the reform was originally estimated as 376, but it turned out to be much lower, around 238. See the 1981 Oxfam America *Impact Audit*, page 9.

40. The reforms, and in particular the U.S. role in El Salvador's land reform, are described by Bonner in *Weakness and Deceit*, chapter 9.

41. ibid., page 188.

42. Montgomery, *Revolution in El Salvador* (first edition), page 167.

43. ibid, pages 167–168.

44. Villacorta's resignation statement was included in *El Salvador: A Struggle for Democracy* (1980). Like most of the other documents there, it was presumably published elsewhere as well.

45. *La voz de los sin voz*, pages 286–292.

46. Romero, *Su Diario*, page 454.

47. *Piezas para un retrato*, page 369.

48. Interview with Antonio Cabrales, San Salvador, December 1996.

49. *Piezas para un retrato*, page 370.

50. *La voz de los sin voz*, page 293.

51. *Piezas para un retrato*, page 383.

52. ibid.

53. *Excelsior*, April 18 1980, page 32-A. Judge Ramírez Amaya received death threats and survived a serious attempt on his life; as a result he had to abandon the investigation and leave El Salvador.

54. *Report*, pages 269–270.

55. *Piezas para un retrato*, page 384.

56. MIPTES statement dated March 26, 1980 in mimeographed form (private communication from M. Silva).

57. Bonner, *Weakness and Deceit*, page 179.

58. *New York Times*, 3/31/80. Of course the number is uncertain, and other reports offered much larger estimates. The tragedy at the funeral is also described in the fiction of Sandra Benítiz; see again her novel *The Weight of All Things*.

59. Jorge Lara-Brand, *Christianity and Crisis*, May 12, 1980.

60. *El Independiente*, April 19 1980, pages 1 and 2, reported by FBIS on April 21.

61. Telegram from the U.S. Embassy in San Salvador to Washington, number 80SANSA02417, April 1980.

62. I have been told that the coincidence of the initials of the *Frente Democrático Revolucionario* with those of the great U.S. president was not an accident. I'm not sure this is true since that name was a natural choice in any event.

63. Telegram from U.S. Embassy to State, number 80SANSA02820. Noting that the *Coordinadora* had a majority of four on the seven-man executive committee and that the FDR incorporated the program of the CRM into its own, Ambassador Robert White commented in the telegram that the "liberal sectors provide little more than window-dressing for the CRM," a theme which U.S. officials would repeat many times. But White added something more positive: "It would seem, from our perspective, to be unwise to seek to discredit the group as a potential confrere in a Salvadoran internal political dialogue." There is no doubt that White was sincerely dismayed by the later murder of the top FDR leaders.

64. April 20 1980, page 15-A.

65. Pinto, *El Grito del Más Pequeño*, page 288.

66. The document was reprinted in *ECA*, March/April 1980, page 346.

67. Interview with Lino Osegueda, December 1996, at finca *El Jobo* near Sonsonate.

68. Interview with Antonio Cabrales, San Salvador, December 1966.

69. U.S. Embassy telegram to State Depart-

ment, April 21, 1980, number 80SANSA02855. The "rightwing terrorists" story was of course a lie, but it is also a chilling prevision of the murder of Enrique and his comrades in November.

70. Interview with Mauricio Silva, op cit.

71. Embassy telegram 80SANSA02871, April 22 1980.

72. *La Prensa Gráfica,* April 22 (for Enrique's arrest and release) and April 19 (photo of the FDR leaders). It was typical of the major Salvadoran press that while some events were noted (and many others were not), no context or analysis was offered to the reader.

73. It has so far proved impossible to find a complete file of copies of *El Independiente.* Apparently no library in El Salvador or the United States has kept them. Photocopies of a few key issues are available in the NACLA archive, and I have copies of several others thanks to a chance encounter in a San Salvador bookstore. Fortunately some of the gaps are filled by Pinto's autobiographical book *El Grito del Más Pequeño.*

74. *El Salvador's Decade of Terror,* page 40.

75. *El Grito Del Más Pequeño,* pages 288 and 294.

76. A great deal has been written about the 1980 agricultural reform in El Salvador. A comprehensive account of the reform is beyond the scope of this book, and we will focus mainly on the opinions and analysis of Enrique Alvarez and the FDR. For the views of outside observers see the books by Bonner and Montgomery, plus the Oxfam America "Impact Audit" cited in the bibliography.

77. The interview took place on April 29 and was reported briefly the next day in Mexico by *Uno Más Uno,* page 8. The relevant issue of *El Independiente* is unfortunately not available, but Enrique's comments were quoted in *El Grito del Más Pequeño,* pages 289–294, from which this account is taken. It is presented here in a condensed version.

Chapter 8

1. Alan Riding, "Salvador dissidents seeking aid abroad," *New York Times,* 6/5/80.

2. Reported by the Xinhua News Agency and by Armstrong and Shenk in *El Salvador: The Face of Revolution,* pages 168–169.

3. White and Oulahan are quoted by Bonner in *Weakness and Deceit,* page 203.

4. Armstrong and Schenk call Majano "the colonel with a conscience." The name is a bit ironic. They write that in the first days after the October coup, Majano "went around to police headquarters and ordered the release of those detained ... he tried to undo the dirty work of his fellow officers. But he could never bring the corpses back to life." (*El Salvador: The Face of Revolution,* page 120.)

5. Stanley, *The Protection Racket State,* page 200.

6. In fact D'Aubuisson was arrested after the coup along with other officers whom the reformers wanted to place on trial for corruption. García released them all and there were no trials; D'Aubuisson went temporarily into exile, traveling between Guatemala and the United States.

7. Karen DeYoung, "Salvadoran rightist eludes ban against entering U.S.," *Washington Post,* July 2, 1980, page 1.

8. Absurd, that is, to the outside world which dealt in facts. Ideologically, D'Aubuisson and the ultra-right defined "communist" to mean anyone or anything working for social change in favor of the poor. A connection with Moscow or with the PCS, or even a belief in socialism, was quite beside the point.

9. Interview with Robert White, Sommerville MA, October 1995. A subsequent Congressional staff report contains this remarkable admission: "White reports giving the documents to the Chief of Station, and requesting that CIA examine them closely. After this, their whereabouts is unknown." The documents were never analyzed by U.S. intelligence and were ignored by policymakers. See Staff Report, Subcommittee on Oversight and Evaluation, Permanent Select Committee on Intelligence, September 22, 1982.

10. The fullest account is given in Stanley, *The Protection Racket State,* pages 201–205.

11. Christopher Dickey, "Suspects in plot freed in El Salvador," May 15, 1980.

12. Karen DeYoung, op.cit.

13. *El Salvador: The Face of Revolution,* pages 168–169.

14. Interview with Rubén Zamora, Stanford CA, June 1996.

15. July 28, 1980.

16. Interview with Mauricio Silva, San Salvador, March 1999.

17. Ibid.

18. Mark Starr, "Salvadorans warn U.S.: Keep out," *Chicago Tribune,* August 1, 1980.

19. A recording of this FDR press conference was given to me by Dr. Tommie Sue Montgomery. The conference was one among several which the delegation held in Washington, D.C.—at Georgetown University and the National Press Club, among others. The dates of those two conferences were July 23 and July 25, respectively.

20. Interview with Mauricio Silva.

21. Ruben Zamora interview, Stanford, CA, June 1996.

22. Outgoing telegram to U.S. Embassies in Europe, July 31, 1980.

23. Interview with Mauricio Silva.

24. *Theology in the Americas,* Conference papers, page 2 plus pages 58–61.

25. Pinto, *El Grito del Más Pequeño,* page 317. To me this characterization of Napoleón Duarte seems too harsh, especially for that moment when the civil war was still pending. I see Duarte as having been partially blinded by ambition and trapped in his sad decision to front for the armed forces in the government — but not as a fascist of any stripe. Whatever his motives, however, Duarte's role during the 1980s contributed to the devastation of his country by prolonging the war and legitimating massive U.S. intervention.

26. Adolfo Gilly, *Uno Más Uno*, June 26, 1980, reprinted in his book *Guerra y política en El Salvador,* pages 111–114.

27. A Canadian commentery on U.S. reporting about El Salvador was "The department of 'misinformation'" by Anne Nelson, *MacLean's* magazine, Sept. 1, 1980. Gilly's article on the summer's second strike appeared in *Uno Más Uno* on August 21 and was reprinted in *Guerra y política en El Salvador*, pages 115–119.

28. Interview with Ruben Zamora, June 1996

Chapter 9

1. *Uno Más Uno*, December 10, 1980, reprinted in *Guerra y política en El Salvador,* page 147.

2. Interview with Salvador Sánchez Cerén, San Salvador, November 1999. Today Sánchez Cerén is an important leader of the FMLN, now the major political party of the left.

3. Interview with Coralia and Ana María Godoy, San Salvador, December 1996.

4. Interviews with Lino Osegueda, 12/1996 and 8/2002.

5. Report of the Commission on the Truth (*ECA*), page 224. Figueroa Morales was acting under the orders of higher ranking officers, also named in the report. He was later killed in combat against real guerrillas.

6. Interviews with Lino Osegueda and with Antonio Longhares (8/2002).

7. The four were Ita Ford, Maura Clarke, Dorothy Kazel, and Jean Donovan; the first three were nuns and Donovan was a lay missioner. As a result of intense U.S. pressure (especially from Congress) to solve the case, five enlisted men were convicted in 1984 and sentenced to prison; they were subsequently freed in an amnesty. The men were known to have acted under superior orders, but those responsible were never charged. or investigated. See the Truth Commission's *Report (ECA)*, pages 213–217.

8. *Duarte: My Story,* page 120.

9. *Report,* page 217.

10. Montgomery, *Revolution in El Salvador,* edition 1, page 178.

11. This account is from the interview with Lino Osegueda in August, 2002.

12. The bombings of the houses of Mauricio Silva and of Ana del Carmen Alvarez were described to me during interviews with them in San Salvador in March 1999 and in December 1996 respectively.

13. January 16, 1981.

14. This section is based on my interview with Antonio Longhares at El Jobo in August, 2002.

15. Interview with Coralia Godoy, op cit.

16. Interview with Salvador Sánchez Cerén, op cit.

17. *El Grito del más pequeño,* page 326.

18. *Guerra y política en El Salvador,* page 150.

19. *Uno Más Uno,* November 28, page 10.

20. *Weakness and Deceit,* pages 211–212.

21. *Uno Más Uno,* op cit.

22. *New York Times,* November 16, 1980.

23. *Maclean's Magazine,* 12/8/1980. The *New York Times* reported the promises of increased aid on page 1, but did not quote Jeane Kirkpatrick's odious remark.

24. The journalist was John Sullivan, a freelancer. He checked into the Hotel Sheraton in December and promptly disappeared. His body was found two years later. The next two U.S. victims were Michael Hammer and Mark Pearlman, both from the American Institute of Free Labor Development (AIFLD) and acting as advisors to the agrarian reform program. Both were serving U.S. government policy, and at least one of them had ties to the CIA. They were having lunch with José Rodolfo Viera, the head of ISTA, in the dining room of the Sheraton hotel when soldiers walked up and shot all three to death. The officers who gave the orders were never tried, despite some U.S. pressure.

25. *New York Times,* November 30, 1980, page 20.

26. Robert White, "Central America: The problem that won't go away," *New York Times Magazine,* 7/18/1982, page 21. White was removed from his post in El Salvador soon after Ronald Reagan's inauguration, and left the Foreign Service a few months later.

27. Bonner, *Weakness and Deceit*, page 209.

28. This building was damaged beyond repair by the earthquake which hit San Salvador in 1986. The same quake damaged the U.S. Embassy, which was sold (it is now a bank) and replaced by an enormous fortified compound a few miles from downtown.

29. Robert White, declassified Embassy telegram to State Department, November 29, 1980.

30. Declassified report from the State Department, Nov. 29, 1980.

31. This and subsequent comments attributed to Martel are from an interview which took place in San Salvador on November 28, 1996 — the 16th anniversary of Enrique's murder. In 1980 Martel was a leader of the new party formed by disident Christian Democrats who had broken with the PDC over its decision to remain in the government. This group (the MPSC) then joined the FDR.

32. In Central America it is common to distinguish the "intellectual authors" and the "material authors" when discussing a crime. In cases involving political murders the material authors— those who actually commit the crime — were often low-ranking soldiers acting under orders, so the identity of the intellectual authors is the important question.

33. The statement was issued on November 28 and reported in *La Prensa Gráfica* on the next day. It is quoted in an Embassy telegram to the State Department dated November 30, 1980.

34. White telegram to State Department, Nov. 29, 1980.

35. Interview in San Salvador, August 2002.

36. White, *New York Times Magazine*, 7/18/1982.

37. Martel interview, op cit.

38. November 29, 1980, page 8. Possibly this bomb helps explain the differing descriptions (below) of the condition of Enrique's corpse, since Cabrales saw it before and Pinto after the explosion.

39. Interview with Antonio Cabrales, December 1996, San Salvador.

40. Longhares, op cit.

41. Pinto Jr., *El Grito del más pequeño*, pages 328–329.

42. *New York Times*, December 3, 1980, page 3.

43. Interview with Antonio Cabrales, August 2002, San Salvador.

44. Gilly, op cit., pages 148–151.

45. Medardo Ernesto Gómez, *Latinoamerica: Testimonio de vida y esperanza*, page 287.

46. *Piezas para un Retrato*, page 9 (preface).

47. Juan José Martel, op cit.

48. Longhares, op cit.

Epilogue

1. The facts about the women's murder are outlined in the report of the Truth Commission immediately following the description of the FDR killings. A moving account of the ministry and death of the four, focusing on the life of the youngest of them, Jean Donovan, is *Salvador Witness* by Ana Carrigan.

2. The State Department's "white paper" was dated February 23, 1981. For an account of claims and counterclaims about "foreign intervention," including the critiques of the white paper, see John Lamperti, *What are we afraid of?*, chapter 4. The Robert White quotation is from "The problem that won't go away," *New York Times Magazine*, July 18, 1982, page 43.

3. Two post-war books describe the El Mozote atrocity in convincing and horrifying detail. They are Mark Danner, *The Massacre at El Mozote: A Parable Of The Cold War*, and Leigh Binford, *The El Mozote Massacre: Anthropology And Human Rights*. Raymond Bonner, then a reporter for the *New York Times*, visited the scene and wrote about the massacre soon after it had occurred. (See *Weakness and Deceit*, chapter 6, especially pages 112–113.) The *NY Times* carried his report about El Mozote, but other papers, notably the *Wall Street Journal*, accepted the Salvadoran and U.S. governments' lies and denied that anything had happened. The FMLN radio station *Radio Venceremos* reported the crime accurately but was not co nsidered a "reliable source" by the U.S. Embassy.

4. As 2005 begins the economy, including increasing poverty and high unemployment, occupies first place in public opinion as El Salvador's worst problem.

5. In 1989 it was again soldiers of the Atlacatl Battalion who murdered Father Ignacio Ellacuría and five other Jesuit leaders of the UCA plus their housekeeper and her teenage daughter. This atrocity significantly strengthened the opposition to continued aid to the Salvadoran government and military within the U.S. Congress.

Appendix

1. This "letter" is included in *El Salvador: A Struggle for Democracy.*

Bibliography

Books

Alas, José Inocencio. *Iglesia, Tierra y Lucha Campesina: Suchitoto, El Salvador, 1968–1977.* San Salvador: Asociación de Frailes Franciscanos OFM de C.A., 2003.

Alegría, Claribel, and Darwin Flakoll. *Ashes of Izalco* (novel). Willimantic, CT: Curbstone Press, 1995. (This is the English edition; the original title was *Cenizas de Izalco*, 1987).

_____. *No me agarran viva: La mujer salvadoreña en la lucha.* San Salvador: UCA Editores, 1998 (7th edition).

Alvarez Geoffroy, Mauricio (ed.). *Los Alvarez: Recuerdos de una Familia.* Privately printed, 1995.

Anderson, Thomas P. *Matanza,* 2nd edition. Willimantic, CT: Curbstone Press, 1992. A Spanish translation recently published in El Salvador under the title *El Salvador, 1932* (San Salvador: CONCULTURA, 2001) contains additional contributions by Héctor Pérez Brignoli and Erick Ching.

_____. *The War of the Dispossesed.* Lincoln, NE, and London: University of Nebraska Press, 1981.

Arias Gómez, Jorge. *Farabundo Martí: Esbozo Biográfico.* San José, Costa Rica: EDUCA, 1972. A revised and amplified version, entitled simply *Farabundo Martí,* was published in 1996, again by EDUCA. Page references are to this more complete edition.

Armstrong, Robert, and Janet Shenk. *El Salvador: The Face of Revolution.* Boston: South End Press, 1982.

Baloyra, Enrique. *El Salvador in Transition.* Chapel Hill and London: University of North Carolina Press, 1982.

Benítez, Sandra. *Bitter Grounds* (novel). New York: Hyperion, 1997.

_____. *The Weight of All Things* (novel). New York: Hyperion, 2000.

Bonner, Raymond. *Weakness and Deceit: U.S. Policy and El Salvador.* New York: Times Books, 1984.

Bosch, Brian. *The Salvadoran Officer Corps and the Final Offensive of 1981.* Jefferson, NC: McFarland, 1999.

Browning, David. *El Salvador: Landscape and Society.* London: Oxford University Press, 1971.

Buckley, Tom. *Violent Neighbors: El Salvador, Central America, and the United States.* New York: Times Books, 1984.

Carrigan, Ana. *Salvador Witness.* New York: Ballantine Books, 1984.

Clements, Charles, M.D. *Witness to War: An American Doctor in El Salvador.* New York: Bantam Books, 1984.

Dalton, Roque. *Las Historias Prohibidas del Pulgarcito,* 9th edition. San Salvador: UCA Editores, 1988.

_____. *Miguel Mármol.* Willimantic, CT: Curbstone Press, 1987 (English edition; original Spanish edition, 1982).

Devine, Frank. *El Salvador: Embassy Under Attack.* New York: Vantage Press, 1981.

Duarte, José Napoleón (with Diana Page). *Duarte: My Story.* New York: Putnam, 1986.

Ellacuría, Ignacio. *Veinte Años de Historia en El Salvador (1969–1989)* (3 vols.). San Salvador: UCA Editores, 1993.

Escalante Arce, Luis. *Sacrificíos Humanos Contra Derechos Humanos,* 3rd edition. San Salvador: Libros de Centroamérica, 1995.

Los Escuadrones de la Muerte en El Salvador. "El Salvador": Editorial Jaragua, 1993.

Gettleman Marvin et al. *El Salvador : Central America in the New Cold War.* New York: Grove, 1987.

Gilly, Adolfo. *Guerra y politica en El Salvador.* Mexico: Nueva Imagen, 1981.

Gómez, Medardo Ernesto. *Latinoamérica: Testimonio de Vida y Esperanza.* San Salvador: Iglesia Luterana Salvadoreña, 1993.

Izaguirre Ruiz, Rafael P. *La Conexión Gringa* (novel). San Salvador: UCA Editores, 1995.

Krehm, William. *Democracies and Tyrannies of the Caribbean.* Westport, CT: Lawrence Hill, 1984. This book was published in Mexico in 1948 in a Spanish translation, but the original only appeared in English 36 years later.

Lamperti, John. *What Are We Afraid Of? An Assessment of the "Communist Threat" in Central America.* Boston: South End Press, 1986.

Lernoux, Penny. *Cry of the People: The Struggle for Human Rights in Latin America — the Catholic Church in Conflict with U.S. Policy.* New York: Penguin, 1982.

López Vigil, María. *Piezas para un Retrato.* San Salvador: UCA Editores, 1993. An English version has appeared recently: *Oscar Romero: Memories in Mosaic,* translated by Kathy Ogle. Washington, D.C.: EPICA, 2000.

Masferrer, Alberto. *Ensayos.* San Salvador: Biblioteca Basica de Literatura Salvaoreña, vol. 2. San Salvador: Concultura, 1996.

McNeil, Frank. *War and Peace in Central America.* New York: Scribners, 1988.

Montgomery, Tommie Sue. *Revolution in El Salvador: Origins and Evolution.* Boulder, CO: Westview, 1982. Also the second edition, *Revolution in El Salvador: From Civil Strife to Civil Peace.* Boulder, CO: 1995. (This second edition was really a new book, emphasizing events since the first edition was published.)

Paige, Jeffery. *Coffee and Power.* Cambridge: Harvard University Press, 1997.

Parkman, Patricia. *Nonviolent Insurrection in El Salvador: The Fall of Maximiliano Hernández Martínez.* Tucson: University of Arizona Press, 1988.

Pearce, Jenny. *Promised Land: Peasant Rebellion in Chalatenango, El Salvador.* London: Latin America Bureau, 1986.

Pinto, Jorge, Jr. *El Grito del Más Pequeño.* Mexico: Editorial Cometa, 1985.

Ramírez, Sergio. *Adios Muchachos: Una memoria de la revolución sandinista.* Mexico: Aguilar, 1999.

Romero, Oscar Arnulfo. *Monseñor Oscar Arnulfo Romero: su diario.* San Salvador: the archdiocese, 1990.

_____. *La voz de los sin voz: La palabra viva de Monseñor Romero* (5th edition). San Salvador: UCA Editores, 1999.

Russell, Phillip L. *El Salvador in Crisis.* Austin, TX : Colorado River Press, 1984.

Stanley, William. *The Protection Racket State.* Philadelphia: Temple University Press, 1996.

Webre, Stephen Andrew. *José Napoleón Duarte and the Christian Democratic Party in Salvadoran Politics, 1960–1972.* Baton Rouge: Louisiana State University Press, 1979.

West, Cornel, et al., editors. *Theology in the Americas: Detroit IL, Conference Papers.* Maryknoll, NY: Orbis, 1982.

Williams, Philip, and Knut Walter. *Militarization and Demilitarization in El Salvador's Transition to Democracy.* Pittsburgh: University of Pittsburgh Press, 1997.

White, Alister. *El Salvador.* New York: Praeger, 1973.

Woodward, Ralph Lee, Jr. *Central America: A Nation Divided,* 2nd edition. New York: Oxford University Press, 1985.

Articles

Note: Estudios Centroamericanos (ECA) is a journal of events and opinion published by San Salvador's Jesuit university, Universidad Centroamericana (UCA). Material from this journal is usually referenced simply by volume and page number, especially in the case of editorials and reprints of documents. Some individual articles are listed by author and or title, however, either below or in the notes. A special issue contains the Report of the post-war Commission on the Truth (below). The national university, *Universidad de El Salvador* (UES), likewise publishes a journal which is called *La Universidad*. In 1970 a special issue was devoted to that year's agrarian reform congress (see below and chapter 4).

Ching, Erick. "Los archivos de Moscu: Una nuevza apreciación de la insurrección del 32." *Tendencias* 44 (San Salvador), September 1995. This article was included in the Salvadoran edition of Thomas Anderson's book *Matanza.*

_____, and Virginia Tilley. "Indians, the Military and the Rebellion of 1932 in El Salvador." *Journal of Latin American Studies* 30 (1998), pp. 121–156.

Gómez, Leonel, and Bruce Cameron. "El Salvador: The Current Danger." *Foreign Policy,* Jan/Feb 1982, pp. 71–78.

Keogh, Dermot. "The Myth of the Liberal Coup: The United States and the 15 October Coup in El Salvador." *Millennium: Journal of International Studies,* Vol. 13, pp. 153–183.

Marden, Luis. "Coffee Is King in El Salvador." *National Geographic*, November 1944, pp. 575–608.

Nairn, Allan. "Behind the Death Squads." *The Progressive,* May 1984. This article and another by Nairn, plus articles by Craig Pyes, Christopher Dickey, and Douglas Farah and Tom Gibbs, were published in Spanish translation in a book entitled *Los Escuadrones de la Muerte en El Salvador* (see book section). That book also contains "A historical sketch of the death squads, with case studies" written in 1992 by "anonomous intelligence officers of the Armed Forces."

Paige, Jeffery. "Coffee and Power in El Salvador." Latin American Research Review, Vol. 28 (1993), No. 3, pp. 7–40.

de Sebastian, Luis. "El Congreso de Reforma Agraria." *ECA*, 1970, pp. 51–56.

Reports and Testimony

United Nations Report: *Comisión de la Verdad: De la Locura a la Esperanza. La Guerra de Doce Años en El Salvador. (Commission on the Truth: From madness to hope. The twelve year war in El Salvador.)* Reprinted in *ECA*, March 1993 (special issue). The commission of three international jurists was headed by Belisario Betancur, ex-president of Colombia; the other two members were Reinaldo Figueredo, the foreign minister of Venezuela, and Prof. Thomas Buergenthal of the United States, formerly president of the Inter-American Court of Human Rights. The text of the Report can also be found on the internet at this address: www.usip.org/library/tc/doc/reports/el_salvador/tc_es_03151993_toc.html, which is part of the website of the U.S. Institute of Peace.

Reforma Agraria en El Salvador, the proceedings of the First National Congress on Agrarian Reform. A special issue of *La Universidad* (the journal of the Universidad de El Salvador, or the UES), January/February 1970.

El Salvador Land Reform: 1980–1981: Impact Audit, by Laurence Simon, James Stephens, Jr., and Martin Diskin, Oxfam America, 1982 (approximately 70 pages).

Report on Human Rights in El Salvador, report by Americas Watch and the American Civil Liberties Union. New York: Vintage, January 1982.

Condoning the Killing: Ten Years of Massacres in El Salvador. Washington, D.C.: EPICA, 1990.

El Salvador's Decade of Terror: Human Rights Since the Assassination of Archbishop Romero, report by Americas Watch. New Haven: Yale University Press, 1991.

Communist Interference in El Salvador, U.S. Department of State Special Report no. 80, Feb. 23, 1981. Critiques of this "white paper" were published by Berryman (American Friends Service Committee, March 3, 1981), Petras (*The Nation*, March 28, 1981), Kwitney (*Wall Street Journal* June 8, 1981) and Kaiser (*Washington Post,* June 9, 1981), among others.

El Salvador: A Struggle for Democracy. A

collection of documents, statements, letters and articles; most of this material is reprinted from other publications. Published in both English and Spanish by the Frente Democrático Revolucionario, San Salvador, 1980.

U.S. Congressional Hearings

"Human rights in Nicaragua, Guatemala, and El Salvador: Implications for U.S. policy," *Hearings* before the Subcommittee on International Organizations of the Committee on International Relations, U.S. House of Representatives, June 8 and 9, 1976.

"The recent presidential elections in El Salvador: Implications for U.S. foreign policy," *Hearings* before the above committee, March 9 and 17, 1977.

"Religious persecution in El Salvador," *Hearings* before the above committee, July 21 and 29, 1977.

*Persons Interviewed**

Fr. José Inocencio (Chencho) Alas
Damián and Carolina Alegría
Francisco Altschul
Ana del Carmen Alvarez
Ernesto Alvarez Córdova
Dr. Emilio Alvarez (by telephone)
Mauricio Alvarez
Salvador Arias Peñate
Allan Bell (letter)
Dean Brackley S.J.
Antonio Cabrales
Fabio Castillo Figueroa
Mario Cerna
Raúl Ernesto Chapitón
Carlos Henríquez Consalvi
Freeman Day Jr. (letters)
Alberto Harth Déneke
Martin Diskin
Rolando Duarte
Mr. and Mrs. Perry Edgar
Carl Fleming (letter)
Gertrudis Flores Paz
Heather Foote
Santiago García
Adolfo Gilly
Coralia Godoy
Ana María Godoy
Leonel Gómez
Bishop Medardo Ernesto Gómez
Shafik Handal
José Antonio Longhares Díaz
Ana María López
Mauricio Marín
Juan José Martel
Gersón Martínez
Román Mayorga Quiroz
Katherine Miller
Tommie Sue Montgomery
Orlando Mungía
Jerry Nolan
Salvador Núñez
Lino Osegueda
Leon Pierce (telephone)
Enrique Restrepo Siguí
Cecile Rodríguez
José Napoleón Rodríguez Ruiz
Dr. Rafael Ruiz Izaguirre
Salvador Sánchez Serén
Theodor Schroeder (letter)
Rev. Luis Serrano
Mauricio Silva
Jorge Simán
José Simán
Jack Spence
Mons. Ricardo Urioste
Jorge Gilberto Villacorta
Victor Villeda
Ambassador Robert White
Haven Whiteside (letter)
Ambassador William Walker
Joy Bartula Wyse (email correspondence)
Rubén Zamora Rivas

**I have not included academic titles such as "Dr." or "lic." (except for religious, government or medical ones) since I was not always sure who had earned which degree and did not want to offend by selective omissions. Titles or no, I am most grateful to all who cooperated with this project. Of course none of them are responsible for opinions expressed in this book or for errors it may contain. J.L.*

Index